USING OPEN EDUCATIONAL RESOURCES TO PROMOTE SOCIAL JUSTICE

EDITED BY **CJ IVORY**
AND **ANGELA PASHIA**

Association of College and Research Libraries
A division of the American Library Association
Chicago, Illinois 2022

The paper used in this publication meets the minimum requirements of American National Standard for Information Sciences–Permanence of Paper for Printed Library Materials, ANSI Z39.48-1992. ∞

Library of Congress Control Number: 2022945369

Copyright ©2022 by the Association of College and Research Libraries.

All rights reserved except those which may be granted by Sections 107 and 108 of the Copyright Revision Act of 1976.

Printed in the United States of America.

26 25 24 23 22   5 4 3 2 1

Table of Contents

v   Introduction

SECTION I. THEORY AND PROBLEMATIZING

3   Chapter 1. The Unrealized Promise of OER: An Exploration of Copyright, the Open Movement, and Social Justice
Shanna Hollich

23   Chapter 2. Repairing the Curriculum: Using OER to Fill Gaps
Kevin Adams and Samantha Dannick

41   Chapter 3. On Being Visible: The Hidden Curriculum of Heteronormativity and Open Educational Resources
Thomas Weeks

SECTION II. OPEN PRAXIS

57   Chapter 4. Centering Justice in Content Development: A Case Study of the Police Brutality Teach-Out
Julia Maxwell, Katya Gorecki, Ryan Henyard, and Benjamin Morse

79   Chapter 5. Pay It Forward: Realizing The Promise of OER for the Next Generation of Learners
Kimberly S. Grotewold, Karen L. Kohler, and Elisabeth M. Krimbill

109   Chapter 6. Reframing Social Work Education Using OER
Jennifer Wood and Mary Jo Orzech

125   Chapter 7. Deconstructing Textbooks for Equity: Open Educational Resources and Culturally Responsive Pedagogy
Elissah Becknell and Rebecca March

SECTION III. DECOLONIZING LEARNING IN THE GLOBAL SOUTH

141   Chapter 8. Open Textbooks, Intuitive Pedagogy, and Social Justice
Glenda Cox, Bianca Masuku, and Michelle Willmers

169 Chapter 9. Opportunities and Challenges in the Development and Usage of Open Textbooks in Institutions of Higher Learning to Promote Social Justice
Josiline Phiri Chigwada

183 Chapter 10. Where Are We on the Map? The State of Open Educational Resources (OER) in Africa
Alkasim Hamisu Abdu

SECTION IV. SCALING UP WITH INSTITUTIONAL POLICIES (APPROACHES)

201 Chapter 11. Reflecting on the Institutional Organization of Academic "Knowledge" as a Barrier to OER Construction and Adoption in Higher Education Curricula
Emily M. Doyle, Kristin Petrovic, Tanya Mudry, and Murray Anderson

217 Chapter 12. Beyond Affordability: Developing Policy to Encourage Faculty to Explore OER as a Means to Create More Diverse, Inclusive, and Socially Conscious Course Materials
Dawn (Nikki) Cannon-Rech

229 Chapter 13. OER, Social Justice, and Online Professional Development to Enhance Equity, Diversity, and Inclusion at a University
Samantha Harlow and Melody Rood   229

SECTION V. BUILDING AND DECOLONIZING OER PLATFORMS

249 Chapter 14. Decolonizing Wikipedia
Ian Ramjohn

263 Chapter 15. Using Open Educational Resources (OER) to Bring Marginalized Voices into the Music Theory Curriculum
Barbara Murphy and Claire Terrell

285 Chapter 16. An Institute-Based Approach to OER in Digital Caribbean Studies
Perry Collins, Hélène Huet, Laurie Taylor, Brittany Mistretta, Hannah Toombs, Anita Baksh, Nathan H. Dize, Juliet Glenn-Callender, Ronald Angelo Johnson, Aaron Kamugisha, K. Adele Okoli, Laëtitia Saint-Loubert, and Keja Valen

301 About the Authors

INTRODUCTION

Introduction

As so often is the case, the idea for this book came from a twisting path. Not long after we began collaborating and presenting together at conferences, we were invited to draft a chapter on critical race theory (CRT) in academic libraries. An invited chapter is, of course, very flattering, so we proceeded without much thought to who the publisher would be. Angela had been working on social justice issues for a while at that point, while CJ had a wealth of expertise on open educational resources (OER). We merged our two areas of expertise in drafting that chapter, discussing OER as an opportunity to not only save students money but incorporate CRT into the curriculum—both in content and in practice.

We submitted the final draft and were dismayed when we received the publication agreement. The publisher was unwilling to allow us to retain the copyright, even after we shared the licensing agreement that the Association of College & Research Libraries (ACRL) Press uses as an example. In discussing how to proceed—should we submit this chapter somewhere else?—we realized that we were really excited about extending the discussion of OER beyond just ensuring that all students can afford to access their course materials. So we pitched the idea of an edited volume on this topic to a publisher that we know has publishing practices we support (chapter authors retain copyright and select the Creative Commons license they prefer for their work), and here we are!

Our entrance to academic work on social justice was through a focus on CRT. We outline this background here but wish to emphasize that it explicitly addresses only one aspect of social justice. For us, the structural understanding of racism in the United States creates a foundation upon which to understand other structures of oppression as well as intersectionality.

Social Justice through a CRT Lens

Critical race theorists have been critiquing the ways white supremacy as an ideology is embedded within academia for decades. The Black Lives Matter (BLM) movement has done a great deal to bring those discussions of institutional

v

racism to a wider audience, leading to more conversation in mass media, on social media, and in academic literature about the ways racism has shaped our institutions.

Alicia Garza, Patrisse Cullors, and Opal Tometi created #BlackLivesMatter in response to specific acts of violence—the killing of Trayvon Martin and the assassination of his character during the subsequent prosecution of his killer.[1] The hashtag gained wider recognition during the protests in Ferguson, Missouri in response to Michael Brown's killing in August 2014 and in demonstrations across the US following the non-indictment of his killer in November 2014. Though the initial protests focused on issues of police brutality and extrajudicial killings, conversation using the #BlackLivesMatter hashtag on Twitter included topics ranging from details about protests in response to extrajudicial killings to underlying structural issues like residential segregation and redlining, local histories, and intersectionality[2]—particularly the ways misogyny and homophobia compound racism in the treatment of Black trans women.

Student-led protests at academic institutions shifted the popular dialog to include the outcomes from a legacy of white supremacist ideology in academia. In fall 2015, students at the University of Missouri led a high-profile protest in response to an insufficient institutional response to racist acts on campus. This inspired students at several other colleges and universities to lead protests as well, issuing lists of demands related to addressing "institutional racism in faculty hiring and student admissions, racially themed fraternity parties, and racial profiling on campus."[3] Many of the specific issues mentioned in student protest demands will sound familiar to those who study CRT in relation to academia, as these are issues that have been discussed in the literature for decades.[4-6]

The #BlackLivesMatter movement coincided with an increase in professional attention among librarians to the ways white supremacy is embedded within our library spaces and services. This timing also coincided with a shift toward applying more critical approaches in scholarship on librarianship, so it is difficult to attribute this increased attention to any one factor. However, we can attest that the BLM movement influenced us to focus more deeply on critical race theory.

Structures of Whiteness in Academia

Academic libraries reflect, record, and help to sustain the structures of inequality found throughout academia. This can be seen in many ways, including the lack of diversity among librarians,[7] the ways library spaces are physically designed,[8] how library materials are organized,[9] and our library instruction practices.[10]

Gusa's framework of white institutional presence (WIP) provides a useful way to discuss these structures throughout academia. WIP is a set of customary ideologies and practices rooted in the institution's design and the organization of its environment and activities. WIP, as a construct, names the racialized influences on discourses between and among students, between student and teacher, and between students and academic resources.[11]

This framework draws on research in critical race theory, focusing specifically on the ways whiteness shapes the norms and policies of academia and scholarly communications. Within this framework, "Whiteness is not based on complexion; rather it is a socially informed ontological and epistemological orientation."[12] This point distinguishing between physiological characteristics and socially constructed racial categories is important to highlight because it enables us to "approach race as a formation produced in and through the exercise of power rather than as a natural, pre-existent, and unchanging demographic attribute around which 'race relations' are organized."[13] WIP in academia means that efforts to diversify the demographic characteristics of our students, faculty, and even administrators will be insufficient alone, as whiteness still retains "the ability to set the terms by which other groups and classes must operate,"[14] making a willingness to conform to WIP a prerequisite for entry into those positions. As with many of the behavior patterns examined in the CRT literature, WIP is upheld in countless little interactions in which those reinforcing the norms and expectations of whiteness do not necessarily recognize the racialized structure underlying their assumptions about appropriate communication and behaviors.

Systems of Scholarly Communication

Open educational resources (OER) exist within the larger context of our systems of scholarly communications, which have been shaped by WIP. This includes everything from textbook and scholarly journal publishing practices to biases in funding and in which items librarians choose to buy, both of which then influence what students have available to use in their research.

Among librarians, there is an increasing awareness of the need to go beyond established methods of collection development to seek out diverse perspectives. However, library collections have and often still reinforce whiteness, as well as maleness and heterosexuality, as the standard "default" category, with others clearly marked as "other." This can be seen in the subject terms applied to materials, which determine the ways materials are organized on the bookshelves. For example, the Library of Congress Subject Headings, used by most academic libraries, effectively segregate books on educating Black/African Americans from books on the same topic that do not specify demographics. Of course, there is no category listed for white or Caucasian, reinforcing whiteness as the default category.[15] Thomas Weeks expands on this "hidden curriculum of heteronormativity" in the context of OERs in chapter three.

In addition to the role of librarians in purchasing and organizing materials, WIP is reinforced through privileging the scholarly sources—books and journal articles written by researchers for researchers. This is reasonable, as students are learning to participate in scholarly conversations, so they need to learn the norms of scholarly discourse—how to evaluate research studies, incorporate (and properly cite) previously published research, determine appropriate levels of detail to provide, and so on. However, it is important to recognize the ways this can reinforce WIP when not combined with discussions about ways to incorporate a wider range of perspectives into original research projects. Open pedagogy, and especially practices that encourage students to participate in building or localizing OER, as discussed in several chapters in this volume, can provide an avenue through which to build these discussions into the curriculum.

This emphasis on scholarly sources raises the question of which voices are represented in those materials, which are largely written by faculty and graduate students in academia and largely privilege authors from the Global North. According to 2018 data from the US National Center for Education Statistics, 75 percent of full-time faculty in "degree-granting postsecondary institutions" were white.[16] Working and publishing in the United States, we have primarily focused on these figures, but taking a global perspective requires further attention to publishing divides between the Global North and Global South. In addition to the need for more publications from marginalized populations in the Global North, several chapters in this volume examine the need for more locally created and relevant materials in and about the Global South.

The whiteness of faculty in higher education has ramifications beyond the biases (whether implicit or explicit) inherent in their own writing. Those who wish to perform and publish research "on marginalized populations often [receive] negative reactions, accusations of 'me-search' and questions about resonance or importance to the broader (read: dominant) world."[17] "Me-search" is a term used to dismiss research that is aligned with a scholar's marginalized identity, though it is rarely applied to white scholars doing research on white populations. The suggestion inherent in this term is that this alignment between marginalized identity and research focus makes the researcher less objective and therefore inferior within the epistemology of whiteness. The effects of this bias can be seen in levels of departmental support for a graduate student or junior faculty member,[18] tenure and promotion structures,[19] each step of the peer review process,[20] and funding apparatuses. For example, in one study, researchers found that Black scholars are around 10 percent less likely to receive a grant from the US National Institutes of Health than their white peers, even after controlling for a range of potentially confounding variables.[21] However, this othering of research on marginalized groups by marginalized scholars omits the fact that many respected research publications follow the same pattern of scholars studying populations that resemble their own identities—except that the identities in those instances are not marginalized.

Each instance of a decision that upholds WIP in scholarly research and publications may feel relatively minor, but they add up to a skewed scholarly record. This means we need to look beyond "traditional" scholarly and academic publications in order to challenge WIP in the curriculum. Open educational resources have the potential to move us beyond these "traditional" structures, to celebrate research done by marginalized populations in the context of their own communities, to amplify the voices of those who have the knowledge but have been excluded from formal prestige networks, and to engage students as co-creators of learning content that is relevant and respectful of their cultural contexts.

Open Educational Resources

Open educational resources are commonly described as any instructional material (usually in digital format) that is adaptable, reusable, and most importantly free to share without restrictions. These possibilities are only available with content in the public domain or that has been published under an open licensing agreement. The growing popularity of OER in higher education can be attributed to the potential cost savings for students and increased access to education. No- or low-cost textbook alternatives are a good solution when rising textbook costs from traditional publishers have become a barrier to student success. Increasing student access and affordability are noteworthy goals, but that is just the beginning of what is possible with OER-enabled pedagogy.

Wiley outlines five criteria that have become the standard for identifying open learning materials. These five permissions, facilitated by open licensing, allow educators to freely incorporate content created by others for their own instructional purposes.[22] The 5Rs described by Wiley include:

1. retain: the right to make, own, and control copies of the resources;
2. reuse: the right to use the content in a wide range of ways;
3. revise: the right to adapt, adjust, modify, or alter the content itself;
4. remix: the right to combine the original or revised content with other material to create something new; and
5. redistribute: the right to share copies of the original content, your revisions, or your remixes with others.

Adhering to the 5Rs does not inherently ensure diversity or inclusion in the development of open educational content. While this volume is filled with examples of the ways OER and open pedagogy can be used to support social justice in education, it is important to acknowledge that open learning is not equivalent to equitable or inclusive learning. Any application of the 5R framework must also be accompanied by a discussion about its challenges in achieving diversity and inclusion in academic knowledge production. OER implementation focused on increasing access without careful consideration of social justice implications will only perpetuate systemic inequities. Therefore, we begin this text with a section on theory and problematizing that take a critical look at the 5R framework and suggest alternative approaches to gauge openness that will increase access as well as achieve social justice goals.

Overview of This Book

The chapters in this volume cover a wide range of topics, from theoretical critiques to examples of OER development in practice to examinations of institutional support for OER development.

The first section, Theory and Problematizing, chapters 1 through 3 provide a theoretical foundation and critique of concerns related to OER. Hollich examines the ways OER to date have fallen short in promoting social justice and proposes ways to better fulfill that promise. Adams and Dannick critique the Western Curriculum more broadly, including the ways it excludes voices and perspectives, and discuss how OER can fill those gaps. These chapters also problematize the 5R definition of OER, outlining some reasons people may not want to share full permission to remix and revise all content. Weeks applies a queer theory lens to this critique, examining the implicit heteronormative messages in existing texts.

The next section, Open Praxis, chapters 4 through 7, describe examples of putting these theoretical approaches into practice. Maxwell, Gorecki, Henyard, and Morse describe the development of a Teach-Out model for an open course addressing police brutality in the United States. Grotewold, Kohler, and Krimbill discuss the impact of OER in PreK-12 education and outline how they incorporate lessons about OER into teacher education and educational leadership programs. Wood and Orzech examine the ways OER can make social work education more equitable. Becknell and March use culturally responsive pedagogy to inform the development of open course material for an information literacy course.

Next, Decolonizing Learning in the Global South, chapters 8 through 10, focus on OER development and use in Africa. Cox, Masuku, and Willmers reveal how educators across multiple disciplines used intuitive pedagogy to develop and implement a curriculum that addresses social injustice in the South African higher education system. Chigwada analyzes interviews of librarians involved with archiving open textbooks in Sub-Saharan Africa as well as interviews of students about their experience with open texts to identify opportunities and challenges faced by stakeholders. Hamisu Abdu presents the results of a survey of teacher educators about their knowledge about OERs in Nigeria.

The next section, Scaling Up with Institutional Policies (Approaches), chapters 11 through 13, examine the impact of institutional support on faculty development of OER. Doyle, Petrovic, Mudry, and Anderson outline several structural barriers that need to be addressed in order to support a wider, more equitable range of faculty in developing OER. Cannon-Rech describes a structural approach to embedding OER within a campus diversity and inclusion plan and the ways that enabled greater support for faculty of all ranks who choose to develop OER for their courses. Harlow and Rood shift that structural lens to a more pragmatic focus on developing training modules for faculty.

The final section, Building and Decolonizing OER Platforms, chapters 14 through 16, discuss efforts to create and decolonize OER platforms—collections that are more than just a textbook for a specific course. Ramjohn discusses Wikipedia, including critiques and efforts to decolonize the content. Murphy and Terrell describe the development of a resource for open content for those who teach music theory, including creating recordings of musical performances when the score is in the public domain but no recording of a performance of that score exists in the public domain. And Collins et al. describe a collaborative approach to building a collection of materials for teaching Caribbean studies.

Endnotes

1. Alicia Garza, "A Herstory of the #BlackLivesMatter Movement," in *Are All the Women Still White? Rethinking Race, Expanding Feminisms*, ed. Janell Hobson (Albany, NY: State University of New York Press, 2016), 23–28.
2. Kimberle Crenshaw, "Demarginalizing the Intersection of Race and Sex: A Black Feminist Critique of Antidiscrimination Doctrine, Feminist Theory and Antiracist Politics," *University of Chicago Legal Forum* 1989, no. 1 (1989), Article 8, available at https://chicagounbound.uchicago.edu/uclf/vol1989/iss1/8.
3. Roderick A. Ferguson, *We Demand: The University and Student Protests* (Oakland: University of California Press, 2017), 3.
4. Diane Lynn Gusa, "White Institutional Presence: The Impact of Whiteness on Campus Climate," *Harvard Educational Review* 80, no. 4 (January 1, 2010): 464–90, https://doi.org/10.17763/haer.80.4.p5j483825u110002.
5. Sylvia Hurtado, Alma R Clayton-Pedersen, Walter Recharde Allen, and Jeffrey F Milem, "Enhancing Campus Climates for Racial/Ethnic Diversity: Educational Policy and Practice," *The Review of Higher Education* 21, no. 3 (March 1, 1998): 279–302, doi:10.1353/rhe.1998.0003.
6. Daniel Solorzano, Miguel Ceja, and Tara Yosso, "Critical Race Theory, Racial Microaggressions, and Campus Racial Climate: The Experiences of African American College Students," *The Journal of Negro Education* 69, no. 1/2 (January 1, 2000): 60–73.

7. Chris Bourg, "The Unbearable Whiteness of Librarianship," *Feral Librarian* (blog), March 3, 2014, https://chrisbourg.wordpress.com/2014/03/03/the-unbearable-whiteness-of-librarianship/.
8. Freeda Brook, Dave Ellenwood, and Althea Eannace Lazzaro, "In Pursuit of Antiracist Social Justice: Denaturalizing Whiteness in the Academic Library," *Library Trends* 64, no. 2 (February 18, 2016): 246–84, doi:10.1353/lib.2015.0048, http://hdl.handle.net/1773/34983.
9. Emily Drabinski, "Queering the Catalog: Queer Theory and the Politics of Correction," *The Library Quarterly: Information, Community, Policy* 83, no. 2 (April 1, 2013): 94–111, doi:10.1086/669547, http://www.jstor.org/stable/10.1086/669547.
10. Angela Pashia, "Examining Structural Oppression as a Component of Information Literacy: A Call for Librarians to Support #BlackLivesMatter through Our Teaching," *Journal of Information Literacy* 11, no. 2 (December 2017): 86–104, https://doi.org/10.11645/11.2.2245.
11. Gusa, "White Institutional Presence," 467.
12. Ibid., 468.
13. David James Hudson, "On 'Diversity' as Anti-racism in Library and Information Studies: A Critique," *Journal of Critical Library and Information Studies* 1 (2017): 20.
14. Gusa, "White Institutional Presence," 469.
15. Pashia, "Examining Structural Oppression."
16. "Characteristics of Postsecondary Faculty," National Center for Education Statistics (NCES), last modified May 2020, https://nces.ed.gov/programs/coe/indicator/csc.
17. J. E. Sumerau, "Research on the Margins," *Inside Higher Ed* (October 14, 2016), https://www.insidehighered.com/advice/2016/10/14/challenges-publishing-research-marginalized-communities-essay.
18. Eric Anthony Grollman, "'Playing the Game' for Black Grad Students," *Inside Higher Ed* (February 24, 2017), https://www.insidehighered.com/advice/2017/02/24/lessons-learned-black-phd-student-essay.
19. Heather Castleden, Paul Sylvestre, Debbie Martin, and Mary McNally, "'I Don't Think That Any Peer Review Committee… Would Ever "Get" What I Currently Do': How Institutional Metrics for Success and Merit Risk Perpetuating the (Re)Production of Colonial Relationships in Community-Based Participatory Research Involving Indigenous Peoples in Canada," *International Indigenous Policy Journal* 6, no. 4 (September 1, 2015), doi:10.18584/iipj.2015.6.4.2.
20. Stephanie A. Fryberg and Ernesto Javier Martínez, "Constructed Strugglers: The Impact of Diversity Narratives on Junior Faculty of Color," in *The Truly Diverse Faculty: New Dialogues in American Higher Education*, ed. Stephanie A. Fryberg and Ernesto Javier Martínez (New York: Palgrave Macmillan, 2014), 3–24.
21. Donna K. Ginther, Beth Masimore, Faye Liu, Joshua Schnell, Laurel L. Haak, Raynard Kington, and Walter T. Schaffer, "Race, Ethnicity, and NIH Research Awards," *Science* 333, no. 6045 (January 1, 2011): 1015–19, doi:10.1126/science.1196783.
22. David Wiley, "Defining the 'Open' in Open Content and Open Educational Resources," Open-Content, accessed September 27, 2021, https://opencontent.org/definition/.

Bibliography

Bourg, Chris. "The Unbearable Whiteness of Librarianship." *Feral Librarian* (blog), March 3, 2014. https://chrisbourg.wordpress.com/2014/03/03/the-unbearable-whiteness-of-librarianship/.

Brook, Freeda, Dave Ellenwood, and Althea Eannace Lazzaro. "In Pursuit of Antiracist Social Justice: Denaturalizing Whiteness in the Academic Library." *Library Trends* 64, no. 2 (February 18, 2016): 246–84. doi:10.1353/lib.2015.0048.

Castleden, Heather, Paul Sylvestre, Debbie Martin, and Mary McNally. "'I Don't Think That Any Peer Review Committee… Would Ever "Get" What I Currently Do': How Institutional Metrics for Success and Merit Risk Perpetuating the (Re)Production of Colonial Relationships in

Community-Based Participatory Research Involving Indigenous Peoples in Canada." *International Indigenous Policy Journal* 6, no. 4 (September 1, 2015). doi:10.18584/iipj.2015.6.4.2.

Crenshaw, Kimberle. "Demarginalizing the Intersection of Race and Sex: A Black Feminist Critique of Antidiscrimination Doctrine, Feminist Theory and Antiracist Politics." *University of Chicago Legal Forum* 1989, no. 1 (1989), Article 8. Available at: https://chicagounbound.uchicago.edu/uclf/vol1989/iss1/8.

Drabinski, Emily. "Queering the Catalog: Queer Theory and the Politics of Correction." *The Library Quarterly: Information, Community, Policy* 83, no. 2 (April 1, 2013): 94–111. doi:10.1086/669547.

Ferguson, Roderick A. *We Demand: The University and Student Protests*. Oakland: University of California Press, 2017.

Fryberg, Stephanie A., and Ernesto Javier Martínez, "Constructed Strugglers: The Impact of Diversity Narratives on Junior Faculty of Color." In *The Truly Diverse Faculty: New Dialogues in American Higher Education*, edited by Stephanie A. Fryberg and Ernesto Javier Martínez, 3–24. New York: Palgrave Macmillan, 2014.

Garza, Alicia. "A Herstory of the #BlackLivesMatter Movement." In *Are All the Women Still White? Rethinking Race, Expanding Feminisms*, edited by Janell Hobson, 23–28. Albany, NY: State University of New York Press, 2016.

Ginther, Donna K., Beth Masimore, Faye Liu, Joshua Schnell, Laurel L. Haak, Raynard Kington, and Walter T. Schaffer. "Race, Ethnicity, and NIH Research Awards." *Science* 333, no. 6045 (January 1, 2011): 1015–19. doi:10.1126/science.1196783.

Grollman, Eric Anthony. "'Playing the Game' for Black Grad Students." *Inside Higher Ed* (February 24, 2017). https://www.insidehighered.com/advice/2017/02/24/lessons-learned-black-phd-student-essay.

Gusa, Diane Lynn. "White Institutional Presence: The Impact of Whiteness on Campus Climate." *Harvard Educational Review* 80, no. 4 (January 1, 2010): 464–90.

Hudson, David James. "On 'Diversity' as Anti-racism in Library and Information Studies: A Critique." *Journal of Critical Library and Information Studies* 1 (2017): 1–36. https://doi.org/10.24242/jclis.v1i1.6.

Hurtado, Sylvia, Alma R Clayton-Pedersen, Walter Recharde Allen, and Jeffrey F Milem. "Enhancing Campus Climates for Racial/Ethnic Diversity: Educational Policy and Practice." *The Review of Higher Education* 21, no. 3 (March 1, 1998): 279–302. doi:10.1353/rhe.1998.0003.

National Center for Education Statistics (NCES). "Characteristics of Postsecondary Faculty." Last modified May 2020. https://nces.ed.gov/programs/coe/indicator/csc.

Pashia, Angela. "Examining Structural Oppression as a Component of Information Literacy: A Call for Librarians to Support #BlackLivesMatter through Our Teaching." *Journal of Information Literacy* 11, no. 2 (December 2017): 86–104.

Solorzano, Daniel, Miguel Ceja, Tara Yosso. "Critical Race Theory, Racial Microaggressions, and Campus Racial Climate: The Experiences of African American College Students." *The Journal of Negro Education* 69, no. 1/2 (January 1, 2000): 60–73.

Sumerau, J. E. "Research on the Margins." *Inside Higher Ed* (October 14, 2016). https://www.insidehighered.com/advice/2016/10/14/challenges-publishing-research-marginalized-communities-essay.

Wiley, David. "Defining the 'Open' in Open Content and Open Educational Resources." OpenContent. Accessed September 27, 2021. https://opencontent.org/definition/.

SECTION I
Theory and Problematizing

CHAPTER 1

The Unrealized Promise of OER:
An Exploration of Copyright, the Open Movement, and Social Justice

Shanna Hollich

Introduction and Definitions

The open movement has been around for several decades now, and it's a field that began with high hopes and aspirations. We were going to bring knowledge to the world, to the masses, and we were going to break down the barriers to information, education, and knowledge. This chapter explores the definitions of and promises made by OER; the systems that OER exists in and depends upon, such as copyright law, academia, and the scholarly communication ecosystem; and where the original mission of OER is falling short, particularly in relation to a framework of social justice access, inclusion, and empowerment. Though the final section does envision some general guidelines that will help move the field forward, the main purpose here is in raising questions and making connections that have been hinted at in the literature but have not previously been made explicit.

Figuring out exactly what we mean when we use terms like "open" and "social justice" is difficult, and the literature abounds with explorations and theorizing about these terms.[1] OER exist in a broader ecosystem of open that includes the open (social) movement, open source software and computer systems, open access literature, open pedagogy, open educational practices (OEP), and even related intellectual property issues such as the right to

3

repair. The definition used here is purposely an expansive one that encompasses and includes all aspects of open. Though ostensibly about OER, I argue below that OER are simply a microcosm of broader systemic concerns involving both the open movement and the field of education as a whole, and I frequently use the terms "OER" and "open" interchangeably. Following the lead of Cronin and MacLaren, I tend to think of OER and the open movement as a whole as being grounded in "theoretical foundations in constructivist, social constructivist and connectivist educational philosophies" that "also adopt a critical approach, often with the aim of challenging traditional educational practices."[2]

It is this social constructivist and critical approach to OER that leads naturally to a relationship with social justice. There are perhaps just as many various and even conflicting definitions of social justice as there are of open, but here I primarily utilize the framework outlined by Gidley, which envisions a three-tiered social justice framework centered primarily on inclusion.[3] Factors that directly impact degrees of social inclusion include socioeconomic status, language, religion, geography, gender and sexuality, age, health or disability status, unemployment, homelessness, and incarceration. There are three general levels of social justice, outlined below with additional information about how they specifically relate to educational resources:

1. Social justice/inclusion as access (sometimes also referred to as redistributive justice).[4] Primarily centered on economic justice in a neoliberal framework, this aspect of social inclusion is concerned with issues of access to and affordability of learning materials, especially to learners who may otherwise be excluded due to lack of financial or technological means. In terms of the popular acronym "EDI," this would be the aspect primarily focused on equity.
2. Social justice/inclusion as participation (sometimes referred to as recognitive justice), ensuring that the learning materials and resources we use are truly reflective of and inclusive of folks from marginalized communities. This would be the "diversity" aspect of much EDI work. Once materials are made more widely accessible to a broader range of learners, it is important that those learners see themselves and their own stories reflected in those materials.
3. Social justice/inclusion as empowerment (sometimes referred to as representational justice). This is social justice as true inclusion and is the logical next step in the process of openly creating and sharing educational resources. Not only is it important for

learners to be represented in their educational materials, but it is important that those groups are allowed to speak for and represent themselves, especially when those groups are, like those listed above, ones that are typically and historically marginalized by society.

OER as a field is generally very good at addressing the first dimension of social justice as access. There has been much literature published in the last ten to twenty years about market surveys, the high profit margins of commercial textbook and scholarly journal publishers, and the affordability of education both in terms of tuition and in terms of ancillary materials and fees. More recently, we are starting to see more attention being paid to the second tier of social justice, which focuses on participation. More educators are beginning to realize that increased access to learning materials that perpetuate patriarchal and white supremacist ideologies are not truly having the social justice impacts we may have hoped for, and recent literature that explores the relationship between OER and social justice often place their focus here,[5] but there is danger in perpetuating and entrenching dichotomies between the Global North and the Global South and embracing paternalism as we in the West focus on "delivering" education and knowledge to the "rest of the world."

It is the third dimension—social justice as empowerment—where OER and the open movement have continually fallen short. As OER largely originated in North America and Europe (due to funding capabilities and power structures that we explore in the next sections), there has been a tendency for those of us in the West to see ourselves as holding expertise that others do not have and furthermore to feel an obligation to use that expertise to sometimes speak for others rather than allowing them to speak for themselves. The rest of this chapter is spent exploring the possibilities inherent to and as yet unrealized within the open movement and suggests some avenues toward making OER a truly inclusive and empowering pedagogy for all learners.

The Promise (and Misconceptions) of OER

Before we begin to truly interrogate where OER is currently and where it could go in the future, it is important for us to briefly explore its foundations. The open movement has existed for almost as long as the World Wide Web has, with the foundation of arXiv in 1991. The technological capabilities brought about by a global network of linked computers allowed for easier file sharing and community outreach, but the current open movement truly took off around the turn of the twenty-first century, with the launch of initiatives such as MIT's

OpenCourseWare and Creative Commons. The arguments for "opening knowledge" and the potential benefits of doing so largely echoed the promises made in the early days of the web: we were going to democratize knowledge and bring it to the masses. This spirit found a natural home in the field of education, where it was argued, "By democratizing the processes through which educational materials and processes are designed and delivered, open education allows a greater plurality of voices to be heard and to contribute, and the experiences of groups who are often marginalized may be better heard: perhaps this is what we should really mean when we refer to education as 'open.'"[6]

However, much like the promise of the early internet, this goal is a well-intentioned one that is easier theorized than practiced. OER are not inherently better educational tools than commercial texts, particularly when it comes to aspects of social justice.[7] Democratization, it turns out, is not a "magic bullet" that solves our diversity problems. Opening up access to a space online does not instantly make that space an inclusive one, as marginalized folks well know thanks to their experiences on social media websites and online forums. Similarly, providing an open venue to publish educational materials and other works does not in and of itself serve to amplify or aid marginalized voices.[8] The promise of OER is reliant on its inherent "goodness" as a concept, and this too often results in a failure to critically evaluate its effects. This echoes almost exactly the problem of "vocational awe" identified by Ettarh in the field of librarianship; that is to say, assuming that a field and its practices are inherently good often leads to ignoring the real harms that that community can and does perpetuate, even if unintentionally.[9]

Relatedly, there are a number of misconceptions about OER and the open movement. We still have not settled, as a field, on a single definition for OER, so there is often difficulty in pinning down exactly what "counts" as OER. The most widely used definition is probably the 5R definition first developed by Wiley, but as we will see later, this definition is in itself a problematic one, particularly when analyzed from a social justice framework focused on empowerment.[10] OER fundamentally relies on copyright and intellectual property law, and there are further misunderstandings about the relationship between the two as well as how open licensing schemes such as Creative Commons work across multiple jurisdictions. Additionally, there are misconceptions about exactly who OER are for. A faculty member once told me, "If a student cannot afford their textbooks, they don't deserve to be in college," suggesting that not only is the open movement designed primarily for "poor" people but that perhaps such people do not "deserve" quality educational materials. And it is important to recognize once again the problems inherent to the belief that for something to be "open" means that it is automatically, by default, "good." Open systems, like the internet-enabled systems that they are based on, tend to bias those folks who are already in privileged positions because of their race, class, or gender. As singh notes, "The people calling for open are often in positions of privilege, or have reaped the benefits of being open early on—when the platform wasn't as easily used for abuse, and when we were privileged to create the kinds of networks that included others like us."[11]

Limitations of the Current Conceptions of OER
The Internet, the Open Movement, and the 5Rs

OER do not exist in a vacuum. They exist in an ecosystem that relies on intellectual property law, the internet and technological capability, academic freedom, educational pedagogy, and scholarly publishing, and the open movement is reliant on each of these systems in order to exist. As a result, the problems of systemic bias and injustice that are endemic to these systems become inherited by OER. We cannot begin to address social justice and OER without also addressing social justice in our related systems and institutions.

There are many examples of this, particularly in relation to technology and the internet. As online spaces such as Twitter, Reddit, and Slack have discovered, it isn't enough to simply designate a space as "open" and leave users to the wolves. These spaces require infrastructure; they require moderation, guidelines, and support.[12] Without these, the ugliest sides of human nature often predominate, and privilege remains free to propagate unchecked. The democratization potential of OER echoes the democratization arguments made about the early internet, but what these arguments fail to recognize is that opening up communications and networks to a global audience brings the entire world inside your open space—and the entire world includes good actors, bad actors, bias, privilege, and white supremacy.[13] Similarly, as many OER are digitally based, they tend to inherit the same problems that all web-based materials have, including lack of investment in infrastructure, indexing, and discoverability, which can make OER siloed, difficult to find, and demanding of a certain level of expertise to evaluate and implement.[14] How do we bring OER to jurisdictions where digital artifacts are subject to widespread and government-sanctioned censorship, e.g., China? How do we empower such societies to participate in a truly open educational environment?

OER's reliance on technology brings with it some other potential pitfalls. Educational technology, like all technology, is coded with privilege and a specific set of values.[15] As Watters points out, "Data is not neutral. Data—its collection, storage, retrieval, usage—is not neutral."[16] Simply opening up data and resources does not automatically ameliorate problems of privilege. Concerns about privacy, personality, publicity, and other types of rights and ethical considerations are also fundamental to any digital ecosystem, but the system of copyright upon which OER is built is not equipped to address these areas.[17] In 2019, IBM made headlines because of their use of openly licensed images to train AI datasets in facial recognition applications.[18] Not only were these images used without consent from the copyright holders (which was not technically, legally required), but the algorithmic bias that runs throughout machine-learning applications such as this one is inextricably bound with societal bias as well.[19] Context is everything here. The images were openly licensed in the specific context of sharing with family and friends online through the social media site Flickr; however, the owners of these images were not able to predict that a tech company might harvest them and use them in a completely different context, and that context matters greatly when we consider issues of privacy and ethics.

Creative Commons as an organization acknowledges that their open licenses are not able to adequately address issues of privacy, security, and confidentiality.[20] If copyright is not a good instrument for addressing privacy and OER are reliant wholly upon copyright to legally be created and shared, then we must find an alternate method to ensure the privacy and confidentiality of folks using OER. As of this writing, there are currently no widespread systems or guidelines in place for the open community to do so. Open licenses do not make specific accommodations for traditional or indigenous knowledge artifacts—for example, when they are not already covered by existing intellectual property laws. There are no built-in protections for marginalized communities. The assumption made by the open community is that sharing is always a good thing and always happens in the public interest, but we are beginning to see more examples, such as the ethics of sharing queer histories and videotape raised by Mattson, where the calculus is more complex.[21] In this example, an archivist working to digitize collections from the Educational Video Center encountered a VHS recording of a complete television episode that had aired in the 1990s on the Manhattan Neighborhood Network. The episode was a show hosted by a transgender African-American woman, but the broadcast was made in a time long before digital streaming video and on a television network with a very narrow broadcast area, so its initial and intended context was to be viewed at a specific time, on a specific day, and only in a specific geographic area (just the borough of Manhattan). Digitizing and putting this material online makes it accessible in a whole new way, to a much broader audience, and potentially releases sensitive information and imagery about an individual, with much broader implications than they could have envisioned when they first created the material.

The lack of protection for marginalized communities within the field of OER is perhaps made most clear by a closer examination of the 5Rs. This framework says that an educational resource can only truly "count" as open if its licensing/copyright status meets all five of the following qualifications: ability to **reuse** the content in its unaltered form; ability to **retain** copies of the content indefinitely; ability to **revise** the content or adapt, adjust, modify, or alter it to suit one's specific needs; ability to **remix** the content with other content to create something new; and ability to **redistribute** the content and share it with others in either its original or altered format.[22] However, this leaves a large chunk of openly licensed content outside the realm of OER—namely, any content that is licensed with a Creative Commons No Derivatives (CC ND) restriction. Bossu et al. explicitly ask, "Would there be certain values of ideological positions that the OER community will not embrace and not include?"[23] And the answer, apparently, is a resounding yes: if you want to retain your work in its whole and unaltered form, then you cannot consider it truly open. Those most likely to be affected by this restriction, however, are members of marginalized groups. Imagine, for example, an open textbook that contains narratives of students from various marginalized groups. Those students tell their stories in their own words, using vernacular and vocabulary that is appropriate to their social groups, and they feel it is important that their words remain whole and that they are not able to be remixed, revised, or altered for fear of being taken out of context. Given these valid concerns, they choose an ND license for this material, but with the 5R definition of OER, they are excluded from the OER movement. Similar objections exist for works of creative art, such as poetry, whose meaning and value are dependent upon the holistic context in which they were first published and whose authors may wish them to remain unaltered.

Embedded in this definition of OER is an assumption that technology is a natural solution to problems of access. However, as Lambert points out, "Technological determinism is a problematic and ultimately ineffective approach to technology implementations, which assumes that the particular capabilities of new technologies will always improve the situations into which they are brought."[24] Most current definitions of OER are almost entirely focused on technology and finances, and as we will see in the next few sections, this does not go far enough. Ensuring low- or no-cost access, and even solving some of the problems of accessibility with respect to hiding OER behind datawalls or other privacy-stripping measures, may be a solution to social justice as access, but it does not address social justice as participation or empowerment.

OER is Primarily About Access and/or Students

The vast majority of arguments about the benefits of OER, particularly with respect to social justice, are focused on student access and rooted in neoliberalism and a deficit model of education.[25] The biggest consequence of this assumption is that it brings with it a slew of additional (and biased) assumptions about the viability of education and creation in the Global North (also referred to here as the West) and the Global South. When we consider simply providing access to material to be a quick fix to comprehensive education, we ignore that educational materials must also be inclusive and empowering in order to be maximally effective.

Current OER center largely on white male topics from a white male lens, because the vast majority of OER are authored in countries in North America and Europe where there is time, privilege, and funding accessible to support this work.[26] But OER themselves do not necessarily result in positive effects, even when they are created and shared with the best of intentions. As Crissinger points out, "The creation of OER by Western institutions is not in itself a bad thing. However, it becomes troubling when these institutions promise that their OER will be useful or applicable to all learners globally for educational purposes."[27] Furthermore, when the West foists OER upon countries it sees as educationally "impoverished" in much the same way we foist our used clothes, print books, and electronics onto them, we may in fact perpetuate real harm on the very folks we are hoping to serve.[28] Simply making things "accessible" does not in and of itself break down systemic barriers of oppression.[29]

Similarly, when we talk about access and OER, we are talking primarily about access for students/learners. However, issues of access are also relevant to educators and creators, particularly in terms of who has access to the time, privilege, and support to produce and integrate these resources into their work. Even aside from these broader issues, the focus on access only reaches the first tier of the social justice framework outlined at the beginning of this chapter. There are some scholars working toward social justice as participation with respect to OER, and this work is laudable. If we want to focus on the effects of OER on students but work toward true social justice as empowerment, we should be asking questions such as:

- Are students also free of bias? OER often advocates for student-centered pedagogy, but what are the cultural ramifications of students, even those from a marginalized background, perpetuating existing stereotypes?[30] Whose voices are we making space for in our classrooms?
- What are we giving learners access to, exactly? Clement argues, "While the affordability of OER can increase accessibility for marginalized learners,

implementing OER in the classroom that are heavily colonized and center a white patriarchal epistemology does nothing to increase or foster equity for marginalized learners. It merely gives marginalized students increased access to an educational environment that continues to systematically devalue them."[31] She then goes on to ask how equitable it really is to ask marginalized students to engage with materials that do not reflect their own experiences and their own communities. What are we doing to support educators from the Global South, for example, to create their own online resources in their own languages?[32]

These questions are integral to all the other limitations discussed throughout this chapter. It is impossible to separate issues of access from issues of privacy, for example, or inclusion. Access is the first tier in the social justice framework, but it is time to ask how we are empowering students and learners not only to be included and represented in the learning materials that they use but also to begin engaging and creating those materials themselves. Additionally, we must examine the context in which we are sharing so as not to permanently entrench a perceived imbalance in knowledge across countries; in our zeal to make all things "open," we may in fact be limiting and even negating the scholarly and academic cultures of non-Western nations. These issues lead us directly to an exploration of the power dynamics inherent to OER, as well as academia and scholarly publishing as a whole, and to ask questions about not only if student learners have access to educational materials but also if faculty and staff educators have access to create and implement them in the first place.

Politics of Labor and Power

One of the largest areas of exploration and research in the OER literature involves the politics of labor and power in OER creation and publishing. Whether it's the discussion of tenure-track versus non-tenure-track faculty, faculty versus staff labor, or academic freedom versus work-for-hire and ownership of copyrighted materials, there are a number of complexities at play here that we will only be able to touch on briefly.

Perhaps the simplest place to start is again at the lower tiers of our social justice framework, regarding access. There are political realities of OER that not only determine who has access to use and learn from these materials but also, and more fundamentally, determine who has the ability to create and share them. The vast majority of OER creators are large non-profit institutions, NGOs, or institutions of higher education. Large nonprofits and higher education institutions wield large donor banks and groups of political lobbyists, which gives them the power to uphold whatever status quo system of privilege they seek to uphold and leaves the rest of us at the mercy of their potential benevolence.[33] This means that certain projects, particularly those involving maintaining legacy initiatives or supporting marginalized social groups, may never receive an adequate level of funding or material support to ever come to fruition. There is much criticism in the literature regarding commercial textbook publishers making decisions about what information is worth inclusion in an educational resource, but even open publishers must make these choices, and their choices are not automatically more inclusive or more empowering by virtue of being open. Which OER are actually indexed and discoverable in search engines, who gets access to what repositories, and who gets cited in the scholarly literature are all functions of who wields power and influence in a given community. To put it another way, all of the problems of power and privilege that are endemic to scholarly communication as a whole are also inherited and potentially perpetuated by open scholarly communication as well.[34]

It has been noted that to make learning materials that can effectively support students in all social groups at all stages of development, educators "must take on constant self-education in contemporary social issues."[35] However, this support for lifelong learning is not available at all institutions and to all educators. One study found that the vast majority of OER initiatives were spearheaded by tenured and tenure-track faculty, presumably because contingent faculty such as lecturers and adjuncts do not have the institutional support or financial backing to create such learning materials.[36] Not only are there no monetary rewards for OER work, but creators may not actually even own the objects that they create or be able to take them along to a new institution, depending on their work-for-hire status and the institution's intellectual property policies. Moreover, though some higher education institutions have implemented grant programs for OER adoption and creation, not only are these almost always short-term programs with limited funding, but there have yet been no grant programs designed specifically to make open texts more diverse or more accessible to marginalized groups.[37] What we fund speaks directly to what we value and what we prioritize.

Similarly, there is a fair amount of work that notes how difficult it is for faculty to find, download, use, adapt, create, and upload OER materials.[38] However, not all of this work explores the extant divisions between tenured and contingent faculty at higher education institutions or those between faculty and staff. Librarians, who have faculty status at some institutions but staff status at others, along with other support staff roles such as instructional designers, often have specific expertise relevant to the entire OER lifecycle, from use to creation, from copyright to course design. Unfortunately, workers in staff or contingent faculty roles, particularly those that do not hold doctorate degrees, are not always seen as valuable contributors in the educational process, and their expertise is often discounted. Additionally, those who are in staff or non-tenure faculty roles at higher education institutions may not have the privilege of academic freedom, which means they may be even more reluctant to create or use OER that focus on social justice inclusion and empowerment, particularly if those materials are seen as antithetical to the institutional status quo.

Essentially, all aspects of scholarly publishing, including open publishing, require labor and support. The time that educators spend to create and utilize educational materials must be compensated; an infrastructure must be available to publish, host, and distribute these materials as well as to create metadata for indexing and discoverability; and care must be taken to ensure that these materials are truly representative of the communities we are seeking to serve. All of these efforts require funding and labor, and institutions that have more access to funding and skilled labor are going to find themselves at an advantage. Many OER practitioners see these issues as primarily belonging to commercial entities, and though there is rightful criticism of "open washing" and the co-opting of open materials to be exploited by commercial entities, providers and publishers of open materials are not immune to these pressures. Again, as OER are embedded in a broader system of scholarly communication and digital technology, they will necessarily inherit the problems endemic to those systems. While a commercial entity may co-opt an OER and put it behind a login or even a paywall, forcing users to forgo their privacy and confidentiality in order to access the resource, many open communities are also now requiring logins or other technological infrastructure in order to interact with their content. How many open publishing servers, for instance, are hosted by Amazon Web Services, which raises questions about privacy, security, and confidentiality of data for the folks who utilize those systems? How invasive is the user tracking implemented by nonprofit and university repositories? Even beyond these basic privileges of access, there are unanswered questions around the privilege of authorship and publication, where one must often be affiliated with an institution of higher education or other nonprofit in order to publish in a highly visible outlet or to provide peer reviews. Providing additional opportunities to publish or use OER is not enough if the environment itself is rife with the potential for exploitation and if the system itself is not yet equitable; instead, these additional opportunities and incentives (such as promotion and tenure or grant funding) will simply go to those with the inherent privilege to take advantage of them.

Finally, Tang and Bao bring to light important issues regarding social influence and its effect on what labor is seen as valued by the academy and what is not.[39] They found, for example, that teachers in Japan consider the effect of social influence when adopting OER, but teachers in Korea are more likely to be driven by how OER can improve their job performance, and teachers in the

United States are almost entirely motivated by the monetary value and potential cost savings of OER. To truly achieve social inclusion in our OER, and to effectively empower others to create and utilize OER most effectively, we must do more work to understand different societal motivations behind OER to understand what solutions will be most effective in different societal contexts. There is evidence that teachers in highly individualistic societies, for example, have a higher likelihood of using OER in their courses. What are the implications of a finding like this? Countries with greater gender parity are also more likely to use OER. If nothing else, this again goes to show how social justice issues are inextricably linked with the open movement. If we do not take cultural differences into account in terms of things such as response to power structures and individualism versus collectivism, our global initiatives will fail. We cannot analyze OER in a vacuum, and we cannot continue to think about, create, and use OER without social justice in mind.

Where We Go From Here

At this point, I'd like to turn the focus of this chapter toward the future by identifying some further questions that can frame the exploration of OER and social justice and to propose some possible avenues where individual OER practitioners can incorporate higher tiers of social inclusion, especially social justice as empowerment, into their work.

Understand and Utilize the True Capacity of CC Licensing

Despite the limitations of copyright and open licensing, particularly in terms of privacy, confidentiality, security, ethics, and surveillance, there are some advantages to Creative Commons licensing that are seldom explored and not widely known. The most relevant to OER and social justice is the capacity for CC-licensed materials to allow for format shifting, even in jurisdictions where a shift in format would normally constitute an adaptation or derivative work, and even in certain cases where the content is licensed with a No Derivatives restriction. Particularly in terms of inclusion with respect to cognitive diversity, the ability to take an openly licensed text and convert it to an audio format or an alternative format that interfaces more easily with text-to-speech software, for example, is vital. Because, in the United States at least, converting a printed text to an audio format is a right granted exclusively to the copyright holder, many OER stakeholders do not realize that such format shifting is allowable and built in to all of the CC licenses by default and that this is a huge step in the right direction when it comes to accessibility of open course materials. Though this is primarily an issue of social justice as access, it is a transitional phase toward increased social justice as participation for cognitively diverse folks as well.

Context is Key

OER are "produced, used, and shaped by important historical and cultural contexts," and those contexts do not just go away when we share and remix them.[40] It is important to remember that context is vital here, as it is in all facets of social justice. There's a common saying in the open movement that "information wants to be free," but information is better off contextualized, truly localized and understood, and culturally relevant.[41] The relevant social justice framework here is one that goes beyond even participation, to be more than just respect for and acknowledgment of difference and diversity, and to be a truly critical endeavor that disrupts the dominant narratives that promote discrimination and bias.[42]

Providing truly contextualized learning materials is no small feat, and it relates directly to the previous discussion of power and funding. Simply translating OER into a local language, for example, is not sufficient for true empowerment; rather, we need to fully adapt OER to local contexts and respect cultural differences. In this way, though there is much focus on gaining additional technology skills to better create and use OER in education, the real challenge will be to increase cultural competency in order to provide full value to these materials. A fully integrative and socially just OER will empower learners by recognizing and harnessing students' experiences, by including space for self-reflection so that we can do more than just pay lip service to diversity, and by recognizing that diversity is multifaceted and intersectional.[43] It is also worth noting that to truly empower marginalized learners means to go beyond our comfort zones and to interface with social groups that have historically been excluded from the open education conversation entirely, such as people who are incarcerated.

Embrace Ambiguity

This may be one of the biggest challenges, particularly for a field that has been arguing over definitions for several decades now. We cannot go beyond social justice as access, however, until we acknowledge that we (meaning educators, PhD-holders, denizens of Western societies, or other members of "expert" levels of society) do not have all the answers. We cannot fall into the trap of paternalism and assume that simply giving people access to knowledge will somehow set them free. Watters argues, and I concur, that "the answer here isn't a clearer definition of 'open'; the answer isn't more fights for a more rigid adherence to a particular license," and that instead the answer may be "more transparency about politics."[44] We cannot continue to act as if open, by its very nature, is politically good or progressive or even neutral. We've figured out the legal logistics, we're chipping away at the issues of technological and economic access, and it is time for us to focus more on a truly participatory open movement that empowers learners from all social groups to drive their own educational journeys and tell their own stories.

Phelan contends that, ultimately, OER raise a question about what it really means to be a learner and what it really means to be an educator.[45] He goes on to ask why we certify learning at all, and though he then proceeds to give a number of arguments about why we should continue to do so, I would encourage an exploration of the opposite. To some extent, we cannot truly know what someone has or has not learned, just as we cannot truly know someone else's mind. We can focus on authentic assessments that respect cultural differences and truly engage a learner and empower them to build knowledge and use information that is vital to their cultural contexts, but doing so goes beyond a set of quiz questions, a digital badge, or a certification. Education is, in and of itself, an ambiguous and socially constructed enterprise, and our educational resources remain so even when we make them open.

Focus on Social Justice as Empowerment

Finally, I'd like to briefly explore what an OER that is truly situated in social justice as empowerment might look like. Arinto et al. suggest that "OER creation as a form of empowerment for educators and students… is fostered by professional development, membership in a community of practice and personal qualities and motivations related to personal histories as well as professional identities."[46] To truly engage in and support that level of empowerment across a wide variety of cultural contexts would involve a more concerted investment in open infrastructure, particularly in terms of time and financial support. Phelan cites a case study where OER materials were designed and shared to support safe birthing practices in remote communities in low-income countries of Latin America.[47] It is unclear whether these materials were developed in true partnership and consultation with members of the community, perhaps acknowledging local cultural practices and traditional medicine. In any case, a project like this, particularly if it is done in solidarity with the community, with actual community members having ownership of the creation and distribution of these materials, begins to look a lot like social justice as empowerment, and it begins to look a lot closer to realizing the democratization and knowledge sharing environment that OER promises.

It is important, as we train and empower folks in their local communities, that we do not veer into paternalism or white saviorism. It is important to engage in a dialogue that allows people to envision their own futures and to express their own cultural values in a way where they can feel that their beliefs and practices are being truly honored. Fully enabling communities to make their own choices in this way means focusing on access and participation as well as empowerment, and it means providing an infrastructure of funding and support. It also involves a certain amount of embracing ambiguity, in that true empowerment is about enabling people to build their own resources, even if their vision of those resources does not match our own. It means that we may not get the results that we expect and that our definitions of open need to be expansive and inclusive enough to make room for hegemonies beyond those of North American and European societies, even if it results in definitions, cultural resources, and OER materials that we ourselves do not fully value or understand

Endnotes

1. Catherine Cronin and Iain MacLaren, "Conceptualising OEP: A Review of Theoretical and Empirical Literature in Open Educational Practices," *Open Praxis* 10, no. 2 (April 20, 2018): 127–43; Robert Farrow, "Open Education and Critical Pedagogy," *Learning, Media and Technology* 42, no. 2 (April 3, 2017): 130–46, https://doi.org/10.1080/17439884.2016.1113991; Audrey Watters, "From 'Open' to Justice," in *Open at the Margins*, ed. Maha Bali, Catherine Cronin, Laura Czerniewicz, Robin DeRosa, and Rajiv Jhangiani (Rebus Community, 2020), https://press.rebus.community/openatthemargins/chapter/from-open-to-justice/; Marco Seiferle-Valencia, "It's Not (Just) About the Cost: Academic Libraries and Intentionally Engaged OER for Social Justice," *Library Trends* 69, no. 2 (2020): 469–87, https://doi.org/10.1353/lib.2020.0042; Jennifer Gidley, Gary P. Hampson, Leone Wheeler, and Elleni Bereded-Samuel, "Social Inclusion: Context, Theory and Practice," Semantic Scholar, 2010, 16.
2. Cronin and MacLaren, "Conceptualising OEP," 137.
3. Gidley et al., "Social Inclusion."
4. Sarah R. Lambert, "Changing Our (Dis)Course: A Distinctive Social Justice Aligned Definition of Open Education," *Journal of Learning for Development* 5, no. 3 (2018): 225–44; Seiferle-Valencia, "It's Not (Just) About the Cost."
5. Cheryl Ann Hodgkinson-Williams and Henry Trotter, "A Social Justice Framework for Understanding Open Educational Resources and Practices in the Global South," *Journal of Learning for Development* 5, no. 3 (2018): 204–24; Patricia Arinto, Cheryl Hodgkinson-Williams, and Henry Trotter, "OER and OEP in the Global South: Implications and Recommendations for Social Inclusion," in *Adoption and Impact of OER in the Global South. Cape Town & Ottawa: African Minds, International Development Research Centre & Research on Open Educational Resources for Development*, eds. C. Hodgkinson-Williams and P. B. Arinto, retrieved from http://dx.doi.org/10.5281/zenodo.1043830; Seiferle-Valencia, "It's Not (Just) About the Cost."
6. Farrow, "Open Education and Critical Pedagogy."
7. Amy T. Nusbaum, "Who Gets to Wield Academic Mjolnir?: On Worthiness, Knowledge Curation, and Using the Power of the People to Diversify OER," *Journal of Interactive Media in Education* (May 1, 2020), https://doi.org/10.5334/jime.559.

8. Jonathan Tennant et al., "A Tale of Two 'Opens': Intersections Between Free and Open Source Software and Open Scholarship," SocArXiv, 2020, https://doi.org/10.31235/osf.io/2kxq8.
9. Fobazi Ettarh, "Vocational Awe and Librarianship: The Lies We Tell Ourselves," *In the Library with the Lead Pipe* (January 10, 2018), http://inthelibrarywiththeleadpipe.org/2018/vocational-awe.
10. David Wiley and John Levi Hilton III, "Defining OER-Enabled Pedagogy," *International Review of Research in Open and Distributed Learning* 19, no. 4 (2018), https://doi.org/10.19173/irrodl.v19i4.3601; Marcos D. Rivera et al., "'Open'-Ing Up Courses for Diversity and Deeper Learning," *International Journal of Open Educational Resources* (November 28, 2020), https://www.ijoer.org/open-ing-up-courses-for-diversity-and-deeper-learning/; Seiferle-Valencia, "It's Not (Just) About the Cost."
11. sava saheli singh, "The Fallacy of 'Open,'" in *Open at the Margins*, ed. Maha Bali, Catherine Cronin, Laura Czerniewicz, Robin DeRosa, and Rajiv Jhangiani (Rebus Community, 2020), https://press.rebus.community/openatthemargins/chapter/the-fallacy-of-open/.
12. Rajiv S. Jhangiani, *Delivering on the Promise of Open Educational Resources: Pitfalls and Strategies. MOOCs and Open Education in the Global South* (Oxfordshire, UK: Routledge, 2019), https://doi.org/10.4324/9780429398919-7.
13. Hodgkinson-Williams and Trotter, "A Social Justice Framework."
14. Arinto, Hodgkinson-Williams, and Trotter, "OER and OEP in the Global South."
15. Sarah Crissinger, "A Critical Take on OER Practices: Interrogating Commercialization, Colonialism, and Content," *In the Library with the Lead Pipe* (October 1, 2015), https://doaj.org.
16. Watters, "From 'Open' to Justice."
17. "Frequently Asked Questions—Creative Commons," Creative Commons," accessed February 25, 2021, https://creativecommons.org/faq/#artificial-intelligence-and-cc-licenses; "Should CC-Licensed Content Be Used to Train AI?" Creative Commons, March 4, 2021, https://creativecommons.org/2021/03/04/should-cc-licensed-content-be-used-to-train-ai-it-depends/.
18. "Facial Recognition's 'Dirty Little Secret': Social Media Photos Used without Consent," NBC News, accessed January 27, 2021, https://www.nbcnews.com/tech/internet/facial-recognition-s-dirty-little-secret-millions-online-photos-scraped-n981921.
19. Safiya Noble, *Algorithms of Oppression* (New York: NYU Press, 2018), https://nyupress.org/9781479837243/algorithms-of-oppression.
20. Brigitte Vézina, "WIPO Consultation on Artificial Intelligence and Intellectual Property Policy," DACS, n.d., 7.
21. Rachel Jurinich Mattson, "Queer Histories, Videotape, and the Ethics of Reuse," in *Open at the Margins*, ed. Maha Bali, Catherine Cronin, Laura Czerniewicz, Robin DeRosa, and Rajiv Jhangiani (Rebus Community, 2020), https://press.rebus.community/openatthemargins/chapter/queer-histories-videotape-and-the-ethics-of-reuse/.
22. Wiley and Hilton III, "Defining OER-Enabled Pedagogy."
23. Carina Bossu et al., "How to Tame a Dragon: Scoping Diversity, Inclusion and Equity in the Context of an OER Project," Commonwealth of Learning (COL), September 2019, 6, http://oasis.col.org/handle/11599/3349.
24. Lambert, "Changing Our (Dis)Course," 229.
25. Gidley, "Social Inclusion: Context, Theory and Practice."
26. Kristina Clement, "Interrogating and Supplementing OER Through a Decolonized Lens," OER and Beyond, accessed March 6, 2021, https://ijoerandbeyond.org/interrogating-and-supplementing-oer-through-a-decolonized-lens/.
27. Crissinger, "A Critical Take on OER Practices."
28. Maha Bali, Catherine Cronin, and Rajiv S. Jhangiani, "Framing Open Educational Practices from a Social Justice Perspective," *Journal of Interactive Media in Education* 2020, no. 1 (May 11, 2020): 10, https://doi.org/10.5334/jime.565.
29. Arinto, Hodgkinson-Williams, and Trotter, "OER and OEP in the Global South."
30. Hodgkinson-Williams and Trotter, "A Social Justice Framework."
31. Clement, "Interrogating and Supplementing OER," para. 1.

32. Monty King, Mark Pegrum, and Martin Forsey, "MOOCs and OER in the Global South: Problems and Potential," *International Review of Research in Open and Distributed Learning* 19, no. 5 (November 2018): 1–20.
33. Hodgkinson-Williams and Trotter, "A Social Justice Framework."
34. Nusbaum, "Who Gets to Wield Academic Mjolnir?"
35. Rivera et al., "'Open'-Ing Up Courses."
36. Shanna Hollich and Jacob Moore, "Open Pedagogy Big and Small: Comparing Open Pedagogy Efforts in Large and Small Higher Education Settings," in *Open Pedagogy Approaches*, ed. Kimberly Davies Hoffman and Alexis Clifton (Geneseo, NY: Milne Publishing, 2021), accessed March 5, 2021, https://milnepublishing.geneseo.edu/openpedagogyapproaches/chapter/open-pedagogy-big-and-small-comparing-open-pedagogy-efforts-in-large-and-small-higher-education-settings/.
37. Nusbaum, "Who Gets to Wield Academic Mjolnir?"
38. Hengtao Tang and Yu Bao, "Social Justice and K-12 Teachers' Effective Use of OER: A Cross-Cultural Comparison by Nations," *Journal of Interactive Media in Education* (May 1, 2020), https://doi.org/10.5334/jime.576; Rivera et al., "'Open'-Ing Up Courses for Diversity and Deeper Learning"; Hollich and Moore, "Open Pedagogy Big and Small."
39. Tang and Bao, "Social Justice and K-12 Teachers."
40. Crissinger, "A Critical Take on OER Practices."
41. Ibid.
42. Bossu et al., "How to Tame a Dragon."
43. Christine Hockings, Paul Brett, and Mat Terentjevs, "Making a Difference—Inclusive Learning and Teaching in Higher Education through Open Educational Resources," *Distance Education* 33, no. 2 (August 1, 2012): 237–52, https://doi.org/10.1080/01587919.2012.692066.
44. Watters, "From 'Open' to Justice," 15.
45. Liam Phelan, "Politics, Practices, and Possibilities of Open Educational Resources," *Distance Education* 33, no. 2 (August 2012): 279–82.
46. Arinto, Hodgkinson-Williams, and Trotter, "OER and OEP in the Global South."
47. Phelan, "Politics, Practices, and Possibilities."

Bibliography

Arinto, Patricia, Cheryl Hodgkinson-Williams, and Henry Trotter. "OER and OEP in the Global South: Implications and Recommendations for Social Inclusion." In *Adoption and Impact of OER in the Global South. Cape Town & Ottawa: African Minds, International Development Research Centre & Research on Open Educational Resources for Development*, edited by C. Hodgkinson-Williams and P. B. Arinto. Retrieved from http://dx.doi.org/10.5281/zenodo.1043830.

Bali, Maha, Catherine Cronin, and Rajiv S. Jhangiani. "Framing Open Educational Practices from a Social Justice Perspective." *Journal of Interactive Media in Education* 2020, no. 1 (May 11, 2020): 10. https://doi.org/10.5334/jime.565.

Bossu, Carina, Judith Pete, Paul Prinsloo, and Jane-Frances Agbu. "How to Tame a Dragon: Scoping Diversity, Inclusion and Equity in the Context of an OER Project." Commonwealth of Learning (COL). September 2019. http://oasis.col.org/handle/11599/3349.

Clement, Kristina. "Interrogating and Supplementing OER Through a Decolonized Lens." OER and Beyond. Accessed March 6, 2021. https://ijoerandbeyond.org/interrogating-and-supplementing-oer-through-a-decolonized-lens/.

Creative Commons. "Frequently Asked Questions—Creative Commons." Accessed February 25, 2021. https://creativecommons.org/faq/#artificial-intelligence-and-cc-licenses.

———. "Should CC-Licensed Content Be Used to Train AI? It Depends." March 4, 2021. https://creativecommons.org/2021/03/04/should-cc-licensed-content-be-used-to-train-ai-it-depends/.

Crissinger, Sarah. "A Critical Take on OER Practices: Interrogating Commercialization, Colonialism, and Content." *In the Library with the Lead Pipe* (October 1, 2015). https://doaj.org.

Cronin, Catherine, and Iain MacLaren. "Conceptualising OEP: A Review of Theoretical and Empirical Literature in Open Educational Practices." *Open Praxis* 10, no. 2 (April 20, 2018): 127–43.

Ettarh, Fobazi. "Vocational Awe and Librarianship: The Lies We Tell Ourselves." *In the Library with the Lead Pipe* (January 10, 2018). http://inthelibrarywiththeleadpipe.org/2018/vocational-awe.

Farrow, Robert. "Open Education and Critical Pedagogy." *Learning, Media and Technology* 42, no. 2 (April 3, 2017): 130–46. https://doi.org/10.1080/17439884.2016.1113991.

Gidley, Jennifer, Gary P. Hampson, Leone Wheeler, and Elleni Bereded-Samuel. "Social Inclusion: Context, Theory and Practice." Semantic Scholar. 2010, 16.

Hockings, Christine, Paul Brett, and Mat Terentjevs. "Making a Difference—Inclusive Learning and Teaching in Higher Education through Open Educational Resources." *Distance Education* 33, no. 2 (August 1, 2012): 237–52. https://doi.org/10.1080/01587919.2012.692066.

Hodgkinson-Williams, Cheryl Ann, and Henry Trotter. "A Social Justice Framework for Understanding Open Educational Resources and Practices in the Global South." *Journal of Learning for Development* 5, no. 3 (2018): 204–24.

Hollich, Shanna, and Jacob Moore. "Open Pedagogy Big and Small: Comparing Open Pedagogy Efforts in Large and Small Higher Education Settings." In *Open Pedagogy Approaches*, edited by Kimberly Davies Hoffman and Alexis Clifton. Geneseo, NY: Milne Publishing, 2021. Accessed March 5, 2021. https://milnepublishing.geneseo.edu/openpedagogyapproaches/chapter/open-pedagogy-big-and-small-comparing-open-pedagogy-efforts-in-large-and-small-higher-education-settings/.

Jhangiani, Rajiv S. *Delivering on the Promise of Open Educational Resources: Pitfalls and Strategies. MOOCs and Open Education in the Global South.* Oxfordshire, UK: Routledge, 2019. https://doi.org/10.4324/9780429398919-7.

King, Monty, Mark Pegrum, and Martin Forsey. "MOOCs and OER in the Global South: Problems and Potential." *International Review of Research in Open and Distributed Learning* 19, no. 5 (November 2018): 1–20.

Lambert, Sarah R. "Changing Our (Dis)Course: A Distinctive Social Justice Aligned Definition of Open Education." *Journal of Learning for Development* 5, no. 3 (2018): 225–44.

Mattson, Rachel Jurinich. "Queer Histories, Videotape, and the Ethics of Reuse." In *Open at the Margins*, edited by Maha Bali, Catherine Cronin, Laura Czerniewicz, Robin DeRosa, and Rajiv Jhangiani. Rebus Community. 2020. https://press.rebus.community/openatthemargins/chapter/queer-histories-videotape-and-the-ethics-of-reuse/.

NBC News. "Facial Recognition's 'Dirty Little Secret': Social Media Photos Used without Consent." Accessed January 27, 2021. https://www.nbcnews.com/tech/internet/facial-recognition-s-dirty-little-secret-millions-online-photos-scraped-n981921.

Noble, Safiya. *Algorithms of Oppression*. New York: NYU Press, 2018. https://nyupress.org/9781479837243/algorithms-of-oppression.

Nusbaum, Amy T. "Who Gets to Wield Academic Mjolnir?: On Worthiness, Knowledge Curation, and Using the Power of the People to Diversify OER." *Journal of Interactive Media in Education* (May 1, 2020). https://doi.org/10.5334/jime.559.

Phelan, Liam. "Politics, Practices, and Possibilities of Open Educational Resources." *Distance Education* 33, no. 2 (August 2012): 279–82.

Rivera, Marcos D., Kaity Prieto, Shanna Smith Jaggars, e alexander, and Amanda L. Folk. "'Open'-Ing Up Courses for Diversity and Deeper Learning." *International Journal of Open Educational Resources* (November 28, 2020). https://www.ijoer.org/open-ing-up-courses-for-diversity-and-deeper-learning/.

Seiferle-Valencia, Marco. "It's Not (Just) About the Cost: Academic Libraries and Intentionally Engaged OER for Social Justice." *Library Trends* 69, no. 2 (2020): 469–87. https://doi.org/10.1353/lib.2020.0042.

singh, sava saheli. "The Fallacy of 'Open.'" In *Open at the Margins*, edited by Maha Bali, Catherine Cronin, Laura Czerniewicz, Robin DeRosa, and Rajiv Jhangiani. Rebus Community. 2020. https://press.rebus.community/openatthemargins/chapter/the-fallacy-of-open/.

Tang, Hengtao, and Yu Bao. "Social Justice and K-12 Teachers' Effective Use of OER: A Cross-Cultural Comparison by Nations." *Journal of Interactive Media in Education* (May 1, 2020). https://doi.org/10.5334/jime.576.

Tennant, Jonathan, Ritwik Agarwal, Ksenija Baždarić, David Brassard, Tom Crick, Daniel J. Dunleavy, Thomas R. Evans, et al. "A Tale of Two 'opens': Intersections Between Free and Open Source Software and Open Scholarship." SocArXiv. 2020. https://doi.org/10.31235/osf.io/2kxq8.

Vézina, Brigitte. "WIPO Consultation on Artificial Intelligence and Intellectual Property Policy." DACS. n.d. 7.

Watters, Audrey. "From 'Open' to Justice." In *Open at the Margins*, edited by Maha Bali, Catherine Cronin, Laura Czerniewicz, Robin DeRosa, and Rajiv Jhangiani. Rebus Community. 2020. https://press.rebus.community/openatthemargins/chapter/from-open-to-justice/.

Wiley, David, and John Levi Hilton III. "Defining OER-Enabled Pedagogy." *International Review of Research in Open and Distributed Learning* 19, no. 4 (2018). https://doi.org/10.19173/irrodl.v19i4.3601.

CHAPTER 2

Repairing the Curriculum:
Using OER to Fill Gaps

Kevin Adams and Samantha Dannick

Introduction

"A curriculum provides a way of identifying the knowledge we value. It structures the ways in which we are taught to think and talk about the world."[1] Students in a formal education system are not only taught content; they are indoctrinated into a way of thinking. In the traditional Western education system, which has spread throughout the world, this way of thinking includes a mindset that there are credentialed experts from whom—and only whom—others learn. In this chapter, we use the term "Western curriculum" to refer to this traditional, formal education system born in Western Europe and spread throughout the world.

Open educational resources (OER) have the potential to provide an avenue and an impetus to look at curricula with fresh eyes. OER, most of which are created and shared digitally, offer flexibility in what media and modality learning objects can be. They offer teachers local control over the resources used in the classroom and the freedom to adapt and create instead of simply passing along commercial products. And, perhaps most importantly, they offer students the opportunity to effect change on teaching materials, shifting the student role from mere recipient to co-creator.

Western Curriculum

As products of the Western formal education system, it is difficult to even frame some of this conversation. Some biases are so firmly entrenched that they just seem to be "the way things are." Consider Sönke Bartling and Sascha Friesike's basic account of the beginning of knowledge creation in *Opening Science: The Evolving Guide on How the Internet is Changing Research, Collaboration and Scholarly Publishing*:

> The history of human knowledge is closely linked to the history of civilization—one could even argue that the history of civilization is in large parts based on knowledge creation and its dissemination. In prehistoric times, knowledge was passed from one generation to the next one orally or by showing certain techniques.... The creation of this knowledge was not yet structured and it was not recorded, except for occasional drawings like cave paintings. The drastic change in knowledge creation was the invention of a writing system.[2]

An attitude of the superiority of written accounts over oral knowledge dissemination is already apparent, and it only becomes more firmly entrenched. However, is the preference for the written modality really deserved, or is it a preference of convenience that we have all bought into?

In the standard narrative of knowledge creation, the first scientific revolution saw the development of academic disciplines and our current publishing system.[3] In this narrative, the development of the notion that knowledge creation is a distinct task performed by professionals is another distinctive step. It is also notable that at this point, in seventeenth-century Europe, these professional knowledge creators were, generally, members of a small, privileged in-group.

> It was the development of a journal publication system that drastically changed publishing in research and gave appropriate credits to researchers.... Based on this core concept of publishing, myriads of partially institutionalized, partially commercialized structures grew. These structures developed constitute the cultural, political, and fundamental background in which academic knowledge creation works still today.[4]

These structures were born of the journal model, which fostered and grew the practice of refereed journals and which later gave birth to the peer-reviewed publication. The formative example of refereed publishing is the Royal Society of London and its creation of *Philosophical Transactions* in 1665.[5] The motivation for refereeing publications depended on the context of the publication, but the motivation differed from the modern goals of peer review. As Noah Moxham and Aileen Fyfe argue, the original purposes of the refereed journal model were the protection of finances, reputations, and awarding prestige within the Royal Society.[6] Despite the shift in motivation of peer review away from upholding social and financial structures, the foundational motivation of ensuring that only the "right" people participate in the system remains. The modern peer-review process serves some of the same functions of anointing specific voices while dismissing others.[7]

Today there is an industry of knowledge creation, with publishers getting monetary compensation and researchers (professional knowledge creators) getting credit. The assurance of receiving proper credit, in the academic currency of citations, is the incentive for researchers to share their knowledge (via publishers). This system of exchange and the entities that facilitate and benefit from it remain the accepted status quo. Bartling and Friesike point out that this transition has been largely facilitated by the internet:

> Currently, we can see a transition in knowledge dissemination set off by the Internet that enables scientists to publish in forms unimaginable only a few years ago.... The Internet offers new answers to many challenges which the first scientific revolution overcame hundreds of years ago. And it is the task of today's researchers to assess and evaluate those newly created options, to bridge the legacy gap, and to lay a path towards the second scientific revolution.[8]

The suggested next step in scientific progress, a move toward "open science," is simultaneously progressive, seeking to end the reliance on the traditional publishing industry as researchers share their knowledge, and still firmly entrenched in the hierarchical system—the notion of the knowledge class, who will share the knowledge that they've created with other researchers and the world (who will receive it) is still taken as a given. The intersection of freely disseminated knowledge with the recognition that even a non-expert can actively engage with it is where open science will hopefully meet OER.

Gaps in the Curriculum

In Paulo Freire's *Pedagogy of the Oppressed*, Freire lays out his conception of the banking model of education, in which students are empty receptacles to be filled with information by the teacher. The teacher imparts a structured flow of knowledge into the uncritically receiving student:

> Education thus becomes an act of depositing, in which the students are the depositories and the teacher is the depositor. Instead of

communicating, the teacher issues communiques and makes deposits which the students patiently receive, memorize, and repeat. This is the "banking" concept of education, in which the scope of action allowed to the students extends only as far as receiving, filing, and storing the deposits.[9]

Without agency, students do not interact with, create, or in many cases retain the knowledge meant for them.

This education system is largely based on the print-based system described above.[10] As digital humanities and scholarly communications researcher Spencer Keralis explains, "When you stick to models of scholarly communication that are over a hundred years old and models of peer review that encode bias and abuse and insist on citation politics where the same old white men get cited over and over in order to establish your credibility: that's not creativity, and that's not innovation. It's profoundly anti-intellectual."[11]

As Keralis suggests, the gaps in the curriculum do not simply impact classroom pedagogy but also impact the types and modes of knowledge that are used to construct our reality. This erasure of non-normative knowledge types and modes has a three-pronged impact: erasure of non-normative voices, dismissal of non-normative modes of knowledge production and communication, and propagation of knowledge and narratives that uphold false and unjust histories, constructions, practices, and hierarchies.[12]

Erasure of Non-normative Voices

In a system that nearly exclusively values recognized expert voices—those put through a gauntlet of vetting by other anointed experts—many voices are marginalized, while others are explicitly expunged. This erasure primarily targets people that do not fit the normative model of cisgender, heterosexual, white, and male.

One tactic used to maintain normative voice is plagiarism and citation erasure. Trudy (who goes by one name) is an artist, indie creator, author, writer, photographer, curator, and social critic.[13] She played an important role in theorizing and popularizing the term *misogynoir*, originally created by her colleague Moya Bailey. Trudy originally encountered the term in the Crunk Feminist Collective. "Misogynoir describes the anti-Black racist misogyny that Black women experience."[14] It applies to the ways that Black women are mistreated in society writ large but more explicitly in knowledge production. "Misogynoir guarantees anyone socially/economically 'above' an unaffiliated Black woman will be praised for the things Black women theorize and write."[15]

In an ironic and unfortunately unsurprising turn, Trudy's theorization of misogynoir was plagiarized across multiple platforms and formats. Perhaps most damning, she saw her work plagiarized by academics for both opportunistic and punitive purposes.[16] Trudy explains:

> Since I am an unaffiliated writer—or in other words, I write independently and without mainstream media, academic or corporate support and without the accompanying social status, yet I have an extremely visible presence in social media—I face the phenomenon of people plagiarizing my work in very public and grotesque ways. People who do this know that since I am without institutional support and resources, they will face no repercussions.[17]

Trudy's experience is just one example of the way that non-normative voices are (sometimes violently) erased from the curriculum. An examination of this type of erasure in scholarship was written about in 1984 by Richard Delgado in an article titled "The Imperial Scholar: Reflections on a Review of Civil Rights Literature."[18] Scholars of color have identified and pointed out this phenomenon for over thirty years, yet it continues. The practice is so common that it can happen without the intent of the researcher. Initiatives such as Cite Black Women were created to combat such erasure.[19] Movements like this one encourage researchers to make an explicit effort to ensure that non-normative voices are not ignored or unacknowledged.

Another valuable set of voices is frequently passed over by the Western curriculum: the voices of students. While it is impossible for students to bring the same kind of subject knowledge that comes with years of experience, they bring their own experience and expertise. Foundational thinkers in critical pedagogy like bell hooks and Paulo Freire have argued for one of the key themes of OER: effective education happens *with* students. "Knowledge emerges only through invention and re-invention, through the restless, impatient, continuing, hopeful inquiry human beings pursue in the world, with the world, and with each other."[20] If scholarship is really about conversation, innovation, and growth, then the exclusion of a valuable set of participants can only hurt the curriculum.

Propagation of False Narratives

Erasure within the curriculum is not limited to the voices and identities of those not deemed worthy but also works to eradicate the contents, narratives, and histories that do not fit the accepted narrative. *An Indigenous People's History of the United States*, Roxanne Dunbar-Ortiz's unflinching look at the ways in which the history of the United States is inextricably intertwined with genocide propagated by settler-colonialism, points out that historically false narratives may go unquestioned in the official historical canon. "Traditionally, historians of the United States hoping to have successful careers in academia and to author lucrative school textbooks became protectors of this origin myth."[21]

Some historians have revisited the origin myth with a critical eye. However, they have not shaken the foundation of the neoliberal education system. In the 1960s, historians sought "objectivity and fairness" through a "dispassionate and culturally relative approach."[22] While cultural relativity may have been a new development of scholarship, we see the use of objectivity, fairness, and dispassionate research and analysis as a throwback to the origins of academic scholarship. These values were established alongside the canon of Western knowledge sharing and creation in the Enlightenment.

In this mirroring, we also see enforcement of the model that platforms selected experts who follow an accepted narrative and work to uphold the origin myth of the United States. Heterodox narratives, no matter how truthful, find themselves minimized as "advocacy" by the values of objective and dispassionate analysis. As Dunbar-Ortiz puts it, "Scholars, both Indigenous and a few non-Indigenous, who attempt to rectify the distortions, are labeled advocates, and their findings are rejected for publication on that basis."[23]

Yet, not all narratives with an "agenda" are summarily dismissed from the mainstream. The difference lies in the story that is being promoted. Those that seek to absolve the United States of its settler colonial histories find a home in mainstream legislature and state-sanctioned texts. US history textbook authors and publishers have made politically conservative falsifications of the historical narrative in the past decade. These changes have sought the further erasure of some of the same histories, voices, and people that Dunbar-Ortiz focuses on. In 2010, Texas state history standards for curriculum were amended to deliberately introduce severe oversights that amounted to the state-sanctioned negation of histories of Native Americans, slavery, and Jim Crow.[24] Thus, we can see that the modification of the accepted historical narrative of the United States may be accepted but only in favor of further whitewashing.[25]

Methodology Erasure

The canon of knowledge production and sharing goes even further to control the modes of knowledge dissemination that are sanctioned as acceptable. As we illustrate in the above section, there is a strong proclivity for the written word, specifically, a preference for the academic journal model. This strict structuring of acceptable knowledge modes works to obscure and erase other important modes of knowing. We break these modes of knowing into forms of inquiry and knowledge modalities.

FORMS OF INQUIRY

In her insightful book *Braiding Sweetgrass*, Robin Wall Kimmerer establishes a dichotomy between indigenous wisdom (also referred to as traditional knowledge) and scientific knowledge. In a poignant vignette, "Goldenrods and Asters," Wall Kimmerer shares her personal experience of being driven away from indigenous knowledge by the scientific methods of the academy. "To walk the science path, I had stepped off the path of Indigenous Knowledge."[26]

As Wall Kimmerer strove to find an intersection between the worlds of indigenous wisdom and scientific knowledge, her professors discouraged her, equating her desires for indigenous wisdom with an artistic drive that had no place in the sciences. "And if you want to study beauty, you should go to art school."[27] This siloing of studies, sanctioning of specific inquiries, and enforcement of a patriarchal approval model all mirror the epistemic model of the academic journal that is so strongly entrenched in the Western curriculum.

Wall Kimmerer concludes her vignette by pointing out that her questions of beauty do have a place in the scientific model. By bringing together her two worlds, she was able to explain the biological, artistic, and botanical reasons that the beautifully complementary plants, yellow goldenrods and purple asters, grow together: the beauty that is so alluring to the human eye also attracts bees, allowing for increased pollination and growth when the two plants grow together.[28]

KNOWLEDGE MODALITIES

There are countless objects and modalities for sharing knowledge that are excluded from the traditional Western curriculum, including oral histories, zines, counter maps, and, frequently, student work. In our brief investigation of the Western curriculum, we see a strong preference for the written word that is apparent in narratives about knowledge creation. As the Western world expanded its colonial reach, its methods of epistemic control moved beyond preference for the written word, and into a preference for the written word shared (or hidden behind logistical and monetary barriers) in specific modes, especially the academic text. With this control on modality, alternative publications and creations were marginalized by higher education only seen as useful primary sources for studying specific cultures. But why aren't these knowledge modalities and objects respected in their own right? We argue that the varied means of sharing knowledge that are sidelined in academia have valuable contributions to make.

Oral histories have proved to help understand geographic history where there was no written history. Indigenous peoples in Australia have passed down oral histories for over 10,000 years and across over 400 generations that accurately tell the stories of flooded islands. These stories include the original names of the islands. The use of oral histories to tell the stories of changes in the landscape is not unique to Australia. Researchers are also investigating oral history accounts and traditions of geography in the United States and India.[29]

Another knowledge container which is vital in different cultures and communities for sharing knowledge is the zine. Zines "are do-it-yourself, handmade magazines that come in all different shapes, sizes and formats. Many are handwritten, photocopied and stapled, while some may be magazine-like publications and professionally printed."[30] Zines have been vital to a variety of counter-culture communities for sharing information and knowledge that pertain to community safety and well-being as well as ideologies, histories, and research.

More specific to higher education, a knowledge type that is rarely accepted into the curriculum is student work. As critical and open pedagogues suggest, students play a vital role in the creation of their own knowledge. Through this process, they create countless modes of expressing this knowledge—papers, forum posts, reflections, presentations, draft proposals, etc. And yet, these creations are frequently treated as what David Wiley has dubbed, "disposable assignments." Upon completion, the student is assigned a grade, and then the assignment goes into a file or a trash can, never to be consulted again.[31] In a better case scenario, the student will take the initiative to hold onto and build on their creations, but it is still unlikely that their work will make its way into the actual curriculum. It is a common trope that students are higher education's most valuable asset. But student perspectives are not yet valued and integrated as accepted and accessible knowledge.

The Western curriculum works to obscure, exclude, and erase knowledge that does not fit the normative, accepted canon. This creates gaps in the represented voices, the represented narratives, and the represented knowledge modalities of the curriculum. So, the question becomes, how do we begin to fill the gaps?

Filling Gaps

Technological innovation means that distributing knowledge widely is no longer limited to printed text as a medium. Audio recordings, video files, and images are as easily reproduced and shared as text. These expanded possibilities should be reflected in curricula. Bodies of knowledge and knowledge modalities that are not easily conveyed in writing can and should be shared with students. Students should also be given the opportunity to demonstrate their learning through multiple modalities.

This shift in practicalities must be accompanied by a shift in attitudes. Whose voices count and how much? It is not enough to simply reproduce the dominant voices in academia through more media; knowledge creators who have previously been shut out must be brought in. Not only that, the idea of who is able to and is allowed to create knowledge should be expanded. Open educational resources, especially when combined with a critical pedagogy, open pedagogy, or open educational practices approach, allow for a much-expanded community of knowledge creators.

OER as Gap Filler

One of the hallmarks of OER—as distinct from resources that are simply free to access—is the set of "5R freedoms," often communicated with the use of Creative Commons licenses. Without needing permission from the copyright holder (often the original creator), anyone is free to retain, reuse, revise, remix, and redistribute the resource. With these freedoms, the learning object can become a living resource as opposed to something static or fixed (for better or worse) until the publisher puts a new edition on the market.

There are some established organizations (one might call them publishers) creating and disseminating OER, but they do not maintain the stranglehold on the content that traditional publishers do. Teachers and subject experts make edits in the content for their individual classes and even directly in the original resource. Additionally, and crucially, many individuals and communities create resources and add them to the "Commons" with the intention that other teachers and learners will be able to build on them.

A Guide to Making Open Textbooks with Students is an OER about OER, with a focus on involving students as knowledge creators. Centering (or co-centering, along with experts) the student as a knowledge creator is empowering for the learner, it benefits the overall body of knowledge by integrating new voices and perspectives, and it allows for a more complete learning process. As Robin DeRosa and Rajiv Jhangiani articulate:

> Embedded in the social justice commitment to making college affordable for all students is a related belief that knowledge should not be an elite domain. Knowledge consumption and knowledge creation are not separate but parallel processes, as knowledge is co-constructed, contextualized, cumulative, iterative, and recursive.[32]

Taking knowledge (and knowledge resource) development as a process, creation is not the only stage at which a variety of voices can be integrated. In the world of OER, there is recognition of the importance of revising and adapting resources. Students can be invited to take part in adapting a resource for their class. This approach reinforces the concept that education is a two-way street, involving active participation from learners. Students are also often more in-tune with what will facilitate learning for themselves and their peers than subject matter experts who have forgotten what it was like to be a beginner. Integrating this student insight can result in not only better-rounded but also more effective teaching/learning objects.

In commercial operations, there is pressure to be first with a new idea or otherwise outpace the competition—it's a zero-sum game. There is also incentive to cater to a broad swath of the market to maximize production efficiency. The American K-12 textbook market is an example of this phenomenon (albeit less so now than once was the case): states with the largest school districts impacted the content of everyone's books.[33]

Because the objective of OER is not to make a profit, learning objects can be hyper-local or localizable. Examples or case studies can feature concepts or issues meaningful to the community of learners utilizing the resource. They can also be used to highlight the background and history, both visible and invisible, extant and erased, that shaped the learning community or locality. Consider the example of a (hypothetical) United States history text:

> As Europeans expanded their influence in the newly "discovered" land, they displaced through treaties, military force, and resource destruction native populations such as the Iroquois, Navajo, and Hopi.

Now consider how that text might be localized to add meaning and impact:

> As Europeans expanded their settler colonial expansion in the newly "discovered" land, they killed and displaced native populations through treaties, intentional spread of disease, military force, and resource destruction. In the northeast, the Haudenosaunee (Iroquois) were the predominant group. Alfred University, where we study now, is on the traditional and ancestral lands of the Onöndowa'ga:' (Seneca).

Similar to the importance of localization for contextualization, community subject knowledge is vital to ethically using and understanding information.

When it comes to citation erasure and the exclusion of marginalized voices, OER offer an opportunity to combat and fix some of the failures. One specific instance of citation erasure happened on social media. The famous singer Katy Perry used the term misogynoir in a popular tweet without giving credit to Moya Bailey for the creation of the term. By Bailey's account, it was Black women on Twitter and other social media platforms that did the legwork to make sure that Bailey's name was associated with the term.[34] In a similar way, OER allow communities to take direct corrective action where necessary. Or better yet, to be involved from the beginning to prevent the need for corrective action.

OER can expand the knowledge modalities of the Western curriculum by opening the door to new information objects. Zines are not always created as openly licensed resources to be remixed, but they can be. In a Library Science 101 course, Cynthia Mari Orozco developed a capstone project in which students created an openly licensed zine about information literacy. By using this format, students constructed information resources using methods taught and passed down by subcultures throughout the world, thus helping to broaden the conception of accepted information resources in the Western curriculum. Not only does this open up the curriculum to new formats, but it also shifts OER production away from its traditional digital format into the analog realm.[35]

In a more traditional sense, OER allow for the integration of new media and information containers into the textbook format. A University of Arkansas OER, *Moving Pictures: An Introduction to Cinema* by Russell Leigh Sharman, covers similar content to a standard for-profit textbook. In addition to the book being free of charge, it also integrates media directly into the text. The chapter "Women in Cinema" looks at representations of women in the history of cinema, and in addition to images, it has embedded YouTube videos.[36] The visual representations in this section, and others throughout the OER, help to further illustrate and bring to life the points in the text of the chapter. The opportunities for incorporating new educational media do not stop at videos but could include audio such as archival recordings, podcasts, and musical recordings. This expansion of the curriculum into new forms of information containers works to open doors for representation of new voices, images, and identities that may not have found a historic home in written text(book)s.

Not a Cure-All and Not Without Risk

OER in the Western education system, if utilized without conscientious adherence to critical and open pedagogy, could very easily continue to propagate the same inaccuracies, erasures, and traditional hierarchies that have historically existed in the Western curriculum. For this reason, and a handful of others that we will highlight below, OER cannot be considered a panacea.

Not all knowledge modalities that fall outside of the Western curriculum comfortably transition into the OER framework. Robin DeRosa suggests, "Feminist and indigenous scholars, in particular, have pointed out the ways in which 'open' is not *necessarily* aligned with values that support sustainable, diverse, and equitable knowledge communities. And privacy advocates have critiqued the notion that public spaces are spaces in which privacy must be forfeited."[37] And, as is pointed out in Kimberly Christen's article, "Does Information Really Want to be Free? Indigenous Knowledge Systems and the Question of Openness," privacy plays a vital role for specific indigenous ways of knowing.[38] While OER may open one door to integrating new ways of knowing into the curriculum, they should not serve to integrate knowledge that is not meant for the Western curriculum.

Because OER require that those who put them out into the world relinquish a not-insignificant amount of control over what happens to them, there is risk. We are not referring here to the risk of bad actors intentionally misusing the work. Frankly, if someone was going to blatantly act in bad faith, it's unlikely that the threat of copyright infringement would be much of a deterrent either. Instead, we are referring to naive, maybe well-intentioned users who may separate OER content from its context, creating opportunities for misunderstanding and misinterpretation. Or someone who (over)shares knowledge that was not theirs to give. Creators—either originators or adapters—of OER have a responsibility to ensure that they are acting intentionally and respectfully. In integrating historically marginalized voices and knowledges, they must be diligent in working to understand how their actions interact with the past and have implications for the future.

Problems also arise with the audience and intent of OER. Who is it for? What is it doing? How will OER be made accessible in a meaningful way to those that are already marginalized by the Western curriculum and education system? As we mention above, OER are primarily possible and operated via technological advances that allow us to move away from a reliance on text. Unfortunately, these technological advances are built upon a capitalistic neoliberal system driven by white masculinity. In "Who Killed the World? White Masculinity and the Technocratic Library of the Future," Rafia Mirza and Maura Seale present an argument that problematizes the uncritical use of technology in library efforts to progress:

> Technocratic visions of the future of libraries aspire to a world outside of politics and ideology, to the unmarked space of white masculinity, but such visions are embedded in multiple layers and

axes of privilege. They elide the fact that technology is not benevolently impartial but is subject to the same inequities inherent to the social world. They hide the physical and emotional labor of the precariat, who are frequently gendered, racialized, or otherwise marginalized, behind discourses of freedom, progress, and the disruptive potential of the digital.[39]

Similarly, OER cannot escape this marred technological landscape. Instead, creators and adapters will constantly have to critically analyze the inequitable systems in which they are embedded in order to try to combat the erasive tactics of their foundational technologies.[40]

As Mirza and Seale point out, the erasive tactics of these technologies often manifest by obscuring the physical and emotional labor of marginalized groups. OER are at particular risk in this regard. While much of the scholarship in academia is unpaid, by the nature of OER being free, their production is also often unpaid. This unduly affects the livelihood of those marginalized in our society who may create and adapt OER.

Further unpacking the thematic questioning of "Who is OER for?," Kelly Hurst encourages practitioners of open education practices to always ask themselves, "Who will benefit from it?" and "Who will be burdened by it?"[41] "If what we are considering is trying to have an equitable way of doing that work, that if we do it from a dominant cultural centered way of being, we are going to benefit whiteness once again."[42] Hurst goes on to point out that it has been a common practice for dominant cultures to use marginalized communities as resource-rich landscapes for extraction.[43] We would like to apply this insight to the use of voices, identities, and modes of knowing as well. If OER use these as resources to enrich the Western curriculum, without truly benefiting the communities they are taking from, then OER become a tool of intellectual colonialism.

Even well-intentioned practitioners of critical pedagogy are guilty of this co-opting and de-contextualization. Take, for example, the work of Paulo Freire. The foundation of Freire's dialogic method of education is grounded in a revolutionary pedagogy of the oppressed. This pedagogy works in two stages: first unveiling the world of oppression and commitment to transforming this reality; second, through working with the people to implement a pedagogy whose end goal is permanent liberation. Freire goes so far as to incorporate aspects of Mao's Cultural Revolution to establish the importance of combating the culture of domination present in liberal capitalist regimes.[44]

The work of Freire is used throughout higher education to promote an equitable classroom—a classroom where all students can engage with the teacher by embracing elements of the dialogical method: cooperation, unity, and organization.[45] However, the foundation of this method is not always implemented and is often declawed at best, fully lacking the revolutionary context. Rather than focusing on liberatory praxis, classrooms will educate students on how to survive in the systems that already exist. For example, in a higher education context, conversations about elevating oppressed voices rarely acknowledge that those conversations are made possible by the continued oppression of others. In contrast, Freire emphasizes revealing the reality of global oppression. In these instances, educators have taken the practice meant to liberate marginalized communities and removed it from its context. This enables the neoliberal education system to enhance its image as a benevolent equitable system without actually implementing sustainable, liberatory praxis.

Conclusion

The Western curriculum as it is usually implemented in North American and European institutions was built on a narrow idea of who has the authority to create knowledge and which channels can be used to disseminate that knowledge. The task of formal education is to impart that "official" knowledge to students, who must absorb it until they are credentialed as experts and are thus authorized to create knowledge themselves.

The use of OER and open pedagogy are expanding the notion of what a learning object is and how it can be used. One no longer needs to be authorized by the "traditional" system to create knowledge that will be used to teach others. Voices and perspectives that have historically been marginalized can enter the conversation without having to appease gatekeepers. Students can see themselves as active knowledge creators, not only as knowledge receptacles, and be empowered to have a hand in their learning. A variety of media can be utilized to convey ideas and invite engagement. Resources can be easily and regularly revised, reinforcing the reality that knowledge is not stagnant or fixed in time but rather is a continuing conversation.

However, with possibility comes responsibility. OER creators and adapters may, if not working conscientiously, simply perpetuate current (problematic) systems rather than make change. The questions should always be asked: Whose voices are represented here? Whose voices are missing? Who is this resource for and in what context? Am I the right person to be telling this story? Could/should I collaborate with someone else to make this resource better? OER users and developers should be intentional and conscientious but not let the existence of risk dissuade them from making progress.

This examination of how OER interacts with the curriculum—filling gaps, perpetuating systems, and everything in between—is incomplete because the world of OER is really a world of potential. By design and by definition, there is a multitude of ways in which scholars, teachers, and learners can use OER. Our hope is that readers will consider the themes and examples presented here as they continue building their praxis.

Endnotes

1. R. Ferguson et al., *Innovating Pedagogy 2019*, The Open University, 2019, https://www.learntechlib.org/p/207292/.
2. Sönke Bartling and Sascha Friesike, "Towards Another Scientific Revolution," in *Opening Science: The Evolving Guide on How the Internet Is Changing Research, Collaboration and Scholarly Publishing*, ed. Sönke Bartling and Sascha Friesike (Cham: Springer International Publishing, 2014), 3–15, https://doi.org/10.1007/978-3-319-00026-8_1.
3. Bartling and Friesike, "Towards Another Scientific Revolution."
4. Ibid.
5. Noah Moxham and Aileen Fyfe, "The Royal Society and the Prehistory of Peer Review, 1665–1965," *The Historical Journal* 61, no. 4 (2018): 864.
6. Moxham and Fyfe, "The Royal Society," 866.
7. Richard Delgado highlights the function of race in a vicious cycle of publication privilege describing how white law professionals repeatedly left out and passed over the work of their colleagues of color in "The Imperial Scholar." Richard Delgado, "The Imperial Scholar: Reflections on a Review of Civil Rights Literature," *University of Pennsylvania Law Review* 132, no. 3 (1984): 561–78, https://doi.org/10.2307/3311882. Laura Czerniewicz explores global inequities in scholarship that reflect the privilege of those in the "Global North." Laura Czerniewicz, "Inequitable Power Dynamics of Global Knowledge Production and Exchange Must Be Confronted Head On," in *Open at the Margins*, ed. Maha Bali et al. (Rebus Community, 2020), https://press.rebus.community/openatthemargins/chapter/repost-inequitable-power-knowledge/.
8. Bartling and Friesike, "Towards Another Scientific Revolution."
9. Paulo Freire, *Pedagogy of the Oppressed*, trans. Myra Bergman Ramos, 30th Anniversary Edition (New York: Continuum International Publishing Group Inc., 2000), 72.
10. Bartling and Friesike, "Towards Another Scientific Revolution," 7.
11. Mallory Untch, "It Takes Spencer Keralis," It Takes a Campus, Illinois Library, accessed December 4, 2020, https://www.library.illinois.edu/sc/podcast/it-takes-spencer-keralis/.
12. "Decolonising SOAS," Decolonising SOAS Working Group, University of London, accessed December 1, 2020, https://blogs.soas.ac.uk/decolonisingsoas/.
13. "About," Trudy, accessed January 29, 2021, http://www.thetrudz.com/about.
14. Moya Bailey and Trudy, "On Misogynoir: Citation, Erasure, and Plagiarism," *Feminist Media Studies* 18, no. 4 (March 13, 2018): 762–63, https://doi.org/10.1080/14680777.2018.1447395.
15. Bailey and Trudy, "On Misogynoir," 765.
16. Ibid., 765–66.
17. Ibid., 766.
18. Delgado, "The Imperial Scholar."
19. "Cite Black Women," Cite Black Women, accessed February 19, 2021, https://www.citeblackwomencollective.org/.
20. Freire, *Pedagogy of the Oppressed*, 72.
21. Roxanne Dunbar Ortiz, *An Indigenous Peoples' History of the United States* (Boston: Beacon Press, 2014), 4.
22. Dunbar Ortiz, *An Indigenous Peoples' History*, 4.
23. Ibid., 13.

24. Kritika Agarwal, "Texas Revises History Education, Again: How a 'Good Faith' Process Became Political," *American History Association Perspectives on History* (January 11, 2019), https://www.historians.org/publications-and-directories/perspectives-on-history/january-2019/texas-revises-history-education-again-how-a-good-faith-process-became-political.
25. Texas school curriculums have since been guilty of revisionist history that minimizes slavery as a cause of the Civil War and eliminates conversation about historical women figures such as Hillary Clinton.
26. Robin Wall Kimmerer, *Braiding Sweetgrass: Indigenous Wisdom, Scientific Knowledge, and the Teachings of Plants* (Minneapolis, MN: Milkweed Editions, 2013), 44.
27. Wall Kimmerer, *Braiding Sweetgrass*, 41.
28. Ibid., 46.
29. John Upton, "Ancient Sea Rise Tale Told Accurately for 10,000 Years," *Scientific American* (January 26, 2015), https://www.scientificamerican.com/article/ancient-sea-rise-tale-told-accurately-for-10-000-years/.
30. "Zines at The New York Public Library," The New York Public Library, June 27, 2020, https://www.nypl.org/about/divisions/general-research-division/periodicals-room/zines.
31. David Wiley, "What Is Open Pedagogy?," *Leveraging Open to Improve Learning* (blog), October 21, 2013, https://opencontent.org/blog/archives/2975.
32. Robin DeRosa, Rajiv Jhangiani, and University Teaching Fellow in Open Studies at Kwantlen Polytechnic University, "Open Pedagogy," in *A Guide to Making Open Textbooks with Students* (The Rebus Community for Open Textbook Creation, 2017), https://press.rebus.community/makingopentextbookswithstudents/chapter/open-pedagogy/.
33. Margaret Crocco, "Texas, Textbooks, and the Politics of History Standards," *Green & Write* (blog), Michigan State University, November 26, 2014, https://education.msu.edu/green-and-write/2014/texas-textbooks-and-the-politics-of-history-standards/.
34. Bailey and Trudy, "On Misogynoir," 764.
35. Cynthia Mari Orozco, "Informed Open Pedagogy and Information Literacy Instruction in Student-Authored Open Projects," in *Open Pedagogy Approaches* (Rochester, NY: Milne Publishing, 2020), accessed December 11, 2020, https://milnepublishing.geneseo.edu/openpedagogyapproaches/chapter/informed-open-pedagogy-and-information-literacy-instruction-in-student-authored-open-projects/.
36. Russell Sharman, "Women in Cinema," in *Moving Pictures*, University of Arkansas, 2020, https://uark.pressbooks.pub/movingpictures/chapter/women-in-cinema/.
37. Robin DeRosa, "Foreword by Robin DeRosa," in *Open Pedagogy Approaches* (Rochester, NY: Milne Publishing, 2021), accessed February 19, 2021, https://milnepublishing.geneseo.edu/openpedagogyapproaches/front-matter/foreward-by-robin-derosa/.
38. Kimberly A. Christen, "Does Information Really Want to Be Free? Indigenous Knowledge Systems and the Question of Openness," *International Journal of Communication* 6, no. 0 (November 30, 2012): 24.
39. Rafia Mirza and Maura Seale, "Who Killed the World? White Masculinity and the Technocratic Library of the Future," in *Topographies of Whiteness: Mapping Whiteness in Library and Information Science*, ed. G. Schlesselman-Tarango, Series on Critical Race Studies and Multiculturalism in LIS (Sacramento: Library Juice Press, February 5, 2020), 187.
40. Similarly, access to technology is privileged. As cited by Meredith Jacob in *Working Towards Antiracism and Culturally Responsive Teaching in Open Education*, students from lower socioeconomic backgrounds were disproportionately positively impacted by the use of OER in the study Nicholas B. Colvard, C. Edward Watson, and Hyojin Park, "The Impact of Open Educational Resources on Various Student Success Metrics," *International Journal of Teaching and Learning in Higher Education* 30, no. 2 (2018): 262–76. However, Jacob points out, accessing OER for those same students may be more difficult than those who have easy access to internet and digital devices.
41. Meredith Jacob et al., *Working Towards Antiracism and Culturally Responsive Teaching in Open Education*, 2020, https://www.youtube.com/watch?v=ZVat4bcwpMg&feature=youtu.be.

42. Meredith Jacob et al., *Working Towards Antiracism*.
43. Ibid.
44. Freire, *Pedagogy of the Oppressed*, 54.
45. Ibid., 8.

Bibliography

Agarwal, Kritika. "Texas Revises History Education, Again: How a 'Good Faith' Process Became Political." *American History Association Perspectives on History* (January 11, 2019). https://www.historians.org/publications-and-directories/perspectives-on-history/january-2019/texas-revises-history-education-again-how-a-good-faith-process-became-political.

Bailey, Moya, and Trudy. "On Misogynoir: Citation, Erasure, and Plagiarism." *Feminist Media Studies* 18, no. 4 (March 13, 2018): 762–68. https://doi.org/10.1080/14680777.2018.1447395.

Bartling, Sönke, and Sascha Friesike. "Towards Another Scientific Revolution." In *Opening Science: The Evolving Guide on How the Internet Is Changing Research, Collaboration and Scholarly Publishing*, edited by Sönke Bartling and Sascha Friesike, 3–15. Cham: Springer International Publishing, 2014. https://doi.org/10.1007/978-3-319-00026-8_1.

Christen, Kimberly A. "Does Information Really Want to Be Free? Indigenous Knowledge Systems and the Question of Openness." *International Journal of Communication* 6, no. 0 (November 30, 2012): 24.

Cite Black Women. "Cite Black Women." Accessed February 19, 2021. https://www.citeblackwomencollective.org/.

Colvard, Nicholas B., C. Edward Watson, and Hyojin Park. "The Impact of Open Educational Resources on Various Student Success Metrics." *International Journal of Teaching and Learning in Higher Education* 30, no. 2 (2018): 262–76.

Crocco, Margaret. "Texas, Textbooks, and the Politics of History Standards." *Green & Write* (blog), Michigan State University. November 26, 2014. https://education.msu.edu/green-and-write/2014/texas-textbooks-and-the-politics-of-history-standards/.

Czerniewicz, Laura. "Inequitable Power Dynamics of Global Knowledge Production and Exchange Must Be Confronted Head On." In *Open at the Margins*, edited by Maha Bali, Catherine Cronin, Laura Czerniewicz, Robin DeRosa, and Rajiv Jhangiani. Rebus Community. 2020. https://press.rebus.community/openatthemargins/chapter/repost-inequitable-power-knowledge/.

Decolonising SOAS Working Group. "Decolonising SOAS." University of London. Accessed December 1, 2020. https://blogs.soas.ac.uk/decolonisingsoas/.

Delgado, Richard. "The Imperial Scholar: Reflections on a Review of Civil Rights Literature." *University of Pennsylvania Law Review* 132, no. 3 (1984): 561–78. https://doi.org/10.2307/3311882.

DeRosa, Robin. "Foreword by Robin DeRosa." In *Open Pedagogy Approaches*. Rochester, NY: Milne Publishing, 2021. Accessed February 19, 2021. https://milnepublishing.geneseo.edu/openpedagogyapproaches/front-matter/foreward-by-robin-derosa/.

DeRosa, Robin, Rajiv Jhangiani, and University Teaching Fellow in Open Studies at Kwantlen Polytechnic University. "Open Pedagogy." In *A Guide to Making Open Textbooks with Students*. The Rebus Community for Open Textbook Creation. 2017. https://press.rebus.community/makingopentextbookswithstudents/chapter/open-pedagogy/.

Dunbar Ortiz, Roxanne. *An Indigenous Peoples' History of the United States*. Boston: Beacon Press, 2014.

Ferguson, R., T. Coughlan, K. Egelandsdal, M. Gaved, C. Herodotou, G. Hillaire, D. Jones, et al. *Innovating Pedagogy 2019*. The Open University. 2019. https://www.learntechlib.org/p/207292/.

Freire, Paulo. *Pedagogy of the Oppressed*. Translated by Myra Bergman Ramos. 30th Anniversary Edition. New York: Continuum International Publishing Group Inc., 2000.

Jacob, Meredith, et al. *Working Towards Antiracism and Culturally Responsive Teaching in Open Education*. 2020. https://www.youtube.com/watch?v=ZVat4bcwpMg&feature=youtu.be.

Mirza, Rafia, and Maura Seale. "Who Killed the World? White Masculinity and the Technocratic Library of the Future." In *Topographies of Whiteness: Mapping Whiteness in Library and Information Science*, edited by Gina Schlesselman-Tarango, 171–97. Sacramento, CA: Library Juice Press, 2017.

Moxham, Noah, and Aileen Fyfe. "The Royal Society and the Prehistory of Peer Review, 1665–1965." *The Historical Journal* 61, no. 4 (2018): 863–89.

New York Public Library, The. "Zines at The New York Public Library." June 27, 2020. https://www.nypl.org/about/divisions/general-research-division/periodicals-room/zines.

Orozco, Cynthia Mari. "Informed Open Pedagogy and Information Literacy Instruction in Student-Authored Open Projects." In *Open Pedagogy Approaches*. Accessed December 11, 2020. Rochester, NY: Milne Publishing, 2020. https://milnepublishing.geneseo.edu/openpedagogyapproaches/chapter/informed-open-pedagogy-and-information-literacy-instruction-in-student-authored-open-projects/.

Sharman, Russell. "Women in Cinema." In *Moving Pictures*. University of Arkansas. 2020. https://uark.pressbooks.pub/movingpictures/chapter/women-in-cinema/.

Trudy. "About." Accessed January 29, 2021. http://www.thetrudz.com/about.

Untch, Mallory. "It Takes Spencer Keralis." It Takes a Campus. Illinois Library. Accessed December 4, 2020. https://www.library.illinois.edu/sc/podcast/it-takes-spencer-keralis/.

Upton, John. "Ancient Sea Rise Tale Told Accurately for 10,000 Years." *Scientific American* (January 26, 2015). https://www.scientificamerican.com/article/ancient-sea-rise-tale-told-accurately-for-10-000-years/.

Wall Kimmerer, Robin. *Braiding Sweetgrass: Indigenous Wisdom, Scientific Knowledge, and the Teachings of Plants*. Minneapolis, MN: Milkweed Editions, 2013.

Wiley, David. "What Is Open Pedagogy?" *Leveraging Open to Improve Learning* (blog), October 21, 2013. https://opencontent.org/blog/archives/2975.

CHAPTER 3

On Being Visible:
The Hidden Curriculum of Heteronormativity and Open Educational Resources

Thomas Weeks

In a 2019 policy briefing, New America, a liberal think tank focusing on technology and social change, wrote that open educational resources (OER) are a way forward in promoting inclusion of LGBTQ+ curriculum in K-12 schools because of their low cost and easy shareability.[1] New America sees OER as a way to challenge "the lack of representation [students] see in curricula and the unconscious bias with which they are often taught."[2] However, as the author of the report discusses, some states that promote the use of OER also have "no promo homo" laws, which outlaw the discussion of issues related to sexuality and gender identity in public schools. How can we understand this contradiction between openness and invisibility? While OER are often touted, as New America shows, as ways forward to issues of social justice and inclusion in education, they can also help to reproduce certain ideological patterns that oppress those such as the LGBTQ+ community. How does this happen? To understand OER in this context, in this chapter I explicate the concept of the hidden curriculum and how it works to reproduce certain oppressive ideologies through schooling. Specifically, I explore the ways that education generally and educational materials specifically have been built around a hidden curriculum of heteronormativity, which seeks to maintain dominant beliefs and practices of gender and sexuality. Further, I argue how the hidden curriculum of heteronormativity interacts with open education and the ways in which OER have been positioned as a way to open access to knowledge production, but without careful implementation

41

may continue to reproduce harmful ideological structures against marginalized people.

The Hidden Curriculum

In order to think through OER in a queer lens, the hidden curriculum is a useful concept in which to frame educational resources broadly as ways in which social structures are reproduced; in other words, the ways educational experiences are structured in patterns that reproduce structural inequalities found outside of schools.[3] Michael Apple and Peter McLaren, two key thinkers in how educational experiences reproduce social inequality, tie this process explicitly to the hidden curriculum.

A key question to ask when starting a discussion of social reproduction and the hidden curriculum is "Whose meanings are collected and distributed?"[4] This question was asked by the groundbreaking curriculum theorist Michael Apple, who posits that schools function primarily to organize social relations around hegemonic ideologies—that is, education acts as a function of our social world to teach students how the world works but tend to privilege those with power and their dominant visions of the social world. As Apple explains, "Hegemony acts to 'saturate' our very consciousness, so that the educational, economic and social world we see and interact with, and the commonsense interpretations we put on it, becomes the world *tout court*, the only world."[5] Hegemony, then, functions invisibly as a kind of filter through which to understand the world without seeing the social and economic oppression endemic to it. Education, as a project of those with power, helps to teach ideological structures which further hegemony's control. Schools thus engage in knowledge-building projects, arranging knowledge in ways that benefit those in power. But educators can push back by asking questions such as, "Whose knowledge is it? Who selected it? Why is it organized and taught in this way? To this particular group?"[6] This process of reproducing hegemonic ideologies through educational methods is the hidden curriculum.

As Apple defines it, "The tacit teaching to students of norms, values, and dispositions that goes on simply by their living in and coping with the institutional expectations and routines of schools...."[7] While this is not necessarily overt on the part of the school or teachers, it is embedded in the structures of education itself. Thus, the hidden curriculum acts as an ideological tool to reproduce certain social and economic structures useful for the powerful to maintain that power. McLaren defines the hidden curriculum as "the unintended outcomes of the schooling process," which often manifest in "textbooks, curriculum materials, course content, and social relations embodied in classroom practices" and how these "benefit dominant groups and exclude subordinate ones."[8] For McLaren, the hidden curriculum seems like a natural product of the bureaucratic nature of education. However, embedded in this bureaucracy are codes that send messages about our broader cultural politics. In this way, the hidden curriculum is a form of cultural politics—"an introduction to, preparation for, and legitimation of particular forms of social life."[9] Like Apple, McLaren sees the hidden curriculum working primarily through hegemony, ideology, and social reproduction in which the hidden curriculum carries the messages of the dominant powers by making these messages seem banal and even harmless. McLaren gives the example of how teachers may treat boys and girls differently in the early grades, such as boys being allowed more independence in interpreting rules or girls being reprimanded more frequently for aggressive behaviors than boys. While this may be unintended at first, it stems from how we ultimately grant more "power and privilege to men over women"[10] in our broader culture, both reproducing and reinforcing such cultural attitudes of the dominant group (in this case, the patriarchy). Through this, we can understand that hegemonic and ideological social reproduction through education may not be intended and often seems like the natural choice, which is precisely how it operates to further harmful and oppressive systems.

Apple and McLaren both note that the hidden curriculum plays out in the ways that knowledge is organized, presented, and legitimated through textbooks and other educational resources.[11] We can understand traditional models of educational resources as attempting to structure knowledge as worthy through both economic and cultural means. As Apple explains, "The past histories of gender, class, and race relations, and the actual local political economy of publishing, set the boundaries within which these decisions are made and in large part determine who will make the decisions."[12] Textbook publishers take their cues from the dominant culture's ideological positions and communicate their worth through their reputation to maintain these positions. They have an interest in reproducing certain kinds of information, even if that information is incomplete or reproduces social inequities.

One way to understand OER in this context is how it attempts to disrupt the hidden curriculum of textbooks and other commercial educational materials as part of the broader disruption of education through open education. As we learn from Apple, McLaren, and others, education is never apolitical or value-neutral; thus, OER is not merely an improved delivery modality but can be understood as a critique of economic and social barriers reinforced by hegemonic ideologies. While open education is often positioned in this way, as the theme of this publication suggests, it can always contain its own hidden curricula functioning to reproduce dominant ideologies.[13] As Terry Anderson discusses, "Educational programming developed in one culture and exported over large geographic areas inevitably carries within it numerous cultural and epistemological overlays or hidden curriculum ideologies."[14] Open education and OER have the propensity to reproduce hegemonic ideologies as well, and not just within our local or national cultures but transnationally as well. How we understand OER in the context of the hidden curriculum and how we decide (if we can) which knowledge is of most economic and cultural worth is of major concern to social justice and other human rights paradigms.

The Hidden Curriculum of Heteronormativity

Like other areas of social life, sexuality is also enmeshed in this system of hegemony and ideology that forms the hidden curriculum. James Sears notes, "Sexual ideology is more than the observance of certain sexual mores or the expression of particular sexual beliefs; sexual ideology reflects the hegemonic power that dominant social groups have to control the body politic, and also reflects the limits of this power."[15] The hidden curriculum orders the ways in which students have access to knowledge about sexuality and gender and the kinds of knowledge available to learn. For Sears, education has historically been organized to privilege certain kinds of sexual knowledge—namely male, white, middle-class, heterosexual, and cisgender. What would a questioning of these assumptions yield? An important first step is to explore the concept of heteronormativity. First explored by Michael Warner, heteronormativity is the organization of the social world that privileges heterosexuality and cisgender identities and the associated assumptions about the world that go along with this privilege. Heteronormativity in this way is the function of ideology and hegemony when applied to understanding how sexuality structures our worlds. Because heteronormativity works invisibly and sexuality and gender difference do not necessarily constitute an easily definable class (as, say, in the case of race or religion), sexuality and gender difference are often overlooked as a site of contestation.[16] As Warner explains, social theory has often excluded discussions of queerness in their analyses of social and economic inequalities. They state,

> Social theory, moreover, must begin to do more than occasionally acknowledge the gay movement because so much of heterosexual privilege lies in heterosexual culture's exclusive ability to interpret itself as society. Even when coupled with a toleration of minority sexualities, heteronormativity has a totalizing tendency that can only be overcome by actively imagining a necessarily and desirably queer world.[17]

Gust Yep, building on Warner's ideas, explains, "When the view is that institutionalized heterosexuality constitutes the standard for legitimate, authentic, prescriptive, and ruling social, cultural, and sexual arrangements, it becomes heteronormativity."[18] Because heteronormativity requires that all experiences are rewritten through its totalizing lens, it recasts experiences not meeting its requirements as invisible, pathological, or deviant. And, as Yep details, "heteronormativity is violent and harmful to a range of people across the spectrum of sexualities, including those who live within its borders."[19] Furthermore, because heteronormativity is enmeshed in the dominant culture's broader hegemonic ideologies, practices and material cultures having nothing to do with sex or sexuality specifically "are implicated in the hierarchies of property and propriety that we will describe as heteronormative."[20] For example, while homeownership may seem to be a neutral, even advantageous act, it can also be understood when viewed through the lens of heteronormativity as a practice that supports the nuclear, heterosexual family. Homeownership as an idea, and the legal and economic apparatuses that bolster it, are premised on the existence of a nuclear family and meant to reinforce the normative structures that strengthen the hetero family bond. While not inherently negative, this example shows how deeply heteronormative structures can be embedded within our cultural politics.

We can see, then, how the hidden curriculum, which functions as a way for hegemony and ideology to be reproduced in schools, and heteronormativity, which functions as the set of beliefs formed by hegemonic and ideological controls, work together to form the hidden curriculum of heteronormativity, which functions to reproduce heteronormative beliefs in education. Donn Short discusses how "…dominant gender codes are promoted and reaffirmed in the values, morals, and structures that inform heteronormative schools… hegemonic masculinity imbues males with power and prestige at the expense of 'Others' [gender and sexual minorities]."[21] As Short notes, the hidden curriculum of heteronormativity is not the same as homophobia or overt violence in education but works in subtle ways to privilege certain kinds of knowledge and knowledge structures over others, reproducing social attitudes toward gender and sexuality. Short particularly notes in his work with teachers and students the assumption of heterosexuality and cisgender identity as the default or normal state, even among queer people.[22] This is how the hidden curriculum of heteronormativity functions at an invisible level in organizing educational structures and rewarding dominant social norms. Borrowing from the earlier homeownership example, we can start to pick apart how these structures operate in our normally taken-for-granted activities. In the last section, we saw how textbooks are implicated as sites of hegemonic and ideological control. We can also read textbooks through a heteronormative lens.

How do textbooks contribute to the hidden curriculum of heteronormativity? First, textbooks, as discussed by Apple and McLaren, organize certain forms of knowledge as authoritative, positioning themselves as arbiters of facts. Because they are a commodity, they reproduce facts that also conform to dominant social beliefs or that are the least offensive to the most people. This organization and legitimation of knowledge is an inherently patriarchal position that imbues textbooks with seemingly natural qualities of truth they do not possess, as they, like all other knowledge products, merely organize accepted knowledge, not create it. Second, the knowledge that is created is done so under systems that reproduce hegemonic ideologies such as heteronormativity. Thus, textbooks organize knowledge in such a way that leaves many people invisible in their narrative. This process by which the system of production chooses content aligned with dominant ideologies to maintain certain power structures and commodifies its knowledge organization in order to lend legitimacy to its project is how the hidden curriculum functions through educational resources as objects, not only by way of school activities. However, this is a fraught process, as teachers and students often push pack against these control mechanisms.[23] As open education becomes more prevalent and many states and institutions push for more adoption of OER, this becomes an area of contestation between the old hegemony of textbooks and other educational resources that had the power necessary to reproduce ideological dominance and the new open movement, which has less ideological power but is gaining institutional support through state and local programs.

One place we can look to understand this tension between old and new forms of ideological power through a queer lens is social media and, in particular, trolling. Trolling is defined as "antagoniz[ing] others online by deliberately posting inflammatory, irrelevant, or offensive comments or other disruptive content."[24] Social media has expanded the ways in which people are able to access and engage in communication online, leading to an increase in what many consider vile behavior such as trolling. However, as Whitney Phillips discusses, trolling reflects larger ideological tensions in our society, especially around racism, sexism, and homophobia.[25] For Phillips, online trolls do not come from nowhere; they illuminate fissures in our society's ideological fault lines. Trolls repeat hegemonic ideologies in their most base terms. Matthew Thomas-Reid takes this further, reading trolling behavior as a queer activity.[26] It is important to note here the use of queer in its academic sense, meaning actions that reject normative understandings of the social world. As Thomas-Reid describes, "Queer theory requires an understanding that normative, or dominant, culture is not fixed, and therefore the approaches to challenging these dominant structures also cannot remain fixed."[27] In this context, we can actively "queer" something—to make it strange or to challenge its place in normative discourse. Thomas-Reid, using this paradigm, reads trolling as a queer activity because it challenges the ways in which ideology is communicated through traditional power structures. Traditional media has long communicated ideological messages, but social media and the changes it engenders have complicated how ideology functions within these structures. As Thomas-Reid explains, "A queer perspective illustrates how virtual spaces harbor particular manifestations of identity that do not fit in normative discursive spaces."[28] The virtual space, for Thomas-Reid, offers new ways of understanding how ideology and hegemony work through discourse to reproduce certain normative beliefs. I would argue that trolling breaks through the hidden curriculum of heteronormativity by queering online discourses through leveraging the system against itself.

While trolling may seek to do more harm than good (though they may argue otherwise), this same logic can be applied to OER. How can we "queer" OER and extricate it from the hidden curriculum of heteronormativity? If we think of traditional textbooks and educational resources as the heteronormative discourse of the hidden curriculum, we can queer it by challenging the ways it communicates its ideological commitments—that is, through queering the legitimating structures of knowledge organization and content creation. This, however, is easier said than done.

The Promises and Perils of Openness

Open education as a space for social justice, much less radical liberation, continues to be a hotly contested topic. Because of their free availability, OER have long been championed as a tool for social justice and equity in education—an answer to the ways the hidden curriculum works to reinforce existing power structures.[29] However, as Amy Nusbaum explains, "There is no concrete evidence that OER are any better than commercial texts at addressing issues of diversity, equity, and inclusion."[30] They continue to explain that the creation of OER "can and often does continue to reinforce structural inequalities that exist in the wider educational world,"[31] but that the ability to reuse and change content within OER makes them worth exploration. Amy Collier and Jen Ross take issue with OER for their totalizing assumptions about learners, explaining, "Open content and open educational resources in particular embed values of access, standardization, and deinstitutionalization. Their emphasis on replication presumes the uniformity of the learner."[32] Similarly, Pat Lockley explores how OER can act as imperialistic tools, as most OER are produced by the Western academy.[33] For him, even the idea of openness is a Western idea, as copyright is a colonial project, and open education does not eliminate copyright claims, just shifts the idea of rights to new paradigms. They implore us to ask, "Does openness tend toward serving a hegemonic public while claiming to work for everyone?"[34]

Gourlay conceptualizes the answer to this question through Foucault's notion of the heterotopia.[35] A heterotopia is a kind of utopia that attempts to solve perceived problems in society by creating compensatory measures (e.g., Foucault includes boarding schools and retirement communities). For Gourlay, OER attempt to fix the perceived problem of unequal access to organized knowledge through creating a heterotopia (or an "enacted utopia," which they use interchangeably). As they state, "OERs and the interactions they generate could be read as an attempt to create an 'enacted utopia' which is created and maintained to compensate for what is regarded as a morally imperfect and corrupt mainstream."[36] However, heterotopias tend to also exclude because they "presume the uniformity of the learner"[37] and cater to a "hegemonic public."[38] We can see here the relationship between the heterotopic nature of OER and the heteronormative nature of the hidden curriculum. Both presume a homogeneous audience in order to function as a structure on which to base experience.

If OER can thus be implicated as reproducing the hidden curriculum even within its open context, what are the ways forward? I would like to follow up on Nusbaum's hope in the idea of the reuse of content. I believe this area is where the usefulness of a queer approach to OER is most useful. Like trolls are able to use social media to queerly expose ideological cracks in our society's hegemonic edifice, so too can educators leverage OER to expose similar cracks in an educational resource's reliance on both knowledge organization and content creation, which enact heterotopias and ultimately reproduce social inequities. Like Nusbaum, I believe the way to queer OER is to continue to question the ways educational resources have historically functioned as tools of the hidden curriculum of heteronormativity—that is, through legitimizing knowledge organization and content creation. By asking questions such as "Who is represented in this work?" or "Who benefits from this narrative?" but also "Who does this format privilege?" and "Why did I choose this organizational structure?," we can begin to queer OER and reject the hidden curriculum imbued within all educational endeavors.

To explore this idea more fully, I want to take a look at a few extant OER that perhaps illuminate some of these ideas more fully. It should be noted that this criticism is not meant to take away from the usefulness of these works or the time invested in them, but to understand them through a queer lens in order to see the hidden curriculum and challenge the ways OER can and does exclude. The question of OER content can be a tricky one. However, as discussed by Nusbaum, OER's ability to be remixed and reused can help support the inclusion of content traditionally left out of textbooks by publishers. As they explain, "Influential textbook writers hold the power to curate knowledge for entire generations of learners.... Using OER to expand textbook writing/editing opportunities serves to isolate knowledge from power."[39] This aspect of OER does help to make visible LGBTQ+ people in the curriculum, as discussed by New America.[40] But there is still the question of knowledge organization. Most OER do not radically rethink the ways traditional educational resources organize and legitimate knowledge and rely instead on heteronormative tropes of authority and the heterotopic assumption of a unified audience. For example, the *U.S. History* textbook from OpenStax[41] has content that covers LGBTQ+ issues as well as the ability to modify the content if necessary. However, it does not radically rethink the knowledge organization and legitimization scheme of the traditional textbook. Similarly, the *LGBTQ+ Studies: An Open Textbook*[42] has content solely focused on LGBTQ+ issues but still relies on the traditional schemes to present its content. Both examples illustrate the ways in which OER can present as a fully open and accessible medium that subverts the power of commodified knowledge but still rely on many of the same organizational and legitimating structures of traditional educational resources.[43] This, in turn, can reinforce these structures as natural and dominant, recreating the hegemonic ideologies of knowledge organization without actually changing anything. As Thomas-Reid and Phillips discuss, while trolling exploits ideological fissures in how hegemonic power is distributed, the messages themselves are not all that different, just more explicit.[44] We see here a similar paradigm within OER. To truly queer OER and make it visible within the hidden curriculum, we must radically rethink our reliance on normative conceptions of knowledge organization and legitimization that traditional models bestow on us. How do we do this? Much like any project, this is still an evolving answer.

Next Steps

One possible way to move toward a queer OER is to disentangle it from the traditional knowledge organization and legitimization structures by asking, "Whose knowledge?" and "Why that structure?" If the answer is "Because that is how it is always done," then the structure most likely is operating as a hegemonic device with embedded ideological complications. Textbooks, whether traditionally published or open licensed, continue to be structured the same way and thus replicate hegemonic knowledge structures. To embrace OER's queer potential, we must move away from such materials. One example of how to do this is the *Mapping the Gay Guides* project by Amanda Regan and Eric Gonzaba.[45] This project "aims to understand often ignored queer geographies using the *Damron Address Books*, an early but longstanding travel guide aimed at gay men since the early 1960s."[46] Using geographic information systems (GIS) mapping software, the creators use the locations of queer establishments listed in *Damron Address Book* from the 1960s to the 1980s. They also include "vignettes," or information about certain locations, which situates it within the historical, political, and economic context and includes additional images, videos, and further readings. Through the map and the vignettes, users can see how queer life has changed geographically and temporally with a changing political, economic, and cultural landscape. The knowledge contained is not made to reproduce ideological commitments but is knowledge that was originally created to undermine homophobic norms. Its organization and legitimization arise not from heteronormative power structures but through a commitment to the knowledge itself and the best ways to represent the knowledge in ways that illustrate its usefulness. While *Mapping the Gay Guides* does not offer a comprehensive educational resource, it offers a queer text that rejects traditional educational resource's commitments to reproducing certain hegemonic ideologies through the hidden curriculum by making visible previously invisible knowledge, doing so through a structure that opens and queers knowledge organization. Paired with additional resources, such projects offer new ways forward.

Conclusion

Through this chapter, I hope to offer a way forward to how we conceptualize and understand OER in the context of the hidden curriculum and how a queer approach can help illuminate certain invisible aspects of our current usage. Through conscientious and deliberate creation and implementation of OER projects, the ways in which OER reproduce the narratives of the dominant culture through the hidden curriculum can be challenged and radically changed. While all forms of OER through their commitment to openness have the potential for social justice, it is through continually interrogating their commitment to liberation that we can move toward a more just and equitable educational system.

Endnotes

1. Sabia Prescott, "Supporting LGBTQ-inclusive Teaching: How Open Digital Materials Can Help," New America (October 22, 2019), http://newamerica.org/education-policy/reports/supporting-lgbtq-inclusive-teaching.
2. Prescott, "Supporting LGBTQ-inclusive Teaching," 8.
3. William F. Pinar et al., *Understanding Curriculum: An Introduction to the Study of Historical and Contemporary Curriculum Discourses* (New York: Peter Lang, 1995).
4. Michael A. Apple, *Ideology and Curriculum*, 2nd ed. (New York: Routledge, 1990), 46.
5. Apple, *Ideology and Curriculum*, 5.
6. Ibid., 7.
7. Ibid., 14.

8. Peter McLaren, *Life in Schools: An Introduction to Critical Pedagogy in the Foundations of Education* (New York: Longman Publishing, 1994), 191.
9. McLaren, *Life in Schools*, 168.
10. Ibid., 192.
11. Apple, *Ideology and Curriculum*; Michael W. Apple, "The Culture and Commerce of the Textbook," in *The Curriculum: Problems, Politics, and Possibilities*, ed. Landon A. Beyer and Michael A. Apple (Albany, NY: State University of New York Press, 1998); McLaren, *Life in Schools*.
12. Apple, "The Culture and Commerce of the Textbook," 171.
13. Terry Anderson, "Revealing the Hidden Curriculum of E-learning," in *Distance Education and Distributed Learning*, ed. Vrasidas Charalambos and Gene V. Glass (Greenwich, CT: Information Age, 2002).
14. Anderson, "Revealing the Hidden Curriculum," 128.
15. James T. Sears, "Dilemmas and Possibilities of Sexuality Education: Reproducing the Body Politic," in *Sexuality and the Curriculum: The Politics and Practices of Sexuality Education*, ed. James T. Sears (New York: Teachers College Press, 1992), 15.
16. Michael Warner, "Fear of a Queer Planet," *Social Text* 29 (1991).
17. Warner, "Fear of a Queer Planet," 8.
18. Gust A. Yep, "The Violence of Heteronormativity in Communication Studies: Notes on Injury, Healing, and Queer World-Making," *Journal of Homosexuality* 45, no. 2/3/4 (2003): 13.
19. Yep, "The Violence of Heteronormativity," 48.
20. Lauren Berlant and Michael Warner, "Sex in Public," *Critical Inquiry* 24 (1998).
21. Donn Short, "Not Keeping a Straight Face: Heteronormativity and the Hidden Curriculum," in *"Don't Be So Gay!": Queers, Bullying, and Making Schools Safe* (Vancouver, BC: University of British Columbia Press, 2013), 119.
22. Short, "Not Keeping a Straight Face."
23. Ibid.
24. "Troll," *Merriam-Webster*, s.v. accessed July 20, 2021, https://www.merriam-webster.com/dictionary/troll.
25. Whitney Phillips, *This Is Why We Can't Have Nice Things: Mapping the Relationship Between Online Trolling and Mainstream Culture* (Cambridge, MA: MIT Press, 2015).
26. Matthew Thomas-Reid, "Queering Text: Literacies Surrounding Cyber Trolling," in *Negotiating Place and Space Through Digital Literacies: Research and Practice*, ed. Damiana G. Pyles, Ryan M. Rish, and Julie Warner (Charlotte, NC: Information Age, 2019).
27. Thomas-Reid, "Queering Text," 42.
28. Ibid., 47.
29. Amy T. Nusbaum, "Who Gets to Wield Academic Mjolnir?: On Worthiness, Knowledge Curation, and Using the Power of the People to Diversity OER," *Journal of Interactive Media in Education* 2020, no. 1 (2020), https://doi.org/10.5334/jime.559; Lesley Gourlay, "Open Education as a 'Heterotopia of Desire,'" *Learning, Media and Technology* 40, no. 3 (2015), https://doi.org/10.1080/17439884.2015.1029941; Amy Collier and Jen Ross, "For Whom, and For What? Not-yetness and Thinking Beyond Open Content," *Open Praxis* 9, no. 1 (2017), https://openpraxis.org/articles/10.5944/openpraxis.9.1.406/; Pat Lockley, "Open Initiatives for Decolonising the Curriculum," in *Decolonising the University*, ed. Gurminder K. Bhambra, Dalia Gebrial, and Kerem Nişancıoğlu (London: Pluto Press, 2018).
30. Nusbaum, "Who Gets to Wield Academic Mjolnir?," 2.
31. Ibid., 2.
32. Collier and Ross, "For Whom, and For What?," 8.
33. Lockley, "Open Initiatives for Decolonising the Curriculum."
34. Ibid., 146.
35. Gourlay, "Open Education as a 'Heterotopia of Desire.'"
36. Ibid., 316.
37. Collier and Ross, "For Whom, and For What?"
38. Lockley, "Open Initiatives for Decolonising the Curriculum."

39. Nusbaum, "Who Gets to Wield Academic Mjolnir?," 3.
40. Prescott, "Supporting LGBTQ-inclusive Teaching."
41. *U.S. History*, OpenStax, 2014, accessed February 26, 2021, https://openstax.org/details/books/us-history.
42. *LGBTQ+ Studies: An Open Textbook*, Lumen Candela, SUNY, 2020, accessed February 26, 2021, https://courses.lumenlearning.com/suny-lgbtq-studies/.
43. Gourlay, "Open Education as a 'Heterotopia of Desire'"; Collier and Ross, "For Whom, and For What?"; Lockley, "Open Initiatives for Decolonising the Curriculum."
44. Thomas-Reid, "Queering Text"; Phillips, *This Is Why We Can't Have Nice Things*.
45. "Mapping the Gay Guides," updated August 10, 2020, accessed February 26, 2021, https://www.mappingthegayguides.org/.
46. Regan and Gonzaba, "Mapping the Gay Guides."

Bibliography

Anderson, Terry. "Revealing the Hidden Curriculum of E-Learning." In *Distance Education and Distributed Learning*, edited by Vrasidas Charalambos and Gene V. Glass, 115–33. Greenwich, CT: Information Age, 2002.

Apple, Michael W. *Ideology and Curriculum*. 2nd ed. New York: Routledge, 1990.

———. "The Culture and Commerce of the Textbook." In *The Curriculum: Problems, Politics, and Possibilities*, edited by Landon A. Beyer and Michael W. Apple, 157–76. Albany, NY: State University of New York Press, 1998.

Berlant, Lauren, and Michael Warner. "Sex in Public." *Critical Inquiry* 24 (1998): 547–66.

Collier, Amy, and Jen Ross. "For Whom, and for What? Not-Yetness and Thinking Beyond Open Content." *Open Praxis* 9, no. 1 (2017): 7–16. https://openpraxis.org/articles/10.5944/openpraxis.9.1.406/.

Gourlay, Lesley. "Open Education as a 'Heterotopia of Desire.'" *Learning, Media and Technology* 40, no. 3 (2015): 310–27. https://doi.org/10.1080/17439884.2015.1029941.

Lockley, Pat. "Open Initiatives for Decolonising the Curriculum." In *Decolonising the University*, edited by Gurminder K. Bhambra, Dalia Gebrial and Kerem Nişancıoğlu, 145–70. London: Pluto Press, 2018.

Lumen Candela. "LGBTQ+ Studies: An Open Textbook." SUNY, 2020, accessed February 26, 2021, https://courses.lumenlearning.com/suny-lgbtq-studies/.

Mapping the Gay Guides. "Mapping the Gay Guides." Updated August 10, 2020, accessed February 26, 2021, https://www.mappingthegayguides.org/.

McLaren, Peter. *Life in Schools: An Introduction to Critical Pedagogy in the Foundations of Education*. New York: Longman Publishing, 1994.

Nusbaum, Amy T. "Who Gets to Wield Academic Mjolnir?: On Worthiness, Knowledge Curation, and Using the Power of the People to Diversity OER." *Journal of Interactive Media in Education* 2020, no. 1 (2020): 1–9. https://doi.org/10.5334/jime.559.

OpenStax. *U.S. History*. 2014. Accessed February 26, 2021, https://openstax.org/details/books/us-history.

Phillips, Whitney. *This Is Why We Can't Have Nice Things: Mapping the Relationship between Online Trolling and Mainstream Culture*. Cambridge, MA: MIT Press, 2015.

Pinar, William F., William M. Reynolds, Patrick Slattery, and Peter M. Taubman. *Understanding Curriculum: An Introduction to the Study of Historical and Contemporary Curriculum Discourses*. New York: Peter Lang, 1995.

Prescott, Sabia. "Supporting LGBTQ-Inclusive Teaching: How Open Digital Materials Can Help." New America (October 22, 2019). http://newamerica.org/education-policy/reports/supporting-lgbtq-inclusive-teaching.

Sears, James T. "Dilemmas and Possibilities of Sexuality Education: Reproducing the Body Politic." In *Sexuality and the Curriculum: The Politics and Practices of Sexuality Education*, edited by James T. Sears, 7–33. New York: Teachers College Press, 1992.
Short, Donn. "Not Keeping a Straight Face: Heteronormativity and the Hidden Curriculum." In *"Don't Be So Gay!": Queers, Bullying, and Making Schools Safe*, 105–22. Vancouver, BC: University of British Columbia Press, 2013.
Thomas-Reid, Matthew. "Queering Text: Literacies Surrounding Cyber Trolling." In *Negotiating Place and Space through Digital Literacies: Research and Practice*, edited by Damiana G. Pyles, Ryan M. Rish, and Julie Warner, 41–57. Charlotte, NC: Information Age, 2019.
Warner, Michael. "Fear of a Queer Planet." *Social Text* 29 (1991): 3–17.
Yep, Gust A. "The Violence of Heteronormativity in Communication Studies: Notes on Injury, Healing, and Queer World-Making." *Journal of Homosexuality* 45, no. 2/3/4 (2003): 11–59.

SECTION II
Open Praxis

CHAPTER 4

Centering Justice in Content Development:
A Case Study of the Police Brutality Teach-Out

Julia Maxwell, Katya Gorecki, Ryan Henyard, and Benjamin Morse

Introduction

This chapter introduces the Teach-Out model: free, short, open learning experiences focused on a single salient social issue and made available to global audiences through online education platforms like FutureLearn or Coursera. In July 2020, the Center for Academic Innovation at the University of Michigan launched the Police Brutality in America Teach-Out as a rapid response to the murders of George Floyd, Breonna Taylor, and other Black victims of police violence and to the surging Civil Rights movement in the United States over the summer of 2020. We situate this Teach-Out within the historical and theoretical contexts of the Teach-In movement of the 1960s–70s and discuss why and how the Teach-Out was chosen as the model of choice for an open learning experience focused on exploring police brutality and anti-Black racism in America. We then follow this with an in-depth examination of the logistical affordances of the experience, during which we attempted to center the experiences of those communities most impacted by police violence, namely invoking American Black, Indigenous, and People of Color (BIPOC) expertise to inform learning content. We also explore the learner response to the launched OER and detail the ways in which we planned for various learner responses, including those that could be considered divisive or potentially racist. Lastly, we reflect on the limitations of our model, the impact the Teach-Out had, and the potential for future work in this area.

Origins of the Teach-Out Model

Historical Underpinnings of the Teach-Out

Informal learning builds on the traditional and contemporary efforts of scholars and institutions to offer open educational resources (OERs) to extend impact and fulfill their missions. The Teach-Out model was inspired by the Teach-Ins of the 1960s–70s at the University of Michigan (U-M) and was designed to create an engaged online learning experience centered around salient social issues. The Teach-In movement was born at the University of Michigan in March 1965 in protest of President Lyndon Johnson's escalation of US involvement in the Vietnam War.[1,2] U-M faculty and students recognized power in collective action and sought to activate public concern and elevate discourse around affecting change within complex social issues. The original Teach-Ins were organized by a mix of faculty and students who came together with their local communities to learn about, discuss, and consider actions they could take around pressing social issues (i.e., war and environmental problems), an approach that quickly spread to institutions like Columbia University and the University of California, Berkeley. The Teach-In movement continued to gain momentum in March and April of 1970 as the world prepared for the first Earth Day on April 22 of that year. The Teach-In became an opportunity to not only reimagine the learning modality of the time but also to redefine how higher education responds in pressing social moments.

The Teach-Out model was developed in March 2017 to build on this history and create opportunities for diverse experts to come together and discuss society's most pressing issues with a broad global audience of non-experts. With a bias toward action, the online model strives to create a virtual "town hall" where learners can discuss new ideas and suggest ways to remedy societal issues regardless of background or expertise. Grounded in several foundational learning theories and best practices in online learning, the Teach-Out model was developed to further connect learners and scholars within online learning environments and provide novel ways to promote engagement.[3]

Literature Review

There are several underlying frameworks that inform the Teach-Out model, including social constructivism, community of inquiry, conversation theory, and social learning theory. Social constructivism emphasizes collaborative approaches to developing knowledge and views knowledge as something that is constructed by learners in response to social and situational stimuli as well as an individual's personal interpretations of those stimuli.[4] This theory is of particular importance within online learning environments—those without face-to-face interactions between instructors and learners—as we risk losing the foundational social learning processes that underpin knowledge creation. In lieu of assessment, the Teach-Out model favors discourse.

The community of inquiry (COI) framework stipulates a process of collaborative knowledge-building, where each learner assumes various instructional roles throughout the learning experience and subsequently contributes to a collective experience. Within this framework there exist three core elements: social presence, cognitive presence, and teaching presence, all of which are key to creating meaningful learning experiences.[5] Social presence is defined by Garrison et al. as "the ability to project oneself and establish personal and purposeful relationships."[6] Lowenthal relays social presence as the explanation for "how people present themselves as being 'there' and 'real' while using a communication medium."[7] Cognitive presence is defined as the "exploration, construction, resolution and confirmation of understanding through collaboration and reflection in a community of inquiry."[8] The final element, teaching presence, is defined as the design, facilitation, and direct instruction of learning experiences, noting that "without leadership (facilitation and direction) and structure (design)," it may be difficult to reach higher-order learning outcomes.[9] The community of inquiry framework can have meaningful applications within online learning. The Teach-Out model emphasizes the role of the learner as a co-creator of knowledge within the learning experience through intentional decisions made during the scoping, design, and creation phases of the process by encouraging learners to share their experiences and expertise on the topic. This bi-directional model for learning empowers learners to establish personal and professional relationships among peers and subject experts and allows for an exploratory and constructivist learning environment.

Conversation theory, defined as a system where one or more individuals interact through conversation about a concept and co-create a shared understanding of that concept,[10] aligns closely with this community of inquiry. In the Teach-Out model, these conversations occur directly in the content (usually during a video interview). Some Teach-Outs use a "host" to serve as the interviewer for conversations, guiding the learners through the content, and acting as a surrogate learner to ensure accessibility of content during filming sessions. Teach-Outs also use discussion forums, which are discussed later in this chapter.

The last pedagogical inspiration for the Teach-Out model is Albert Bandura's social learning theory, which posits that people learn from one another through observation, imitation, and modeling.[11] Literature suggests that modeling impacts how learners engage with one another in discussion threads;[12] Garrison

& Cleveland-Innes found that when there is a model interacting with learners in an online learning experience, and that model offers examples of how to reflectively engage in critical discourse, learners experienced deeper and more meaningful learning.[13] Bandura's social learning theory can offer valuable insight into how to design Teach-Outs that have a strong behavioral change component. In the Police Brutality in America Teach-Out, for example, academics, law enforcement officers, and community activists were interviewed to offer a range of models for learners as they consider action in their own contexts.

The theoretical foundations for the Teach-Out model were made more operational by developing a design framework that includes eight key design tenets. These define Teach-Outs as open, brief, engaged, inclusive, diverse, connected, bridging, and actionable. Tenets are aspirational while offering guiding requirements. See table 4.1 for a description of each tenet.

Tenet	Description
Open	Teach-Outs are free, with no paid element. They should be accessible worldwide with no primary content behind a paywall. All original content should be able to be repurposed in other educational contexts. All Teach-Outs are licensed under Creative Commons (CC-BY - SA 4.0).
Brief	Following the model of the Teach-In, the Teach-Out features a short, highly participatory, event-oriented design. The total participant engagement should be 1–4 hours, and Teach-Outs are time-bound learning events, lasting between 2–6 weeks.
Engaged	In lieu of assessments, Teach-Outs focus on participatory discussion and interaction with the other Teach-Out participants.
Inclusive	Teach-Outs are accessible to a global audience of non-experts from a broad range of cultural, socioeconomic, and educational backgrounds.
Diverse	Teach-Out content features a diverse range of voices and perspectives, drawing on expertise both from within an institution as well as the broader community beyond campus.
Connected	Where possible, Teach-Outs feature a corollary event on campus or in the local geographic community.
Bridging	Given the short duration of Teach-Outs, additional resources serve as a bridge to further engagement.
Actionable	Teach-Outs culminate in a call to action that allows the participants to put their knowledge and values into practice.

Table 4.1
Teach-Out design tenets and descriptions.

The Police Brutality in America Teach-Out

Inception of the Teach-Out

This section was written solely by author Ryan Henyard, whose experiences, expertise, and ideas fueled the inception of the Police Brutality in America Teach-Out.

Police brutality has deeply impacted marginalized communities in the United States for generations, and while there have been occasional incidents that pierced the veil of indifference in white communities—Tamir Rice, Amadou Diallo, Rodney King—the tragic killings of George Floyd, Breonna Taylor, and Tony McDade in the summer of 2020 created an unprecedented national and global outcry. The Black Lives Matter activists and civil rights leaders that have fought to change the violence of policing were once again thrust into a familiar pattern of rallying their communities while bracing for the seemingly inevitable failure to hold the officers involved accountable. The images of Black death at the hands of those sworn to serve and protect helped millions of people see the depth of this problem for the first time in a way they haven't truly reckoned with before, and they were fervently reaching out for resources to understand what they have witnessed. Unfortunately, the burden of that demand for understanding and knowledge historically falls on the victims of systemic oppression, adding the frustrating and demoralizing responsibility on top of the weight they already carry.

Like others in my community, I found myself inundated with messages of support, concern, and requests for answers during the uprisings of 2020 from friends, colleagues, and teammates. The decision to create a learning experience centered around police brutality in that moment was driven by three primary goals:

- Ensure BIPOC people who are disproportionately impacted should be centered in discussions about police violence and have their deep knowledge and history acknowledged and uplifted.
- Create enduring educational resources to reduce the emotional labor that impacted communities are asked to undertake whenever a police brutality incident enters the news cycle.
- Advance the national and global conversation about police violence beyond the incremental (and often unsubstantial) reforms, empowering activists with the knowledge to push for change locally.

The decision to create this learning experience as a Teach-Out flowed naturally out of the initial slate of design goals. We saw an opportunity to marry the public-facing nature of the Teach-Out model with the unprecedented number of demonstrations that took place across both the United States and numerous other countries. The Teach-Out model could be used in service of an educational need for those joining the movement to end police violence to truly understand the demands of activists and organizers. The emergent situation and the corresponding opportunity to press for changes in policing and shift the cultural acceptance of police violence necessitated a rapid response—something the University of Michigan has accomplished for such topics as the COVID-19 pandemic and the 2020 presidential impeachment proceedings. We also recognized that reaching the intended audiences required a shorter learning experience aimed at a wide range of potential learners and focused more on calling learners to action rather than formal certification of knowledge.

Building Deep Understanding of a Movement

Even in early conceptions of the learning experience, there was an intentional effort to build foundational knowledge necessary for understanding the crisis of police violence through the lived experience and scholarship of marginalized people. Holding space in the course to highlight disparities beyond killings of unarmed Black men normally discussed in the national conversation around police brutality—gendered violence at the hands of police, the ongoing epidemic of violence against transgender men and women, etc.—was vital to the vision for the course, and we worked to ensure they would be represented in the content. The concepts underlying the demands of Black Lives Matter protesters were frequently misunderstood by good- and bad-faith commentators alike, and ensuring that Teach-Out learners understood the ideological lineage of police abolition and abolitionist efforts to dismantle the prison industrial complex emerged as an important pillar of the course materials.

Similarly, being able to differentiate between some of the existing reform efforts and calls to defund the police were critical learning objectives. Defund and re-invest discussions naturally led learners to ask what should receive funding instead. The Teach-Out design team sought out community groups and leaders whose work proactively addressed the root causes of poverty, addiction, homelessness, and instability that produce crime as opposed to the reactive nature of violent policing. Above all, I recognized that the Teach-Out needed to spark the imaginations of learners: *What does it mean to create a world where police don't kill anyone?* What social structures, institutions, and systems of oppression are entangled with policing that also need to be dismantled? To make progress toward these goals, learners needed to see that there were decades of intellectual thought undergirding the popular protest signs and prepare them to imagine a future built around community care and support rather than punishment and imprisonment.

Scope and Content Conceptualization

The Teach-Out learner base features individuals from more than eighty countries, with much higher engagement (quantified by discussion board posts) than the typical University of Michigan MOOC.[14] This diverse and highly-engaged learner base fit the profile of many of the newcomers to the fight against police brutality, and even though they weren't centered in the creation of the Teach-Out, we envisioned that would deliver necessary perspective across different levels of learner understanding and previous investment.

Police brutality intersects with many different issues, so a concerted effort was made to determine what should be in scope for the initial Teach-Out, keeping in mind that the format calls for a brisk-paced learning experience. In order to build understanding of the lasting impacts of police brutality, we recognized the need to meet learners where they are; the Teach-Out accomplished that by conceptualizing the discussion on police violence through several different cultural lenses. Learners with an affinity and attachment to music would hopefully become more invested after hearing Dr. Eugene Rogers guiding them through a U-M Men's Glee Club performance of Seven Last Words of the Unarmed,[15] while those drawn to sports may respond directly to Dr. Ketra Armstrong's examination of the historical precedents for Colin Kaepernick's anti-brutality protests in the National Football League.[16]

Obstacles to Conception

Educating about police brutality, for both myself and for our expert contributors who have experienced violence or harassment by police, is an emotionally fraught endeavor. To prevent invoking traumatic episodes, the course design consistently sought to elevate the systemic and structural aspects of the issue above individual stories of misconduct and loss. This served the goal of establishing links between the historical preceding events and the current social movement but was primarily done in the interest of protecting contributors and learners from undue harm.

Some of the scholars whose work was foundational to the original vision were, like many Black academics during 2020, facing a deluge of requests for their time and dramatic increases in interest around their scholarship addressing structural racism. The rapid response timeline combined with the sudden rush of mainstream interest meant that we weren't able to feature their contributions in the course. We sought to have their scholarship represented by other expert presenters or searched for existing materials created by those faculty members (accessible articles, videos, podcasts, etc.) to include in the learning experience.

Design and Development

Phase 1: Scoping and Design

The initial design step refined the proposed Teach-Out scope in the context of the rapid timeline, resources, and expertise available. Our goal was to provide a concise but substantive overview of policing in the United States to contextualize current events. We identified history, theories of abolition and of police reform, policing alternatives, and how to take action against police violence as key areas to guide our selection of contributors and experts.

An early challenge was determining the correct tone to present this work. Being seen to take an explicit political stance, particularly in work by a public university, may have been seen as inappropriate, could discourage substantive dialogue among a diverse learner group, and potentially increase the potential for bad-faith actors in the Teach-Out. On the other hand, presenting all perspectives on the issue as equally valid might risk validating racist and damaging narratives around policing. The Teach-Out model mitigates this by presenting a wide range of experts in an academic fashion and inviting learners to respond with their own reactions in a respectful manner. Teach-Outs are typically designed around a series of brief videos recorded by multiple expert contributors. This allows the project to show a wide range of perspectives from a range of fields and experiences without explicitly endorsing any particular view. Resources are not presented prescriptively and dialogue among learners is encouraged. We designed around the assumption that most learners considered police violence an issue, which allowed us to focus on different perspectives on solutions and avoid a debate about the existence of police brutality, particularly racist violence, as that had been widely addressed in public conversation elsewhere.

This was reflected in speaker selection as well. We included experts from law enforcement, policymakers, social workers, scholars of police abolition, artists responding to police violence, and historians on racial conflict in the United States. No speakers were included that did not agree that police brutality was a problem on some level because it did not fall within the scope of the project and conflicted with the prevailing opinions of experts themselves.

Phase 2: Outreach and External Contributors

These general topic areas informed our outreach to experts in phase two. The development team contacted experts in their personal and professional networks as well as the University of Michigan system relating to key subject areas. This strategy inherently led to a bias toward perspectives from Michigan, particularly the Ann Arbor and Detroit areas where both staff and faculty connections were localized and potential contributors were more likely to engage with our office as representatives of a local, public research university. We were, however, able to leverage alumni and our own personal networks to include others outside of Michigan, and many of our contributors were regular participants to national conversations on the subject and could speak to the broader contexts of policing although the subject matter centered US experiences and law. Though a drawback in the sense that the details might not connect with the experiences of all learners on a global platform like Coursera, it allowed us to focus on concrete examples of how an issue was understood and addressed within a consistent context. For example, a series of videos from workers at Avalon Housing—a supportive housing development[17] in Ann Arbor, MI—about their experiences spoke to the lived reality of low-income communities interacting with the police. When these are placed alongside videos from state-wide representatives and policymakers as well as those speaking to the national context, learners were able to see multiple levels of experience within the same issue.

The outreach process was the most formative of the project's design. We asked experts to contribute one or two shorts (three-to-five-minute videos, although this could vary) and any supporting materials for learners. While we determined speakers based on our own assessment of what the Teach-Out should look like, its final form was dependent on who was able to participate and what their interests were. Members of the development team worked with interested contributors in scoping calls to establish the key points they felt most urgently needed to be shared with a public, non-expert audience. This approach allowed us to center experts' voices in the project.

Outreach was also shaped by newly implemented honoraria policies. Teach-Outs are not paid experiences and therefore do not generate revenue, but they benefit the institution that produces them in other, less tangible ways. A Teach-Out may generate traffic for other (paid) learning experiences, increase the visibility of the institution, and/or contribute to the institutional reputation. In addition, DEI-related work, in higher education and many other fields, is disproportionately carried out by underrepresented groups, including faculty of color and women, whose efforts may not be reflected in pay or in tenure review.[18,19] The work of activists, organizers, and community workers also tend to be underpaid, if they are paid at all. Our honoraria policies enacted recognition of the non-financial benefits to the university of producing such work in an environment with existing gender, race, and class inequities.

Each contributor was offered an honorarium for their work, regardless of their employment status with the university as their contributions were outside the scope of their normal position.[20] Our intention was that these efforts would curtail our work from contributing to the undervaluing of community work or existing pay inequities within higher education. Many contributors did elect not to receive their honoraria or shared that they would be donating their payment to causes organizing in response to police brutality. Nonetheless, these policies are a valuable step to bring social justice work in higher education in line with the recognition and pay received for doing other forms of intellectual labor both for workers in higher education and in the broader community.

Phase 3: Build, Launch, and Live Engagement

The rest of the Teach-Out, including discussion prompts and external resources, was designed around the confirmed contributors and their interests. Content was organized according to topic groupings that would allow learners to progress through foundational material, into specific topic areas, and finally end on content that would help them create an action plan. We also included a live event during the course where learners could engage with Teach-Out experts. Within each section, discussion questions guided learners to reflect on the material in response to questions that could be shared in discussion forums associated with each question, as discussed at length in the next section.

Action Plan and External Resources

The final module of the Teach-Out concluded on a call to action asking learners to apply what they learned to their communities. The development team collaborated with specialists in behavioral sciences to create a guided action plan and curated list of external resources that fit different tiers of engagement. The sample action plan developed by members of CAI's behavioral science team and the design team (see figure 4.1) allowed learners to self-assess their current capacity and activity level in key areas, establish goals, and establish a concrete action plan to reach those goals.

The curated external resources allowed learners to explore suggested ways to get involved. Each tier was presented using an "I" statement that corresponded to how a learner might be feeling about their capacity. Tiers included were: "I'm ready to take action," "I need to learn more about the issues," "I want to have conversations about the issues," and "I've been taking action and need to prevent my own burnout," and each statement directed learners to a page with next steps of how to engage at that level. For example, "I'm ready to take action" guided learners to a page with foundational guidance about making action against police brutality a sustainable habit followed by links to external organizations, policy efforts, and other opportunities to get involved.

Centering Justice in Content Development 67

SAMPLE ACTION PLAN

Use the action plan below to:

1. Assess how confident and active you are in each category
2. Set general goals for each category
3. Identify concrete action steps you'll take to get there
4. Choose when you want to take action

You can print this plan or click File > Make a Copy in the menu bar to make an editable copy to fill out.

My Monthly Action Plan				
Category	**Learn & Listen**	**Have discussions**	**Take action**	**Take care of yourself**
How active or confident do you feel in this category?				
What are your general goals for this category?				
What concrete action(s) will you take?				
By when do you want to take this action?				

At the end of the month, reflect on:
- What worked well for you?
- What felt impactful?
- What barriers did you experience?
- How might you change your personal plan to help get past these barriers?

Figure 4.1
The sample guiding action plan for learners.

Live Event

The Teach-Out ran for four weeks during July 2020. During the third week, the development team hosted a live town hall event via a Zoom webinar that allowed learners to ask questions of selected Teach-Out experts. More than 1,600 learners registered for the event and an estimated 473 learners attended. We selected four experts that represented a range of perspectives, including professors of law, history of race and policing, as well as law enforcement officials and advocates for police oversight. The panel responded to pre-sourced questions collected from a form within the Teach-Out, curated by the development team for clarity and prioritization of the most frequent or substantive questions as well as questions collected during the live webinar.

Including this live event allowed us to engage with learners to address an evolving subject. While the content from the Teach-Out focused on more stable content such as history, theoretical approaches, or more high-level discussions about police brutality, the live event allowed experts to comment on examples specific to that moment that were currently unfolding. For example, while there had been widespread protests in Portland, OR, in response to the murder of George Floyd and Breonna Taylor beginning in late May of 2020, these escalated when federal officers were deployed in early July.[21] The deployment of federal agents, the use of force on protesters, including tear gas and flash grenades, shifted the national conversation around police brutality and particularly the role of federal law enforcement in policing protestors. This shift was important to address within the context of the movement to end police brutality but could not have been anticipated by the design team. The live event offered experts a space to contextualize emerging information into the larger issues covered in the Teach-Out.

Learner Engagement
Learner Interactions in the Teach-Out Model

The Teach-Out tenet of engagement specifies that learners are encouraged to contribute to large-group discussions as a means of community and knowledge-building within the online learning experience. Discussions are prompted through forums embedded in the Teach-Out's learning platform, Coursera, with questions guiding reflection on learning content. Internal data gathering efforts from prior Teach-Outs characterized learner audiences as highly engaged and markedly honest in their responses to prompts and in dialogue with other learners and moderators. We anticipated especially high enrollment in this Teach-Out due to the timeliness of the subject, high learner enrollment rates in previous Teach-Outs, the open nature of the Teach-Out, and the documented desire for individuals to involve themselves in anti-racist work in and beyond the summer of 2020.[22,23] We were eager to create a discussion space that would serve to foster important, honest, and pivotal discussions on the subjects of police brutality and anti-Black racism in the United States but were cognizant of the unique challenges that would accompany engaging a global public on this necessary but too often polarizing subject.

All Teach-Out discussion forums require a certain degree of moderation and attention, usually conducted by one or two members of the Teach-Out development team. We anticipated that most learners would be present to learn and educate themselves on the topic, but the content would be challenging for many. Our experts explored the anti-Blackness at the foundations of policing in the US and the white supremacist nature of many American social structures. Some learners might demonstrate discomfort or anger in response to these topics while others might join the course as bad-faith actors intent on trolling or otherwise agitating productive learner conversation. With these factors in mind, we developed a more comprehensive and scaled approach to discussion moderation and facilitation within the Police Brutality in America Teach-Out as compared to prior learning experiences. We began by sending out a call for volunteer moderators within the Center for Academic Innovation's digital channels. With eight respondents able to fortify our moderation team, we began implementing training strategies to help volunteers become comfortable and confident facilitators within the Teach-Out's discussion forums.

Moderator Training

Training focused on several key goals to ensure that moderators understood their purpose in the forums, knew when and how to interact with learners, and were able to recognize and respond to divisive, offensive, or otherwise bad-faith behavior. To accomplish these goals, we created documentation (including videos, charts, and a manual), gathered external resources, created channels for communication, and held question-and-answer sessions for the volunteers.

To establish moderators' sense of purpose within the forums, we created an engagement guide that clearly delineated moderator roles by gathering all documentation and external resources into one manual. This guide, while used for all Teach-Outs, was tailored to help the moderators of the Police Brutality Teach-Out navigate the unique specifications of this learning experience. Moderators were guided by engagement outcomes tailored to the online discussion space (see figure 4.2). We included general goals that apply to all Teach-Out experiences, followed by more specific goals tailored to the Police Brutality Teach-Out. The general goals, used for every Teach-Out, include these objectives:

- learners engage with each other in dialogue and conversation;
- learners engage with experts (i.e., through discussion forums or by submitting questions for experts to answer in live events); and
- learners engage with Teach-Out engagement staff (i.e., Teach-Out team mentors, student fellows, course operations specialists).

To achieve these goals, the Teach-Out moderation team traditionally has a noticeable and established presence using "likes," encouraging comments/feedback/interaction, clear signaling or acknowledgment that moderators are "listening" to the learners as they contribute, and by sharing updates with expert contributors and encouraging them to join the learning experience on the platform.

These goals provide a high-level understanding of moderator actions; the goals specified for the Police Brutality Teach-Out (shown below in table 4.2) served to point moderators' interactions with learners toward salient learning outcomes.

Engagement outcome ("Learners will...")	Moderator action ("Facilitators will encourage learners to...")
... articulate issues causing and stemming from police brutality in the US (i.e., history and origins) and how race and the history of systemic racism in America factor into violent police actions.	... identify, articulate, and relate their commented thoughts and opinions about current events as analyzed in the learning segments to segments that cover the historical context of policing and racism.
... identify different perspectives and opinions on police violence and will be exposed to various modern strategies for mitigating police violence in the US.	... apply content to their surroundings: how can these concepts and perspectives be actionable in their own communities? ... reflect on what has changed about their perceptions of these opinions and strategies throughout the learning experience. ... reflect on how they came to their current conclusions about police violence and how their thinking has changed due to the learning experience in the Teach-Out. ... share their lived experiences as they are comfortable and will encourage listening learners to honor, learn from, and support those who share.
... understand how the concepts of police violence, race, systemic racism, and history apply to their own lives and communities.	... articulate how they became interested in participating in this learning experience. ... specify how the information in the Teach-Out has contributed to changes in their perceptions and actions.
... be motivated to take action.	... seek to educate themselves further after the Teach-Out experience concludes. ... speak about police violence and systemic racism with those in their personal and professional circles. ... take civic action against police brutality and similar injustices in their own communities.

Table 4.2
Learning engagement outcomes and moderator actions for the Police Brutality Teach-Out.

Planning for Discomfort and Incivility

Ground rules are shared with the learner when entering the Teach-Out and, like other standard components of Teach-Out documentation, were tailored to include more specific language surrounding what we envisioned could be possible outcomes of antiracist conversation. They also served as another clear guide for moderators, along with a powerful tool that could be used to encourage learners to challenge themselves and others in respectful and constructive ways. The ground rules read, in part:

> Challenge the idea and not the person. If you want to respond to a discussion forum post, you may respond with thoughts on what was said but not about the person who posted.
>
> Keep your passion positive. Strong feelings are great and sharing them politely keeps discussion forums friendly. Avoid using all caps, too many exclamation points, or aggressive language.
>
> Acknowledge discomfort. The topics discussed in this specific Teach-Out can be hard to talk about, for many reasons and from many perspectives. Stick with it and remember the benefits of having these tough conversations.
>
> In this Teach-Out, we will specifically be monitoring for language that could be considered inflammatory, uncivil, racist, or otherwise unacceptable for this learning space, and we will remove language deemed such.

We held two unique objectives in mind when writing these ground rules: the mitigation of divisive or uncivil language in the discussion forums and the encouragement of racially privileged learners to lean in to predicted discomfort that might arise from challenging privilege and white supremacist structures.[24]

The Teach-Out development team wanted moderators to possess the tools to recognize and take appropriate action against any trolling, hate speech, or other confrontational content within the forums. We took the possibility of such instances of incivility very seriously, as trolling and other online harassment tactics are a digital form of the racism and discrimination found in non-digital social environments.[25] Documentation included in the moderator manual took three distinct forms: collected resources on how to recognize trolling, a list of potential divisive scenarios along with ways to respond to those scenarios, and a decision tree that helped moderators decide what to do when encountering uncivil or confrontational content in the forums.

The process of identifying trolling or hate speech is not always linear or clear,[26] especially in online environments with thousands of learners. We predicted the potential forms of confrontational learner-posted content based on personal experience and through the collected resources provided to moderators. We also recognized that some inflammatory or confrontational discussion posts could be an opportunity to shift learners toward more antiracist mindsets. This provided a unique challenge: how do we give moderators the tools to determine when a post constituted hate speech and needed to be removed, when a post was a learning opportunity and could be engaged, or when a post was trolling and was best left ignored?

We created a decision tree to delineate situations and empower decision-making between the types of questionable posts a moderator might encounter (figure 4.2). We found that moderators had great success using this as a general guide for decision-making and determination of the "type" of questionable post they were encountering. We also created suggested responses that moderators used to engage with posts that were determined to be potential learning opportunities rather than hate speech or trolling. For instance, if a learner asserted that "all lives matter" in a discussion thread, the template response was:

> We agree that everyone's lives matter, but the statement "All Lives Matter" can minimize and devalue the history and lived experiences of what Black communities have experienced. "Black Lives Matter" raises awareness that systemic racism[27]—slavery and its afterlives, policies concentrating poverty along racial lines, policing practices, and so on—have meant that Black lives have historically meant less within those systems. The claim is not to discount the lives of others, but to reaffirm the value of lives that have historically and continue to be devalued.

We encouraged moderators to consider these responses to adapt these standardized approaches to best fit their communication styles and situations. These standardized responses allowed the moderation team to have clear and unified language options when encountering predicted scenarios and minimized anxieties moderators might experience over crafting responses in divisive situations.

Centering Justice in Content Development 73

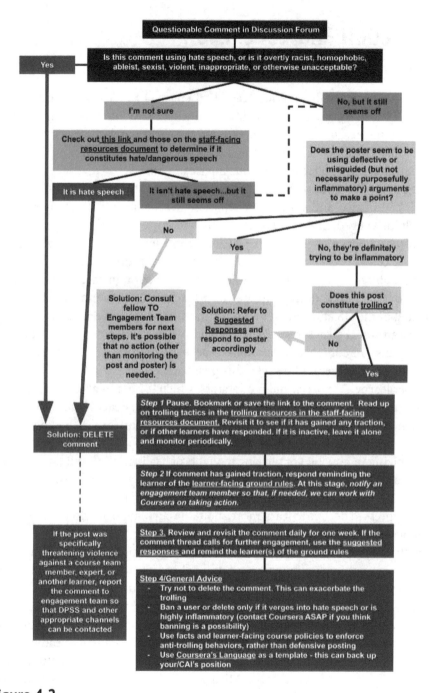

Figure 4.2
The decision tree for moderators to determine a post's potential for hate speech, trolling, or a learning opportunity.

Reflection and Conclusion

Impact

The Police Brutality in America Teach-Out engaged 5,375 learners and generated 4,755 discussion posts at the time of conclusion. While success in the OER space can be measured in a variety of ways, the sheer number of participants in the learning experience demonstrates the interest in and need for an OER that directly addresses police brutality in America.

Learners were varied in perspective, country, race, age, gender, culture, career, politics, ethnicity, and spiritual belief. Many learners could be categorized as racially privileged, and these learners, by and large, used their experience in the Teach-Out to recognize their privilege, confronting the role racial bias has in instances of police brutality in America. Many addressed the necessity of learning about the topic in order to take further action in their communities. With content that so deeply explored anti-Blackness as a foundational piece of policing in the US and sought to discuss the white supremacist nature of many American social structures, learners sometimes felt uncomfortable or pushed back against the content and solutions (especially against the concept of defunding the police). Overall, however, this pushback was explored and challenged by other learners, experts, and moderators, which led to remarkable changes in knowledge, mindset, and perspective by the end of the Teach-Out.

Many Black learners and learners of color shared stories of their experiences with police violence. Other learners created a safe space for these stories by empathizing (if possible) or offering thoughts of healing. While our engagement model didn't require or suggest sharing personal stories, the safe learning space created by the learning community led to this dialogue. Learners across the globe expressed desires to learn more about the current police violence issues in America and wished to develop anti-racist action plans to prevent police brutality in their communities and committed to making plans of direct action to fight racism, community disempowerment, and police violence in their communities.

Although the live learning experience concluded on July 31, 2020, the Police Brutality in America Teach-Out lives on in a free, open-access archival format available on Michigan Online.[28] All course content, excluding discussion prompts, is available in this format. The individual segments (readings and videos) of the Teach-Out are also available in various themed collections, also freely available and open access on Michigan Online.[29] This Teach-Out was also the basis for an expanded Community Awareness course, the first-ever created by the University of Michigan, which launched in October 2020. This version made the original Teach-Out content available, including discussion prompts, on Coursera on an ongoing basis alongside updated and expanded external resources. In addition to distributing and sharing the learning materials with community organizations and activist groups, the team created a K-12 teaching guide that links each video and module in the Teach-Out to relevant Common Core standards to support instructors who wish to teach students about the topics covered in the learning experience.

Limitations

One salient barrier we would like to address is the difficulty of moving learners toward taking concrete action on controversial issues. The call to action included in the Teach-Out called for people to take significant actions above and beyond the typical response of book clubs and symbolic gestures. While many learners described modules as impactful and enlightening, they were less willing to commit to supporting efforts to end police brutality that carried what they viewed to be social or reputational risk. In later project iterations, the project team explored the possibility of creating an interactive online simulation that would allow learners to practice engagement as a stepping-stone to real-world action. This work would build on the evolving use of gaming and virtual reality used to inspire critical reflection and inspire real-world action.[30]

We also recognize the inherent inequalities and inequities that accompany digital learning, usually termed the "digital divide."[31,32] While the Teach-Out model ameliorates some of the barriers to digital learning—such as cost—barriers surrounding digital learning preparedness, online access, and digital literacy cannot be ignored in this or any digital learning experience. In addition, there may also be cultural or linguistic barriers. Contributors are encouraged to use inclusive language that does not presuppose technical or field-specific knowledge and speaks to a global audience, but the local specificity of how an issue like police brutality manifests in a particular community may conflict with accessibility goals. In this case, most contributors and the development team were located in the United States; therefore, our content focused on policing in the United States. As an OER from the University of Michigan, there was also an emphasis on issues impacting the state of Michigan since that was closest to both many contributors and the development teams' experience. The team approached this limitation, where it appeared, as an example illustrating larger trends in the United States, although this prevented the Teach-Out from addressing more national examples or police violence internationally. The participation of global learners did diversify the available perspectives, but these were not reflected in Teach-Out content directly.

In future OER development, we would like to continue to broaden our definition of expertise to include more diverse backgrounds and perspectives, including students, community members, and activists. We also will be continuing to find innovative ways to present paths toward action that will convert learners from online engagement to offline action. We also feel that it is important to continue to question our own internal development processes and procedures by taking on feedback from our learners, community partners, and fellow developers of online learning experiences. It is our hope that this chapter can introduce readers to a new form of OER in the Teach-Out model and will inspire future antiracist open learning initiatives.

Endnotes

1. Louis Menashe and Ronald Radosh, "Teach-Ins: USA, Reports, Opinions, Documents," *History of Education Quarterly* 9, no. 1 (1969): 99–101.
2. Marshall Sahlins, "The Teach-Ins: Anti-War Protest in the Old Stoned Age," *Anthropology Today* 25, no. 1 (2009): 3–5, https://doi.org/10.1111/j.1467-8322.2009.00639.x.
3. Benjamin Morse and Molly Maher, "Teach-Outs: A Framework for Public Engagement in Online Learning," In *EDULEARN20 Proceedings* (2020), 5027–35, https://doi.org/10.21125/edulearn.2020.1314.
4. L. S. Vygotsky, *Mind in Society: The Development of Higher Psychological Processes* (Cambridge, MA: Harvard University Press, 1980).
5. D. Randy Garrison, Terry Anderson, and Walter Archer, "Critical Inquiry in a Text-Based Environment: Computer Conferencing in Higher Education," *The Internet and Higher Education* 2, no. 2–3 (March 1999): 87–105, https://doi.org/10.1016/S1096-7516(00)00016-6.
6. D. Randy Garrison, "Online Community of Inquiry Review: Social, Cognitive, and Teaching Presence Issues," *Journal of Asynchronous Learning Networks* (2007): 61–72.
7. P. R. Lowenthal, "A mixed methods examination of instructor social presence in accelerated online courses," in *Handbook of Research on Strategic Management of Interaction, Presence, and Participation in Online Courses* (2016), 147–59.
8. Garrison, "Online Community of Inquiry Review," 65.
9. Ibid., 67.
10. G. Pask, *Conversation Theory. Applications in Education and Epistemology* (Berkeley, CA: Elsevier, 1976).
11. A. Bandura, R. H. Walters, *Social Learning Theory* (Englewood Cliffs, NJ: Prentice-Hall, 1977).
12. J. R. Hill, L. Song, R. E. West, "Social Learning Theory and Web-based Learning Environments: A Review of Research and Discussion of Implications," *The American Journal of Distance Education* (2009): 8–103.
13. D. Randy Garrison and M. Cleveland-Innes, "Facilitating Cognitive Presence in Online Learning: Interaction is Not Enough," *The American Journal of Distance Education* (2005): 33–48.
14. Morse and Maher, "Teach-Outs: A Framework," 5033.
15. Eugene Rogers, "Seven Last Words of the Unarmed," Michigan Online, 2020, http://www.online.umich.edu/teach-outs/police-brutality-in-america-teach-out/lessons/eugene-rogers-seven-last-words-unarmed/.
16. Ketra Armstrong, "Ketra Armstrong: Lessons from Colin Kaepernick," Michigan Online, 2020, https://www.online.umich.edu/teach-outs/police-brutality-in-america-teach-out/lessons/armstrong-lessons-kaepernick/.

17. Avalon Housing is a nonprofit housing provider that provides housing, emotional and physical health, and community services to more than 800 formerly homeless individuals in Washtenaw County, Michigan. See more at https://www.avalonhousing.org/.
18. Miguel F. Jimenez, Theresa M. Laverty, Sara P. Bombaci, Kate Wilkins, Drew E. Bennett, and Liba Pejchar, "Underrepresented Faculty Play a Disproportionate Role in Advancing Diversity and Inclusion," *Nature Ecology & Evolution* 3, no. 7 (July 2019): 1030–33. https://doi.org/10.1038/s41559-019-0911-5.
19. Patricia A. Matthew, ed., *Written/Unwritten: Diversity and the Hidden Truths of Tenure* (Chapel Hill: The University of North Carolina Press, 2016).
20. The development team was also paid as this work fell within the scope of their regular duties as staff or student fellows.
21. Mike Baker, Thomas Fuller, and Sergio Olmos, "Federal Agents Push Into Portland Streets, Stretching Limits of Their Authority," *The New York Times* (July 25, 2020).
22. Michael Tesler, "Analysis | The Floyd Protests Have Changed Public Opinion about Race and Policing. Here's the Data," *Washington Post* (June 9, 2020), https://www.washingtonpost.com/politics/2020/06/09/floyd-protests-have-changed-public-opinion-about-race-policing-heres-data/.
23. Constance Grady, "Do the Soaring Sales of Anti-Racism Books Signal a True Cultural Shift?," Vox, June 11, 2020, https://www.vox.com/culture/2020/6/11/21288021/anti-racism-books-reading-list-sales-figures.
24. Tonya Mosley, "'Lean Into Discomfort' When Talking About Race," WBUR, June 9, 2020. https://www.wbur.org/hereandnow/2020/06/09/taking-about-race.
25. Stephanie M. Ortiz, "Trolling as a Collective Form of Harassment: An Inductive Study of How Online Users Understand Trolling," *Social Media + Society* 6, no. 2 (April 1, 2020): 2056305120928512, https://doi.org/10.1177/2056305120928512.
26. Elise Moreau, "Here's What You Need to Know About Internet Trolling," Lifewire, November 12, 2019, https://www.lifewire.com/what-is-internet-trolling-3485891.
27. In the original template response, we linked to the following article: Katie O'Malley, "History of Slavery Professor Explains the Mistake in Saying 'All Lives Matter,'" *ELLE* (June 10, 2020), https://www.elle.com/uk/life-and-culture/culture/a32800835/all-lives-matter-fake-equality/.
28. The archived version can be accessed at https://www.online.umich.edu/teach-outs/police-brutality-in-america-teach-out/.
29. Browse the collections at https://www.online.umich.edu/collections/.
30. Ian Bogost, *Persuasive Games: The Expressive Power of Videogames* (Cambridge: MIT Press, 2007).
31. Doug Lederman, "Study Offers Data to Show MOOCs Didn't Achieve Their Goals," *Inside Higher Ed* (January 16, 2019), https://www.insidehighered.com/digital-learning/article/2019/01/16/study-offers-data-show-moocs-didnt-achieve-their-goals.
32. John B. Horrigan, "Digital Literacy and Learning in the United States," Pew Research Center, September 20, 2016, https://www.pewresearch.org/internet/2016/09/20/digital-readiness-gaps/.

Bibliography

Armstrong, Ketra. "Ketra Armstrong: Lessons from Colin Kaepernick." Michigan Online. 2020. https://www.online.umich.edu/teach-outs/police-brutality-in-america-teach-out/lessons/armstrong-lessons-kaepernick/.

Baker, Mike, Thomas Fuller, and Sergio Olmos. "Federal Agents Push Into Portland Streets, Stretching Limits of Their Authority." *The New York Times* (July 25, 2020).

Bandura, Albert. *Social Learning Theory*. Englewood Cliffs, NJ: Prentice-Hall, 1977.

Bogost, Ian. *Persuasive Games: The Expressive Power of Videogames*. Cambridge: MIT Press, 2007.

Garrison, D. R. "Online Community of Inquiry Review: Social, Cognitive, And Teaching Presence Issues." *Journal of Asynchronous Learning Networks* 11, no. 1 (2007): 61–72. https://doi.org/10.24059/olj.v11i1.1737.

Garrison, D. Randy, Terry Anderson, and Walter Archer. "Critical Inquiry in a Text-Based Environment: Computer Conferencing in Higher Education." *The Internet and Higher Education* 2, no. 2–3 (March 1999): 87–105. https://doi.org/10.1016/S1096-7516(00)00016-6.

Garrison, D. Randy, and Martha Cleveland-Innes. "Facilitating Cognitive Presence in Online Learning: Interaction Is Not Enough." *American Journal of Distance Education* 19, no. 3 (September 1, 2005): 133–48. https://doi.org/10.1207/s15389286ajde1903_2.

Grady, Constance. "Do the Soaring Sales of Anti-Racism Books Signal a True Cultural Shift?" Vox. June 11, 2020. https://www.vox.com/culture/2020/6/11/21288021/anti-racism-books-reading-list-sales-figures.

Hill, Janette R., Liyan Song, and Richard E. West. "Social Learning Theory and Web-Based Learning Environments: A Review of Research and Discussion of Implications." *American Journal of Distance Education* 23, no. 2 (May 19, 2009): 88–103. https://doi.org/10.1080/08923640902857713.

Horrigan, John B. "Digital Literacy and Learning in the United States." Pew Research Center. September 20, 2016. https://www.pewresearch.org/internet/2016/09/20/digital-readiness-gaps/.

Jimenez, Miguel F., Theresa M. Laverty, Sara P. Bombaci, Kate Wilkins, Drew E. Bennett, and Liba Pejchar. "Underrepresented Faculty Play a Disproportionate Role in Advancing Diversity and Inclusion." *Nature Ecology & Evolution* 3, no. 7 (July 2019): 1030–33. https://doi.org/10.1038/s41559-019-0911-5.

Lederman, Doug. "Study Offers Data to Show MOOCs Didn't Achieve Their Goals." *Inside Higher Ed* (January 16, 2019). https://www.insidehighered.com/digital-learning/article/2019/01/16/study-offers-data-show-moocs-didnt-achieve-their-goals.

Lowenthal, Patrick Ryan. "A Mixed Methods Examination of Instructor Social Presence in Accelerated Online Courses." In *Handbook of Research on Strategic Management of Interaction, Presence, and Participation in Online Courses*, 147–59. Hershey, PA: IGI Global, 2016. http://www.igi-global.com/chapter/a-mixed-methods-examination-of-instructor-social-presence-in-accelerated-online-courses/140644.

Matthew, Patricia A. *Written/Unwritten: Diversity and the Hidden Truths of Tenure*. Chapel Hill: University of North Carolina Press, 2016. https://uncpress.org/book/9781469627717/writtenunwritten/.

Menashe, Louis, and Ronald Radosh. "Teach-Ins: USA, Reports, Opinions, Documents." *History of Education Quarterly* 9, no. 1 (1969): 99–101.

Moreau, Elise. "Here's What You Need to Know About Internet Trolling." Lifewire. November 12, 2019. https://www.lifewire.com/what-is-internet-trolling-3485891.

Morse, Benjamin, and Molly Maher. "Teach-Outs: A Framework for Public Engagement in Online Learning." In *EDULEARN20 Proceedings* (2020), 5027–35. https://doi.org/10.21125/edulearn.2020.1314.

Mosley, Tonya. "'Lean Into Discomfort' When Talking About Race." WBUR. June 9, 2020. https://www.wbur.org/hereandnow/2020/06/09/taking-about-race.

O'Malley, Katie. "History of Slavery Professor Explains The Mistake In Saying 'All Lives Matter.'" *ELLE* (June 10, 2020). https://www.elle.com/uk/life-and-culture/culture/a32800835/all-lives-matter-fake-equality/.

Ortiz, Stephanie M. "Trolling as a Collective Form of Harassment: An Inductive Study of How Online Users Understand Trolling." *Social Media + Society* 6, no. 2 (April 1, 2020): 2056305120928512. https://doi.org/10.1177/2056305120928512.

Pask, Gordon. *Conversation Theory: Applications in Education and Epistemology*. Berkeley, CA: Elsevier, 1976.

Rogers, Eugene. "Seven Last Words of the Unarmed." Michigan Online. 2020. http://www.online.umich.edu/teach-outs/police-brutality-in-america-teach-out/lessons/eugene-rogers-seven-last-words-unarmed/.

Sahlins, Marshall. "The Teach-Ins: Anti-War Protest in the Old Stoned Age." *Anthropology Today* 25, no. 1 (2009): 3–5. https://doi.org/10.1111/j.1467-8322.2009.00639.x.

Tesler, Michael. "Analysis | The Floyd Protests Have Changed Public Opinion about Race and Policing. Here's the Data." *Washington Post* (June 9, 2020). https://www.washingtonpost.com/politics/2020/06/09/floyd-protests-have-changed-public-opinion-about-race-policing-heres-data/.

Vygotsky, L. S. *Mind in Society: The Development of Higher Psychological Processes*. Cambridge, MA: Harvard University Press, 1980.

CHAPTER 5

Pay It Forward:
Realizing The Promise of OER for the Next Generation of Learners

Kimberly S. Grotewold, Karen L. Kohler, and Elisabeth M. Krimbill

Pay it Forward: A Ripple Effect

"Pay it forward" became a commonly used phrase and sociocultural fixture after Catherine Ryan Hyde's 1999 novel of the same name and the subsequent movie released in 2000 featuring prominent actors and celebrities. Particularly in the United States, society recognizes the phenomenon of people paying for occupants' orders in the next car at drive-through windows as enactments of the pay-it-forward mindset. This is largely due to news media outlets publicizing long chains of cars lasting multiple hours at well-known commercial establishments such as Starbucks.[1] According to the former Pay It Forward Foundation's website, the foundation was established "as a catalyst to inspire growth for the Pay It Forward philosophy, acts of kindness among strangers, generating a ripple effect from one person to the next, one community to the next."[2] The benefits of open educational resources (OER) adoption, modification, creation, and use in various education settings clearly extend beyond what one would categorize as a "kindness," and specifically in the context of PreK-12 education, it is possible to truly imagine the power and potential of a "ripple effect" spreading community-to-community but also from one generation of learners to the next.

Cost Savings for PreK-12 Students

As some readers are likely aware, the United Nations Educational, Scientific, and Cultural Organization (UNESCO) defines OER as "teaching, learning and research materials in any medium—digital or otherwise—that reside in the public domain or have been released under an open license that permits no-cost access, use, adaptation, and redistribution by others with no or limited restrictions."[3] Part of what initially attracts interest in OER is the "no-cost" aspect.

Cost reduction for individual students and the collective student body is a benefit associated with the adoption and use of OER to replace expensive textbooks and other instructional materials in higher education. There have been various, widely publicized reports on the huge increases in textbook prices for college students, looking at ranges of years from 1978–2013 and 2006–2016, and OER is seen as an option for reducing individual students' expenditures.[4] Because students in PreK-12 public schools in the United States are often not required to purchase their textbooks or curriculum resources themselves, it is harder to recognize and perhaps realize reduced costs as a benefit. One 2017 calculation of the average spending on textbooks and instructional materials by K-12 school systems was $250/student annually, although this number seems to be based on 2013/2014 data.[5] Another article puts K-12 non-digital curriculum spending at $10.4 billion for the 2014–2015 academic year and $1.8–$4.8 billion[6] of spending on digital content in the previous year. For large school systems, this adds up to significant funds expenditures. Particularly for school systems in economically challenged areas, OER could be a district-level cost-saving measure. A 2017 study of school systems in the United States and the factors that drive curriculum materials adoption decisions found that the cost of the materials was of more concern when larger percentages of the school's student population had been identified as living in poverty.[7] At least, in theory, funds that are not being spent on instructional materials could be diverted toward other resources in support of students, which may be particularly important in schools serving impoverished students and families.

During the fall of 2015 and early 2016, the United States Department of Education launched its #GoOpen initiative. A main goal of the initiative was to promote access to and creation of "high-quality openly licensed educational resources" and supports—specifically, free resources with the "5R" permissions fully enabled. These 5R permissions allow users to retain, reuse, revise, remix, and redistribute the materials to best suit their needs.[8] The #GoOpen website advocates that "switching to openly licensed educational materials has enabled school districts to repurpose funding typically spent on textbooks for other pressing needs, such as investing in the transition to digital learning."[9] During the current COVID-19 pandemic, it is relatively easy to envision how funding saved from textbook purchases might be used to purchase additional computers for students' home use, MiFi units, or augmented WiFi access at schools and surrounding areas. Prior to the #GoOpen initiative, the Office of Educational Technology issued a Dear Colleague Letter to clarify that federal funding could be used to "support innovative technology-based strategies" across four areas:

1. improving and personalizing professional learning and other supports for educators;
2. increasing access to high-quality digital content and resources for students;
3. facilitating educator collaboration and communication; and
4. providing devices for students to access digital learning resources.[10]

Within this letter, open educational resources were specifically noted in a section on using Title II-A funds for providing teachers with training on finding and adapting relevant openly licensed college- and career-ready resources.[11]

Within the #GoOpen initiative framework, there are both #GoOpen States and #GoOpen Districts. There were originally fourteen #GoOpen States, a number that eventually grew to twenty.[12] Among #GoOpen Districts, there have been both Launch Districts and Ambassador Districts, with the total number of participating districts beginning at sixteen and growing to more than 120. Ambassador Districts are districts with more experience in adopting and developing OER, which serve as mentors to the Launch Districts.[13] Additionally, as part of its open education efforts, the Department of Education has issued regulations to require that all Department of Education grant awardees must openly license and make available to the public all copyrightable intellectual property that was created with the grant funding. While works created under an awarded grant may have initially been designed to benefit specific students, the department concluded that "the resources are such that other education stakeholders would significantly benefit from being able to access them, reuse them, and in some cases, modify them to address their needs and goals."[14] These important initiatives have the potential to improve educational resources, allow for more equitable access, and disrupt a funding system in which textbook publishing monopolies have exerted disproportionate influence over curriculum materials for decades.

El Paso Independent School District (ISD) in Texas, currently listed among the #GoOpen Ambassador Districts, began its work with OER in 2013, at a time when it had just adopted new science curriculum materials. Purchases of textbooks for 18,000 students to address the curricular changes were projected to cost $2 million, pushing school system administrators to consider whether there might not be better ways to provide students with access to the needed content while expending scarce resources differently. The district began working with the CK-12 Foundation to develop OER science instructional materials covering the disciplines of chemistry, biology, and physics and aligned to the Texas state curriculum standards. Later, El Paso ISD teachers also curated materials from other sources, such as OpenStax, to develop open resources for more subjects, including math and social studies.[15] Digital textbooks (called Flexbooks), online study guides, simulations, and gamified exercises (called PLIXs—Play Learn Interact Explore) are among the materials available for use and modification on the CK-12 website.[16] Tim Holt, El Paso ISD's executive director of blended learning at the time, described a meaningful process shift when he noted, "Instead of us matching our curriculum to a pre-made textbook, we've done it the other way. We've made the textbook to match our curriculum."[17] Creating or selecting a textbook that aligns with the curriculum is the approach that best mirrors the instructional planning practice of starting with intended student learning objectives and then selecting materials and activities to facilitate that learning.

Culturally Responsive Teaching

The remixing right, which is one of the 5R permissions inherent in open educational resources, sets forth the promise that teachers can adapt instructional materials to best meet the needs of their specific students with all their unique characteristics. Researchers, particularly those affiliated with the Open University in the United Kingdom, have studied efforts to "localise" [sic] content in India and Sub-Saharan Africa in part to determine what supports are most likely to produce successful collaborative efforts and meaningful content adaptation or reinvention and how the practices of the educators' who worked on the "localisation" projects shifted to be more child-centered.[18]

In the United States, culturally responsive teaching includes similar efforts to localize instructional content. Dating back to the 1970s, educators, such as Geneva Gay, advocated for culturally responsive teaching practices in America's PreK-12 schools. These practices are closely connected to funds of knowledge and asset-based pedagogy in that the emphasis is placed on educators seeing culture and diversity as assets rather than deficits, which children bring to the classroom.[19] Many researchers use culturally relevant, responsive, and culturally sustaining teaching and pedagogy interchangeably; it is important to note the nuances between culturally relevant teaching and pedagogy. Teaching focuses on competence and practice, while pedagogy affects disposition and attitude.[20] For the purpose of this chapter, we use the term culturally responsive teaching (CRT) as defined by Gay:

Culturally responsive teaching is the behavioral expression of knowledge, beliefs, and values that recognize the importance of racial and cultural diversity in learning. It is contingent on seeing cultural differences as assets; creating caring learning communities where culturally different individuals and heritages are values; using cultural knowledge of technically diverse cultures, families, and communities to guide curriculum development, classroom climates, instructional strategies, and relationships with students; challenging racial and cultural stereotypes, prejudices, racism, and other forms of intolerance, injustice, and oppression; being change agents for social justice and academic equity; mediating power imbalances in classrooms based on race, culture, ethnicity, and class; and accepting cultural responsiveness as endemic to educational effectiveness in all areas of learning for students from all ethnic groups.[21]

CRT demands a shift in teachers' practices. No longer could it be enough for a school merely to celebrate particular heritage months during the academic year. Instead, CRT calls teachers to ensure that the vastly rich cultural experiences, identities, demographics, racial, and historical backgrounds of students in the classroom are reflected in the curriculum. Doing so means that all students have the opportunity to feel valued and engaged in unbiased, cultural instructional materials. Gay suggested that teachers evaluate textbooks as one way to become competent in implementing CRT.[22] OER presents teachers with opportunities to transform existing materials into curricular content that recognizes and uplifts students' own experiences. Traditional textbooks may not fit the unique cultural, demographic makeup of a classroom, so replacing them with more readily adaptable OER can help educators make materials more inclusive and accessible.

The state of Washington has adopted this change in thinking and created the Washington K-12 Open Educational Resource Project, which is housed within the Washington Office of Superintendent of Public Instruction (OSPI), "the primary agency charged with overseeing public K–12 education in Washington state."[23] Washington state's OER work began in 2012 and continues today. The state has curated an impressive collection of OER in its Washington OER Hub (an OER library) through collaborative efforts across PreK-12 districts, universities, and organizations statewide. Within the Washington OER Hub, there are resources to introduce teachers to OER and help them effectively search and adapt materials.[24] Also of note, the Washington OSPI provides financial grants to support K-12 OER content development.[25] One notable OER project features the American Indian and Native Alaskan population who made up approximately 1.9 percent of the population of Washington state in 2019.[26] The OSPI worked with various agencies and the federally recognized tribes of Washington to create the materials for the project, which carries the name "Since Time Immemorial: Tribal Sovereignty in Washington State." The "Since Time Immemorial" (STI) resources are predominantly open-licensed and serve as learning materials for students ranging from Pre-K through high school and allow teachers to meet the state requirements for teaching tribally developed curriculum. The STI curriculum website also includes implementation resources for teachers and information about how the curriculum must be integrated into teacher and administrator preparation programs in Washington state. One approach to the curriculum content is inquiry-based learning focused on essential questions where teachers and students are encouraged to consider the questions in relation to the tribes in their communities.[27]

Textbooks produced by commercial educational publishers cannot accurately represent every cultural background that may be part of a school or classroom community. Even attempts by large publishers to create state-specific editions of curriculum materials are likely to miss the mark of full inclusivity. Nor can such textbooks incorporate real-time news in the making as it occurs—the COVID-19 pandemic being an obvious example. OER can mitigate these shortfalls because teachers can contextualize content and align it with curricular goals to address students' interests and actual cultural backgrounds.[28] Teachers can take this practice of ensuring curricular materials represent their students a step further by directly incorporating students' voices and work. David Wiley, often considered the founder of OER, would likely recognize such a practice as moving toward non-disposable, "renewable assignments," assignments or activities that have value beyond their submission for a score or grade and which often reach a broader audience than just the teacher and a single class of students.[29] OER is an excellent solution to infuse CRT practices into the classroom. States like Washington have been, and remain, at the forefront of building OER awareness among educators, providing access to locally developed, culturally responsive resources, and offering training on effectively finding and using openly licensed materials.

OER as Way to Provide Pre-service Teachers with Access to Currently Adopted Instructional Materials

The concept of what constitutes an effective educator preparation program has been and still is the subject of research and debate. Search library databases and catalogs for resources on this topic and lists of thousands of articles and books are retrievable. Additionally, PreK-12 education professional organizations have developed numerous sets of teacher, administrator, and other specialist standards that influence instruction in higher education programs designed to prepare college students for these roles.[30] Additionally, individual states establish educator credentialing requirements, which also drive teacher preparation curricula. Less open to argument is the idea that the goal of educator preparation programs is to generate high-quality professionals ready to work with students to promote learning.

In March 2020, the global epidemic of COVID-19 forced an unprecedented number of PreK-12 school systems to shift their mode of instructional delivery to primarily online, at least for a period of two to three months. Recent data showed that across North America, PreK-12 schools were closed or partially closed to in-person learning for thirty-one to forty weeks between January 2020 and January 2021.[31] After the close of the 2019–2020 academic year, many school systems elected to offer their families the options of fully online or hybrid learning. While this rapid shift of operations affected a huge swath of the global population of PreK-12 students and communities, some districts and systems already had the infrastructure and technologically competent teachers to meet the challenges of the new educational environment. Even prior to COVID-19, numerous school systems worldwide had already been making use of online instructional materials and learning management systems; however, this was not necessarily the norm.

Access to quality resources plays an important role in teacher preparation. Pre-service teachers who are students in college/university educator preparation programs have their academic library materials available to them. They may also have access to a specialized curriculum library through their education department, depending on its size. Curriculum libraries often contain resources such as print copies of teacher and student editions of PreK-12 textbooks and workbooks, manipulative kits, classroom reading collections, educational models, puppets, etc.[32] When school systems adopt online instructional materials for use with their students, they typically purchase licenses through large educational publishers, such as Pearson or McGraw Hill. While portions of these resources may be available without a license, access is typically highly restricted. Frequently, curriculum libraries are unable to secure licensing for pre-service teachers who are unaffiliated with a specific PreK-12 school system. The result is that for at least part of their preparation programs, these teacher candidates will not have access to the instructional materials that are being used in the districts where they are likely to be working in the future.[33] Of course, pre-service teachers can use other materials for their lesson planning and curriculum-related course assignments, but having access to materials currently in use, and in the correct media format, would arguably be highly advantageous for their preparation.

The adoption of OER by a PreK-12 school system or state solves the problem of pre-service teachers' limited access to curriculum materials that are currently in use. The Affordable Learning Georgia initiative and the GALILEO Open Learning Materials site are well-known to those working with OER in higher education.[34] What may be less known is that in 2016, Georgia was one of fourteen states to make a #GoOpen commitment during the first state-focused round of the Department of Educational Technology/ISKME OER partnership targeting PreK-12 education.[35] The Georgia Virtual Resources/Georgia Virtual Learning (GaV) site was an outcome of the #GoOpen project.

According to the GaV site, "589+ Georgia and out of state schools used GaV in 2019–2020."[36] The GaV site organizes materials by subject and grade level. Within each grade level, standards-aligned shared resources are offered. One of the larger groupings is Middle School Language Arts, 6th Grade, which includes twenty-one instructional modules.[37] The first module in this section provides an example of how the content is organized. It is titled "Introduction and Novel: *The Watsons Go to Birmingham*." The module's opening screen includes a column on the right where relevant standards are linked. In this case, the links are to a Georgia-specific set of Novel Introduction Standards for 6th Grade English Language Arts and to a Technology Standards document from the International Society for Technology in Education (ISTE).[38] The modules are generally structured for independent learning, although some have discussion topics and other activities that encourage interaction and collaboration. Additional modules are provided across the secondary (grades 6–12) subject areas of math, science, fine arts, social studies, world languages, and career and technical education. The GaV site additionally offers professional development learning modules aimed at a teacher audience. There are no license barriers to pre-service teachers in Georgia (or elsewhere), preventing them from adopting and using these materials in their coursework, teaching demonstrations, and other preparation program activities.

OER and Digital Equity for Pre-service Teachers

The adoption of OER by PreK-12 school districts can benefit pre-service teachers doing their teacher preparation in those communities by giving them free access to the same instructional materials as employed teachers are using with their students. This access alone is one step toward equity; however, because OER are typically online instructional materials, there are issues around technology, which need to be considered. Terms, such as "digital divide," have frequently been used too simplistically to describe the differences between communities where students' families are likely to have internet and computer access at home versus those where computers and connectivity are less prevalent.[39] More recently, and particularly as the COVID-19 pandemic has gripped the world, educators and scholars have grown increasingly aware of the multifaceted challenges inherent in achieving greater digital equity and inclusion among schools, students, and families. Beyond access to computers and other technological devices, PreK-12 teachers' competencies in effectively integrating technology into their instructional practices have become part of the conversation around digital equity. In their book *Closing the Gap: Digital Equity for Teacher Prep Programs*, a publication of ISTE, authors Howard, Schaffer, and Thomas make a strong case that in education, digital equity includes "skilled, digitally literate teachers comfortable with incorporating technology into instruction"[40] Comfort level likely influences teachers' motivation and willingness to use technology in instruction, and while there may be correlations between teachers' self-reported comfort level and their frequency of technology usage in instructional situations, frequent technology use does not necessarily equate to the effective integration of technology.

Some scholars suggest that teachers' effective technology integration differs from successful technology use by other professionals, or even that successful technology integration by teachers has particular subject-specific dimensions. For example, art teachers' instructional technology use should not look exactly like that of science teachers. Approximately twenty-five years ago, Shulman made the argument that teachers' pedagogical content knowledge (PCK) would vary by discipline so that pedagogy and content must be considered together in teacher preparation.[41] Later, Mishra and Koehler extended this idea and introduced a technological component into the model, thereby converting the acronym and the framework to TPCK and, finally, to TPACK. It is helpful to see a visual representation of the TPACK framework (figure 5.1) to fully understand how the proposed teacher-required knowledge areas intersect.

Looking at the TPACK diagram, it becomes useful to think about where OER fit into the picture. As previously noted, OER are generally understood to be accessed online and then remixed and redistributed digitally.[42] Therefore, to access, and more importantly, to use OER successfully, teachers need to have some level of technological expertise. This technological expertise is represented most basically in the TPACK figure by the T circle, which demonstrates overlap with both the content (C) circle and the pedagogical (P) circle. One of the groundbreaking aspects of TPACK was the emphasis on the areas of intersection in the model. Rather than considering each of the knowledge types as functioning

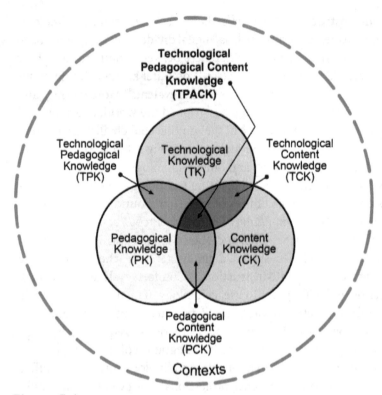

Figure 5.1
TPACK diagram reproduced with permission of the publisher, © 2012 by tpack.org.[43]

independently in instructional practice, all the intersection points are worthy of attention—so pedagogical content knowledge is different from what pedagogical knowledge and content knowledge represent in isolation. Mishra and Koehler describe the overlap of all three circles or the culminating level of the model—Technological Pedagogical Content Knowledge—as involving "a nuanced understanding of the complex relationships between technology, content, and pedagogy and using this understanding to develop appropriate, context-specific strategies and representations. Productive technology integration in teaching needs to consider all three issues not in isolation but rather within the complex relationships in the system defined by the three key elements."[44]

We, the authors of this chapter, propose that understanding of OER and OER-enabled practices be recognized as an additional subset of knowledge within the Technological Pedagogical Content Knowledge region. See the addition shown on the TPACK diagram in figure 5.2.

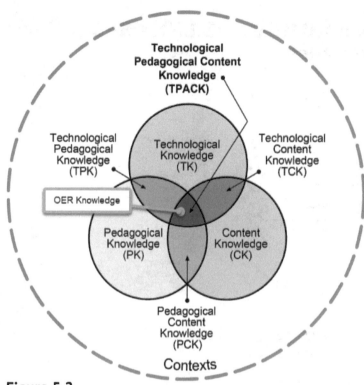

Figure 5.2
TPACK diagram reproduced with permission of the publisher, © 2012 by tpack.org[45] with addition by Grotewold, Kohler, and Krimbill, 2021.

In order to know what types of reuse and remixing are allowed regarding identified OER, educators should have a basic understanding of "traditional" copyright and alternative forms of content licensing. Creative Commons.org has developed the most common form of alternative licensing. Understanding the varying levels of permissions can be challenging and requires study and practice.

The chart in figure 5.3 explains the ways users can employ materials that display the Creative Commons (CC) licensing symbols and the corresponding expectations regarding crediting the creator, making changes, and re-sharing the works. The specific information in the chart is likely not widely known by the general public nor by pre-service and in-service teachers. Training opportunities to learn about existing CC-licensed materials and OER resource repositories could broaden teachers' awareness of these tools and their possibilities. Still, repeated exposures and consistent use are likely needed for teachers to truly incorporate them into their regular practices.

Creative Commons Licenses
Quick Reference

	COPY & PUBLISH	ATTRIBUTION REQUIRED	COMMERCIAL USE	MODIFY & ADAPT	CHANGE LICENSE
Public Domain	✓		✓	✓	✓
Attribution (CC BY)	✓	✓	✓	✓	✓
Attribution-ShareAlike (CC BY-SA)	✓	✓	✓	✓	
Attribution-NoDerivs (CC BY-ND)	✓	✓	✓		✓
Attribution-NonCommercial (CC BY-NC)	✓	✓		✓	✓
Attribution-NonCommercial-ShareAlike (CC BY-NC-SA)	✓	✓		✓	
Attribution-NonCommercial-NoDerivs (CC BY-NC-ND)	✓	✓			✓

Figure 5.3
Creative Commons Licenses Quick Reference Chart image by SUNY OER Services is licensed as CC BY.[46]

The Open High School of Utah, founded in 2007 by David Wiley, was an early attempt to engage teachers and students in the regular adoption, modification, and creation of new OER for use as the sole instructional materials for courses. Wiley and colleagues Tonks, Weston, and Barbour described the history of online learning in K-12 education, which led to the launch of Open High School and analyzed Open High's first four years of operation with students from 2009–2013. The high school differed from other online schools at the time because it stated in its original operating policies that it would rely entirely on OER for its instructional materials rather than purchasing commercial publisher materials. Its charter also indicated that it would make its courses freely available online. In their analysis, the authors noted advantages of OER curricula, such as quick adaptability for meeting students' learning needs—specifically special education students' requirements for content in multiple formats and potential cost savings associated with the whole school functioning openly. Conversely, they also saw logistical challenges. One of the final statements in the article articulated the potential issues surrounding teachers' technological competencies and knowledge of licensing:

> We hope every teacher possesses the skills necessary to successfully use curriculum materials and educational media in support of student learning. However, successfully using OER requires teachers

to possess additional information literacies that will enable them to find and evaluate the quality of OER and additional technical skills that will enable them to take full advantage of the "4R" permissions granted by open educational resources.[47]

Other researchers, and particularly Kimmons, who is currently a colleague of Wiley's, have explored teachers' use of technology as it applies to open educational practices and specifically OER-enabled practices.[48] Kimmons carried out a study while at the University of Idaho on how best to develop teachers' "open education literacies." At the time, he found "Open education is a new concept to most K-12 teachers and administrators, and knowledge and skills necessary for effectively utilizing and creating open educational resources are not standard topics of teacher education courses or professional development trainings."[49] To address this gap, Kimmons and colleagues planned and carried out three-day-long Technology and Open Education Summer Institutes. Pre- and post-survey data gathered and analyzed from eighty K-12 teachers revealed that participants tended to over-estimate their prior knowledge of concepts like copyright, fair use, and open licensing. Then, it was through professional development that they learned what these terms actually mean. Kimmons explained why this finding suggests a possible obstacle in the way of connecting teachers with additional learning covering OER-related practices and therefore may be damaging to momentum in the PreK-12 OER movement: "If teachers already believe that they understand copyright and fair use, for instance, then they have no impetus to learn about these concepts and may consider themselves to be open educators when in fact they have very little understanding of what this entails and what it means to share in open ways utilizing copyleft or Creative Commons licensing."[50]

Kimmons' subsequent work individually and with colleagues tended to be more encouraging regarding teachers' establishment of a knowledge framework that would allow them to realize the pedagogical benefits associated with OER use. Mason and Kimmons conducted a mixed-methods study, which included surveys and interviews of 7th–12th-grade teachers using open science textbooks. They found that most study participants rated the open textbook as better than the publisher-supplied textbook they had previously used. They also reported positive changes in their instructional practices resulting from their switch to an online OER, such as increased collaboration with other teachers. Finally, although the instructors recognized the value of remixing the OER content, some reported reluctance to make "in-the-moment" changes due to lack of time or an instance where a technical issue caused changes not to show up.[51] This again suggests a need for teachers to be technologically savvy or for there to be support systems in place to help them navigate potential issues.

Pre-Service Teachers and Administrators at Our Institution

The authors of this chapter are Kimberly Grotewold, an academic librarian and subject research specialist for education (a.k.a. the Education Librarian); Dr. Karen Kohler, an assistant professor of curriculum and instruction; and Dr. Elisabeth Krimbill, an assistant professor of educational leadership, who all work at the same young, urban, regional university. This university is recognized as a minority-serving institution (MSI) and, more specifically, an Hispanic-serving institution (HSI), with 72 percent of the student body identifying as Hispanic/Latino and 77 percent as first-generation college students.[52] The institution has strong ties to the community in which it is geographically located, and the university president regularly affirms a commitment to elevate and provide increased educational and economic opportunities for this community. The student body demographics at the university, and more specifically within the College of Education and Human Development, largely reflect those of the surrounding local community and rapidly expanding metropolitan areas beyond it.[53] We, the authors, feel that it is essential to situate our OER-related efforts within this context.

During the past two years at our institution, we have engaged in a dual-faceted approach to building awareness of OER and its promises for PreK-12 education. One of the facets has involved introducing pre-service teachers to Creative Commons licensing, public domain resources, fair use concepts, and OER during a legal and ethical issues in education course taken by all undergraduate education majors. The other spur of our efforts has employed OER and other freely available materials to replace commercially published textbooks in a graduate-level educational leadership course.

OER Instruction and Research Collaboration: Kimberly Grotewold, Education Librarian with Dr. Karen Kohler and Undergraduate Education Students

New to the position of education librarian at the university in summer 2018 and coming from a vastly different institution, I was initially cautious in my library instruction undertakings, generally keeping session topics and explorations similar to what I thought had been done in the past. One of these was the "copyright for teachers" lesson. After presenting the lesson a number of times, mainly using lecture format in a face-to-face classroom setting, I yearned to move away from an emphasis on avoiding copyright infringement and toward a more positively framed approach that would present alternatives to "traditional" copyright, such as the open licensing options developed by Creative Commons.org. I was also thinking about experimenting with creating an online tutorial to teach the content. Around this time, I met Dr. Karen Kohler, assistant professor of curriculum and instruction, who was also relatively new to the university and is another author of this chapter. Together, we embarked on a partnership that incorporated both changes—the development of an interactive, online instructional tutorial and a shift in the material covered to include Creative Commons licensing and OER. Our collaboration also led to a successful grant proposal in spring 2019 and, with additional teammates, the construction of an OER module for pre-service and in-service teacher professional development. The grant was funded by an organization that aims to increase diversity in the teaching profession through support of teacher preparation programs at MSIs across the country.[54] The grant-sponsored training prompted us to consider how to address assessment of OER in relation to equity in both our module and in our instructional unit and inspired our inclusion of content on visual literacy.

In another extension of this OER work, we drafted a plan for a research study to (1) determine our educator preparation program students' awareness of, and specific knowledge concerning, Creative Commons licensing, public domain, fair use, and OER before and after they experience the new instructional tutorial and corresponding in-class activities, and (2) evaluate the effectiveness of the tutorial plus synchronous instruction session approach in teaching this content. By the time this chapter is published, we will have completed a pilot round, and a slightly modified, expanded round of our study. Both rounds of the study consisted of five major parts: (1) a pre-instruction survey, (2) an online tutorial,[55] (3) an in-class review and group activity, (4) a post-survey, and (5) written student reflections. The total number of students who engaged in at least one aspect of either round of the study was more than one hundred.

From the first pilot study, Dr. Kohler and I noted that the participating education students did not have a strong understanding of the relationships between copyright, fair use, Creative Commons, and OER, both before and after completing the tutorial. We adjusted our in-class instructional approach and increased the time between pre-survey and post-survey implementation for the next semester, and we hoped to collect improved and more robust data from a second iteration of the study. Unfortunately, due to a weakness in the pre- and post-survey data collection, we could not accurately analyze our data for change.

An additional challenge was that we received approximately half the number of completed post-surveys as pre-surveys, so there was a marked drop-off in participation at the end of the study.

Based on our interactions with students during the synchronous class instruction sessions and reading through students' end-of-unit reflections, Dr. Kohler and I made informal observations on students' reactions and sentiments about the unit. First, one student commented that the content related to copyright, public domain, fair use, Creative Commons, and OER was very "dense." Students taking the legal and ethical issues course in which we situated the unit generally come from various specialties across our institution's educator preparation programs, and few students seemed to have prior knowledge of the content related to Creative Commons licensing and other content sharing options presented in the unit. Second, while the majority of the online tutorial was on alternatives to traditional copyright, such as CC licensing, and how to appropriately attribute images and other content, students' reflections emphasized concern about legal ramifications for violating copyright and school districts possibly owning work they have created. Third, education students' apparent distress at potentially not having ownership of lessons or activities they develop shows some movement toward recognition of themselves as content creators, but so far we have seen students express limited enthusiasm for the benefits of remixing openly licensed materials and the value of sharing their work using the permissions afforded by CC-licensing. We recommend further study of this issue in the future. We are not aware of these topics being covered in many, if any, of students' other educator preparation courses. We are left wondering if more sustained exposure to the topics of copyright, public domain, fair use, Creative Commons, and OER throughout educator preparation curricula could be influential in shifting future teachers' perceptions and attitudes.

Dr. Elisabeth Krimbill's Experience Implementing OER with Pre-service Administrators

The other author of this chapter is Dr. Elisabeth Krimbill, assistant professor of educational leadership, who has grown in awareness of OER and has revamped her courses to realize the benefits of OER and OER-enabled practices. Here is her story:

I was introduced to open educational resources (OER) during a college faculty meeting. As a previous K-12 administrator, I was unaware of the depth and breadth of the variety of openly licensed educational resources available to me in my new role as a college professor. I was impressed by the content, quality, and availability of the OER textbooks relevant to the courses I teach. One, in particular, *Social Science Research: Principles, Methods, and Practices*,[56] seemed to be a perfect fit for my course. Although it was framed broadly to cover various types of social science research, it covered all of the key content specific to educational leadership and was available to my students free of charge. The standard textbooks often used for this course ranged between $85 and $150, and this book was free! My students were so excited to have access to this content, particularly in light of the financial burdens they were already encountering in the degree program.

The OER allowed me to provide the text, plus professor-created outlines, key content presentations, and assignments that I created to assist in student mastery of the material, in a cost-effective manner. This OER encouraged users to add material, thereby expanding the resources available to my students and others who might find and adopt the text. This collaborative approach has the potential to impact social justice initiatives by providing students in under-funded, under-represented communities with the resources they need to access greater educational opportunities.

For one of the assignments I created to align with the text, the students created their own OER resource file of educational research data sets and analysis worksheets. The students had a unique opportunity to publish their own work in an OER learning environment, which allowed them to share their own voices and research interests in the field of education. Under-represented populations may not be included in the development of traditional textbooks, but in an OER environment, they can explore and add to the body of knowledge in a manner previously unavailable to students and most professors.

OER can be very useful for professors and teachers at every level. Table 5.1 is an example of how I implemented the 5R OER permissions[57] and engaged in OER-enabled practices with my pre-service school administrators.

Step	Description	Activity
Step 1	Retain: The right to make, own, and control copies of the content.	Professor searched for appropriate OER materials. • OER Commons • OASIS • Merlot • Vimeo • Open Textbook Library Professor reviewed carefully and to ensure alignment with course standards and objectives.
Step 2	Reuse: The right to use the content in a wide range of ways.	Professor created supporting resources to support student access and generated a greater variety of modalities to support student learning. • Outlines of each chapter • Narrated PowerPoint presentations to review the content in audiovisual format
Step 3	Revise: The right to adapt, adjust, modify, or alter the content itself.	Professor added material for other users. • Terminology matching cards • Action Research Procedure Guide
Step 4	Remix: The right to combine the original or revised content with other material to create something new.	Professor developed three online tests (multiple-choice and T/F) to assess student mastery of the content. • Students collaboratively created note-taking tools and worksheets. • Students were allowed to use their notes on the tests.
Step 5	Redistribute: The right to share copies of the original content, your revisions, or your remixes with others.	Professor set up structure for students to add content to OER. • Students created their own data sets and statistical analysis worksheets and uploaded them to a resource file for classmates to complete.

Table 5.1

An example of OER-enabled practices.

Next Steps: OER in Pre-service Teacher Programs in the United States

In the process of researching for this chapter and the other OER work happening within our own college of education, we have noticed a few patterns. OER awareness, adoption, modification, and use in PreK-12 education seems to be higher and generally of greater interest to countries outside the United States, particularly in countries where access to education is not as ubiquitous.[58] The International Association for K-12 Online Learning (iNACOL) released a report in 2013 touting the potential for OER to address a need in the United States for collaboratively reimagined curricular materials to align with the establishment of Common Core State Standards while also noting possible obstacles.[59] Four years later, a Babson Survey Research Group report from 2017, which analyzed data on curriculum materials adoption processes from representative K-12 school systems in the United States, found that only 16 percent of districts had adopted "open licensed full-course" curricular materials.[60] Blomgren's and MacPherson's conclusion in 2018, based on their systematic review of the previously published research literature, was that OER in K-12 education in the United States in Canada was in the "nascent" phase corroborates this finding.[61]

Another recent, intriguing study included the United States, among many other nations, both Western- and non-Western, and situated OER adoption and use for particular purposes in the context of cultural characteristics. Tang and Bao (2020) examined survey results from 675 K-12 teachers representing seventy-two countries to try to better understand which societal and cultural factors might affect successful OER adaptation and use. Of particular note was the researchers' application of Hofstede's six cross-cultural dimensions to explain societal differences among countries. Through regression analyses of the survey data, interesting positive correlations emerged: Teachers from countries where individualism is prioritized over collectivism were more likely to face both issues with access to OER and problems with adaptation, perhaps due in part to a lack of coordinated and supportive policies. Second, using Hofstede's masculinity versus femininity dimension, their analysis found a positive relationship among high masculinity countries and difficulty with successful OER integration. They speculated that the focus of masculine-oriented countries on competition and assessment, often tied to state or national standards, may pose obstacles for OER adoption.[62] Because Hofstede's dimensions can be judged as subjective, it is difficult to claim definitive conclusions based on the Tang and Bao study, but it does present a different lens through which to view the evaluation of OER utilization in K-12 education, and it encompasses data from around the world, which should not be ignored.

A second pattern in the research to emerge is that most attention in the United States has been paid to developing practicing teachers' OER knowledge. Kimmons, Wiley, Hilton, and others who are well-known names in the North American OER landscape have tended to center their efforts on employed teachers in K-12 classrooms.[63] Research involving college and university students who are studying to become teachers and school administrators is less abundant. Two years ago, we, as authors of this chapter, surmised a lack of OER awareness among our local educator preparation program faculty members and students, which catalyzed our interest in both building awareness at our institution and adding to the body of literature. At the beginning of our efforts, we became aware of an academic librarian-educator preparation faculty duo, Katz (librarian) and Van Allen (education faculty member) doing inspiring work through CUNY in New York. Their work has so far yielded a decision-making framework for the process of replacing commercial curriculum materials with OER in educator preparation courses and some strong qualitative reflections from students on their engagement with the OER materials.[64] Other work of interest to us is a 2018 literature review by Kim, which describes possibilities for integrating OER into teacher education programs using distributed cognition and example-based learning modalities.[65] Van Allen and Katz's efforts in New York, a state like Texas in that it was never was listed as a #GoOpen state, may offer us helpful insight into how to develop and support pre-service teachers in OER use and creation without the direct scaffolding of the #GoOpen model.

Although the endeavor is not without challenges, we hope that introducing pre-service teachers and administrators to OER and OER-enabled practices builds foundations for greater digital equity and amplifies teachers' and students' lesser-heard voices. Acquainting students in educator preparation programs with OER and its potential for customization and working with them to acquire content licensing knowledge and the requisite technological proficiency will allow these students to step into the profession of teacher or school administrator with a specialized toolkit. The tools in this kit can help them reframe school budget conversations to evaluate priorities more effectively when it comes to adopting and/or purchasing curricular materials, ensuring that the value is at least commensurate with the cost. These new professionals may advocate for increased sharing of resources and expertise to most effectively meet the needs of their schools and communities. Ultimately, as OER-enabled teachers and school leaders, they may pass this understanding on to their students, who can carry on an open knowledge and innovation cycle, paying the benefits forward to the next generation of learners.

Authors' Statement

The authors acknowledge that we are writing from the perspective of privilege. We hope that others, particularly those whose voices have been marginalized, are able to authentically build on or reimagine our work in a way that is most empowering for them and their communities.

Endnotes

1. Paulina Firozi, "378 People 'Pay It Forward' at Starbucks," *USA Today* (August 21, 2014), https://www.usatoday.com/story/news/nation-now/2014/08/21/378-people-pay-it-forward-at-fla-starbucks/14380109/; Jon Delano, "Dozens Participate In Spontaneous Pay-It-Forward At Starbucks Drive-Thru," KDKA CBS Pittsburgh, April 18, 2017, https://pittsburgh.cbslocal.com/2017/04/18/bethel-park-starbucks-pay-it-forward/.
2. "Pay It Forward Foundation: About Us Page," Pay it Forward Foundation, Pay It Forward Foundation, last updated date 2017, https://www.payitforwardfoundation.org/about. Based on the most current dates on the website, it appears that the foundation ceased operations in 2017.
3. "Open Educational Resources (OER)," United Nations Educational, Scientific, and Cultural Organization (UNESCO), 2019, https://en.unesco.org/themes/building-knowledge-societies/oer.
4. Chris Zook, "Infographic: Textbook Costs Skyrocket 812% in 35 Years," Applied Educational Systems, September 7, 2017, https://www.aeseducation.com/blog/infographic-the-skyrocketing-cost-of-textbooks-for-schools-students; "College Tuition and Fees Increase 63% since January 2006," United States Bureau of Labor Statistics, August 30, 2016, https://www.bls.gov/opub/ted/2016/college-tuition-and-fees-increase-63-percent-since-January-2006.htm. Online news articles describing the escalating course materials costs for students include Ben Popken, "College Textbook Prices Have Risen 1,041 Percent Since 1977," NBC News, August 6, 2015, https://www.nbcnews.com/feature/freshman-year/college-textbook-prices-have-risen-812-percent-1978-n399926; Herb Weisbaum, "Students are Still Saddled with Soaring Textbook Costs, Report Says," NBC Business News, last modified February 10, 2016, https://www.nbcnews.com/business/business-news/students-are-still-saddled-soaring-textbook-costs-report-says-n516011; Jennifer Ma, Matea Pender, and C. J. Libassi, "Trends in College Pricing and Student Aid 2020," College Board, 2020, https://research.collegeboard.org/pdf/trends-college-pricing-student-aid-2020.pdf.
5. Zook, "Infographic: Textbook Costs Skyrocket."
6. LeiLani Cauthen, "Perspective: How Big is the K-12 Digital Curriculum Market?," The Learning Counsel, accessed March 1, 2021, https://thelearningcounsel.com/article/how-big-k-12-digital-curriculum-market.
7. "Districts that have over 25% of their population aged 5 to 17 living in poverty cite cost as critical to the decision process twice as often as districts where less than 10% of the population aged 5 to 17 live in poverty," I. Elaine Allen and Jeff Seaman in "What We Teach: K-12 School District Curriculum Adoption Process," Babson Survey Research Group, September 2017, 13, https://www.onlinelearningsurvey.com/reports/k12oer2017/whatweteach_2017.pdf.
8. "U.S. Department of Education Recognizes 14 States and 40 Districts Committing to #GoOpen with Educational Resources," United States Department of Education, February 26, 2016, https://www.ed.gov/news/press-releases/us-department-education-recognizes-13-states-and-40-districts-committing-goopen-educational-resources; "Welcome to #GoOpen," United States Department of Education, Office of Educational Technology, ca 2016, https://tech.ed.gov/open/districts/launch/welcome/.

9. "#GoOpen States," United States Department of Education, Office of Educational Technology, accessed March 1, 2021, https://tech.ed.gov/open/states/.
10. Richard Culatta and United States Department of Education, Office of Educational Technology, "Dear Colleague Letter: Federal Funding for Technology," November 19, 2014, 1, https://files.eric.ed.gov/fulltext/ED584158.pdf.
11. Culatta, "Dear Colleague Letter," 2.
12. "U.S. Department of Education Recognizes," United States Department of Education; "#GoOpen States," United States Department of Education.
13. The resource that names the sixteen original #GoOpen Districts, both Launch Districts and Ambassador Districts, is United States Department of Education, "U.S. Department of Education Launches Campaign to Encourage Schools to #GoOpen with Educational Resources," October 29, 2015, https://www.ed.gov/news/press-releases/us-department-education-launches-campaign-encourage-schools-goopen-educational-resources. The most current listing of #GoOpen Districts can be found in United States Department of Education, Office of Educational Technology, "#GoOpen Districts," accessed March 1, 2021, https://tech.ed.gov/open/districts/.
14. "Open Licensing Requirement for Competitive Grant Programs," United States Education Department, January 19, 2017, 7376, https://www.federalregister.gov/documents/2017/01/19/2017-00910/open-licensing-requirement-for-competitive-grant-programs.
15. Tim Holt, "Why and How El Paso ISD Went Open," TechNotes, Texas Computer Education Association, December 22, 2017, https://blog.tcea.org/el-paso-isd-went-open/.
16. "CK-12 Teacher Site," CK-12 Foundation, accessed March 1, 2021, https://www.ck12.org/teacher/.
17. Holt as quoted in Jennifer Bergland, "It's Time: #Go Open," TechNotes, Texas Computer Education Association, October 23, 2016, under "Districts Leading the Way," https://blog.tcea.org/goopen/.
18. Leigh-Anne Perryman, Alison Hemings-Butler, and Tim Seal, "Learning from TESS-India's Approach to OER Localisation Across Multiple Indian States," *Journal of Interactive Media in Education* 2, no. 7 (2014): 1–11, http://doi.org/10.5334/jime.af; Freda Wolfenden and Lina Adinolfi, "An Exploration of Agency in the Localisation of Open Educational Resources for Teacher Development," *Learning, Media and Technology* 44, no. 3 (2019): 327–44, https://doi.org/10.1080/17439884.2019.1628046.
19. Geneva Gay, *Culturally Responsive Teaching: Theory, Research, and Practice*, 2nd ed., (New York: Teachers College Press, 2010).
20. Brittany Aronson and Judson Laughter, "The Theory and Practice of Culturally Relevant Education: A Synthesis of Research Across Content Areas," *Review of Educational Research* 86, no. 1 (March 2016): 167, https://doi.org/10.3102/0034654315582066.
21. Gay, *Culturally Responsive Teaching*, 31.
22. Geneva Gay, "Teaching to and Through Cultural Diversity," *Curriculum Inquiry*, 43 (2013): 48–70, https://doi.org/10.1111/curi.12002.
23. "About OSPI," Washington Office of Superintendent of Public Instruction (OSPI), February 2021, https://www.k12.wa.us/about-ospi.
24. "Washington OER Hub," Washington OSPI & ISKME, OER Commons, accessed February 26, 2021, https://www.oercommons.org/hubs/washington.
25. Barbara Soots, contact staff for "Washington OSPI, Open Educational Resources," accessed February 26, 2021, https://www.k12.wa.us/student-success/learning-standards-instructional-materials/open-educational-resources. See specific announcement of recent grant awardees at Washington Open Educational Resources Project 2020-2021 OER Project Grant Awards at https://www.k12.wa.us/sites/default/files/public/oer/pubdocs/2020%20OER%20Project%20Grant%20Awards.pdf.
26. "Quick Facts: Washington," United States Census Bureau, 2019 data, accessed March 1, 2021, https://www.census.gov/quickfacts/fact/table/WA/RHI625219#RHI625219.

27. See the website for complete information. "Since Time Immemorial: Tribal Sovereignty in Washington State," Washington OSPI, 2020/2021, https://www.k12.wa.us/student-success/resources-subject-area/time-immemorial-tribal-sovereignty-washington-state.
28. Constance Blomgren, "OER Awareness and Use: The Affinity Between Higher Education and K-12," *International Review of Research in Open & Distributed Learning* 19, no. 2 (April 2018): 60–62, http://www.irrodl.org/index.php/irrodl/article/view/3431/4614.
29. David Wiley, "What is Open Pedagogy?," *Improving Learning* (blog), October 13, 2013, https://opencontent.org/blog/archives/2975; David Wiley and John Hilton, "Defining OER-enabled Pedagogy, *International Review of Research in Open & Distributed Learning* 19, no. 4 (September 2018): 133–47, http://www.irrodl.org/index.php/irrodl/article/view/3601.
30. National Council of Teachers of English, National Council of Teachers of Mathematics, American Association of School Librarians, American Association of School Administrators, International Society of Technology in Education, etc.
31. "UNESCO Figures Show Two Thirds of an Academic Year Lost on Average Worldwide Due to Covid-19 School Closures," United Nations Educational, Scientific, and Cultural Organization (UNESCO), January 25, 2021, https://en.unesco.org/news/unesco-figures-show-two-thirds-academic-year-lost-average-worldwide-due-covid-19-school.
32. This statement is based on the author's experience as an education subject specialist librarian and other librarian and instructor positions she has held.
33. This observation is based primarily on the author's experience as an education subject specialist librarian and her communication with others employed in this role.
34. Readers can visit the Affordable Learning Georgia website at https://www.affordablelearninggeorgia.org/. The GALILEO Open Learning Materials website is a Digital Commons site affiliated with the University System of Georgia and accessible at https://oer.galileo.usg.edu/.
35. "U.S. Department of Education Recognizes," US Department of Education.
36. "Georgia Virtual Learning," Georgia Department of Education, 2021, http://www.gavirtuallearning.org/.
37. "OER MS LA 6th Grade," Georgia Department of Education, Georgia Virtual Learning, Shared Content, http://www.gavirtuallearning.org/Resources/SharedMSLA6(MSCopy).aspx.
38. The sample module described is: Georgia Virtual Learning, Shared Content, "OER, MS LA 6th Grade, Introduction and Novel: *The Watsons Go to Birmingham*–1963, http://cms.gavirtualschool.org/Shared/Language%20Arts/6thGradeLA/IntroductionAndNovel/index.html; the Novel Introduction Standards for 6th Grade Language Arts in Georgia which are addressed in the module are viewable at http://cms.gavirtualschool.org/Shared/Language%20Arts/6thGradeLA/IntroductionAndNovel/Module1_NovelIntroduction_Standards.pdf. The module also includes a link to the International Society for Technology in Education (ISTE), "ISTE NETS-S," ca 2007, http://cms.gavirtualschool.org/Support/NETSSStandards/netssstandardsCurrent.pdf. NETS-S stands for the National Educational Technology Standards for Students, which have been renamed as the "ISTE Standards for Students" and are available at https://www.iste.org/standards/for-student in their current version.
39. Anique Scheerder, Alexander van Deursen, and Jan van Dijk, "Determinants of Internet Skills, Uses and Outcomes: A Systematic Review of the Second- and Third-level Digital Divide," *Telematics & Informatics* 34, no. 8 (2017): 1607–24, https://doi.org/10.1016/j.tele.2017.07.007. This article defines digital equity in reference specifically to Internet skills, seemingly because they found Internet access and used to be dominant in the literature. However, in its definition of the digital divide, it includes other technology skills which could, but do not necessarily involve an internet connection, such as creating spreadsheets.
40. Nicol R. Howard, Regina Schaffer, and Sarah Thomas, *Closing the Gap: Digital Equity Strategies for Teacher Prep Programs* (La Verne: ISTE, 2018), ix.
41. Lee S. Shulman, "Those Who Understand: Knowledge Growth in Teaching," *Pedagogical Content Knowledge*, a special issue of *The Journal of Education* 193, no. 3 (2013): 1–11, https://www.jstor.org/stable/24636916. This is a reprint of the article with permission from *Educational Researcher* 15, no. 2: 4–14.

42. "Open Educational Resources Initiative, 2006," William & Flora Hewlett Foundation, https://hewlett.org/wp-content/uploads/2016/08/HewlettFoundationOER.pdf, 2. This statement in the chapter refers to Hewlett Foundation's grant work since 2002 in which OER are described as "high-quality digitized educational materials offered freely and openly for anyone with access to the Internet."
43. Punya Mishra and Matthew J. Koehler, "Technological Pedagogical Content Knowledge: A Framework for Teacher Knowledge, *Teachers College Record* 108, no. 6 (June 2006): 1017–54, https://www.punyamishra.com/wp-content/uploads/2008/01/mishra-koehler-tcr2006.pdf; Matthew J. Koehler, "TPACK explained," TPACK.org, September 24, 2012, http://matt-koehler.com/tpack2/tpack-explained/. The downloadable version of the TPACK diagram is available on this 2012 website.
44. Mishra and Koehler, "Technological Pedagogical Content Knowledge," 1029.
45. Matthew J. Koehler, "TPACK explained."
46. "Creative Commons Licenses Quick Reference," SUNY OER Services, February 2, 2019, https://knilt.arcc.albany.edu/File:Oer.jpg.
47. DeLaina Tonks, Sarah Weston, David Wiley, and Michael K. Barbour, "'Opening' a New Kind of High School: The Story of the Open High School of Utah," *International Review of Research in Open and Distance Learning* 14, no. 1 (2013): 267–68. The entire article runs from 255–71. Note that Wiley's original definition of OER from 2007 included 4Rs. See David Wiley, "Open Education License Draft," August 8, 2007, https://opencontent.org/blog/archives/355. Then he added the fifth R in 2014 as indicated in David Wiley, "The Access Compromise and the 5th R," Improving Learning, March 5, 2014, https://opencontent.org/blog/archives/3221.
48. Royce Kimmons is now an assistant professor of instructional psychology and technology at Brigham Young University. See https://roycekimmons.com/. Formerly, he was a faculty member at the University of Idaho and was at Idaho when he carried out the 2014 study. See note 49. In addition to other roles he holds, David Wiley is presently an adjunct instructor in instructional psychology and technology at Brigham Young University. See https://davidwiley.org.
49. Royce Kimmons, "Developing Open Education Literacies with Practicing K-12 Teachers," *International Review of Research in Open and Distance Learning* 15, no. 6 (2014): 73, http://www.irrodl.org/index.php/irrodl/article/view/196.
50. Kimmons, "Developing Open Education Literacies," 85.
51. Stacie L. Mason and Royce Kimmons, "Effects of Open Textbook Adoption on Teachers' Practices, *International Review of Research in Open and Distributed Learning* 19, no. 3 (2018): 128–50, http://www.irrodl.org/index.php/irrodl/article/view/3517/4650.
52. "About Texas A&M University-San Antonio," Texas A&M University-San Antonio, ca 2019, https://www.tamusa.edu/about/index.html.
53. "Quick Facts San Antonio," Raise Your Hand Texas data report (confidential), United States Census Bureau, 2019 data, https://www.census.gov/quickfacts/fact/table/sanantoniocitytexas,US/PST045219; US Census data projections for 2019 indicate that more than 64% of San Antonians identify as Hispanic.
54. "Branch Alliance for Educator Diversity: Redefining Quality Educator Preparation," Branch Alliance for Educator Diversity (BranchED), ca 2021, https://www.educatordiversity.org/.
55. Kimberly S. Grotewold, "Teachers as Content Creators: Copyright, Fair Use, Creative Commons, OER, & Visual Literacy," Teachers as Content Creators Tutorial, https://tamusa.libwizard.com/f/creative_commons_oer_for_teachers.
56. Anol Bhattacherjee, *Social Science Research: Principles, Methods, and Practices*, 2nd ed. (Tampa: Textbook Collection, University of South Florida, 2012), https://scholarcommons.usf.edu/cgi/viewcontent.cgi?article=1002&context=oa_textbooks.
57. David Wiley, "Defining the 'Open' in Open Content and Open Educational Resources," Open Content, accessed February 26, 2021, https://opencontent.org/definition/.
58. Examples of non-U.S.-focused studies on OER involving both pre-service and in-service teachers include Pradeep K. Misra, "Training Teachers to Use and Produce Open Educational Resources: A Win-Win Approach," *Journal of Educational Technology* 9, no. 2 (January 2012):

1–7, https://eric.ed.gov/?id=EJ1102031 (India); Patricia Murphy and Freda Wolfenden, "Developing a Pedagogy of Mutuality in a Capability Approach: Teachers' Experiences of Using the Open Educational Resources (OER) of the Teacher Education in Sub-Saharan Africa (TESSA) Programme," *International Journal of Educational Development* 3, no. 3 (May 2013): 263–71, http://dx.doi.org/10.1016/j.ijedudev.2012.09.010 (Africa); Maria-Soledad Ramirez-Montoya, Juanjo Mena, and Jose Antonio Rodriguez, "In-Service Teachers' Self-Perceptions of Digital Competence and OER Use as Determined by a XMOOC Training Course," *Computers in Human Behavior* 77 (December 2017): 356–64, https://doi.org/10.1016/j.chb.2017.09.010 (Mexico and Spain); SuBeom Kwak, "How Korean Language Arts Teachers Adopt and Adapt Open Educational Resources: A Study of Teachers' and Students' Perspectives," *International Review of Research in Open and Distributed Learning* 18, no. 4 (June 2017): 193–211, http://www.irrodl.org/index.php/irrodl/article/view/2977 (South Korea); Cheryl Hodgkins-Williamson and Patricia B. Arinto, eds., *Adoption and Impact of OER in the Global South*, African Minds, International Development Research Centre, and Research on Open Educational Resources for Development, December 2017, https://www.idrc.ca/en/book/adoption-and-impact-oer-global-south (generally, countries outside North America and Europe); Freda Wolfenden and Lina Adinolfi, "An Exploration of Agency in the Localisation of Open Educational Resources for Teacher Development," *Learning, Media, and Technology* 44, no. 3 (July 2019): 327–44, https://doi.org/10.1080/17439884.2019.1628046 (India); Tak-Lam Wong, Haoran Xie, Di Zou, Fu Lee Wang, Jeff Kai Tai Tang, Anthony Kong, and Reggie Kwan, "How to Facilitate Self-regulated Learning? A Case Study on Open Educational Resources," *Journal of Computers in Education* 7 (2019 online/2020): 51–77, https://doi.org/10.1007/s40692-019-00138-4 (Hong Kong); and Gemma Tur, Leo Havemann, Dawn J. Marsh, Jeffrey M. Keefer, and Fabio Nascimbeni, "Becoming an Open Educator: Towards an Open Threshold Framework," *Research in Learning Technology* 28 (March 2020), https://journal.alt.ac.uk/index.php/rlt/article/view/2338 (mainly New Zealand).

59. TJ Bliss and Susan Patrick, "OER State Policy in K-12 Education: Benefits, Strategies, and Recommendations for Open Access, Open Sharing," International Association for K-12 Online Learning (iNACOL), June 2013, https://aurora-institute.org/wp-content/uploads/oer-state-policy.pdf.

60. I. Elaine Allen and Jeff Seaman, "K-12 School District Curriculum Adoption Process, 2017," September 2017, 13, https://www.onlinelearningsurvey.com/reports/k12oer2017/whatweteach_2017.pdf (see note 7).

61. Constance Blomgren and Iain MacPherson, "Scoping the Nascent: An Analysis of K-12 OER Research 2012–2017, *Open Praxis* 10, no. 4 (October–December 2018): 359–75, https://openpraxis.org/articles/10.5944/openpraxis.10.4.905/.

62. Hengtao Tang and Yu Bao, "Social Justice and K-12 Teachers' Effective Use of OER: A Cross-Cultural Comparison by Nations," *Journal of Interactive Media in Education* 2020, no. 9 (May 2020): 1–13, https://doi.org/10.5334/jime.576. All six of Hofstede's cultural dimensions are named and defined on page 4 of the article by Tang and Bao. They also reference Geert Hofstede, "The 6-D Model of National Culture," April 2021, https://geerthofstede.com/culture-geert-hofstede-gert-jan-hofstede/6d-model-of-national-culture/.

63. Wiley, "What is Open Pedagogy?;" Tonks et al.,"'Opening a New Kind of High School"; Wiley, "Defining the Open"; David Wiley and John Hilton, "Defining OER-enabled Pedagogy," *International Review of Research in Open & Distance Learning* 19, no. 4 (September 2018): 133–47, http://www.irrodl.org/index.php/irrodl/article/view/3601; Kimmons, "Developing Open Education Literacies"; Mason and Kimmons, "Effects of Open Textbook Adoption."

64. Jennifer Van Allen and Stacy Katz, "Developing Open Practices in Teacher Education: An Example of Integrating OER and Developing Renewable Assignments," *Open Praxis* 11, no. 3 (January 2019): 311–19, https://eric.ed.gov/?id=EJ1234940; Jennifer Van Allen and Stacy Katz, "Teaching with OER During Pandemics and Beyond," *Journal for Multicultural Education* 14, no. 3 / 4 (June 2020): 209–18, http://dx.doi.org/10.1108/JME-04-2020-0027.

65. Dongho Kim, "A Framework for Implementing OER-Based Lesson Design Activities for Pre-Service Teachers," *International Review of Research in Open and Distributed Learning* 19, no. 4 (September 2018): 148–70, http://www.irrodl.org/index.php/irrodl/article/view/3394.

Bibliography

Allen, I. Elaine, and Jeff Seaman. *What We Teach: K-12 School District Curriculum Adoption Process*. Babson Survey Research Group. September 2017. https://www.onlinelearningsurvey.com/reports/k12oer2017/whateweteach_2017.pdf.

Aronson, Brittany, and Judson Laughter. "The Theory and Practice of Culturally Relevant Education: A Synthesis of Research Across Content Areas." *Review of Educational Research* 86, no.1 (2015). doi: 10.3102/0034654315582066.

Bergland, Jennifer. "It's Time: #Go Open." TechNotes. October 23, 2016. https://www.blog.tcea.org/goopen/.

Bhattacherjee, Anol. *Social Science Research: Principles, Methods, and Practices*, 2nd ed. Tampa: University of South Florida, 2012.

Bliss, TJ, and Susan Patrick. "OER State Policy in K-12 Education: Benefits, Strategies, and Recommendations for Open Access, Open Sharing." International Association for K-12 Online Learning (iNACOL). June 2013. https://aurora-institute.org/wp-content/uploads/oer-state-policy.pdf.

Blomgren, Constance. "OER Awareness and Use: The Affinity Between Higher Education and K-12." *The International Review of Research in Open and Distributed Learning* 19, no. 2 (2018). doi.org/10.19173/irrodl.v19i2.3431.

Blomgren, Constance, and Iain McPherson. "Scoping the Nascent: An Analysis of K-12 OER Research 2012-2017." *Open Praxis* 10, no. 4 (October–December 2018): 359–75. https://openpraxis.org/articles/10.5944/openpraxis.10.4.905/.

Branch Alliance for Educator Diversity. "Redefining Quality Educator Preparation." Branch Alliance for Quality Educator Preparation. Accessed March 1, 2021. http://www.educatordiversity.org/.

Cauthen, LeiLani. "Perspective: How Big is the Digital Curriculum Market?" The Learning Counsel. Accessed March 1, 2021. https://thelearningcounsel.com/article/how-big-k-12-digital-curriculum-market.

CK-12 Foundation. "CK-12 Teacher Site." Last modified February 16, 2021. https://www.ck12.org/teacher/.

Culatta, Richard. "Dear Colleague Letter: Federal Funding for Technology." Office of Educational Technology. November 19, 2014, 1–4. https://tech.ed.gov/wp-content/uploads/2014/11/Tech-Federal-Funds-Final-V2.pdf.

Delano, Jon. "Dozens Participate In Spontaneous Pay-It-Forward At Starbucks Drive-Thru." Pittsburgh CBS Local. April 18, 2017. https://pittsburgh.cbslocal.com/2017/04/18/bethel-park-starbucks-pay-it-forward/.

Firozi, Paulina. "378 People 'Pay it Forward' at Starbucks." *USA Today* (August 21, 2014). https://www.usatoday.com/story/news/nation-now/2014/08/21/378-people-pay-it-forward-at-fla-starbucks/14380109/.

Gay, Geneva. *Culturally Responsive Teaching: Theory, Research, and Practice*, 2nd ed. New York: Teachers College Press, 2010.

———. "Teaching to and Through Cultural Diversity." *Curriculum Inquiry*, 43 (2013): 48–70. doi:10.1111/cuir.12002.

Georgia Department of Education. "Georgia Virtual Learning: Shared Resources: OER MS LA 6th Grade." Accessed March 1, 2021. http://www.gavirtuallearning.org/Resources/SharedMSLA6(MSCopy).aspx.

Georgia Department of Education. "Georgia Virtual Learning: Welcome to Georgia Virtual Learning." Last modified 2020. http://www.gavirtuallearning.org/.

———. "MS Language Arts Grade 6, Introduction and Novel: The Watsons Go to Birmingham—1963." Georgia Virtual Learning. Accessed March 1, 2021. http://cms.gavirtualschool.org/Shared/Language%20Arts/6thGradeLA/IntroductionAndNovel/index.html.

GoOpen Michigan. "Explore Open Content." #GoOpen Michigan. Accessed March 1, 2021. https://goopenmichigan.org/.

Grotewold, Kimberly S. "Teachers as Content Creators: Copyright, Fair Use, Creative Commons, OER, & Visual Literacy." LibWizard Tutorial. Last modified 2022. https://tamusa.libwizard.com/f/creative_commons_oer_for_teachers.

Hodgkinson-Williams, Cheryl, and Patricia Arinto. "Adoption and Impact of OER in the Global South." Creative Commons Attribution 4.0 (2017). doi: 10.5281/ZENADO.1005330.

Hofstede, Geert. "The 6-D Model of National Culture." Geert Hofstede: Culture. Last modified April 2021. https://geerthofstede.com/culture-geert-hofstede-gert-jan-hofstede/6d-model-of-national-culture/.

Holt, Tim. "Why and How El Paso ISD Went Open." *TechNotes: Texas Computer Education Association* (blog), December 22, 2017. https://blog.tcea.org/el-paso-isd-went-open.

Howard, Nicole. R., Regina Schaffer, and Sarah Thomas. *Closing the Gap: Digital Equity Strategies for Teacher Prep Programs.* Portland: International Society for Technology in Education (ISTE). 2018.

International Society for Technology in Education (ISTE). "ISTE NETS-S." Last modified 2007. [These standards have since been updated.] http://cms.gavirtualschool.org/Support/NETSSStandards/netssstandardsCurrent.pdf

Kim, Dongho. "A Framework for Implementing OER-Based Lesson Design Activities for Pre-Service Teachers." *International Review of Research in Open and Distributed Learning* 19, no. 4 (September 2018): 148–70. ISSN 1492-3831.

Kimmons, Royce M. "Developing Open Education Literacies with Practicing K-12 Teachers." *International Review of Research in Open and Distance Learning* 15, no. 6 (2014): 71–92. http://www.irrodl.org/index.php/irrodl/article/view/196.

Koehler, Matt. "TPACK Explained." TPACK.org. September 24, 2012. http://matt-koehler.com/tpack2/tpack-explained/.

Kwak, SuBeom, "How Korean Language Arts Teachers Adopt and Adapt Open Educational Resources: A Study of Teachers' and Students Perspectives." *International Review of Research in Open and Distributed Learning* 18, no. 4 (2017): 193–211. ISSN: 1492-3831.

Ma, Jennifer, Matea Pender, and C. J. Libassi. "Trends in College Pricing and Student Aid 2020." New York: College Board, 2020. https://research.collegeboard.org/pdf/trends-college-pricing-student-aid-2020.pdf.

Mason, Stacie L., and Royce M. Kimmons. "Effects of Open Textbook Adoption on Teachers' Open Practices." *International Review of Research in Open and Distributed Learning* 19, No. 3 (2018): 128–50. http://www.irrodl.org/index.php/irrodl/article/view/3517/4670.

Mishra, Punya, and Matthew J. Koehler. "Technological Pedagogical Content Knowledge: A Framework for Teacher Knowledge." *Teachers College Record* 108, no. 6 (June 2006): 1017–54. https://www.punyamishra.com/wp-content/uploads/2008/01/mishra-koehler-tcr2006.pdf.

Misra, Pradeep Kumar. "Training Teachers to Use and Produce Open Educational Resources: A Win-Win Approach." *Journal of Educational Technology* 9 (July–September 2012): 1–7. ISSN-0973-0559.

Murphy, Patricia, and Freda Wolfenden. "Developing a Pedagogy of Mutuality in a Capability Approach: Teachers' Experiences of using the Open Educational Resources (OER) of the Teacher Education in Sub-Saharan Africa (TESSA) Programme." *International Journal of Educational Development* 33, no. 3 (May 2013): 263–71.

Pay it Forward Foundation. "About Us." Last modified ca 2017. https://payitforwardfoundation.org/about-us/.

Perryman, Leigh-Anne, Allison Hemings-Butler, and Tim Seal. "Learning from TESS-India's Approach to OER Localisation Across Multiple Indian States." *Journal of Interactive Media in Education* 2, no. 7 (2014): 1–11. http://doi.org/10.5334/jime.af.

Popken, Ben. "College Textbook Prices Have Risen 1,041 Percent Since 1977." NBC News. August 6, 2015. https://www.nbcnews.com/feature/freshman-year/college-textbook-prices-have-risen-812-percent-1978-n399926.

Ramírez-Montoya, Maria-Soledad, Juanjo Mena, and Jose Antonio Rodríguez-Arroyo. "In-Service Teachers' Self-Perceptions of Digital Competence and OER Use as Determined by a Xmooc Training Course." *Computers in Human Behavior* 77 (December 2017): 356–64. doi 10.1016/j.chb.2017.09.010.

Scheerder, Anique, Alexander J. A. M. Van Deursen, and Jan A. G. M. Van Dijk. "Determinants of Internet Skills, Uses and Outcomes. A Systematic Review of the Second- and Third-Level Digital Divide." *Telematics & Informatics* 34 (2017): 1607–24.

Shulman, Lee S. "Those Who Understand: Knowledge Growth in Teaching." Pedagogical Content Knowledge, a special issue of *The Journal of Education* 193, no. 3 (2013): 1–11. https://www.jsotr.org/stable/24636916.

Soots, Barbara. "Washington OSPI, Open Educational Resources." Last modified July 2020. https://www.k12.wa.us/student-success/learning-standards-instructional-materials/open-educational-resources.

SUNY OER Services. "Creative Commons Licenses Quick Reference." KNILT. Accessed March 1, 2021. https://knilt.arcc.albany.edu/File:Oer.jpg.

Tang, Hengtao, and Yu Bao. "Social Justice and K-12 Teachers' Effective Use of OER: A Cross-Cultural Comparison by Nations." *Journal of Interactive Media in Education* no. 1 (May 11, 2020). http://jime.open.ac.uk/articles/10.5334/jime.576/.

Texas A&M University-San Antonio. "About Texas A&M University-San Antonio." Last modified 2019. https://tamusa.edu/about/index.html.

Tonks, DeLaina, Sarah Weston, David Wiley, and Michael K. Barbour. "'Opening' a New Kind of High School: The Story of the Open High School of Utah." *International Review of Research in Open and Distance Learning* 14, no.1 (2013): 255–71. https://doi.org/10.19173/irrodl.v14i1.1345.

Tur, Gemma, Leo Havemann, Dawn J. Marsh, Jeffrey M. Keefer, and Fabio Nascimbeni. "Becoming an Open Educator: Towards an Open Threshold Framework." *Research in Learning Technology* 28 (2020). doi 10.25304/rlt.v28.2338.

United Nations Educational, Scientific, and Cultural Organization (UNESCO). "UNESCO Figures Show Two Thirds of an Academic Year Lost on Average Worldwide Due to Covid-19 School Closures." January 25, 2021. https://en.unesco.org/news/unesco-figures-show-two-thirds-academic-year-lost-average-worldwide-due-covid-19-school.

United States Bureau of Labor Statistics. "College Tuition and Fees Increase 63% since January 2006." August 30, 2016. https://www.bls.gov/opub/ted/2016/college-tuition-and-fees-increase-63-percent-since-January-2006.htm.

United States Census Bureau. "QuickFacts San Antonio, City, Texas, United States." Last modified ca July 2019. https://www.census.gov/quickfacts/fact/table/sanantoniocitytexas,US/PST045219

———. "QuickFacts Washington." Last modified ca July 2019. https://www.census.gov/quickfacts/WA.

United States Department of Education. "Open Licensing Requirement for Competitive Grant Programs." January 19, 2017. https://www.federalregister.gov/documents/2017/01/19/2017-00910/open-licensing-requirement-for-competitive-grant-programs.

———. "U.S. Department of Education Launches Campaign to Encourage Schools to #GoOpen with Educational Resources." October 29, 2015. https://www.ed.gov/news/press-releases/us-department-education-launches-campaign-encourage-schools-goopen-educational-resources.

———. "U. S. Department of Education Recognizes 14 States and 40 Districts Committing to #GoOpen with Educational Resources." February 26, 2016. https://www.ed.gov/news/press-releases/us-department-education-recognizes-13-states-and-40-districts-committing-goopen-educational-resources.

———. Office of Educational Technology. "#GoOpen Districts." Accessed March 1, 2021. https://tech.ed.gov/open/districts/.

———. Office of Educational Technology. "#GoOpen States." Accessed March 1, 2021. https://tech.ed.gov/open/states/.

———. Office of Educational Technology. "Open Education." Accessed March 1, 2021. https://tech.ed.gov/open/.

———. Office of Educational Technology. "Welcome to #GoOpen." Last modified ca 2016. https://tech.ed.gov/open/districts/launch/welcome/.

University System of Georgia. "Find Textbooks: Open Textbooks." Affordable Learning Georgia. 2021. https://www.affordablelearninggeorgia.org/find_textbooks/open_textbooks.

Van Allen, Jennifer, and Stacy Katz. "Developing Open Practices in Teacher Education: An Example of Integrating OER and Developing Renewable Assignments." *Open Praxis* 11, no. 3 (January 1, 2019): 311–19. https://eric.ed.gov/?id=EJ1234940.

———. "Teaching with OER During Pandemics and Beyond." *Journal for Multicultural Education* 14, no. 3 /4 (June 2020): 209–18. http://dx.doi.org/10.1108/JME-04-2020-0027.

Washington Office of Superintendent of Public Instruction (OSPI). "About OSPI." February 2021. https://www.k12.wa.us/about-ospi.

———. "Washington OER Hub." OER Commons. Accessed March 1, 2021. https://www.oercommons.org/hubs/washington.

———. "Since Time Immemorial: Tribal Sovereignty in Washington State." Last modified 2020–2021. https://www.k12.wa.us/student-success/resources-subject-area/time-immemorial-tribal-sovereignth-washington-state.

Weisbaum, Herb. "Students are Still Saddled with Soaring Textbook Costs, Report Says." NBC Business News. Last modified February 10, 2016. https://www.nbcnews.com/business/business-news/students-are-still-saddled-soaring-textbook-costs-report-says-n516011.

Wiley, David. "Defining the 'Open' in Open Content and Open Educational Resources." Accessed March 1, 2021. http://opencontent.org/definition/.

———. "Open Education License Draft." August 8, 2007. https://opencontent.org/blog/archives/355.

———. "What is Open Pedagogy?" October 13, 2013. https://opencontent.org/blog/archives/2975.

———. "The Access Compromise and the 5th R." March 5, 2014. https://opencontent.org/blog/archives/3221.

Wiley, David, and John Hilton. "Defining OER-Enabled Pedagogy." *International Review of Research in Open & Distance Learning* 19, no. 4 (September 2018): 133–47. doi 10.19173/irrodl.v19i4.3601.

William and Flora Hewlett Foundation. "Open Educational Resources Initiative." ca 2006, Accessed March 1, 2021. https://hewlett.org/wp-content/uploads/2016/08/HewlettFoundationOER.pdf.

Wolfenden, Freda, and Lina Adinolfi. "An Exploration of Agency in the Localisation of Open Educational Resources for Teacher Development." *Learning, Media and Technology* 44, no. 3 (July 3, 2019): 327–44. https://doi.org/10.1080/17439884.2019.1628046.

Wong, Tak-Lam, Haoran Xie, Di Zou, Fu Lee Wang, Jeff Kai Tai Tang, Anthony Kong, and Reggie Kwan. "How to Facilitate Self-regulated Learning? A Case Study on Open Educational Resources." *Journal of Computers in Education* 7 (2019 online/2020): 51–77. https://doi.org/10.1007/s40692-019-00138-4.

Zook, Chris. "Infographic: Textbook Costs Skyrocket 812% in 35 Years." Applied Educational Systems. September 7, 2017. https://www.aeseducation.com/blog/infographic-the-skyrocketing-cost-of-textbooks-for-schools-students.

CHAPTER 6

Reframing Social Work Education Using OER

Jennifer Wood and Mary Jo Orzech

Social work is, by definition, a profession devoted to the pursuit of social justice and the eradication of oppression, inequity, disparities, and other forms of injustice. Social workers are focused on the empowerment of marginalized people and communities and are expected to adhere to clear standards of ethical and competent practice. Additionally, the title of "social worker" is earned through the successful completion of social work education, either on the undergraduate or graduate levels. These social work programs are, in the United States of America, accredited by the Council on Social Work Education (CSWE), which periodically revises and updates its Educational Policy and Accreditation Standards (EPAS)[1] and monitors the adherence of each accredited program to these standards. Essentially, CSWE determines the learning of every social worker in the United States.

There are many codes for ethical social work practice in the United States, most based on some aspect of social identity (race, ethnicity, religious affiliation). However, the default resource for ethical expectations is the Code of Ethics of the National Association of Social Workers (NASW),[2] a membership-based organization with state, regional, and local chapters throughout the nation. This code sets forth basic ethical principles of the profession, along with detailed and extensive standards for all aspects of practice, and is revised at intervals to reflect changes in culture. Essentially, this code and the CSWE standards guide the profession, its practice, and its development and are meant to further the anti-oppressive goals of the profession.

Both the CSWE standards and the NASW Code of Ethics call for high levels of competency in issues of diversity. The code states, "Social workers should have a knowledge base of their clients' cultures and be able to demonstrate competence in the provision of services that are sensitive to clients' cultures and to differences among people and cultural groups. Social workers should obtain education about and seek to understand the nature of social diversity and oppression with respect to race, ethnicity, national origin, color, sex, sexual orientation, gender identity or expression, age, marital status, political belief, religion, immigration status, and mental or physical ability."[3] Therefore, it would stand to reason that the materials used in social work education should accurately reflect the perspectives and viewpoints of the client systems to ensure some acceptable level of cultural competence.

Similarly, the CSWE educational standards also require prospective social workers to understand and respect diverse identities, experiences, and perspectives. According to the 2015 EPAS, "Social workers understand how diversity and difference characterize and shape the human experience and are critical to the formation of identity.... Social workers apply and communicate understanding of the importance of diversity and difference in shaping life experiences in practice at the micro, mezzo, and macro levels and present themselves as learners and engage clients and constituencies as experts of their own experiences."[4] This competency makes it clear that only members of oppressed communities truly understand their situation and the meaning of their experiences. The EPAS also set forth expectations for how social workers gain knowledge: "Social workers know the principles of logic, scientific inquiry, and culturally informed and ethical approaches to building knowledge. Social workers understand that evidence that informs practice derives from multi-disciplinary sources and multiple ways of knowing. They also understand the processes for translating research findings into effective practice."[5]

When this standard is viewed in the context of professional expectations for engaging and respecting diversity, as well as the ethical imperative to do the same, it shines a light on the need to understand how social work students are learning about the needs of marginalized communities—in particular, communities of racial minority status. We are examining the current sources of social work knowledge in educational programs to determine whether ways of teaching align with the professional ethical principles and standards of professional education.

Social Work Clients

Social workers provide assistance and advocacy for clients on the micro (individual), mezzo (families and groups), and macro (organizations and communities) levels. Many clients experience poverty and structural oppression, which then manifests in community, family, and individual suffering. The Kaiser Family

Foundation's 2019 report[6] showed that Black, Indigenous, and People of Color (BIPOC) experience much higher rates of poverty than their white counterparts. They also experience higher rates of acute medical need, family disruption, and interaction with the justice system as well as poorer educational outcomes. Therefore, BIPOC tend to make up a proportionally greater portion of the clients served by the social work profession, which indicates that social work students must be prepared to competently and ethically serve communities of color. Social work educators must be sure that the materials used to teach future professionals accurately portray the etiology of oppressive conditions as well as the reality of living in an oppressive society. Only by teaching under these circumstances will students become ethical and competent practitioners; otherwise, they have the potential to do grave harm to these already vulnerable client systems.

Diversity in Social Work Education

One way to provide accurate education to social work students is to employ faculties from the communities served by the profession and to have a racially diverse faculty so students from those communities can relate to their educators. However, there is a dearth of faculty members in social work who identify as BIPOC. It is important to note that requirements for accreditation from CSWE, as well as regional accrediting bodies in higher education, result in an increased need for faculty members holding a doctoral degree (a PhD or in the case of social work, a DSW). As of 2017, only 25 percent of Black people had a bachelor's degree or higher, along with 20 percent of Indigenous people and 17 percent of Hispanic people, compared to over 40 percent of white people.[7] This is a reflection of disparities in education that manifest in early childhood. That same report stated that roughly 1 percent of Black people attain doctoral degrees, and this is true for a smaller proportion of people identifying as Indigenous or Hispanic. Therefore, according to current accrediting requirements, there is only a limited number of BIPOC who would even be eligible for full-time faculty status.

There are, as of 2021, hundreds of accredited social work programs in the United States, each requiring faculty members holding doctoral degrees. There are 533 baccalaureate programs, 291 master's programs, 18 DSW (practice doctorate) programs, and 25 PhD programs; those numbers increase each year (CSWE, 2021). According to CSWE (2020),[8] nearly one-half of students attaining an undergraduate social work degree identified as Black, Indigenous, or Hispanic. That number dropped to 34 percent of MSW students. That same year, 36 percent of DSW recipients identified as such, but those individuals rarely go into education. Only 23 percent of PhD graduates identified as BIPOC. In total, there were ninety-two tenure-track faculty positions acquired in 2020 by social work doctoral degree holders of any race, so it can be inferred that relatively few BIPOC found tenure-track appointments, and the dominance of faculty bodies by white educators persists. Additionally, students of color often experience structural racism that intensifies along with the level of study, frequently resulting in a departure from graduate education. This contributes to the issue of poor retention of BIPOC students in doctoral study programs as well as the increasing scarcity of minority faculty members. Faculty members of color, who are already navigating structural racism in the workplace, are then overburdened with increasing service load, particularly the expectation to lead all diversity and inclusion initiatives. This often contributes to faculty burnout and fewer BIPOC faculty members reaching tenure.[9]

The Concept of "Valid Knowledge"

Within many professional fields, there has been a drive to engage in "more scientific" ways of learning and teaching, often citing the buzzwords "evidence-based practice." Social work is no exception and is not alone in the social sciences in the need to prove itself a science as opposed to an art. [10-12] That need and drive are reflected in the classroom, where social work educators tout the merits of "peer-reviewed" sources and "scholarly journal articles." However, we must consider who is writing and reviewing these articles and who has the access to publishing their work.

As previously discussed, only a relatively small number of BIPOC are able to secure tenure-track social work faculty positions that would carry a publishing requirement. Therefore, it is reasonable to assume that the vast majority of these scholarly, peer-reviewed articles—those considered to be valid knowledge for social work practice—are overwhelmingly written by white academics from the perspective of whiteness. The overall tone and direction of discourse on diversity in the social work profession are set during the years of social work education, so it is crucial that future practitioners learn about oppressed communities in a way that allows them to best understand the perspectives and experiences of the members of those communities.[13] Is research done by white academics, using the work of other white academics, truly valid? Does that data, filtered through the lens of whiteness, truly teach social workers how to serve communities of color in an ethical and competent manner? In the absence of diversifying the faculty itself, is there a more effective way to teach future social workers what the reality is of racial oppression?

Critical Race Theory and Social Work Principles

While social work presents itself as a field and profession that fully engages in anti-oppressive work and the relief of injustice, it is still a field dominated by whiteness and white practitioners. It is both a part and product of the white supremacy that guides most systems in the United States. While social workers, overwhelmingly, enter the profession with the intention of improving social conditions, the dynamics of that profession put them in the position to be potentially harmful and oppressive themselves, regardless of intention.[14] Critical race theory[15] (CRT) is a useful and appropriate lens through which to examine issues of inequity and injustice in social work education.

CRT is a framework used to overall examine the fundamental purpose of systems to oppress BIPOC. It was used in the 1990s to investigate and critique educational disparities between institutions educating primarily white children and those educating children of color.[16] While the focus was on K-12 schools, the whitewashing of knowledge and the dominance of white ways of knowing was and is not exclusive to those systems, and it is still seen in post-secondary education. The author states that this "hidden curriculum flagrantly services white students"[17] and serves to, at best, disenfranchise and, at worst, demonize Black and brown students. The majority voices determine the status quo and what is considered "common sense" and "the norm," and anything else is "other." If primarily white academics are designing the curriculum (along with the ethical code and competencies) of social work education, it stands to reason that the "normal" education will not represent the truth and reality as known and experienced by members of the BIPOC communities.

Hackman and Rauscher,[18] in their discussion of CRT, drew attention to the fact that insensitive and inequitable curricula serve to truly marginalize vulnerable students. They set forth the dichotomy of "storytelling" and "counter-storytelling" as two ways of knowing and understanding. Under this framework, the mainstream, whitewashed view of the world is the "storytelling" passed through and down white-dominated systems and framed as common sense, truthful knowledge as "facts." The concept of "counter-storytelling" is both a learning of the truth outside the white experience and an unlearning of what has been commonly accepted as "fact." That "counter-storytelling" comes from members of marginalized communities, whose voices are generally not heard in the current conception of "valid evidence." If the widely accepted practices of disseminating knowledge in social work education are serving to perpetuate the oppression of those communities, how can educators begin introducing the authentic voices of the marginalized and cease the whitewashing of social work education?

An Overview of Open Educational Resources

OER is a powerful and pragmatic way to create novel opportunities for sharing counter-storytelling more easily. An open educational framework is well-suited to encourage inclusive and open-minded observers, attentive listeners, and flexible learners. OER allows social workers, both educators and practitioners, to develop a keen situational awareness that comes from exposure to a range of different experiences. At the same time, OER is a way to think beyond the textbook in recognizing other forms and formats of insightful scholarly communication. OER may include podcasts, blogs, video, government and NGO content, and more. OER offers a valuable opportunity to evaluate how social justice concepts can be put into practice as part of social work instruction.

OER enables the ability to review, reimagine, and potentially revamp social work teaching materials. OER is defined as "teaching, learning and research materials in any medium—digital or otherwise —that reside in the public domain or have been released under an open license that permits no-cost access, use, adaptation and redistribution by others with no or limited restrictions."[19] "Open," as related to OER, is described in terms of the 5Rs, allowing users to retain, revise, remix, reuse, and redistribute content.[20]

Using OER in social work education and practice seems to be an obvious partnership, with shared goals of equity, diversity, and inclusion that are visibly aligned with social work's stated principles and ethics. There is also rich overlap with information literacy frameworks and concepts.[21] This intersection provides a useful foundation for developing course materials that reflect social justice as well as library and social work objectives.

Counter-Storytelling via OER

OER is particularly attractive to instructors seeking to include globally diverse or locally representative voices as appropriate. Insightful OER can be created to reflect communities whose worldviews, experiences, and underlying value systems may not be otherwise explicitly documented. Oral histories, cultural traditions, and relevant anecdotes can be explored in a number of ways through OER. These can help prevent "the danger of a single voice"[22] and discourage deficit thinking.

OER enables the movement of learning and teaching beyond the currently narrow and restrictive channels for becoming academically credentialed and published. It also facilitates discussion and consideration of other ways of knowing besides the exclusive reliance on traditional academic journals or even textbooks. New open (or subscription-based) digital platforms and social media are providing alternative ways to communicate in a quickly changing world.

Incorporating student writing and collaborative scholarship in OER materials results in successful and motivational examples for others. They provide a valuable opportunity to publicly acknowledge and credit student work. They also give agency and standing to more informal or other ways of knowing in contrast to exclusive traditional academic outlets. Conversational language, jargon, and idioms, responsive to specific learners, can make course materials more interesting and understandable. This allows social work students to better relate the curriculum to real-life experience and practice. There is a wealth of knowledge to be gained outside the classroom, recognizing that students approach social work while coming from various disciplines, career entry points, academic backgrounds, and lived experiences.

OER and Student Retention

For OER, 2018 was identified as a breakthrough year in the move to becoming an essential teaching tool.[23] Using open course materials ensures that all students have access on the first day of classes and levels unanticipated barriers that could be detrimental to an optimal learning experience. Saving students money on course materials is a positive move to help keep students in the education pipeline and able to fully participate throughout a course. Additionally, by providing long-term access, materials are available to graduates as part of lifelong learning.

Regarding learning outcomes, a majority of research on OER's efficacy has shown them to be at least as good as traditional textbook-based materials.[24] A study of more than 20,000 students found that students' grades increased using OER, while letter grades of D, F, and withdrawals decreased.[25] OER can be helpful in removing some of the barriers to retention at many points in a student's journey as an undergraduate, during graduate school, and as part of their professional social work experience.

OER Timeliness and Adaptability

The flexibility of OER creation allows for timeliness and sensitivity in responding to current events. It can be frequently refreshed as needed to reflect and react to the needs of specific communities. Keeping materials updated helps ensure that both students and faculty are familiar with topical resources, policies, and procedures. Utilizing current data and addressing contemporary issues models best practice, develops student confidence, and helps instructor effectiveness.

Being able to revise and replace OER as part of continuous improvement allows inclusion of real-world, "ripped from the headlines" examples.

Regular examination and review of content can identify gaps, misappropriations, or biased lenses for learners. Constructivist education theories encourage students to learn by doing and action rather than exclusively relying on passive intake of the words of others. Engaging students in producing OER content for a "frequently asked questions and answers" section or contributing items for quiz banks can add value and increase student ownership of their shared learning environment. OER can leverage resources by utilizing a variety of realistically representative case studies, role-plays, field book scenarios, and community toolkits.[26] This encourages sharing of difficult-to-replicate materials and moving away from single-use, disposable assignments to strengthen, build confidence in, and encourage developing students' professional voices.

Textbook Cost, OER, and Sustainability

Cost and convenience are the most frequently cited benefits of using OER.[27] Open education resources have existed in various forms for many years, although the last two decades have seen a dramatic rise in widespread understanding, funding, and adoption. Creating OER has frequently been motivated by frustration with commercial textbook prices that have risen dramatically well beyond the annual rate of inflation. The high cost of textbooks that change frequently with no added value (or that do not change enough) provide a valid reason to consider alternatives.

Pressure for alternatives to commercial textbooks has been voiced by students[28] and faculty as well as policymakers, grant funders, legislators, and international rights organizations.[29] The desire by authors to control and retain a portion of their copyright has also led to the development of licensing platforms such as Creative Commons. In the US, federal, state, and local OER initiatives have seeded several noteworthy OER projects. The Scholarly Publishing and Academic Resources Coalition (SPARC) and other organizations have helped to initiate and implement programs supporting OER champions and policy advocates to carry the OER message. Student groups have worked on #TextbookBroke campaigns to demonstrate how money for expensive course materials precludes the purchase of other necessities such as food, rent, gas, etc. They have been successful in helping underscore the need for more affordable learning.[30]

Integrating OER and Social Work for Equity

It seems there would be much support for OER in social work education, and inroads are underway.[31] However, DeCarlo notes, "Only one OER social work text is listed in the Open Textbook Library, and that openly available social work resources in Merlot and OER Commons lack organization, faculty review, or a record of widespread adoption."[32] Currently, not as much OER has been developed in social work as in allied disciplines such as psychology,[33] the professions (e.g., education and nursing), or the sciences (e.g., math and physics).

The surprising comparative lack of OER in social work education to date provides enormous opportunity. In social work, "OER enables faculty to localize and decolonize learning materials. For example, textbooks on child welfare might use common core content and localized content based on state regulations, trends, and client populations."[34] Inclusion of images reflective of their community can increase students' feeling of belongingness.[35] These modifications may assist in student persistence to degree and in eventually finding a disciplinary home in the social work field. In this way, OER has significant potential value in widening the pipeline to a more diverse cadre of learners and helping to grow the social work community.

Meaningfully engaging students as OER partners and advocates has several advantages. Participating in OER creation allows social work students to examine and challenge underlying belief systems, values, and motivations in a safe manner. Encouraging students to be part of knowledge creation helps them to gain confidence, enhances their standing, and enables them to model both solution-seeking and sharing with others.

Understanding that OER materials are always available and can be shared allows new social workers to assemble a better suite of tools for real-world work. This is especially true and helpful when graduates may no longer have access to an academic library for paywalled articles or access to a continuing professional education budget to keep up with the field. Teaching students critical information literacy emphasizing OER and open access materials helps prepare graduates to navigate beyond Google for their own use and to assist the clients they serve.

It should be mentioned that one weakness of OER, in general, is that it may not include supplemental materials or other textbook ancillaries such as quizzes, gradebooks, practice exercises, and more. Although some may be critical of quality, OER by definition affords the opportunity to improve, update, and enhance materials as part of the larger professional learning community. Inviting students to contribute to creating additional materials such as quiz banks and exercises can also help them develop their professional voice. In this way, OER not only gives credibility to those who might not otherwise be heard but, more importantly, enables additional ways to respectfully listen and make change.

From a larger perspective, Hodgkinson-Williams and Trotter[36] discuss some of the economic, cultural, and political responses to social injustices. They posit that OER and open educational practice can be categorized as either ameliorative (i.e., remedial) or transformative (i.e., addressing the root causes). They classify straightforward OER adoption as ameliorative, but it becomes transformative when students become more directly involved in developing class structure, activities, readings, and assessment. The acknowledgment of the power of proactive student involvement offers a framework for further examination of underlying pedagogical structures, assumptions, and open practices[37] in social work education and elsewhere.

This framework also leads to a clarion call for deeper empirical research in the use of OER as a means of examining redistributive social justice for underserved students.[38] All OER cannot be embraced uncritically. OER will only be transformative and ensure its sustainability by continuing to ask, "Open for whom?," "Open by whom?," as well as, "Open in what context, for what reason, and for what outcome?"[39]

Incorporating OER in Social Work Education

It is important to acknowledge that integrating OER in social work education is a process and does not happen overnight. Below are some practical ways it can be encouraged.

1. Utilize OER conversation to re-visit other needed changes in curriculum toward being more accessible and inclusive.
2. Find and reward champions from faculty, students, and other stakeholders who have been successful with OER in their courses to help carry the message to others.
3. Work with information literacy experts (e.g., librarians) to ensure students understand how to evaluate open resources and repudiate misinformation.
4. Conduct research that asks students for their perception of OER use and suggestions for improvement. Include and acknowledge student voices whenever possible.
5. "Lean into open" in all areas including open data, open education, and open access journal publishing[40] to break down paywalls and silos.
6. Encourage faculty to recognize and reward the development of OER materials and open educational practices in promotion and tenure guidelines.[41]
7. Advocate for additional OER support at departmental, institutional, association, state, and federal levels.

8. Celebrate by sharing successful programs and initiatives that can be adapted by others.

Social work has historically been a field that has been known for flexibility of thought and method. That flexibility must extend to methods of teaching and learning to allow the profession and its education to change in response to the changing world. One such potential change is rethinking scholarship requirements for tenure and promotion. The ever-present push in academia for articles in "peer-reviewed publications" is a driving force behind elitism in publishing. Additionally, the desperation to publish in a competitive field has facilitated the rise of predatory publishers, charging authors large sums of money to publish articles with little review or oversight.[42] The result of this trend is a flood of potentially low-quality research that is framed as "expert data" to students and practitioners. Rethinking tenure requirements and perceptions of "valid" scholarship would allow faculties more flexibility and creativity in how they conduct research and produce knowledge for consumption.

As previously discussed, social work education and social workers overall should expand the definition of what is considered valid knowledge, including and elevating the words and voices of the communities they serve. That process could begin with the introduction of materials from nontraditional sources, currently often seen as unorthodox and not sufficiently "scholarly" for inclusion in the social work curriculum. These materials could include blogs, podcasts, and posts on social media platforms, as these are channels currently available to members of marginalized communities such as BIPOC.

Conclusion

As a profession, social work prides itself on its focus on social justice, action, and advocacy on behalf of oppressed and marginalized communities. In particular, there has been a recent focus on anti-racist work within social work. Social workers are uniquely poised to provide valuable service to communities such as BIPOC; however, they are also uniquely poised to do harm to these same vulnerable people. Much of the influence that determines this course comes from social work education, so it stands to reason that anti-oppressive work must begin when practitioners are learning their trade. Social workers do not learn best about racism and its impact from white academics within a field dominated by whiteness; true learning comes from the voices of those whose lives are impacted by racism. The development and use of OER not only broadens the scope of information available to educators and students, it also reflects the ethical principles of the profession.

Many of the issues plaguing social work education are not unique to that discipline; tenure requirements, accreditation standards, and the exclusion of BIPOC from academia are problems identified throughout higher education. However, social workers, by virtue of their interaction with vulnerable human beings, have a unique imperative to adapt their pedagogy to the changing needs of their students and the world around them. Through the use of OER, social work education can better reflect its values and ethics and impart those, along with a better understanding of client needs, to future practitioners.

Endnotes

1. "Educational Policy and Accreditation Standards," Council on Social Work Education, 2015, https://www.cswe.org/accreditation/standards/2015-epas/.
2. "Code of Ethics," National Association of Social Workers, 2017, https://www.socialworkers.org/About/Ethics/Code-of-Ethics/Code-of-Ethics-English.
3. "Standards and Indicators for Cultural Competence in Social Work Practice," National Association of Social Workers, 2015, 14–15. https://www.socialworkers.org/LinkClick.aspx?fileticket=7dVckZAYUmk%3D&portalid=0.
4. "Educational Policy and Accreditation Standards," Council on Social Work Education.
5. Ibid., 8.
6. "Poverty Rate by Race/Ethnicity," Kaiser Family Foundation, 2020, https://www.kff.org/other/state-indicator/poverty-rate-by-raceethnicity/?currentTimeframe=0&sortModel=%7B%22colId%22:%22Location%22,%22sort%22:%22asc%22%7D.
7. Lorelle Espinosa, et al., "Race and Ethnicity in Higher Education: A Status Report," American Council on Education (Washington, DC: American Council on Education, 2019): 8. https://1xfsu31b52d33idlp13twtos-wpengine.netdna-ssl.com/wp-content/uploads/2019/02/Race-and-Ethnicity-in-Higher-Education.pdf.
8. Council on Social Work Education, 2019 statistics on social work education in the United States: Summary of the CSWE annual survey of social work programs, 2020, https://cswe.org/getattachment/Research-Statistics/2019-Annual-Statistics-on-Social-Work-Education-in-the-United-States-Final-(1).pdf.aspx.
9. Ain A. Grooms, Mahatmya Duhita and Eboneé T. Johnson, "The Retention of Educators of Color amidst Institutionalized Racism," *Educational Policy* 35, no. 2 (March 2021): 180–212, https://doi.org/10.1177/0895904820986765.
10. Björn Blom, "Knowing or Un-Knowing? That Is the Question: In the Era of Evidence-Based Social Work Practice," *Journal of Social Work* 9, no. 2 (April 2009): 158–77, https://doi.org/10.1177/1468017308101820.
11. Anne E. Fortune, "How Quickly We Forget: Comments on 'A Historical Analysis of Evidence-Based Practice in Social Work: The Unfinished Journey toward an Empirically Grounded Profession," *Social Service Review* 88, no. 2 (2014): 217–33, https://scholarsarchive.library.albany.edu/ssw_sw_scholar/1/.
12. Eileen Gambrill, "Is Social Work Evidence-Based? Does Saying So Make It So? Ongoing Challenges in Integrating Research, Practice and Policy," *Journal of Social Work Education* 52, no. sup1 (July 13, 2016): S110–25, https://doi.org/10.1080/10437797.2016.1174642.
13. Katarzyna Olcoń, Dorie J. Gilbert, and Rose M. Pulliam, "Teaching About Racial and Ethnic Diversity in Social Work Education: A Systematic Review," *Journal of Social Work Education* 56, no. 2 (2020): 215–37, https://doi.org/10.1080/10437797.2019.1656578.

14. Zeus Leonardo, "The story of schooling: critical race theory and the educational racial contract," *Discourse: Studies in the Cultural Politics of Education* 34 no. 4 (2013): 599–610, https://doi.org/10.1080/01596306.2013.822624.
15. Lori D. Patton, "Disrupting Postsecondary Prose: Toward a Critical Race Theory of Higher Education," *Urban Education* 51, no. 3 (March 2016): 315–42, https://doi.org/10.1177/0042085915602542.
16. Nicolas Daniel Hartlep, *Critical Race Theory: An Examination of its Past, Present, and Future Implications* (Milwaukee, WI: University of Wisconsin at Milwaukee, 2009), ED506735, https://files.eric.ed.gov/fulltext/ED506735.pdf.
17. Hartlep, *Critical Race Theory*, 4.
18. Heather Hackman and Laura Rauscher, "A Pathway to Access for All: Exploring the Connections Between Universal Instructional Design and Social Justice," *Education, Equity & Excellence in Education* 37 no. 2 (2004): 114–23, https://doi.org/10.1080/10665680490453931.
19. "Open Educational Resources (OER)," United Nations Educational, Scientific, and Cultural Organization, 2019, https://en.unesco.org/themes/building-knowledge-societies/oer.
20. David Wiley, "Defining the 'Open' in Open Content and Open Educational Resources," 2014, http://opencontent.org/definition/.
21. "Social Work: Companion Document to the ACRL Framework," ACRL/EBSS Social Work Committee, 2020, https://acrl.libguides.com/sw.
22. Chimamanda Ngozi Adichie, "The danger of a single story," TED, 2009, https://www.ted.com/talks/chimamanda_ngozi_adichie_the_danger_of_a_single_story.
23. Mike Silagadze, "OER Had Its Breakthrough in 2017. Next Year, It Will Become an Essential Teaching Tool," *EdSurge News* (December 28, 2017), https://www.edsurge.com/news/2017-12-28-oer-had-its-breakthrough-in-2017-next-year-it-will-become-an-essential-teaching-tool.
24. John Hilton III, "Open Educational Resources, Student Efficacy, and Use Perceptions: A Synthesis of Research Published Between 2015 and 2018," *Education Technology Research Development* (2019): 1–24, https://doi.org/10.1007/s11423-019-09700-4.
25. Nicolas Colvard, C. Edward Watson, and Park Hyojin, "The Impact of Open Educational Resources on Various Student Success Metrics," *International Journal of Teaching and Learning in Higher Education* 30, no. 2 (2018): 262–76, https://www.isetl.org/ijtlhe/pdf/IJTLHE3386.pdf.
26. "About the Community Toolbox," Center for Community Health and Development, University of Kansas, 2021, https://ctb.ku.edu/en.
27. Mathew P. DeCarlo and Kerry F. Vandergrift, "Textbook Cost Burden and Social Work Students," preprint, SocArXiv (December 29, 2019), https://doi.org/10.31235/osf.io/5q289.
28. Caitlyn Nagle and Kaitlyn Vitez, *Fixing the Broken Textbook Market, 3rd Edition* (Washington DC: U.S. PIRG Education Fund, 2021), https://uspirg.org/reports/usp/fixing-broken-textbook-market-third-edition.
29. "UNESCO Recommendation on OER," UNESCO, 2019, https://en.unesco.org/themes/building-knowledge-societies/oer/recommendation.
30. J. Jacob Jenkins et al., "Textbook Broke: Textbook Affordability as a Social Justice Issue," *Journal of Interactive Media in Education* 2020, no. 1 (May 11, 2020): 3, https://doi.org/10.5334/jime.549.
31. Pendell, Kimberly and DeCarlo, Matthew, Open Social Work, n.d., https://opensocialwork.org/.
32. Matthew P. DeCarlo, "Teaching Note: Creating Open Textbooks for Social Work Education," SocArXiv (November 7, 2019): 4.
33. DeCarlo, "Teaching Note," 4.
34. Ibid., 12.
35. Amy T. Nusbaum, "Who Gets to Wield Academic Mjolnir?: On Worthiness, Knowledge Curation, and Using the Power of the People to Diversify OER," *Journal of Interactive Media in Education* no. 1 (2020): 4, http://doi.org/10.5334/jime.559.
36. Cheryl Ann Hodgkinson-Williams and Henry Trotter, "A Social Justice Framework for Understanding Open Educational Resources and Practices in the Global South," *Journal of Learning for Development* 5 no. 3 (2018), https://jl4d.org/index.php/ejl4d/article/view/312.

37. Baha Mali, Catherine Cronin, and Rajiv S. Jhangiani, "Framing Open Educational Practices from a Social Justice Perspective," *Journal of Interactive Media in Education* no. 1 (May 11, 2020): 10, https://doi.org/10.5334/jime.565.
38. Sarah R. Lambert, "Changing Our (Dis)Course: A Distinctive Social Justice Aligned Definition of Open Education," *Journal of Learning for Development—JL4D* 5, no. 3 (2018), https://jl4d.org/index.php/ejl4d/article/view/290.
39. Kimberly Pendell, "Open for whom? Challenging information privilege in social work" (presentation, CSWE 2020 Conference APM, 2020), https://opensocialwork.org/2020/05/07/open-for-whom/.
40. Daniel Dunleavy, "Open Insights: Social Work and the Necessity of Open Access," Open Library of Humanities, January 18, 2021, https://www.openlibhums.org/news/407/.
41. "OER in Tenure and Promotion," DOERS3, 2021, https://www.doers3.org/tenure-and-promotion.html.
42. Marcelo Perlin, Imasato Takeyoshi, and Denis Borenstein, "Is Predatory Publishing a Real Threat? Evidence from a Large Database Study," *Scientometrics* 116, no. 1 (July 2018): 255–73, https://doi.org/10.1007/s11192-018-2750-6.

Bibliography

ACRL/EBSS Social Work Committee. Social Work: Companion Document to the ACRL Framework. 2020. https://acrl.libguides.com/sw.

Adichie, Chimamanda Ngozi. TED. The danger of a single story. 2009. https://www.ted.com/talks/chimamanda_ngozi_adichie_the_danger_of_a_single_story.

Bali, Maha, Catherine Cronin, and Rajiv S. Jhangiani. "Framing Open Educational Practices from a Social Justice Perspective." *Journal of Interactive Media in Education* no. 1 (May 11, 2020): 10. https://doi.org/10.5334/jime.565.

Blom, Björn. "Knowing or Un-Knowing? That Is the Question: In the Era of Evidence-Based Social Work Practice." *Journal of Social Work* 9, no. 2 (April 2009): 158–77. https://doi.org/10.1177/1468017308101820.

Center for Community Health and Development. "About the Community Toolbox." 2021. University of Kansas. https://ctb.ku.edu/en.

Colvard, Nicolas, C. Edward Watson, and Hyojin Park. "The Impact of Open Educational Resources on Various Student Success Metrics." *International Journal of Teaching and Learning in Higher Education* 30, no. 2 (2018): 262–76. https://www.isetl.org/ijtlhe/pdf/IJTLHE3386.pdf.

Council on Social Work Education. *Educational Policy and Accreditation Standards*. 2015. https://www.cswe.org/accreditation/standards/2015-epas/.

———. 2019 statistics on social work education in the United States: Summary of the CSWE annual survey of social work programs. 2020. https://cswe.org/getattachment/Research-Statistics/2019-Annual-Statistics-on-Social-Work-Education-in-the-United-States-Final-(1).pdf.aspx.

DeCarlo, Matthew P. "Teaching Note: Creating Open Textbooks for Social Work Education." SocArXiv. November 7, 2019. https://doi:10.31235/osf.io/qf3t5.

DeCarlo, Matthew P., and Kerry F. Vandergrift. "Textbook Cost Burden and Social Work Students." Preprint. SocArXiv. December 29, 2019. https://doi.org/10.31235/osf.io/5q239.

DOERS3. "OER in Tenure and Promotion." 2021. https://www.doers3.org/tenure-and-promotion.html.

Dunleavy, Daniel. "Open Insights: Social Work and the Necessity of Open Access." Open Library of Humanities. January 18, 2021. https://www.openlibhums.org/news/407/.

Espinosa, Lorelle L., Jonathan M. Turk, Morgan Taylor, and Hollie M. Chessman. *Race and Ethnicity in Higher Education: A Status Report*. 2019. Washington, DC: American Council on Education. https://1xfsu31b52d33idlp13twtos-wpengine.netdna-ssl.com/wp-content/uploads/2019/02/Race-and-Ethnicity-in-Higher-Education.pdf

Fortune, Anne E. "How Quickly We Forget: Comments on 'A Historical Analysis of Evidence-Based Practice in Social Work: The Unfinished Journey toward an Empirically Grounded Profession.'" *Social Service Review* 88, no. 2 (2014): 217–33. https://scholarsarchive.library.albany.edu/ssw_sw_scholar/1/.

Gambrill, Eileen. "Is Social Work Evidence-Based? Does Saying So Make It So? Ongoing Challenges in Integrating Research, Practice and Policy." *Journal of Social Work Education* 52, no. sup1 (July 13, 2016): S110–25. https://doi.org/10.1080/10437797.2016.1174642.

Grooms, Ain A., Duhita Mahatmya, and Eboneé T. Johnson. "The Retention of Educators of Color Amidst Institutionalized Racism." *Educational Policy* 35 (2) (2021): 180–212. https://doi.org/10.1177/0895904820986765.

Hackman, Heather, and Laura Rauscher. "A Pathway to Access for All: Exploring the Connections Between Universal Instructional Design and Social Justice." *Education, Equity & Excellence in Education* 37 no. 2 (2004): 114–23. https://doi.org/10.1080/10665680490453931.

Hartlep, Nicholas Daniel. *Critical Race Theory: An Examination of its Past, Present, and Future Implications*. Milwaukee, WI: University of Wisconsin at Milwaukee, ED506735, 2009. https://files.eric.ed.gov/fulltext/ED506735.pdf.

Hilton III, John. "Educational Resources, Student Efficacy, and Use Perceptions: A Synthesis of Research Published Between 2015 and 2018." *Education Technology Research Development* (2019): 1–24. https://doi.org/10.1007/s11423-019-09700-4.

Hodgkinson-Williams, Cheryl Ann, and Henry Trotter. "A Social Justice Framework for Understanding Open Educational Resources and Practices in the Global South." *Journal of Learning for Development* 5 no. 3 (2018). https://jl4d.org/index.php/ejl4d/article/view/312.

Jenkins, J. Jacob, Luis A. Sánchez, Megan A. K. Schraedley, Jaime Hannans, Nitzan Navick, and Jade Young. "Textbook Broke: Textbook Affordability as a Social Justice Issue." *Journal of Interactive Media in Education* 2020, no. 1 (May 11, 2020): 3. https://doi.org/10.5334/jime.549.

Kaiser Family Foundation. "Poverty Rate by Race/Ethnicity." 2020. https://www.kff.org/other/state-indicator/poverty-rate-by-raceethnicity/?currentTimeframe=0&sortModel=%7B%22colId%22:%22Location%22,%22sort%22:%22asc%22%7D.

Leonardo, Zeus. "The story of schooling: critical race theory and the educational racial contract." *Discourse: Studies in the Cultural Politics of Education* 34 no. 4 (2013): 599–610. https://doi.org/10.1080/01596306.2013.822524.

Nagle, Cailyn, and Kaitlyn Vitez. *Fixing the Broken Textbook Market*. 3rd ed. Washington DC: U.S. PIRG Education Fund, 2021. https://uspirg.org/reports/usp/fixing-broken-textbook-market-third-edition.

National Association of Social Workers. *Code of Ethics*. 2017. https://www.socialworkers.org/About/Ethics/Code-of-Ethics/Code-of-Ethics-English.

Nusbaum, Amy T. "Who Gets to Wield Academic Mjolnir?: On Worthiness, Knowledge Curation, and Using the Power of the People to Diversify OER." *Journal of Interactive Media in Education* 2020, no. 1 (May 11, 2020): 4. https://doi.org/10.5334/jime.559.

Olcoń, Katarzyna, Dorie J. Gilbert, and Rose M. Pulliam. "Teaching About Racial and Ethnic Diversity in Social Work Education: A Systematic Review." *Journal of Social Work Education* 56, no. 2 (2020): 215–37. https://doi.org/10.1080/10437797.2019.1656578.

Patton, Lori D. "Disrupting Postsecondary Prose: Toward a Critical Race Theory of Higher Education." *Urban Education* 51, no. 3 (March 2016): 315–42. https://doi.org/10.1177/0042085915602542.

Pendell, Kimberly. "Open for whom? Challenging information privilege in social work." Presentation, CSWE 2020 Conference APM, 2020. https://opensocialwork.org/2020/05/07/open-for-whom/.

Pendell, Kimberly, and Matthew DeCarlo. Open Social Work. n.d. https://opensocialwork.org/.

Perlin, Marcelo S., Takeyoshi Imasato, and Denis Borenstein. "Is Predatory Publishing a Real Threat? Evidence from a Large Database Study." *Scientometrics* 116, no. 1 (July 2018): 255–73. https://doi.org/10.1007/s11192-018-2750-6.

Silagadze, Mike. "OER Had Its Breakthrough in 2017. Next Year, It Will Become an Essential Teaching Tool." *EdSurge News* (March 13, 2018). https://www.edsurge.com/

news/2017-12-28-oer-had-its-breakthrough-in-2017-next-year-it-will-become-an-essential-teaching-tool.

United Nations Educational, Scientific, and Cultural Organization. Open Educational Resources (OER). 2019. https://en.unesco.org/themes/building-knowledge-societies/oer.

———. UNESCO Recommendation on OER. 2019. https://en.unesco.org/themes/building-knowledge-societies/oer/recommendation.

Wiley, David. "Defining the 'Open' in Open Content and Open Educational Resources." OpenContent.org. 2014. http://opencontent.org/definition/.

CHAPTER 7

Deconstructing Textbooks for Equity:
Open Educational Resources and Culturally Responsive Pedagogy

Elissah Becknell and Rebecca March

Equity of Cost

Our introduction to open education was through an initiative in our college system to address textbook costs with open education resources (OER). Faculty were asked to adopt or adapt OER textbooks to use with their students and share with other instructors across the system. Adopting and adapting an OER textbook has radically changed our relationship with our course materials. We have become authors of our own textbook, which gives us power over content and delivery. Open education is not merely OER course materials, but most adoptions of OER in higher education are motivated by an attempt to address the cost of education by empowering faculty to create OER textbooks, assessments, multimedia, and ancillary materials. Critically thinking about the economic barriers students experience when trying to access higher education reveals that course materials are just a small part of the overall cost. However, course material costs are something that educators directly control and can help ameliorate for their students. An educator's commitment to OER course materials can be their contribution to a larger discussion about all economic barriers students face as they pursue higher education.[1]

Open education offers more than just economic benefits to students. Definitions of open education pedagogy (OEP) vary widely; however, most modern

125

conceptions are grounded in the free or open sharing of knowledge on the internet. The Cape Town Open Education Declaration proclaims that this technology is "planting the seeds of a new pedagogy where educators and learners create, shape and evolve knowledge together, deepening their skills and understanding as they go."[2] An ethos of free sharing is combined with the creation of OER under open licensing, typically Creative Commons licenses, which allows educators across the world to share the best of their teaching practice with others for free. This collaboration is not merely between educators, it explicitly invites students into the process of creation and sharing. Educators and students consume and create knowledge together, engaging in a learning process that is "co-constructed, contextualized, cumulative, iterative, and recursive."[3]

We teach credit-bearing information literacy, research skills, and research methods courses at a community college. Over the years, we have taken many students through a research process from topic development to research portfolio in a classroom community. Adopting first an OER and then OEP has reaffirmed our values and expectations about the future of academic scholarship. We believe that the best academic scholarship will be grounded in anti-oppressive research methods that invite researchers to work with communities of interest on problems that matter. Technology should be at the heart of scholarship and research in the twenty-first century, but we need to be critical of how we implement technology in these processes.

Equity of Pedagogy

Open education pedagogy (OEP) is an emerging digital pedagogy that draws from many theories of learning, teaching, technology, and social justice.[4] This flexibility makes it compatible with many existing teaching philosophies and practices. Social justice is what drew us deeper into OEP. Before we heard of OEP, we were practitioners of critical information literacy and culturally responsive pedagogy. We believe that these pedagogical approaches create effective learning environments that center students as they learn academic research.

Information Literacy

Information literacy is a set of foundational concepts in librarianship, and all librarians must construct philosophies of information literacy to inform their work. In recent years, academic librarians have coalesced around the Association of College and Research Libraries' *Framework for Information Literacy for Higher Education* (*Framework*).[5] This framework is important because it is somewhat informed by critical scholarship on how students become enculturated into an

academy that constructs meaning and belonging through specific research practices and attitudes. The *Framework* is organized into six frames:
- Authority Is Constructed and Contextual
- Information Creation as a Process
- Information Has Value
- Research as Inquiry
- Scholarship as Conversation
- Searching as Strategic Exploration

Each frame is a threshold concept central to information literacy as practiced in the academy. These frames have definitions that discuss knowledge practices and dispositions that learners should develop as they become information literate within the domain of the academy. The *Framework* acknowledges the role of students in academic knowledge production and dissemination, not merely as information consumers. The *Framework* also encourages students to develop critical approaches to information environments, not merely skills to apply to information problems. This is an improvement on the standards that came before.

However, one important critique of this framework is that identity is not explicitly mentioned; there is no discussion of how race, gender, sexuality, ability, culture, or class impact how students engage with the institution of higher education.[6] The *Framework* is silent about the importance of structural or historical oppression within American institutions—oppression that impacts culturally and linguistically diverse students more than white students. The *Framework* is a good start for defining information literacy in the academy, but in order to address the impact of identity and structural or historical oppression more fully, librarians must add in critical pedagogy. We use two critical pedagogical approaches in our teaching practice: critical information literacy and culturally responsive pedagogy.

Critical Information Literacy

Critical information literacy (CIL) is concerned with definitions of information literacy and developing critical pedagogical approaches to delivering information literacy. Definitions of information literacy are important; however, let us assume that we are teaching information literacy within the ACRL *Framework for Information Literacy for Higher Education*. This discussion is about critical pedagogy.

Practitioners of critical pedagogy assert that schools enact the dominant ideology of their societies.[7] Schools are not passive transmitters of knowledge; they create culture and shape student consciousness. Instructors must be cognizant of how dominant ideologies function in their society and then resist reenacting domination by developing alternative approaches to different cultural, social, economic, and political agendas. Neutrality is not possible in this situation. For the critical information literacy practitioner, we must encourage students to engage with and act on the power structures underpinning information production and dissemination.[8]

In his work, *Pedagogy of the Oppressed*, Paulo Freire imagines education as a dialogic process between students and instructors, students and students, and students and themselves. People involved in this education must actively engage their embodied and enlightened experience to help one another see reality. Freire takes this dialogic process further and demands that instructors articulate and solve problems with their students. "Problem posing education is revolutionary futurity. Hence, it is prophetic (and, as such, hopeful). Hence, it corresponds to the historical nature of humankind. Hence, it affirms women and men as beings who transcend themselves, who move forward and look ahead, for whom immobility represents a fatal threat, for whom looking at the past must only be a means of understanding more clearly what and who they are so that they can more wisely build the future."[9] A librarian can instantly recognize their discipline in this form of education. Research, at its best, is about articulating and solving problems. More importantly, Freire demands that this exploration be hopeful, imaginative, futurist, prophetic, and transcendent. Liberation for oneself and one's community is the goal of this approach to education and research.

Librarians who take this approach to education seriously must encourage students to research significant problems in their world. These students should be empowered with agency and community support as they conduct research. Their experience and knowledge must be honored and invited into the research process. There is a place for basic information literacy and research skills, but the primary focus needs to be on developing an identity as a fully realized academic scholar capable of solving the world's problems and making a difference to oppressed communities. These students are invited to the library to conduct research and create meaning for themselves, not merely to find the correct answers about the way the world is.

Michelle Holschuh Simmons points out that academia is a foreign culture to most students. Librarians should develop an anthropologist's sensitivity to this culture to share their insights about the academy with students. Simmons is a strong proponent of genre pedagogy informing how libraries teach academic research, theorizing genre pedagogy as a dialogic that involves the student, the teacher, and the institution of academic research. Understood this way, academic research is a genre of research with particular discourse and conventions. Students who master the discourse and conventions are uniquely positioned to critique or effect change within the academy, instead of "learning how to conform to the established patterns within a particular 'community of practice' or academic discipline."[10] Students need to see that academic culture is fluid and dynamic and that it is enmeshed in the larger cultural, social, economic, and political agendas of society.

Students come into the classroom with an embodied identity and lived experience. They already understand tribalism and their place in the social reality. What they need to see in the academy, is how scholars use embodied and lived experience to propose theory and frame research questions. Students need to understand how academics engage in conversation, build community, and solve problems. They must learn academic conventions around discourse, research, intellectual freedom, and intellectual property. Research is at the heart of academic discourse because academic knowledge is constructed by what can be observed and measured in the world.

Librarians can be guides, mediators, mentors, and peers to their students. The dialogic relationship makes it clear that we are in the pursuit of knowledge together. An honest examination of academic culture points out the problems and contradictions along with the strengths and accomplishments. Students need to see themselves in the academy, and in the twenty-first century, there is no excuse for ignoring the scholarly contributions of every person represented in your classroom.

Culturally Responsive Pedagogy

Culturally and linguistically diverse students are a growing demographic in schools. These students, who have many racial and ethnic identities, have encountered an education system that systematically fails to help them achieve at the same rates as white middle- and upper-classed students. It is important for librarians to understand the impact of identity and culture in education and to develop pedagogical approaches that address achievement gaps between cultural groups.

Culturally responsive pedagogy (CRP) is the pedagogical approach we use to better engage with our culturally and linguistically diverse students. CRP has roots in dialogic pedagogy and offers clear guidance about the relationship between instructors and students as they engage in teaching and learning. This pedagogy demands that instructors embed consciousness-raising and social justice into all aspects of education. CRP works well with genre pedagogy because it asks instructors to be critical of how students get socialized into learning and school environments. Instructors are asked to develop classroom environments and course materials that are rigorous and engage culturally and linguistically diverse students in meaningful education.

In her book *Culturally Responsive Teaching & The Brain*, Zaretta Hammond acknowledges that the most difficult part of CRP is operationalizing CRP principles into teaching practices. She offers a framework with four core practices that instructors can engage in to develop their CRP practice: awareness, learning partnerships, community-building, and information processing.[11] Using this framework, we are going to explain how an OER textbook can support CPR practice in the classroom. This analysis will include dialogic practices and genre pedagogy from critical information literacy.

Equity of Content

Awareness

CRP starts with instructor reflection and awareness. Culturally responsive instructors are aware of the many forms of oppression in their world, and they are critically aware of the cultural, social, economic, and political forces that create inequitable education outcomes in their society. A culturally responsive instructor knows their cultural identity and social position and can manage their social, emotional, and political response to culturally and linguistically diverse students. When a culturally responsive instructor enters a classroom with culturally and linguistically diverse students, they have a positive view of all the diversity represented and do not seek to change, erase, or minimize a student's culture. These instructors see culture as key to authentic engagement with all students in the classroom.

The language used in academic library instruction describes a discourse style and publishing industry that is foreign to many students. Terminology like scholarly, peer-reviewed, plagiarism, open access, and controlled vocabulary can be alienating to those who are not familiar with these concepts.[12] Cultural features of academic knowledge production, including disciplinary silos, publish-or-perish production, and elitism, do not lend themselves to CRP practices like community building or learning partnerships. These same linguistic and cultural features of academia shape library research environments, adding layers of complexity as novice students navigate database silos, decipher specialized language, assess information quality, evaluate information relevance, and determine expertise or authority. Culturally responsive instructors know that learning how to do academic research is important; the challenge is making academic culture coherent and accessible to culturally and linguistically diverse students.

OER textbooks about academic research need to introduce culturally and linguistically diverse students to academic culture and language. This helps contextualize the problems or peculiarities students run into when conducting academic research like discipline-specific databases, mismatches between colloquial and expert search terminology, the glut of scholarly articles on some topics, and the scarcity of scholarly articles on other topics. At a minimum, an OER textbook about academic research must give students enough information to feel informed and interested in these cultural features of academia and the problems of academic research. These textbooks should explicitly acknowledge that scholarship is a conversation and that a diverse set of voices brings depth and clarity to academic knowledge. A well-written OER textbook about academic research gives students a framework to critique different ways of knowing and producing information. This helps students make critical connections between their cultural practices and knowledge systems to those of academia. A truly culturally responsive OER textbook will explicitly recognize that knowledge created outside the academy has value and can inform academic research, acknowledging that many communities create knowledge and try to make the world a better place.

Beyond the textbook, culturally responsive instructors invite culturally and linguistically diverse students into academic culture, acknowledging the elitism, disciplinary silos, and competitive nature. They accept that academic libraries are constructed and contested, allowing for discussion and critiques. They help students conduct meaningful academic research, creatively working through problems together as they arise.

Learning Partnerships

A culturally responsive instructor develops authentic connections with their students. This practice acknowledges the social and emotional dimensions of learning and teaching. Instructors can nurture connections with individual students by giving emotionally intelligent feedback, supporting self-directed learning, and cultivating a student's academic identity. These instructors also create classroom environments that communicate camaraderie, facilitate mutual respect, and build community.[13]

Twenty-first-century technology allows for free and open sharing of knowledge on the internet. Online social networks facilitate wider sharing of ideas or practices across the world, from "calls to participate" to peer review. The internet makes open access publishing and open scholarship possible. Creative Commons licensing allows copyright holders nuanced and expedient ways of sharing intellectual property. All the traditional features of scholarly information production have been impacted by these innovations. Open pedagogy seeks to make these technologies and innovations known to students. A culturally responsive instructor can see the learning partnership possibilities in this evolving information technology ecosystem.

OER textbooks about academic research need to introduce culturally and linguistically diverse students to the technological innovations happening in scholarship today. It is important to be critical about the limitations of technology to change traditional academic culture. This honesty helps students understand the importance of changing deeper structures within the academy that hold academic culture in stasis. A thoughtful OER textbook about academic research would describe the full complexity of the information environment students navigate and negotiate every day. This gives students the vocabulary and conceptual frameworks to understand fake news, influencing, epistemology, and disinformation. A culturally responsive textbook would contrast Western values of intellectual property ownership with indigenous values around communal ownership of knowledge. This contrast resonates with culturally and linguistically diverse students and can help all students imagine what a more open knowledge society might look like.

In addition to the textbook, a culturally responsive instructor invites culturally and linguistically diverse students to participate in open access research and scholarship. They help students understand the value of sharing knowledge across the world while developing skills in information production, peer review, and licensing. These instructors see cultural and linguistic diversity as assets to building global knowledge. These instructors give students a chance to develop an identity as academic researchers in a larger community.

Community-Building

For the culturally responsive instructor, community-building is about integrating the cultural elements and themes of your students into the classroom environment and course materials. This helps students see themselves and their communities as they are learning. It is important to move beyond mere cultural representation to incorporate deeper cultural practices or orientations in the curriculum. When setting up classrooms and digital course spaces, instructors should establish rituals and routines that help reinforce self-directed learning and academic identity.

It is important to center the experience of culturally and linguistically diverse people in academic research. Librarians and instructors who teach academic research must explicitly and implicitly communicate this truth to students throughout their time in school. Our curricula must include stories and contributions of academic experts from all walks of life. Western positivism has played a central role in the development of research methods in the academy, but that can be critiqued and better understood if anti-oppressive and indigenous research methodologies are present in the curricula. When possible, we should incorporate the experiences and stories of former and current students. Culturally responsive instructors know that their students have an incredible amount of wisdom and experience to share about research, and they make space for student voices.

A culturally responsive OER textbook reflects student culture and communicates a sense of belonging to culturally and linguistically diverse students. Thoughtfully created OER textbooks portray students as capable academic researchers, who employ creativity and critical thought while exploring. CRP-informed textbooks contain accurate representations of culturally and linguistically diverse students who skillfully conduct research that matters to them. Research topics and search strategies resonate with culturally and linguistically diverse students. Expertise is bestowed on people who do careful and critical work as academic researchers, not simply because they have the right credentials or pedigree.

Information Processing

A culturally responsive instructor is interested in learning about all the different cultures in their classroom. They spend time contemplating the deeper elements of culture, which include different worldviews, core beliefs, and group values.[14] Culturally responsive instructors incorporate nonwestern cultural orientations into their teaching practice, such as orality and communalism. These instructors experiment with teaching strategies developed in nonwestern cultures, such as storytelling, call-and-response, provocations, rhythm mnemonics in song or poetry, recursive graphic organizers, metaphors or analogies, and wordplay or humor.[15] They understand that culture impacts how the brain processes information, so they look for culturally congruent ways to help students learn.

More than any other culturally responsive teaching practice, information processing requires instructors to step away from traditional Western approaches to education. Many of the teaching strategies that resonate with culturally and linguistically diverse students are oral or visual in nature, so an instructor has to take a hard look at their physical and digital course materials and in-class lessons. OEP has great potential to improve accessibility for culturally and linguistically diverse students because many web-based technologies are visual in nature and can be embedded with interactive learning activities. Instructors can be experimental as they create OER course materials with their culturally and linguistically diverse students in mind.

A culturally responsive OER textbook about academic research is designed with visual and interactive elements. Instructors who design these textbooks know that many culturally and linguistically diverse students come from cultures that center teaching and learning around oral practices. These instructors do not assume that students will read large chunks of information without graphical representations or images to communicate key concepts and processes in academic research. These textbooks use effective teaching strategies from oral traditions, such as stories, metaphors, provocative questions, rhythm mnemonics, and humor. OER textbook interfaces should work well with accessible text-to-speech technologies, offering students the option to have their textbooks read to them. Videos or interactive activities should be embedded into the textbook, if possible, to reinforce learning and help students practice.

Beyond the textbook, a culturally responsive instructor can improve their teaching practice by breaking up lectures with dialogue, videos, and interactive activities. They can highlight practices in academic research that involve community-building like disciplinary discourse, peer review, open access scholarship, and research teams. These instructors can help culturally and linguistically diverse students develop effective strategies for reading scholarly publications. For example, pointing out how publishing norms, like abstracts, journal article headings, and table of contents, facilitate quicker browsing. A culturally responsive instructor knows that culturally and linguistically diverse students can adapt to the text-based communication style of academia; however, these instructors communicate knowledge and build skills with academic research in culturally congruent ways.

Deconstructing Textbooks for Equity

Thoughtfully produced OER textbooks can help librarians and practitioners of information literacy deepen their practice of equitable teaching and learning. OER can make course content fluid and dynamic because they are adaptable to digital learning environments. Why point students toward a textbook when you can embed the textbook in course management systems, tutorials, activities, and discussions? Ultimately, the Creative Commons licenses that make OER textbooks cheap for students also make the text of these books highly adaptable for instructors who want to engage in culturally responsive teaching approaches.

Instructors can adapt and adopt OER textbook chapters in different creative ways. They might create modules that correspond with and include information from the text chapters in learning content management course shells. They might place the chapter information into an editable, shared document, allowing students to alter, add to, and create new content. An OER chapter can be turned into a Wikipedia page controlled by students who can edit, fact check, and evolve the page during the course and beyond. Instructors can deliver the content in a physical class or an online meeting in dialogue with students, where students can work with the instructor in community to question, clarify, and challenge terms and concepts.

We have turned our OER textbook into a LibGuide for our school and for the general public. LibGuide is a Springshare platform that allows librarians to create and share digital subject guides about topics, collections, services, and courses. LibGuides are web pages that can be embedded into a library's website. Each guide can be organized into pages, and each page can include text, databases, links, images, and videos. Our Research 101 LibGuide is organized by the threshold concepts of the ACRL *Framework for Information Literacy for Higher Education* and includes relevant videos, assignments, and self-assessment quizzes. Unlike course content placed into proprietary content management systems and closed to students at the end of the semester, our LibGuide remains open and accessible to our students, our college, and to the public.

We have moved away from the traditional practice of instructing students to read a chapter followed by proof in the form of assessment. Instead, we embed information from the OER chapters into our virtual learning environment, which is better suited to Zaretta Hammond's CRP model of "Ignite, Chew, Chunk and Review."[16] Igniting introduces new concepts and invites students to connect the new information to culturally meaningful information. Chunking breaks up information into small digestible bites with a 20:10 rule: 20 minutes to learn and 10 minutes to process. Chewing helps the brain process information during downtime. Establishing cognitive routines help learners turn unfamiliar information into usable knowledge. Chewing is encouraged in our digital course environment with zero-stakes games and challenges we create using activity generators compatible with our content management system. We use a platform called H5P to create many of these digital activities, enabling students to practice new ideas and skills with digital flashcards, drag-and-drop exercises, memory games, and fill-in-the-blank exercises. These added activities help students work through "thinking routines" to make sense of new content and establish relationships, perspectives, systems, similarities, and differences.

Beyond the textbook and course materials, classroom practices matter a great deal. In our research courses, we ask students to collect research from traditional academic resources and from resources they consider to be expert, such as community leaders, relatives with lived experience, and instructors they respect. We ask students to seek out and examine research quoted in their everyday lives, from family, friends, or social media. We help students develop their ability to critically summarize, analyze, and evaluate information with the songs, movies, blog posts, and articles chosen from their lived experiences. Students are given the opportunity to deliver their research assignments through writing, video, audio, or personal meetings with the instructor. Class discussions in online classes can be completed with traditional written responses or students can create video or audio posts. Responses in online discussions can be direct interfacing between students or students can interview their friends and family to report back as their discussion response, which is a way to invite the wider community into discussion forums.

Current and future plans for teaching our credit-bearing information literacy courses are rooted in deepening and expanding our culturally responsive practices. Culturally responsive pedagogy recognizes that students' brains are more receptive and willing to engage in productive persistence when they feel safe in a community.[17] That sense of community often comes from live discussion and the ability to express oneself in culturally meaningful ways, whether through writing, oral dialogue, storytelling, or art. Learning builds neural pathways, and the most effective way to build a pathway is to allow learners to anchor new information to personal points of familiar meaning and context, adding and mixing new concepts and vocabulary into foundational frames of meaning.[18]

Conclusion

Adopting OER can change how instructors interact with course content and can dramatically change their pedagogy. We would not have evolved our research skills and research methods courses in such dramatic ways without OER to experiment with. The Creative Commons licenses that make OER textbooks cheap for students also make the text of these books highly adaptable for instructors. OER helped us create relevant, targeted content that we can share with other instructors who edit and alter the text into their own version of student and course-appropriate material. OER and OEP helped us reconsider the meaning of "equitable" teaching and learning and allowed us to deepen our critical information literacy and culturally responsive pedagogy practices. We have come to believe that OER should act as a catalyst for instructors—a springboard for delivering content in a non-textbook format that can be more interactive and engaging for students than traditional course materials.

Endnotes

1. Robin DeRosa and Rajiv Jhangiani, "Open Pedagogy and Social Justice," Digital Pedagogy Lab, Vancouver, accessed 2 March 2021, https://digitalpedagogylab.com/open-pedagogy-social-justice/.

2. "Cape Town Open Education Declaration: Unlocking the Promise of Open Educational Resources," The Cape Town Open Education Declaration, accessed March 2, 2021, https://www.capetowndeclaration.org/read-the-declaration.
3. DeRosa and Jhangiani, "Open Pedagogy and Social Justice."
4. Robin DeRosa and Rajiv Jhangiani, "Open Pedagogy," in *A Guide to Making Open Textbooks with Students*, ed. Elizabeth May (Rebus Community for Open Textbook Creation, 2017), Chap. 1, https://press.rebus.community/makingopentextbookswithstudents/.
5. *Framework for Information Literacy for Higher Education*, American Library Association, 2015, accessed March 13, 2021, http://www.ala.org/acrl/standards/ilframework.
6. Marcia Rapchak, "That Which Cannot Be Named: The Absence of Race in the Framework for Information Literacy for Higher Education," *Journal of Radical Librarianship* 5 (2019): 173–96.
7. James Elmborg, "Critical Information Literacy: Implications for Instructional Practice," *Journal of Academic Librarianship* 32, no. 2 (2006): 193.
8. Eamon Tewell, "A Decade of Critical Information Literacy," *Communications in Information Literacy* 9, no. 1 (2015): 24–43, Library, Information Science & Technology Abstracts with Full Text, 25.
9. Paulo Freire, *Pedagogy of the Oppressed: 50th Anniversary Edition*, trans. Myra Bergman Ramos (New York: Bloomsbury Academic, 2018), 84.
10. Michelle Holschuh Simmons, "Librarians as Disciplinary Discourse Mediators: Using Genre Theory to Move toward Critical Information Literacy," *portal: Libraries and the Academy* 5, no. 3 (July 2005): 297–311, Library, Information Science & Technology Abstracts with Full Text, 302.
11. Zaretta Hammond, *Culturally Responsive & The Brain: Promoting Authentic Engagement and Rigor Among Culturally and Linguistically Diverse Students* (Thousand Oaks, CA: Corwin, 2015), 18–20.
12. Devina Dandar and Sajni Lacey, "Critical Discourse Analysis as a Reflection Tool for Information Literacy Instruction: A Case Study Approach of Library Orientation Sessions," *Journal of Information Literacy* 15, no. 1 (January 2021), 6.
13. Hammond, "Culturally Responsive & The Brain."
14. Ibid.
15. Ibid., 24.
16. Ibid., 128–31.
17. Ibid., 48.
18. Ibid., 131–38.

Bibliography

Bali, Maha, Catherine Cronin, and Rajiv S. Jhangiani. "Framing Open Educational Practices from a Social Justice Perspective." In *Open Education and Social Justice*, edited by Sarah Lambert and Laura Czerniewicz. Special collection, *Journal of Interactive Media in Education* no. 1 (May 2020). https://doi.org/10.5334/jime.565.

Cape Town Open Education Declaration, The. "Unlocking the Promise of Open Educational Resources." Accessed March 2, 2021. https://www.capetowndeclaration.org/read-the-declaration.

Dandar, Devina, and Sajni Lacey. "Critical Discourse Analysis as a Reflection Tool for Information Literacy Instruction: A Case Study Approach of Library Orientation Sessions." *Journal of Information Literacy* 15, no. 1 (January 2021): 3–25.

DeRosa, Robin, and Rajiv Jhangiani. "Open Pedagogy." In *A Guide to Making Open Textbooks with Students*, edited by Elizabeth May. Rebus Community for Open Textbook Creation, 2017, Chap. 1. https://press.rebus.community/makingopentextbookswithstudents/.

———. "Open Pedagogy and Social Justice." Digital Pedagogy Lab, Vancouver. Accessed March 2, 2021. https://digitalpedagogylab.com/open-pedagogy-social-justice/.

Elmborg, James. "Critical Information Literacy: Implications for Instructional Practice." *Journal of Academic Librarianship* 32, no. 2 (2006): 192–99.
Friere, Paulo. *Pedagogy of the Oppressed: 50th Anniversary Edition*. Translated by Myra Bergman Ramos. New York: Bloomsbury Academic, 2018.
Hammond, Zaretta. "Culturally Responsive & The Brain: Promoting Authentic Engagement and Rigor Among Culturally and Linguistically Diverse Students." Thousand Oaks, California: Corwin, 2015.
Hodgkinson-Williams, Cheryl, and Henry Trotter. "A Social Justice Framework for Understanding Open Education Resources and Practices in the Global South." *Journal of Learning for Development* 5, no. 3 (2018): 204–24. https://jl4d.org/index.php/ejl4d/article/view/312.
Ladson-Billings, Gloria. "But That's Just Good Teachings: The Case for Culturally Relevant Pedagogy." *Theory into Practice* vol. 34, no. 3 (Summer 1995): 159–65.
Simmons, Michelle Holschuh. "Librarians as Disciplinary Discourse Mediators: Using Genre Theory to Move toward Critical Information Literacy." *portal: Libraries and the Academy* 5.3 (July 2005): 297–311. Library, Information Science & Technology Abstracts with Full Text.
Tewell, Eamon. "A Decade of Critical Information Literacy." *Communications in Information Literacy* 9, no. 1 (2015): 24–43. Library, Information Science & Technology Abstracts with Full Text.

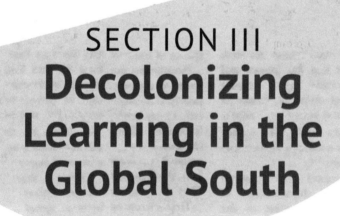

SECTION III
Decolonizing Learning in the Global South

CHAPTER 8

Open Textbooks, Intuitive Pedagogy, and Social Justice

Glenda Cox, Bianca Masuku, and Michelle Willmers

Introduction

The role of open education and open educational resources (OER) in ensuring more equitable access to education is now a mainstream concept in global higher education (HE). In the recent EDUCAUSE Horizon Report,[1] OER was deemed to be a "global movement" and described as part of the emerging technologies and practices that would have a significant impact on the future of HE. Openness has achieved "victories," showing that it "is an effective way to operate"[2] and has saved students millions of dollars in North America.[3] Weller and Allen call on open educators to be brave and hold the line in order to carve out future directions, including those that bring together inclusive practices and values. In line with this approach, the open education movement is growing in its diversity and is becoming increasingly critical in its approach.[4]

This chapter enters into the debate around the issue of the role of open textbooks in promoting social justice, specifically in South African HE. Critical of the role of openness as a lever that can accelerate or impede accessibility to and representation in knowledge production,[5,6] this chapter explores the complex interrelationship between five open textbook authors' layered conceptions of social (in)justice in their classrooms, the pedagogical approaches they develop in response to these injustices, and how this extends into their open textbook development processes.

Access and Representation in South African HE

Students face numerous systemic injustices in South African HE, all of which have been exacerbated by the COVID-19 pandemic. These include significant

141

challenges in terms of lack of access to uninterrupted power supply, devices, and data as well as the necessary skills and a conducive learning environment to engage in online learning. Recent data indicates that "20% of students are not able to charge their devices as needed, more than half (54%) do not have a quiet place to study, and only half (50%) indicate that they have appropriate network connection."[7]

The curriculum transformation and decolonial agenda in South African HE also highlights a range of systemic injustices related to accessibility and inclusivity.[8] These include the need for strategies to address the broader inclusion of marginalised and disabled student cohorts, more democratic epistemic representation in knowledge transfer and HE spaces, and an expanded approach toward multilingualism.[9-11] Within this context, there has been a move toward centering the student experience, "both in terms of pedagogical and larger institutional social justice efforts."[12]

The University of Cape Town (UCT), a highly ranked, traditionally English medium and historically white institution in South Africa with a commitment to promoting African-centric scholarly content,[13] has embedded curriculum transformation and decolonisation in its Vision 2030 statement as part of its institutional transformation effort.[14] Within this context, the decolonial agenda has raised questions within the institution around epistemic positioning, particularly as relates to factors such as whose knowledge is being presented? What/who gets privileged? Whose interests dominate?[15]

This interrogation coincides with a global call to give students more agency in the classroom and, in the process of obtaining their education as a whole,[16] as it is widely acknowledged that engaging students in their own learning processes can lead to improved learning outcomes, a higher level of interest in the course work and a greater sense of responsibility on the part of the learner. Engaging students on a more equal, democratic footing has also been shown to lead to increased knowledge exchange between teachers and students.[17] Pedagogies that include students' "adapting, identities, testing new ideas, making mistakes and learning"[18] can give them agency in the classroom.

Stein et al.[19] point out that students around the world traditionally have no involvement in the choice of textbooks, or any other learning materials, even though they are directly affected by decision-making in this regard. Open textbook development processes provide one means through which to address the power imbalance in the classroom by integrating students in curriculum articulation, textbook selection, production, and peer review.[20]

Opening and democratising textbook creation is one way in which students can have more agency in the classroom, in that it "isolate(s) knowledge from power and allows educators and students to seize the means of textbook production."[21] As such, it provides a means through which to support learner-centred educational design and enhance teaching and learning practice rather than merely being a content delivery strategy or technology.[22]

Intuitive Pedagogy and Open Textbooks

In this study, we understand the pedagogical practices of the open textbook authors we are profiling as "intuitive," in that there is an instinctive aspect to their teaching approach and how they respond to the situations they encounter in their classrooms. Markauskaite and Goodyear[23] point out that "pedagogical ideas and ways of knowing that originate in one's personal experience ('intuitive pedagogy') can be a productive resource in teacher thinking, action and professional learning."

The open textbook authors were in no way steeped in the discourse of learning theory and did not explicitly identify their pedagogical approaches as intuitive—nor, interestingly, as explicitly "socially just." These terms are instead employed by the authors of this chapter as a result of the observation and interview process that informed this study.

Farrow's[24] description of critical pedagogy aligns with the approaches and practices of these participants. They applied an intuitive and critical approach to classroom power dynamics and content creation. Here, "intuitive" pedagogy, a form of critical pedagogical practice, is responsive and focused on the student's lived reality, particularly as relates to principles of access and representation. Farrow[25] argues that a critical pedagogical approach offers strategies that are conducive to "improved understanding of both the conditions and techniques that support knowledge creation and transmission; and a sense of the importance of power relations for the pedagogical process itself." In the context of this study, it also entails giving consideration to the learning materials used as an extension of the classroom space and on how the power dynamics of the classroom extend into and are influenced by these resources.

The concept of "intuitive pedagogy" is not a new one and has previously been used to understand pedagogy and how teachers are thinking.[26,27] In line with our findings, Ahlbom,[28] who founded this form of pedagogy, describes it as being not something random but rather "decisions and actions where both plans and concepts are included as possible directions."

Open textbook production is a means through which to extend intuitive pedagogy into open practice and what Moje[29] refers to as pedagogy for social justice, in that it provides a content creation mechanism that functions as a microcosm of the classroom. The agility which manifests in open textbook authors' approaches toward content development[30] is an extension of their dynamic approach in adopting intuitive, responsive pedagogical practices as they are required. These open textbook authors practice access-oriented, learner-centred "open pedagogy."[31]

While openness shows promise in terms of helping to address inequity in the classroom, it cannot address all the social justice challenges of HE.[32] It is also the case that OER may unintentionally perpetuate injustices if authors do not critically evaluate their motivations for creating open textbooks and carefully consider the purpose of the open textbook as part of curriculum transformation and decolonisation.[33]

Exploring insights gained from interviews with five open textbook authors at UCT, this chapter highlights the role of intuitive pedagogical approaches in addressing injustice in the classroom and draws on the work of critical theorist Nancy Fraser[34,35] to examine the role of open textbooks as a tool for promoting social justice in the South African HE classroom. It also considers the views of open textbook authors in light of Fraser's more recent responses to the decolonial debate.[36]

Theoretical Framework

In the past decade, there has been a continued recognition of social injustices perpetrated within HE, which has led to a need "to reconsider how higher education is privileging some and excluding others."[37] As such, the inclusion of a social justice agenda in HE has prompted critical questioning of how the HE space operates.

Nancy Fraser and Openness for Social Justice

In recent years, there has been a call for the inclusion of political perspective and a social justice interpretation in the understanding of "open" in open education.[38] This call is in line with a growing focus on the need for "an ethics of care, of justice, (and to) not simply assume that open does the work for us."[39] More recently, critical research has emerged questioning "open" and its definitions and arguing for the inclusion of social justice as an embedded concept in all "open" work.[40] Other studies critically examine the relationship between open education and diversity, equity, and inclusion.[41] All of this research holds at its centre the philosophy that as researchers and participants in HE "we have an ethical responsibility to work for greater 'parity of participation.'"[42,43]

In several recent HE studies, the work of Nancy Fraser, a political philosopher, has been used as a framework to understand the role of various forms of "open" (OER, open educational practices, and open textbooks) in supporting social justice.[44-48] This critical turn was influenced by the application of Fraser's framework to OER developed in the Global South by Hodgkinson-Williams and Trotter[49] whose work provided an analysis of the social justice dimensions of "openness."

Nancy Fraser[50,51] provides a philosophical framework that can be used to critically examine HE pedagogy and practices. An underlying principle of this framework is the concept of "participatory parity," which "requires social arrangements that permit all to participate as peers in social life."[52] Her framework identifies inequities along three different dimensions: the economic (maldistribution), cultural (misrecognition), and political (misrepresentation). These three dimensions are entwined and influence each other, and all three need to be addressed for participatory parity to be present in HE.

Fraser's maxim is "no redistribution or recognition without representation."[53] In other words, for a society to be socially just, it is necessary for all the dimensions to be affirmed or transformed. Simply addressing, for example, economic redistribution is insufficient. Within this context, maldistribution refers to the uneven access to resources experienced by aspirant and registered students in HE. Misrecognition pertains to unequal respect for all participants and unequal opportunity for achieving social esteem and respect. Misrepresentation applies when people are denied participation as equals in social interaction and decision-making.

Affirmative responses are a way of remedying some of the social injustices located in current social arrangements; these responses do not address underlying structural issues that cause the injustices. Transformative processes, on the other hand, change the "deep grammar underlying the breadth and depth of contemporary forms of injustice in higher education"[54] by addressing the root causes of the injustice.

Although Fraser provides us with a "global justice ...analytical framework that sits at a high level of abstraction,"[55] her work has provided a language with which to evaluate the sometimes aligned versus the sometimes contradictory role of OER in addressing social justice. For example, the predominance of OER in English compared to other languages[56] represents a contradiction that manifests as cultural misrecognition, where "the current domination of Western-oriented epistemic perspectives and proliferation of hegemonic English-language OER" can only be countered through the production of OER in, or translated into, local languages.[57] Recent research has argued for the diversification of voice in global OER production in order to better include underrepresented groups.[58-62] This form of representational justice enables previously marginalised or unheard voices to contribute to global knowledge production through OER production.

Pedagogy and Curriculum Transformation

The South African HE system, specifically (although arguably this could be extended across the Global South), is under pressure to respond to calls for curriculum transformation and decolonisation in order to prevent the "deepening of structural processes of maldistribution, misrecognition, misrepresentation and misframing."[63-65]

Many students in South African HE arrive at university from an impoverished basic education schooling system and struggle to recognise "underlying disciplinary principles necessary for epistemological access."[66] They are also often required to do so in their second or third language. A study by Garroway and Lange,[67] for example, showed that non-first-language English-speaking students in an extended curriculum course that represented both race and class differences showed a deferential attitude and seemed unable to make decisions or bring forth their own ideas. These students were afraid of being mocked in class because they were not first-language English speakers.[68]

The recently published book *Nancy Fraser and Participatory Parity*[69] focuses on Fraser's work and its relation to HE within the South African context. This work seeks to understand how institutional policy, curricula, and pedagogical practices "may be required to advance just social arrangements and just ways of relating and access so that students and academics feel they belong and can participate on an equal footing in the sector."[70] In this edited volume, Fraser's concept of participatory parity is used to analyse pedagogical approaches to a community psychology module designed using a counter-hegemonic perspective intervention.[71] The author of this study[72] shows how curriculum design can be a "powerful tool to create platforms for participatory parity" and emphasises that it is crucial for lecturers to know the students in their classes.

Knowing students helps to better understand their economic circumstances and the need to move toward distributive justice.[73] Finding sufficient funding for studying, living, and traveling expenses is a barrier to students being able to participate with their better-resourced peers, which affects their ability to progress in HE.[74] This highlights the interconnectedness of maldistribution and misrecognition and the fact that in order to overcome injustice, both aspects need an affirmative but preferably transformative remedy.

Addressing misrecognition entails finding pathways for students to have "epistemological access"[75] through inclusive pedagogies and curriculum change. Epistemological access has "been deployed in numerous papers and publications as a banner to signal intent to move beyond physical or formal access to meaningful access to the goods of the university."[76] As such, pedagogical approaches need to consider "just ways of relating and access so that students and academics feel they belong and can participate on an equal footing."[77]

Decolonisation

The decolonial debate is just starting to be taken up in some regions in the world.[78] However, discussions around the impact of colonialism in South Africa are front and centre in HE and civil society discourse. In relation to open textbook development, Fraser's "critical-theoretical" critique of twenty-first-century capitalism includes engagement with colonialism and decolonialism.[79]

Neoliberalism can be regarded as a mode of coloniality, in that the focus on human capital subordinates people to the pure logic of the market.[80] Today, the prevailing institutional culture at many South African universities continues the production of colonial bureaucracies, control, classification, and commodification of HE.[81] Hölscher, Zembylas, and Bozalek[82] highlight two key aspects of decolonisation: (1) "It resists Eurocentrism and acknowledges the contributions of colonised populations to knowledge, culture and the world in general and (2) it emphasises a moral imperative for righting the wrongs of colonial domination and an ethical stance in relation to justice for those who continue to be affected socially, economically, politically and culturally by persistent forms of coloniality."

The "Africanisation" of HE, as put forward by Makgoba and Seepe,[83] assumes a policy that increases the number of African scholars and can be interpreted as essentialist and exclusionary in its approach. This approach to decoloniality is based on a nationalist African approach that promotes the exclusion of other voices that are not African. This concept of the Africanisation of HE is analysed by Hölscher, Zembylas, and Bozalek as being limited, in that it does not critique or engage with neoliberalism; they suggest that there should instead be an inclusion of "recent scholarship on Black internationalism and …intersections with various other forms of internationalisms."[84] Another way of approaching this epistemic challenge is to not discard the Western canons; instead, we should try to understand how they emerged and what the social and political conditions were that allowed for this dominance.[85]

In Fraser's critique of neoliberalism and imperialism, she argues that it is necessary to consider class and status and the associated injustices of maldistribution and misrecognition. With regard to misrecognition, she rejects the notion of Africanisation-as-decolonisation as being too binary, as it is not possible to exclude all Global North knowledge.[86] Fraser's version of transformation is when the structures that underpin social injustice are broken down and rebuilt. In order to do this, Luckett and Shay[87] call for "access to critical theory and reflexive pedagogic practice for both teachers and learners."

This study gives consideration to the macro debate on power and neoliberalism but is primarily concerned with examining the micro-detail of the engagement between students and educators, the relationship between injustice and pedagogy, and how this relates to open textbook production.

Methodology

This chapter presents data derived from a mixed methods research approach which drew insight from two rounds of in-depth interviews (of approximately 1.5 hours each) with five academics who participated in the Digital Open Textbooks for Development (DOT4D) project at UCT.

The design of the interview schedule was informed by the project's conceptual framework, derived from Fraser,[88,89] which had a specific focus on exploring the economic, cultural, and political dimensions of social injustice in South African HE.

The first interview examined authors' motivations for developing open textbooks, their envisioned content development plans in terms of authorship approach and student involvement, as well as envisioned approaches toward publishing, quality assurance, sustainability, and copyright and licensing.

The second interview, on which this chapter is predominantly based, expanded on its focus. Within this interview, we explored authors' goals in terms of their envisioned open textbook development initiatives, the injustices related to race, gender, and culture that occurred within their classroom contexts, and the different ways in which they endeavoured to address these injustices, their conceptions of curriculum transformation and decolonisation, and the manner in which they situated their open textbook production work in relation to broader global power dynamics and epistemic positioning.

The UCT educators selected for this interview process were all aspiring open textbook authors, who in the course of their teaching careers engaged in varying degrees of OER (including open textbooks) production and open education practice. They were selected as study participants based on disciplinary spread, level of academic expertise, and gender. These factors are, however, not explored in this study.

The five interview participants for this study comprised an associate professor (identified as OTA1), three senior lecturers (OTA2, OTA3, and OTA4), and a head tutor (OTA5).

The data analysis process involved collating the responses from transcriptions of the second interview into an Excel spreadsheet. In this process, the interview questions and the corresponding responses from the interviews were mapped in a spreadsheet. Subsequently, key themes were identified from the interview questions, namely, motivations to produce open textbooks, social injustice in the classroom, educators' understandings of curriculum transformation and decolonisation, and power dynamics related to epistemic positioning in the classroom. Finally, we identified interview responses that were related to or addressed these particular themes and filtered out key insights that spoke to the varying social injustices experienced within the classroom, interpretations of curriculum transformation and decolonisation, as well as the varied practices employed by educators in their responses.

Findings

In this section, we present five UCT open textbook authors' intuitive pedagogical practices as a means to address social injustice in the classroom, their understandings of power dynamics in relation to open textbook production, and the ways in which they extend their pedagogical practice into open textbook production as a means to address social injustices.

Addressing Injustice Through Care and Attention to Difference: Intuitive Pedagogical Practices as a Means to Address Social (In)Justice

In the course of the interview process, the authors identified a series of complex and interrelated social injustices that manifested in their classrooms, including
- lack of access to relevant, affordable teaching and learning materials;
- disparity in educational background, resulting in a lack of digital literacy and a skills gap between secondary and tertiary education;
- scheduling of late classes excluding students who have to travel far distances;
- second- or third-language English speakers receiving instruction in English;
- social dynamics, self-confidence or lack of confidence (personality traits);
- social stress such as anxiety and depression; and
- cultural dynamics perpetuating white, patriarchal, heteronormative ideals and the exclusion of historically marginalised voices.

The open textbook authors in this study displayed a thoughtful, sensitised awareness of misrepresentation, misrecognition, and misrepresentation in the classroom, which correlated with a high level of care in their pedagogical practice.

OTA2 believed that students could not optimally engage if they were stressed and therefore focused on "helping people calm down" within the classroom setting. In addition to this, she worked on helping her students "see each other as human" as a way to eliminate racial and gender-related tensions. She explicitly incorporated error and used failure as part of her teaching strategy, as she believed that acknowledging error helped to promote a more human approach in which both lecturer and students were allowed to make mistakes. This human-focused, "culture of care" approach was echoed by all the other open textbook authors in this study.

OTA1 included paying attention to her students' mental health as part of her teaching practice as a way of understanding the ways in which her students were navigating the myriad pressures they were experiencing in their lives. Her teaching practice involved facilitating group discussions to surface the different perspectives and voices of her students.

OTA5's teaching strategy centred around keeping his interactions with students in the classroom as informal as possible so that they could talk openly about anything, as a way to connect with students on both an academic level and a personal level. He also felt that building and boosting the confidence of the students in his class was a key part of his role and that students did not work as well if they lacked confidence.

As an extension of her culture of care, OTA3's teaching practice involved what she referred to as "social engineering" through group work in order to encourage peer learning. She attempted to mitigate the different levels of literacy in her classroom through "accepting ...different levels of offerings" in the kinds of work that her students produced.

An appreciation for diversity also underpinned OTA4's teaching practice, which was grounded in his need to be more conscious of the social and cultural differences between students and lecturers. In this sense, his entire pedagogical approach was based on prioritising the student in the provision of education and seeing the student as "a client that needs to be better served."

Curriculum Transformation and Decolonisation

The open textbook authors' reflections on curriculum transformation and decolonisation revealed insights into some of the processes and practices they felt they needed to undertake in order to address transformation and power dynamics in the classroom.

Curriculum Transformation

For OTA3, curriculum transformation centred around the notion of pedagogical "responsiveness" in which teaching practices would be "responding to the cohort ...and the diversity of the students" through various kinds of culturally appropriate material and inclusive pedagogical practices. OTA2 described curriculum transformation as making content accessible with regards to the curriculum and exposing "the hidden curriculum" in the discipline through engaging with the language, the thinking, and the methods within the subject. OTA2 felt her open textbook chapters were exploring new territory but that her colleagues did not want to change their way of working with existing prescribed textbooks.

OTA1's understanding of curriculum transformation prioritised "contextuali[sing] what we teach" in ways that are applicable to the African context. This was similar to OTA5's understanding of curriculum transformation as a means to support prioritisation of the local context. OTA4 echoed these sentiments, defining curriculum transformation as "loosening up the tight grip of European and American North points of view" in order to prioritise the wide range of issues and experiences.

DECOLONISATION

The open textbook authors' understandings of decolonisation were generally an extension of their conceptualisation of curriculum transformation and indicated how they were grappling with how to operationalise both concepts.

OTA2 described decolonisation as establishing a greater level of accessibility to knowledge (through developing local content, improved assessments, and supportive structures) in order to enable students to engage with content in more meaningful ways. She also viewed decolonisation as part of creating teaching practices within the classroom that "[make] everybody feel like a valid human." Similarly, OTA5's understanding of decolonisation centred around equitable access, particularly in the context of breaking away from dominant practices in teaching and learning in order to put everyone on an even footing and level the playing field for all students.

OTA3 highlighted that decolonisation was about acknowledging and understanding what colonisation means and finding a way to empower students to engage with the concepts and legacy of colonialism instead of "pretending it's not there." She thoughtfully reflected that her textbook could be seen as reinforcing colonialism and that one of the primary challenges in contributing to the decolonial agenda through her textbook was ensuring that the methods and the approaches to her work were carefully and explicitly defined. As such, she described decolonisation as the primary aspiration of her open textbook and stated that "if it doesn't do that then we will withdraw it." Aware of the tensions within her work, in the course of their open textbook development process,

OTA3 and her team decided to "just keep quiet about what [they were] doing for a while" in order to internally make sense of the decolonising process.

OTA1 shared similar sentiments about decolonisation, with a particular focus on the realities of the developing world, whereby "instead of following in the footsteps of what has been done already, we try and re-imagine where we are and can improve on practices and processes …in a way that is good for us." OTA1 also had the view that "work has to be rooted in Africa." Lastly, OTA4's understanding of decolonisation emphasised acknowledging the disparities between lecturers and students, stating that "your teaching body should reflect your student body" and achieving this change required the removal of "people like [him]," the white male lecturer, whose presence currently dominated the teaching body in his discipline.

SENSE OF POWERLESSNESS TO ADDRESS CURRICULUM TRANSFORMATION AND DECOLONISATION

A number of the open textbook authors expressed a sense of powerlessness in terms of being able to effectively respond to the injustices and transformation imperatives they witnessed in their classrooms and to respond effectively to decolonisation imperatives.

They mentioned the practical circumstances they and their students need to overcome. OTA3 reported that the size of her class often presented constraints in terms of time and capacity, which left her unsure about how to effectively respond to the issues that would arise in her classroom. Similarly, OTA2 noted that although she was aware of the challenge of academic literacy in her classroom, she did not know how to go about solving it—this despite her participation in institutional initiatives investigating the issue.

The authors also spoke of the emotional challenges that went beyond their academic roles. OTA5 reported experiencing challenges in finding ways to boost the confidence and comfort levels of his students in the classroom as well as their ability to actively engage, explaining, "I literally don't know, because it's hard. It's human behaviour." OTA1 shared how, in her attempts to assist her students in their struggles with mental health and academic demands, she assumed roles that were outside of her capacity as a lecturer, which tested the boundaries of her work, stating that "it's a challenge to put yourself in that space, in that guidance space, in that advisory role…. And sometimes I may get into trouble."

In trying to understand the open textbook authors' positionality in terms of the realities they witnessed in their classrooms, they were asked whether they felt complicit in perpetuating particular injustices in the classroom. Four of the five open textbook authors interviewed said that they did feel complicit. OTA2 responded with caution and said that, due to her whiteness, there were "things that I just don't see" and that she felt complicit "by just declaring that something was a 'textbook' that students needed." OTA3 also felt that she was complicit, in that she had not thought about the issue of language or considered translating her work, which she viewed as an injustice in the classroom. OTA5 saw himself as unintentionally complicit in perpetuating the skills gap within the classroom through focusing on students who were more comfortable with him.

At least one author proposed radical action. OTA4 expressed that by merely still assuming his role as lecturer at the university, he was perpetuating the injustices around diversity and representation that he was trying to address through his work. He (OTA4) lamented that he felt unable to address the social justice issues in his classroom and that the only way to affect change with regard to these injustices was through radical action, such as leaving the university as "a point of protest, a point of trying to encourage change." He felt that one of the biggest challenges in addressing injustice was that "people don't have a voice outside of these very slow-moving structured wheels… [and] those slow-turning wheels swallow all attempts at change."

The Power of the Open Textbook: Extending Intuitive Pedagogical Practice into Open Textbook Production to Address Injustice

The awareness of social injustice in the classroom combined with the open textbook authors' intuitive pedagogical approaches extended into their open textbook practice and provided a means through which they felt they could try to address social injustice in the classroom. Within this context, the practices that the authors employed in their pedagogical approaches informed their perceptions of what the affordances of their open textbooks would be. These perceived affordances included the ability of the open textbook to serve as a platform or mechanism through which to incorporate multiple voices and politically challenge the status quo, shift power dynamics and address issues of relevance, and counter existing publishing models.

INCORPORATION OF MULTIPLE VOICES AND CHALLENGING THE STATUS QUO

OTA3's ambition was to create a resource that would reflect the realities of the Global South and challenge the dominance of the Global North in her field in ways that would allow students to be able to relate to the discipline. With this ambition, what concerned her the most was how decisions would be made with regards to the content in her open textbook, as she was attempting to challenge the authority of particular voices. In order to support these ambitions, she adopted a more thoughtful and critical approach to the development of the textbook that would include the work of her students as a means to empower them and make the textbook more applicable.

Through OTA4's open textbook development process, he believed that he was contributing to the shift in power dynamics by actively moving away from having an elitist voice in his content to including different voices that contribute lived experiences and realities. He believed that his open textbook would "speak to the local" and that the diversity of inputs from different voices (including students) would reveal varied ways of explaining and approaching his subject.

OTA2's open textbook process was motivated by her ambition to "train students to engage with academic literature," as her main concern in her teaching was that students were not comfortable in their reading of academic texts because of their varied educational backgrounds. She envisioned her open textbook as a "living document" for students that could be changed and corrected to suit and facilitate their learning. As such, the open textbook and the open movement were sources of empowerment for her.

OTA1's work was motivated by her aspirations to create awareness and facilitate the transfer of knowledge within her discipline in ways that were accessible to students and to industry. As part of her process, she drew on the insights gained from class discussions with her students to develop content not only for her OER but also for her growing body of research in her field.

The main concern behind OTA5's work was the fact that the current textbook in use was in American measurement standards and did not reflect local contexts or the requirements of his field of study in the South African context. As such, his ambition was to create a resource that students could easily use and that aligned with the local measurement standards and requirements of the course. Within his process, OTA5 paid careful attention to student feedback through self-administered course feedback surveys that he conducted in his class in order to make sure that he continued to meet the needs of his students.

SHIFTING POWER DYNAMICS AND ADDRESSING RELEVANCE

OTA3 used her open textbook development process to bring in female and black voices in a very direct attempt at shifting existing power dynamics, with the hope that this would empower students to have a voice, contribute to the canon in their field, and realise the "power in publication." She also expressed how she was using the open textbook as a process through which to change her approach to her course and include "persons' own embodied experience" and their lived realities.

OTA4's work was motivated by the need to address issues around the relevance of the content that was being taught in his discipline. This was driven by his concern that all texts that were currently being used were predominantly oriented around the European and American context and therefore neglected local experiences and practices. He believed that in addition to paying attention to the content of the texts that students were engaging with, there needed to also be a considered prioritisation of the different ways in which content could be delivered in formats that were accessible and appropriate.

OTA1's view was that the content that she produced needed to be "rooted in Africa," and she felt that open education practice gave her the necessary platform through which to engage her students in localised content production. She also extended her teaching focus to investigating local practices, local businesses, and local processes (as well as her students' interpretations of these factors) into her textbook development approach.

OTA5 highlighted that "it's all about the students' will for themselves to engage," calling for the active participation of students in curriculum articulation through the use of open textbooks. He believed that his open textbook would provide students with both access and the confidence to be able to navigate the course and that it would be a great leveler in terms of students' ability to engage with the work presented.

CHALLENGING PUBLISHING MODELS

OTA3 expressed that the development of her open textbook was a means through which she could subvert the power dynamics and authority of traditional publishers. She also believed that her open textbook development process could play in mitigating power dynamics between herself and her students by making content accessible and allowing equal student involvement in the creation of content "[from] those that are struggling and the ones that are flying."

OTA4 echoed OTA3's sentiments around power dynamics related to textbook production and expressed that "publishers are the problem." He did, however, believe that there was some movement away from the powerful grip of publisher hegemony toward the side of knowledge consumers and that a power shift was being realised through the open education movement.

OTA2 also shared the ambition of using her open textbook development process to contribute toward a shift in power dynamics related to open textbook use and felt that she could do so by allowing things to be done differently without the constraints of publishers. She felt that her open textbook could contribute to a deeper understanding of the discipline and enable her students to better engage with the language, thinking, and methods of her subject, thereby allowing her students to better relate to the knowledge presented and providing a means through which to address disparity in the classroom. While she felt strongly that "quality information on topics needs to be free" in order to shift existing global power dynamics, she also highlighted how the ambition of increased access is compromised by the power imbalance that the predominance of English bears on the production of knowledge in her field.

OTA1 stated that there have been global power dynamics in place in the past but felt that with the emergence of OER, the dominant power in control, particularly in publishing, "has all been broken down." As such, voices that would not have been heard before were now surfacing, allowing different narratives to be shared and acknowledged. With this, OTA1 saw her open textbook development process as a way of contributing to the disruption of global power dynamics around knowledge dissemination.

OTA5 expressed that he didn't feel well-versed in understanding the broader dynamics that operated within his field in relation to publisher hegemony, but he felt that there was a constant global movement of information in his discipline and that there wasn't a sense of "specific knowledge reserved for [a] certain type of people," as innovation was a public good that everyone, particularly students, needed to be exposed to. He explained that, although publishers shaped the kinds of innovations being shared, his work with his open textbook was about creating access to knowledge and resources and contextualising global innovations to meet local standards and the needs of our local industries.

Discussion

The reflections of the open textbook authors in this study illustrate the intuitive pedagogy they employ in response to classroom injustices and their visions of just collaborative content creation approaches in response to these injustices. These authors have an agile approach to teaching and have a deep sense of responsibility to their students as human beings. The relationship between pedagogical practice and content appears to be fluid, as does their approach toward content creation.

In line with this approach, the open textbook authors in this study interpret curriculum transformation in the context of being responsive and context-focused. They aim to loosen the grip of Eurocentrism on local knowledge sharing and production, an approach deemed appropriate as a means to acknowledge local contributions to knowledge.[90] Decolonial principles inform their transformation of content; for example, authors placed emphasis on accessibility and a leveling out or balance of epistemic contributions so that students and lecturers were all represented. These authors critically examined their own roles and cautioned that there were dangers in overlooking or pretending that injustices were "solved" and no longer existed.

In response to these curriculum transformation and decolonial imperatives, the authors in this study were motivated to produce open textbooks. They recognised that making their teaching content localised, relevant, and accessible was an essential pathway to redress. Researchers have argued for a careful balance between "Africanisation as decolonisation" (i.e., the outright rejection of Western scholarship) and the critique of Western canons with regard to how these intersect with recent, local scholarship.[91,92] Fraser rejects the idea of binaries and finds the process of purifying and removing everything Western "unhelpful."[93]

Injustices are visible to these educators on a daily basis. Economic injustices include lack of access to teaching and learning materials due to the prohibitive cost of textbooks, disparity in educational background resulting in skills gaps between secondary and tertiary education, and late classes that poorer students struggle to attend as they have to travel long distances to get home. These examples of economic maldistribution[94] translate into students failing or leaving HE.[95] While open textbooks provide free access to resources, these economic barriers are difficult to overcome unless lecturers and better-resourced peers raise awareness of these injustices.[96]

A number of cultural and political injustices are also visible in the classroom in various forms of misrecognition and misrepresentation.[97] Students at UCT arrive with second- or third-language English proficiency and are expected to grasp disciplinary knowledge. They are also expected to deal with a range of social and mental health challenges as well as cultural dynamics perpetuating the current neoliberal regime. Despite having an opportunity to enter the HE arena, students seemed to struggle with confidence and speaking in class. In one example, this proved to be related to race, in that black students struggled to find a voice in the classroom. While open textbooks provide affordances to start to address some of these cultural and political injustices, such as through translation of definitions and texts into other languages,[98,99] true transformation requires deeper structural intervention.

The open textbook authors in this study felt powerless to find ways to solve these problems, a situation compounded by the additional constraint of large class sizes. Two authors also mentioned that their "whiteness" made them feel complicit. One intensely frustrated author felt they were perpetuating the injustice of the lack of representation in the teaching body and subsequently left the university. All of the open textbook authors in this study recognised political misrepresentation and their participation in unjust social arrangements and responded to these injustices through intuitive pedagogical approaches, advancing *just* ways of teaching and *just* ways of selecting and producing content in their open textbooks.

Classroom practices included an ambition that all students participate on an equal footing as far as possible, as the open textbook authors recognised principles of "equal moral worth."[100] They used techniques of mindfulness to help students "calm down" and employed compassion to mitigate the different abilities of students. They consciously prioritised students' needs and made an effort to connect with them. This pedagogy represents cultural recognition "in which people's attributes and their ways of being in, understanding, and acting upon the world are valued."[101]

In the context of this study, open textbook development extends the intuitive pedagogical approach toward achieving social justice in the classroom, moving beyond affirmation toward transformation in the economic sense, in that the open textbook is available free of charge and is easily accessible, enabling economic redistribution. The deeper societal maldistribution, misrecognition, and misrepresentation implicit in the traditional use of textbooks and other teaching and learning materials in South African HE requires deeper intervention. However, the open textbook is one achievable, recommended step toward redress.

The open textbook is especially powerful in that it provides the affordance for students to participate in their own academic journeys. The open textbook development process also allows the educator to carefully consider who the authoring entity is and what their own role is in the authoring process. It allows for the inclusion of student voice, thereby empowering students. This process is potentially the beginning of the overturning of Western neoliberal epistemic hegemony deemed necessary in South African HE.[102] The open textbook authors refer to the open textbook as an opportunity for students to author their own experiences resulting in a resource that they can relate to.

As a "living" document, open textbooks empower the author, giving them a platform to showcase their work and build the resource through many iterations. Classroom insights can be included in the textbook, and the open textbook gives the content creators power in the publishing and dissemination process, subverting traditional publisher hegemony over which voices are traditionally represented. Holding power does however come with risks. Being "open" exposes one's work. These authors are exploring new territory, changing practice, and taking risks in the process.

Social justice and its allied forces of curriculum transformation and decolonisation have been thoughtfully considered by these educators and have become entrenched in their pedagogical practice and open textbook development processes. Intuitive pedagogy comes naturally to these passionate educators and is part of their practice. These covert attempts to address historic and current injustices through open textbooks constitute a change in pedagogical practice and a move away from traditional ways of teaching and learning.

Conclusion

As a way forward to critiquing and understanding the role of OER (specifically open textbooks) in addressing social injustice, Fraser maintains it is necessary to "complicate, deepen, and enrich" in order to explain the nexus of social justice and the decolonial debate in HE.[103] This is what we have attempted in this chapter.

This chapter focuses on the micro-level rather than on the systemic issues that might provide a deeper understanding of the causal mechanisms that form the underlying framing of injustice. We do not feel that open textbooks have managed to "[resolve] the economic and socio-political challenges facing universities and its learners."[104] The open textbook does, however, enable authors to take discernable steps toward transforming the curriculum. We have attempted to give the reader a snapshot into the classroom and to elucidate the complex arenas these open textbook authors negotiate in their classroom contexts.

Can the process of open textbook development reframe economic maldistribution, cultural misrecognition, and political representation? Yes, in the classrooms of these open textbook authors, open textbook creation provides the opportunity to engage with multiple voices. In this sense, open textbooks allow for cultural recognition and political representation not previously witnessed in HE. Within these classrooms, there is more than an affirmative or ameliorative change. Do open textbooks address underlying structures of dominance and subordination? Only if they are created and used across the institution and potentially across South Africa in order to embrace critical reflexivity and pluralism valuing previously excluded knowledge and legitimising indigenous resources. We can't make an argument that through these tactics there is a "dismantling (of) institutional obstacles"[105] or root causes of systemic injustice that underlie the pursuit of participatory parity present in South African HE. The inclusion of students in the authoring, editing, and evaluation of aspects of these open textbooks is a move toward out-flanking traditional ways of working. Is this student representation just and fair? Partially, but we still have a way to go before representation includes equal voice in decision-making.

Looking ahead toward a transformative response to social injustice, the valiant efforts in some classrooms need to extend across the institution and across institutions. Institutional support in the form of open textbook awards, recognising open education work in promotion criteria, empowering academics through intellectual property rights and ownership, and sourcing funding to support the work of educators and students involved in open textbook production are crucial for transformation.

Acknowledgment

The authors are grateful to Cheryl Hodgkinson-Williams for her close reading of and suggested refinements to this chapter.

Endnotes

1. Malcolm Brown et al., *Educause Horizon Report Teaching and Learning Edition* (Louisville, CO: EDUCAUSE, 2020), https://www.learntechlib.org/p/215670/.
2. Martin Weller, *The Battle for Open: How Openness Won and Why It Doesn't Feel Like Victory* (London: Ubiquity Press, 2014), 202, http://oro.open.ac.uk/44363/.
3. Nicole Allen, "Holding the Line on Open in an Evolving Landscape" (presentation, OER19 Conference, Galway Ireland, November 4, 2019), 2019, https://www.slideshare.net/txtbks/holding-the-line-on-open-in-an-evolving-landscape.
4. Rajiv Jhangiani, "For-profit, faux-pen, and critical conversations about the future of learning materials," *Rajiv Jhangiani, Ph.D.* (blog), October 15, 2019, https://thatpsychprof.com/for-profit-faux-pen-and-critical-conversations/.
5. Robert Farrow, "Open Education and Critical Pedagogy," *Learning, Media and Technology* 42 (2017): 130–46.
6. Laura Czerniewicz, "Challenging Open Education," 30th Annual Conference of the Asian Association of Open Universities, Manila, Philippines, October 26, 2016, 2016. http://hdl.handle.net/11427/24686.
7. *Students' Access to and Use of Learning Materials: Survey Report 2020*, Department of Higher Education and Training (DHET), 2020, 7, Pretoria: Government Printer.
8. John Mendy and Maria Madiope, "Curriculum Transformation: A Case in South Africa," *Perspectives in Education* 38 (2020), https://doi.org/10.18820/2519593X/pie.v38.i2.01.
9. Savo Heleta, "Decolonisation of Higher Education: Dismantling Epistemic Violence and Eurocentrism in South Africa," *Transformation in Higher Education* 1, no.1 (2016), http://dx.doi.org/10.4102/the.v1i1.9.
10. Elizabeth Walton, "Decolonising (Through) Inclusive Education?," *Educational Research for Social Change* 7 (2018): 31–45, http://www.scielo.org.za/pdf/ersc/v7nspe/04.pdf.
11. Michalinos Zembylas, "Decolonial Possibilities in South African Higher Education: Reconfiguring Humanising Pedagogies as/with Decolonising Pedagogies," *South African Journal of Education* 38, no. 4 (2018), https://files.eric.ed.gov/fulltext/EJ1204069.pdf.
12. Tamara Shefer, Lindsey Clowes, and Sisa Ngabaza, "Student Experience: A Participatory Parity Lens on Social (In)justice in Higher Education," in *Nancy Fraser and Participatory Parity: Reframing Social Justice in South African Higher Education*, ed. Vivienne Bozalek, Dorothee Hölscher and Michalinos Zembylas, Routledge Research in Education Policy and Politics Series (Abingdon: Routledge, 2020), 63–76.
13. "UCT Libraries' new platform supports publishing of African-centric research," *University of Cape Town News* (January 13, 2021), https://www.news.uct.ac.za/article/-2021-01-13-uct-libraries-new-platform-supports-publishing-of-african-centric-research.
14. Carla Bernado, "Decolonisation in the context of Vision 2030," *University of Cape Town News* (September 28, 2020), https://www.news.uct.ac.za/article/-2020-09-28-decolonisation-in-the-context-of-vision-2030.

15. *UCT Curriculum Change Framework*, Curriculum Change Working Group, Cape Town: University of Cape Town, 2018, https://www.news.uct.ac.za/images/userfiles/downloads/media/UCT-Curriculum-Change-Framework.pdf.
16. Victoria I. Marín, Bárbara de Benito Crosetti, and Antonia Darder, "Technology-Enhanced Learning for Student Agency in Higher Education: A Systematic Literature Review," *IxD&A* 45 (2020), 15–49, http://www.mifav.uniroma2.it/inevent/events/idea2010/doc/45_1.pdf.
17. Tim Unwin, et al., "Involving Marginalised Young People in the Design of Their Own Education," in *Education for the Most Marginalised Post-COVID-19: Guidance for Governments on the Use of Digital Technologies in Education*, report by UNESCO & EdTech Hub, 2020, https://edtechhub.org/education-for-the-most-marginalised-post-covid-19/.
18. Anne Edwards, "Cultural-Historical Approaches to Teaching and Learning in Higher Education: Teaching to Support Student Agency," in *Theorising Learning to Teach in Higher Education*, ed. Brenda Leibowitz, Vivienne Bozalek, and Peter Kahn (London: Routledge, 2017), 124.
19. Sarah Stein, Simon Hart, Phillipa Keaney, and Richard White, "Student Views on the Cost of and Access to Textbooks: An Investigation at University of Otago (New Zealand)," *Open Praxis* 9, no. 4 (2017): 403–09, https://files.eric.ed.gov/fulltext/EJ1165496.pdf.
20. Glenda Cox, Bianca Masuku, and Michelle Willmers, "Open Textbooks and Social Justice: Open Educational Practices to Address Economic, Cultural and Political Injustice at the University of Cape Town," *Journal of Interactive Media in Education* 1, no. 2 (2020): 1–10, https://open.uct.ac.za/handle/11427/31887.
21. Amy T. Nusbaum, "Who Gets to Wield Academic Mjolnir? On Worthiness, Knowledge Curation, and Using the Power of the People to Diversify OER," *Journal of Interactive Media in Education* 1, no. 4 (2020): 1–9, https://jime.open.ac.uk/articles/10.5334/jime.559/print/.
22. Michael Paskevicius and Valerie Irvine, "Practicalities of Implementing Open Pedagogy in Higher Education," *Smart Learning Environments* 6, no. 23 (2019), https://doi.org/10.1186/s40561-019-0110-5.
23. Lina Markauskaite and Peter Goodyear, "Tapping into the Mental Resources of Teachers' Working Knowledge: Insights into the Generative Power of Intuitive Pedagogy," *Learning Culture and Social Interaction* 3, no. 4. (2014): 237.
24. Farrow, "Open Education and Critical Pedagogy."
25. Ibid., 2.
26. Marta Sinclair, "An Integrated Framework of Intuition," in *Handbook of Intuition Research*, ed. Marta Sinclair (Cheltenham, Edward Elgar, 2011), 3–17.
27. Markauskaite and Goodyear, *Tapping into the Mental Resources*.
28. Pär Ahlbom, "Welcome to Intuitive Pedagogy," Intuitive Pedagogy, https://intuitive-pedagogy.com/.
29. Elizabeth B. Moje, "Developing Socially Just Subject-Matter Instruction: A Review of the Literature on Disciplinary Literacy Teaching," *Review of Research in Education* 31, no. 1 (2007): 1–44, https://eric.ed.gov/?id=EJ782450.
30. Cox, Masuku, and Willmers, *Open Textbooks and Social Justice*.
31. Robin DeRosa and Scott Robison, "Pedagogy, Technology, and the Example of Open Educational Resources," *EDUCAUSE Review* (2015), https://er.educause.edu/articles/2015/11/pedagogy-technology-and-the-example-of-open-educational-resources.
32. George Veletsianos, "Open Educational Resources: Expanding Equity or Reflecting and Furthering Inequities?," *Educational Technology Research and Development* (2020), https://doi.org/10.1007/s11423-020-09840-y.
33. Czerniewicz, "Challenging Open Education."
34. Nancy Fraser, "Reframing Justice in a Globalizing World," *New Left Review* 36 (2005): 69–88, https://newleftreview.org/II/36/nancy-fraser-reframing-justice-in-a-globalizing-world.
35. Nancy Fraser, "Feminism, Capitalism and the Cunning of History," *New Left Review* 56 (2009): 97–117, https://newleftreview.org/II/56/nancy-fraser-feminism-capitalism-and-the-cunning-of-history.

36. "Imperialism: Is it Still a Relevant Concept?," The New School for Social Research, May 10, 2017, https://www.youtube.com/watch?v=nRvcGP1ALvI.
37. Dorothee Hölscher and Vivienne Bozalek, "Nancy Fraser's Work and Its Relevance to Higher Education," in *Nancy Fraser and Participatory Parity: Reframing Social Justice in South African Higher Education*, ed. Vivienne Bozalek, Dorothee Hölscher, and Michalinos Zembylas (London: Routledge, 2020), 3–19.
38. Audrey Watters, "From 'Open' to Justice" (keynote presentation, OpenCon 2014), 2014, http://hackeducation.com/2014/11/16/from-open-to-justice.
39. Watters, "From 'Open' to Justice."
40. Sarah R. Lambert, "Changing Our (Dis)course: A Distinctive Social Justice Aligned Definition of Open Education," *Journal of Learning for Development* 5, no. 3 (2018), http://hdl.handle.net/11599/3101.
41. Nusbaum, "Who Gets to Wield Academic Mjolnir?"
42. Kathy Luckett and Suellen Shay, "Reframing the Curriculum: A Transformative Approach," *Critical Studies in Education* (2017), https://doi.org/10.1080/17508487.2017.1356341.
43. Fraser, "Reframing Justice in a Globalizing World."
44. Taskeen Adam, "Between Social Justice and Decolonisation: Exploring South African MOOC Designers' Conceptualisations and Approaches to Addressing Injustices," *Journal of Interactive Media in Education* 1, no. 7 (2020): 1–11, https://doi.org/10.5334/jime.557.
45. Maha Bali, Catherine Cronin, and Rajiv S. Jhangiani, "Framing Open Educational Practices from a Social Justice Perspective," *Journal of Interactive Media in Education* 1, no. 10 (2020), https://doi.org/10.5334/jime.565.
46. Cox, Masuku, and Willmers, "Open Textbooks and Social Justice."
47. Jonathan Funk and Kathy Guthadjaka, "Indigenous Authorship on Open and Digital Platforms: Social Justice Processes and Potential," *Journal of Interactive Media in Education* 1, no. 6 (2020), accessed at https://doi.org/10.5334/jime.560.
48. Kadir Karakaya and Ozlem Karakaya, "Framing the Role of English in OER from a Social Justice Perspective: A Critical Lens on the (Dis)empowerment of Non-English Speaking Communities," *Asian Journal of Distance Education* 15, no. 2 (2020): 175–90, https://doi.org/10.5281/zenodo.4319616.
49. Cheryl Hodgkinson-Williams and Henry Trotter, "A Social Justice Framework for Understanding Open Educational Resources and Practices in the Global South," *Journal of Learning for Development* 5, no. 3 (2018), https://jl4d.org/index.php/ejl4d/article/view/312.
50. Fraser, "Reframing Justice in a Globalizing World."
51. Fraser, "Feminism, Capitalism and the Cunning of History."
52. Ibid., 16.
53. Fraser, "Reframing Justice in a Globalizing World," 282.
54. Hölscher and Bozalek, "Nancy Fraser's Work," 16
55. Luckett and Shay, "Reframing the Curriculum," 6.
56. Karakaya and Karakaya, "Framing the Role."
57. Hodgkinson-Williams and Trotter, "A Social Justice Framework," 2–7.
58. Lambert, "Changing Our (Dis)course."
59. Karakaya and Karakaya, "Framing the Role."
60. Cox, Masuku, and Willmers, "Open Textbooks and Social Justice."
61. Nusbaum, "Who Gets to Wield Academic Mjolnir?"
62. Veletsianos, "Open Educational Resources."
63. Brenda Leibowitz and Vivienne Bozalek, "The Scholarship of Teaching and Learning from a Social Justice Perspective," *Teaching in Higher Education* 21, no. 2 (2016): 109–22.
64. Elizabeth de Kadt, "Promoting Social Justice in Teaching and Learning in Higher Education Through Professional Development," *Teaching in Higher Education* (2019), https://doi.org/10.1080/13562517.2019.1617685.

65. Vivienne Bozalek, Dorothee Hölscher, and Michalinos Zembylas, eds. *Nancy Fraser and Participatory Parity: Reframing Social Justice in South African Higher Education* (London: Routledge, 2020).
66. James Garroway and Janine Lange, "Participatory Parity in South African Extended Curriculum Programmes," in *Nancy Fraser and Participatory Parity: Reframing Social Justice in South African Higher Education*, ed. Vivienne Bozalek, Dorothee Hölscher and Michalinos Zembylas (London: Routledge, 2020), 130.
67. Garroway and Lange, "Participatory Parity."
68. Ibid.
69. Bozalek, Hölscher and Zembylas, *Nancy Fraser and Participatory Parity*.
70. Hölscher and Bozalek, "Nancy Fraser's Work," 4.
71. Ronelle Carolissen, "Becoming a Community (Educational) Psychologist: Enablements and Constraints of Participatory Parity In Student Educational Journeys," in *Nancy Fraser and Participatory Parity: Reframing Social Justice in South African Higher Education*, ed. Vivienne Bozalek, Dorothee Hölscher and Michalinos Zembylas (London: Routledge, 2020), 90.
72. Carolissen, "Becoming a Community (Educational) Psychologist."
73. Susan Gredley, "When It Rains [Our House] Rains Too: Exploring South Africa Students' Narratives of Maldistribution," in *Nancy Fraser and Participatory Parity: Reframing Social Justice in South African Higher Education*, ed. Vivienne Bozalek, Dorothee and Michalinos Zembylas (London: Routledge, 2020), 94–110.
74. Gredley, "When It Rains."
75. Wally Morrow, *Learning to Teach in South Africa* (Pretoria: Human Sciences Research Council, 2007), https://www.hsrcpress.ac.za/books/learning-to-teach-in-south-africa.
76. Johan Muller, "Every Picture Tells A Story: Epistemological Access and Knowledge. *Education as Change* 18, no. 2. (2015): 190, https://www.tandfonline.com/doi/abs/10.1080/16823206.2014.932256.
77. Hölscher and Bozalek, "Nancy Fraser's Work."
78. Eve Tuck and Wayne K. Yang, "Decolonisation is Not a Metaphor," *Decolonisation: Indigeneity, Education & Society* 1, no. 1 (2012): 1–40.
79. Dorothee Hölscher, Michalinos Zembylas, and Vivienne Bozalek, "Neoliberalism, Coloniality and Nancy Fraser's Contribution to the Decolonisation Debate in South African Higher Education: Concluding Thoughts," in *Nancy Fraser and Participatory Parity: Reframing Social Justice in South African Higher Education*, ed. Vivienne Bozalek, Dorothee Hölscher and Michalinos Zembylas (London: Routledge, 2020), 145.
80. Bettina Gruber and Josefine Scherling, "The Relevance of Unmasking Neoliberal Narratives for a Decolonized Human Rights and Peace Education," *International Journal of Human Rights Education* 4(1), 3 (2020), https://repository.usfca.edu/ijhre/vol4/iss1/3/.
81. Hölscher, Zembylas and Bozalek, "Neoliberalism," 145.
82. Ibid., 148.
83. Ibid.
84. Achille Mbembe in Hölscher, Zembylas and Bozalek, "Neoliberalism," 149.
85. Luckett and Shay, "Reframing the Curriculum."
86. Nancy Fraser and Rahel Jaeggi, *Capitalism: A Conversation in Critical Theory* (Cambridge: Polity Press, 2018), 189.
87. Luckett and Shay, "Reframing the Curriculum," 12.
88. Fraser, "Reframing Justice in a Globalizing World."
89. Fraser, "Feminism, Capitalism and the Cunning of History."
90. Hölscher, Zembylas and Bozalek, "Neoliberalism."
91. Achille Mbembe, "Decolonising the University: New Directions," *Arts & Humanities in Higher Education* 15, no. 1 (2016): 29.
92. Luckett and Shay, "Reframing the Curriculum."
93. Fraser and Jaeggi, *Capitalism*, 189.
94. Fraser, "Reframing Justice in a Globalizing World."

95. Nusbaum, "Who Gets to Wield Academic Mjolnir?"
96. Gredley, "When It Rains."
97. Fraser, "Reframing Justice in a Globalizing World."
98. Hodgkinson-Williams and Trotter, "A Social Justice Framework."
99. Karakaya and Karakaya, "Framing the Role."
100. Fraser, "Feminism, Capitalism and the Cunning of History," 16.
101. Hölscher and Bozalek, "Nancy Fraser's Work," 151.
102. Luckett and Shay, "Reframing the Curriculum."
103. Fraser and Jaeggi, *Capitalism*, 7.
104. Mendy and Madiope, "Curriculum Transformation," 2.
105. Fraser, "Feminism, Capitalism and the Cunning of History," 16.

Bibliography

Adam, Taskeen. "Between Social Justice and Decolonisation: Exploring South African MOOC Designers' Conceptualisations and Approaches to Addressing Injustices." *Journal of Interactive Media in Education* 1, no. 7 (2020): 1–11. https://doi.org/10.5334/jime.557.

Ahlbom, Pär. "Welcome to Intuitive Pedagogy." Intuitive Pedagogy. https://intuitive-pedagogy.com/.

Allen, Nicole. "Holding the Line on Open in an Evolving Landscape." Presented at OER19 Conference, Galway Ireland, November 4, 2019. 2019. https://www.slideshare.net/txtbks/holding-the-line-on-open-in-an-evolving-landscape.

Bali, Maha, Catherine Cronin, and Rajiv S. Jhangiani. "Framing Open Educational Practices from a Social Justice Perspective." *Journal of Interactive Media in Education* 1, no. 10 (2020). https://doi.org/10.5334/jime.565.

Bernado, Carla. "Decolonisation in the context of Vision 2030." *University of Cape Town News* (September 28, 2020). https://www.news.uct.ac.za/article/-2020-09-28-decolonisation-in-the-context-of-vision-2030.

Bozalek, Vivienne, Dorothee Hölscher, and Michalinos Zembylas, eds. *Nancy Fraser and Participatory Parity: Reframing Social Justice in South African Higher Education*. London: Routledge, 2020.

Brown, Malcolm, Mark McCormack, Jamie Reeves, D. Christopher Brook, Susan Grajek, Bryan Alexander, Maha Bali, et al. *Educause Horizon Report Teaching and Learning Edition*. Louisville, CO: EDUCAUSE, 2020, 26. https://www.learntechlib.org/p/215670/.

Cape Town: University of Cape Town. Curriculum Change Working Group. UCT Curriculum Change Framework. 2018. https://www.news.uct.ac.za/images/userfiles/downloads/media/UCT-Curriculum-Change-Framework.pdf.

Carolissen, Ronelle. "Becoming A Community (Educational) Psychologist: Enablements and Constraints of Participatory Parity in Student Educational Journeys." In *Nancy Fraser and Participatory Parity: Reframing Social Justice in South African Higher Education*, edited by Vivienne Bozalek, Dorothee Hölscher and Michalinos Zembylas. London: Routledge, 2020, 77–93.

Cox, Glenda, Bianca Masuku, and Michelle Willmers. "Open Textbooks and Social Justice: Open Educational Practices to Address Economic, Cultural and Political Injustice at the University of Cape Town." *Journal of Interactive Media in Education* 1, no. 2 (2020): 1–10. https://open.uct.ac.za/handle/11427/31887.

Czerniewicz, Laura. "Challenging Open Education." *30th Annual Conference of the Asian Association of Open Universities, Manila, Philippines, 2016-10-26*. 2016. http://hdl.handle.net/11427/24686.

de Kadt, Elizabeth. "Promoting Social Justice in Teaching and Learning in Higher Education Through Professional Development." *Teaching in Higher Education* (2019). https://doi.org/10.1080/13562517.2019.1617685.

DeRosa, Robin, and Scott Robison. "Pedagogy, Technology, and the Example of Open Educational Resources." *EDUCAUSE Review* (2015). https://er.educause.edu/articles/2015/11/pedagogy-technology-and-the-example-of-open-educational-resources.

Department of Higher Education and Training (DHET). *Students' Access to and Use of Learning Materials: Survey Report 2020*. Pretoria: Government Printer, 2020, 7.

Edwards, Anne. "Cultural-historical Approaches to Teaching and Learning in Higher Education: Teaching to Support Student Agency." In *Theorising Learning to Teach in Higher Education*, edited by Brenda Leibowitz, Vivienne Bozalek, and Peter Kahn. London: Routledge, 2017, 124.

Farrow, Robert. "Open Education and Critical Pedagogy." *Learning, Media and Technology* 42 (2017): 130–46.

Funk, Jonathan, and Kathy Guthadjak. "Indigenous Authorship on Open and Digital Platforms: Social Justice Processes and Potential." *Journal of Interactive Media in Education* 1, no. 6 (2020). https://doi.org/10.5334/jime.560.

Fraser, Nancy. "Reframing Justice in a Globalizing World." *New Left Review* 36 (2005): 69–88. https://newleftreview.org/II/36/nancy-fraser-reframing-justice-in-a-globalizing-world.

———. "Feminism, Capitalism and the Cunning of History." *New Left Review* 56 (2009): 97–117. https://newleftreview.org/II/56/nancy-fraser-feminism-capitalism-and-the-cunning-of-history.

Fraser, Nancy, and Rahel Jaeggi. *Capitalism: A Conversation in Critical Theory*. Cambridge: Polity Press, 2018.

Garroway, James, and Janine Lange. "Participatory Parity in South African Extended Curriculum Programmes." In *Nancy Fraser and Participatory Parity: Reframing Social Justice in South African Higher Education*, edited by Vivienne Bozalek, Dorothee Hölscher, and Michalinos Zembylas. London: Routledge, 2020, 128–42.

Gredley, Susan. "When It Rains [Our House] Rains Too: Exploring South Africa Students' Narratives of Maldistribution." In *Nancy Fraser and Participatory Parity: Reframing Social Justice in South African Higher Education*, edited by Vivienne Bozalek, Dorothee Hölscher, and Michalinos Zembylas. London: Routledge, 2020, 94–110.

Gruber, Bettina, and Josefine Scherling. "The Relevance of Unmasking Neoliberal Narratives for a Decolonized Human Rights and Peace Education." *International Journal of Human Rights Education* 4(1), no. 3 (2020). https://repository.usfca.edu/ijhre/vol4/iss1/3/.

Heleta, Savo. "Decolonisation of Higher Education: Dismantling Epistemic Violence and Eurocentrism in South Africa." *Transformation in Higher Education* 1, no.1 (2016). http://dx.doi.org/10.4102/the.v1i1.9.

Hodgkinson-Williams, Cheryl, and Henry Trotter. "A Social Justice Framework for Understanding Open Educational Resources and Practices in the Global South." *Journal of Learning for Development* 5, no. 3 (2018). https://jl4d.org/index.php/ejl4d/article/view/312.

Hölscher, Dorothee, and Vivienne Bozalek. "Nancy Fraser's Work and Its Relevance to Higher Education." In *Nancy Fraser and Participatory Parity: Reframing Social Justice in South African Higher Education*, edited by Vivienne Bozalek, Dorothee Hölscher, and Michalinos Zembylas. London: Routledge, 2020, 3–19.

Hölscher, Dorothee, Michalinos Zembylas, and Vivienne Bozalek. "Neoliberalism, Coloniality and Nancy Fraser's Contribution to the Decolonisation Debate in South African Higher Education: Concluding Thoughts." In *Nancy Fraser and Participatory Parity: Reframing Social Justice in South African Higher Education*, edited by Vivienne Bozalek, Dorothee Hölscher, and Michalinos Zembylas. London: Routledge, 2020, 145–58.

Jhangiani, Rajiv. "For-profit, faux-pen, and critical conversations about the future of learning materials." *Rajiv Jhangiani, Ph.D.* (blog), October 15, 2019. https://thatpsychprof.com/for-profit-faux-pen-and-critical-conversations/.

Karakaya, Kadir, and Ozlem Karakaya. "Framing The Role Of English In OER From A Social Justice Perspective: A Critical Lens On The (Dis)empowerment of Non-English Speaking Communities." *Asian Journal of Distance Education* 15, no. 2 (2020): 175–90. https://doi.org/10.5281/zenodo.4319616.

Lambert, Sarah R. "Changing Our (Dis)course: A Distinctive Social Justice Aligned Definition of Open Education." *Journal of Learning for Development* 5, no.3 (2018). http://hdl.handle.net/11599/3101.

Leibowitz, Brenda, and Vivienne Bozalek. "The Scholarship of Teaching and Learning from a Social Justice Perspective." *Teaching in Higher Education* 21, no. 2 (2016): 109–22.

Luckett, Kathy, and Suellen Shay. "Reframing the Curriculum: A Transformative Approach." *Critical Studies in Education* (2017). https://doi.org/10.1080/17508487.2017.1356341.

Markauskaite, Lina, and Peter Goodyear. "Tapping into the Mental Resources of Teachers' Working Knowledge: Insights into the Generative Power of Intuitive Pedagogy." *Learning Culture and Social Interaction* 3, no. 4 (2014): 237.

Marín, Victoria I., Bárbara de Benito Crosetti, and Antonia Darder. "Technology-Enhanced Learning for Student Agency in Higher Education: A Systematic Literature Review." *IxD&A* (2020), 15–49. http://www.mifav.uniroma2.it/inevent/events/idea2010/doc/45_1.pdf.

Mbembe, Achille. "Decolonising the University: New Directions." *Arts & Humanities in Higher Education* 15, no. 1 (2016): 29.

Mendy, John, and Maria Madiope. "Curriculum Transformation: A Case In South Africa." *Perspectives in Education* 38 (2020). https://doi.org/10.18820/2519593X/pie.v38.i2.01.

Moje, Elizabeth B. "Developing Socially Just Subject-Matter Instruction: A Review of the Literature on Disciplinary Literacy Teaching." *Review of Research in Education* 31, no. 1 (2007): 1–44. https://eric.ed.gov/?id=EJ782450.

Morrow, Wally. *Learning to Teach in South Africa*. Pretoria: Human Sciences Research Council, 2007. https://www.hsrcpress.ac.za/books/learning-to-teach-in-south-africa.

Muller, Johan. "Every Picture Tells a Story: Epistemological Access and Knowledge. *Education as Change* 18, no. 2 (2015). https://www.tandfonline.com/doi/abs/10.1080/16823206.2014.932256.

New School for Social Research, The. "Imperialism: Is it Still a Relevant Concept?" May 10, 2017. https://www.youtube.com/watch?v=nRvcGP1ALvI.

Nusbaum, Amy T. "Who Gets to Wield Academic Mjolnir?: On Worthiness, Knowledge Curation, and Using the Power of the People to Diversify OER." *Journal of Interactive Media in Education* 1, no. 4 (2020): 1–9. https://jime.open.ac.uk/articles/10.5334/jime.559/print/.

Paskevicius, Michael, and Valerie Irvine. "Practicalities of Implementing Open Pedagogy in Higher Education." *Smart Learning Environments* 6, no. 23 (2019). https://doi.org/10.1186/s40561-019-0110-5.

Shefer, Tamara, Lindsey Clowes, and Sisa Ngabaza. "Student Experience: A Participatory Parity Lens On Social (In)justice in Higher Education." In *Nancy Fraser and Participatory Parity: Reframing Social Justice in South African Higher Education*, edited by Vivienne Bozalek, Dorothee Hölscher, and Michalinos Zembylas. Routledge Research in Education Policy and Politics Series. Abingdon: Routledge, 2020, 63–76.

Sinclair, Marta. "An Integrated Framework of Intuition," In *Handbook of Intuition Research*, edited by Marta Sinclair. Cheltenham, Edward Elgar, 2011, 3–17.

Stein, Sarah, Simon Hart, Phillipa Keaney, and Richard White. "Student Views on the Cost of and Access to Textbooks: An Investigation at University of Otago (New Zealand)." *Open Praxis* 9, no. 4 (2017): 403–09. https://files.eric.ed.gov/fulltext/EJ1165496.pdf.

Tuck, Eve, and Wayne K. Yang. "Decolonisation is Not a Metaphor." *Decolonisation: Indigeneity, Education & Society* 1, no. 1 (2012): 1–40.

University of Cape Town. "UCT Libraries' new platform supports publishing of African-centric research." *University of Cape Town News* (January 13, 2021). https://www.news.uct.ac.za/article/-2021-01-13-uct-libraries-new-platform-supports-publishing-of-african-centric-research.

Unwin, Tim, Azra Naseem, Alicja Pawluczuk, Mohamed Shareef, Paul Spiesberger, Paul West, and Christopher Yoo. "Involving Marginalised Young People in the Design of Their Own Education." In *Education for the Most Marginalised Post-COVID-19: Guidance for Governments on the Use of Digital Technologies in Education*. Report by UNESCO & EdTech Hub. 2020. https://edtechhub.org/education-for-the-most-marginalised-post-covid-19/.

Veletsianos, George. "Open Educational Resources: Expanding Equity or Reflecting and Furthering Inequities?" *Educational Technology Research and Development* (2020). https://doi.org/10.1007/s11423-020-09840-y.

Walton, Elizabeth. "Decolonising (Through) Inclusive Education?" *Educational Research for Social Change* 7 (2018): 31–45. http://www.scielo.org.za/pdf/ersc/v7nspe/04.pdf.
Watters, Audrey. "From 'Open' to Justice." Keynote presentation, OpenCon 2014. 2014. http://hackeducation.com/2014/11/16/from-open-to-justice.
Weller, Martin. *The Battle for Open: How Openness Won and Why It Doesn't Feel Like Victory*. London: Ubiquity Press, 2014, 202. http://oro.open.ac.uk/44363/.
Zembylas, Michalinos. "Decolonial Possibilities in South African Higher Education: Reconfiguring Humanising Pedagogies as/with Decolonising Pedagogies." *South African Journal of Education* 38, no. 4 (2018). https://files.eric.ed.gov/fulltext/EJ1204069.pdf.

CHAPTER 9

Opportunities and Challenges in the Development and Usage of Open Textbooks in Institutions of Higher Learning to Promote Social Justice

Josiline Phiri Chigwada

Introduction

The development and use of open textbooks had been regarded as an alternative way of dealing with the ever-increasing costs of buying textbooks. In order to excel in their studies, higher education students are required to buy core textbooks that are beyond the reach of many students, especially in developing countries. In South Africa, for example, it was stated that textbook costs rise faster than any other higher education expense, and this is a barrier to accessing or completing tertiary education.[1] The open science movement led to the development of open educational resources (OER), which are learning materials that are accessible online and free to download, use, and modify, taking into account the copyright license. There are five Rs that should be adhered to when using open textbooks and these are retain, reuse, revise, remix, and redistribute. This chapter documents the opportunities and challenges that are encountered in institutions of higher learning in developing and using open textbooks as a way of promoting social justice. The objectives of the chapter are

1. to showcase the opportunities and challenges experienced in the development and use of open textbooks and
2. to point out the roles of different stakeholders involved in the development and use of open textbooks.

Open Educational Resources and Social Justice

There is a call to address social injustice in institutions of higher learning to achieve greater equity in accessing information resources.[2] Students in institutions of higher learning face financial challenges since most of the textbooks are expensive and do not represent local realities. In the United States of America, it has been stated that textbook costs have risen by 1,000 percent in forty years, and the textbooks are not evenly priced across disciplines, which is a major disadvantage to those who buy the books.[3] To deal with these injustices and frustrations, the advent of open textbooks helped to minimize affordability challenges. The use of open textbooks improves the learning outcomes as well as fosters the culture of equity, which is important in dealing with social justice issues. Most of the students are now able to access open textbooks, although there are other challenges that are experienced as well.

Open Textbooks

An open textbook is regarded as a textbook that is created using an open copyright license and shared with no- or low-cost at the point of use for students, teachers, and the members of the public.[4] There are a number of projects that were done to support the open textbook movement, such as the South African Siyavula Education project that was formed in 2002, and the Scholarly Publishing and Academic Resources Coalition (SPARC) has successfully lobbied for $5 million to create open textbooks. In the United Kingdom, the Hewlett-funded UK Open Textbook project was used to raise awareness and encourage wider uptake of open textbooks in the UK and the Digital Open Textbooks for Development of Cape Town.[5] Therefore, these and other organisations, such as the Commonwealth of Learning, Open Educational Resources (OER) Africa, and the William and Flora Hewlett Foundation, should continue supporting the development and use of open textbooks by providing guides and courses in support of open education.[6]

Advantages of Open Textbooks

A study conducted by Dastur, Jhangiani, Grand, and Penner[7] concluded that 65 percent of students at Florida Virtual Campus decided not to buy textbooks because of the high cost. The impact of these high textbook costs prevented some of the students from purchasing textbooks, 35 percent taking fewer courses, 31 percent choosing not to register, 23 percent going without textbooks, 14 percent dropping a course, and 10 percent withdrawing from a course. One major advantage of using open textbooks is the cost reduction of education since students and government use a lot of money on textbooks.[8] In most cases, students end up searching for secondhand textbooks from other students or fail to get the needed textbooks because of the cost implications. OpenEd[9] summarized the importance of open textbooks by pointing out their potential to increase access to higher education by reducing student costs, giving faculty more control over their instructional resources, and moving the open educational resources agenda forward in a meaningful and measurable way. The way that open textbooks are created and shared enhances the accessibility of these instructional resources. This indicates that open textbooks are flexible for educators and free for students as part of education innovation as they are regarded as an affordable, flexible alternative to traditionally published textbooks.[10]

Limitations of Open Textbooks

The limitation of open textbooks is the issue of quality where there is a prejudice that free materials are associated with poor quality. To create original work, there are costs to an author that should be met, including graphics, editing or review, and marketing costs. To deal with this, there is a need for the development of a sustainable business model in the form of a government subsidy or financial support for open textbooks. It has been noted that the adoption of open textbooks does not offer solutions overnight with regard to high textbooks costs.[11] There is a need for institutional investment by allocating funds and getting the buy-in of institutional leaders to be successful. Capacity building cannot be overlooked when introducing such services, and there should be incentives for the faculties who would be willing to take part in the development and use of open textbooks.

Stakeholders in the Development and Use of Open Textbooks

The major stakeholders in the development and use of open textbooks are authors, publishers, institutions of higher learning administrators, policymakers, librarians, and students. The authors are the lecturers who are responsible for teaching certain courses who can choose to work with students to develop open textbooks. The people who work in information communication technology (ICT) are responsible for championing and supporting the integration of ICT into teaching and learning.[12] The developers and platform administrators are involved in installing, setting up, maintaining, and upgrading open textbook platforms.

Librarians are also involved in the development and use of open textbooks. Librarians ensure that there is easy accessibility to these resources by providing solutions to the challenges that might be faced when developing and using open textbooks. In many places, they are responsible for creating awareness among the various stakeholders on the existence of open textbook platforms and how they deal with the various challenges that they might face, such as bringing together open textbooks that are scattered on the internet and helping authors to understand open licenses. Librarians play a major role in the advocacy process to ensure that open textbooks are accepted in institutions of higher learning.

The publishers are responsible for making sure that the books are available for the end-users to access. However, due to the advent of Open Monograph Press and other software, some books are now published online. The inexpensive and free publishing tools enable the faculty and other researchers to assume the role of traditional publishers.[13] There is a need to learn how to use these tools and the tenets of online publishing using various tools. The policymakers are responsible for enacting policies that encourage the adoption of open textbooks in institutions of higher learning. These can be at an institutional, national, regional, or international level. The students are the major beneficiaries of the open textbook movement since they are able to access the information without subscription or purchasing issues that had been hindering access to textbooks in higher education.

Opportunities in the Development and Use of Open Textbooks

There are various issues that are causing an increasing interest in open textbooks, such as increasing awareness, recession, and the COVID-19 pandemic.[14] It was discovered that the authors of open textbooks are taking advantage of the open monograph system to publish their open textbooks. This has improved their visibility and citations since many researchers can easily access their textbooks. The public knowledge project (PKP) developed Open Monograph Press, which is an open source software platform for managing and publishing scholarly books.[15] Open Monograph Press is free to download, use, and modify. The use of the Open Monograph Press software is to manage the editorial workflow for monographs, edited volumes, and scholarly editions through internal and external reviews, editing, cataloguing, production, and publication. The features of Open Monograph Press are pointed out by PKP[16] as the ability to handle edited volumes, with different authors for each chapter; involve editors, authors, reviewers, designers, indexers, and others in book production; see submission through multiple rounds of both internal and external reviews; utilize industry-standard ONIX for bookseller metadata requirements such as Amazon; create document libraries for submissions, recording contracts, permissions; and handle thumbnail covers in the catalog as well as spotlight features.

There is more flexibility in the teaching and delivery of up-to-date knowledge to support learning leading to the acceptance of the use of open textbooks by both students and teaching staff.[17] This leads to improved student success in some areas in terms of course grades and completion rates as a result of the affordability and accessibility of open textbooks. The COVID-19 pandemic was seen as an opportunity by students and instructors to use open textbooks. McKenzie[18] stated that more than 100,000 students and instructors created OpenStax accounts to access free resources associated with OpenStax textbooks. Instructors are redesigning their curricula to work in new modalities and are experimenting with new course materials. McKenzie[19] stressed that instructors and students want low-cost materials that are accessible and flexible, and the economic impact of the COVID-19 pandemic on students' finances has caused an increase in the adoption of OER.

Students are now involved in the development of open textbooks through open pedagogy, leading to the critical role that is played by faculty in making learning accessible.[20] Students are regarded as more adept at understanding their requirements as beginners and can play a leading role in reframing and representing course content in innovative ways. Examples of institutions that worked with students to develop open textbooks are undergraduate students at the Ohio State University who worked on the open textbook *Environmental ScienceBites*.[21]

Students are saving money on buying textbooks, making college more affordable since it has been stated that textbook prices have soared over the years.[22] There is the textbook revolution project, which is a student-led initiative advocating for lectures and professors to adopt and embrace open textbooks in their courses.[23] The Department of Higher Education and Training in South Africa has an open learning site that documents a small list of projects that use open learning materials in technical and vocational education.[24] Accessibility has been improved and open textbooks are said to provide students with a fair and equitable learning environment by providing access to free resources.

Initiatives in the Use of OER

A number of initiatives adopting the use of open textbooks were introduced in various countries, and there are libraries and repositories of open textbooks available online, such as eCampus Ontario, the University of Minnesota Centre for Open Education, BCCampus in British Columbia, and sites that are available at Educational Technology and Mobile learning, in Pakistan, and United Kingdom.[25] This is due to the slight growth of awareness of open educational resources as well as the growth in faculty decisions to use these resources as course materials.

The faculty in some regions must consider additional factors, such as restrictions on access to international materials. In China, for example, some publisher platforms for digital course materials are not accessible where firewalls block international websites. Instructors are taking advantage of the availability of open educational resources by embedding them in the learning management system to be accessible anywhere, regardless of geolocation. There are also open educational resources grants that are available to faculty members who would be willing to adopt, adapt, or create their own openly available resources. McKenzie[26] indicated that three times more applications were received in May 2020 due to the COVID-19 pandemic.

In South Africa, an open access symposium was held from December 2–6, 2019 under the theme "open access and social justice driving African development." The symposium was hosted by the University of Cape Town Libraries, the African Charter of the Scholarly Publishing Academic Resources Coalition (SPARC), together with its Northern American counterpart as well as the Western Cape Universities.[27] It was a week of workshops, engagements, and the presentation of invited papers around open access and social justice to advance African open scholarship within a social justice paradigm. The sponsors were mainly organizations that support open science activities around the world, including MDPI Academic Open Access Publishing, Confederation of Open Access Repositories (COAR), Library Publishing Coalition, and African Journals Online among others.

Challenges in the Development and Use of Open Textbooks

It has been pointed out that the cost of buying textbooks is a barrier to accessing information resources in tertiary institutions, although the South African government is providing financial aid and subsidies.[28] Textbooks are unevenly priced across disciplines and, in most cases, the book is used for a maximum of one year and would not be useful for other courses, holding little or no relevance for future learning. Challenges that were pointed out include quality issues, complex intellectual property and copyright issues, unfamiliarity with the resources, and the time needed to create and locate open textbooks.

Prasad and Usagawa[29] pointed out that students would be able to save money through open textbooks if the lecturers were willing to develop and use them. There is a need for vigorous marketing through workshops, where academics and teaching staff, library staff, ICT people, and senior university executive staff should attend. These would be aimed at contextualizing student experiences and highlighting how it is difficult for them to secure textbooks. As a result, enabling policies should be enacted to deal with such challenges.[30]

Students might face connectivity challenges to access open textbooks due to the technological infrastructure and lack of resources to fully utilize the open textbooks, such as laptops and tablets. In Zimbabwe, for example, although it is said that every student who attends college or university should have a laptop and a smartphone; in reality, most of the learners cannot afford to buy these gadgets. Data is also very expensive in Africa, and most students rely on Wi-Fi that is provided by their higher education institutions. However, due to the COVID-19 pandemic, campuses were closed and students were supposed to learn from home, leading to accessibility challenges. The technological infrastructure is not enabling in most African countries, leading to difficulties in developing and using open textbooks.

Lack of skills and knowledge to develop open textbooks can be a challenge among the authors. Therefore, there is a need to train all the stakeholders so that they are aware of their duties and responsibilities. Lecturers can take advantage of the various guides that are available to understand the concept of developing open textbooks.[31] This can assist the stakeholder to understand the value of open textbooks in teaching and learning, appreciate the potential value of developing an open textbook platform, and select the appropriate technology to build and maintain the platform.

Methodology

To find out how institutions of higher learning are taking advantage of the opportunities offered by textbooks in Sub Saharan Africa, the author conducted telephone interviews with five librarians in five countries to determine if they are involved in archiving and maintaining open textbooks in Zimbabwe, South Africa, Zambia, Botswana, and Malawi. Purposive sampling of those who attended the open access symposium at the University of Cape Town in 2019 to point out the challenges they are experiencing in using the Open Monograph system. Twenty students in institutions of higher learning in Zimbabwe were also interviewed to explain how they are using open textbooks and to explain the challenges that they face. The students were randomly selected from ten institutions of higher learning—five universities and five colleges. The results were analysed and presented thematically using the objectives of the study as the main headings.

Results and Discussion

The findings are categorized thematically according to the interviews that were held with students and librarians. Students were asked whether they use open textbooks in their studies. The findings indicated that the majority of students in institutions of higher learning are now utilizing open textbooks due to the high costs of buying books because of the economic recession that is taking place in most African countries, Zimbabwe included. All the students interviewed indicated that they are using open textbooks to accomplish their academic dreams. In terms of developing open textbooks with their lecturers, the students indicated that they were never involved in the writing process of any books since most of them were not aware of the publishing process. However, they indicated that they are willing to be involved since it seems to be an exciting process. This is an opportunity to enhance the use of open educational resources to promote social justice because incorporating student work improves representation and localized content in the texts. The students promised that if their institutions of higher learning engaged them, they are ready to join in the development of open textbooks.

In terms of the challenges that they face when using open textbooks, the students pointed out that they lack the skills to download the books since some of them had not had information literacy training where they would be taught how to access and use electronic resources. The following were the findings from the students:

Difficulties in Downloading the Books

Most of the students pointed out a lack of skills to download the open textbooks that are available online. One of the students pointed out that "in as much as I want to access the open textbooks, I [do not] have the skills [to] download the books. As a result, I ask for assistance from the librarians to get access to these books and use them." Some of the students pointed out that they do not know where to get such books, although they are available on the internet to be used free of charge. It is therefore important for librarians to roll out information and digital literacy training sessions to all the students in institutions of higher learning to enable them to access and use these useful resources in their academic endeavors.

Difficulties in Using the Books

The students indicated that there is too much information on the internet, and even if they manage to download the open textbooks, they cannot separate the good from the bad books. One student added that "the books are scattered all over the internet and I wish I could find them in one place." Another student stated, "I do not have a laptop to use when I am not on campus to access the open textbooks; I rely on machines in the library." Another added, "My laptop is now like a desktop because of battery problems and I cannot use it when there is a power outage. This makes it difficult for me to use the books in the learning process since there are electricity problems in my country."

Difficulties with Network Connections

Some students pointed out that although they have heard about open textbooks, they do not have the internet to be able to download them and benefit from them. One of the students stated, "Where I stay, I do not have [an] internet connection, and I can only use these books when I am on campus." Another student pointed out that downloading a book is a nightmare due to the poor internet connection. This shows that internet connectivity is one of the challenges faced by students when using open textbooks, emphasized by one student who said, "The internet connection is very poor in my area, and it is difficult to access the open textbooks." Although these books are available free of charge, there are still some costs that must be met by these students for them to be able to utilize the books—costs for an internet connection and the machines such as computers, laptops, smartphones, and storage devices.

Difficulties in Using Electronic Copies

The students indicated that they are used to reading print copies that they borrow from the library, and to them, reading electronic copies is a challenge. They cannot spend a lot of time looking on the computer screen, as stated by one student who said that librarians are very helpful in locating good open textbooks, "but I cannot concentrate for a long time when reading on a computer screen." Those who are facing electricity problems also indicated that they might face challenges in using electronic copies when their batteries are drained. Due to high printing costs, the students are not able to print the open textbooks to use as hard copies.

Impact of the COVID-19 Pandemic

The impact of the COVID-19 pandemic led to the closure of libraries, shifting teaching and learning to online. One student indicated that "we were supposed to learn from home, but we used to benefit from the internet facilities in the library to download and use open textbooks. At home, we were not connected to the internet and it was difficult to access these useful resources." Another student said, "We used to benefit from the computers in the library in using open textbooks, but now the library closed due to the COVID-19 pandemic. Someone added that I do not have enough space to save the open textbooks on my machine because my laptop has low storage capacity, and due to COVID-19, I cannot access my books that I have saved in the cloud since at home I cannot access the internet."

Open Textbooks Not Part of the Reading List

Some students stated that they rely mainly on textbooks that are recommended by their lecturers when they research the teaching and learning process. One student remarked, "My lecturers give us a reading list of books to use for the courses. Sometimes the open textbook titles I come across [were] not part of the reading lists. Therefore, I use them as supplementary reading materials." This shows that lecturers should embrace the use of open textbooks so that they recommend them as part of the reading list on the course outlines. This would increase the usage of these books since students always look for reading materials that they are pointed to by their lecturers.

These findings show that students face a number of challenges in using open textbooks. These include lack of resources, such as internet connectivity, laptops, and smartphones, a lack of skills to access the resources, the closure of libraries that provide computers and internet connection due to the COVID-19 pandemic, lack of storage space to store the textbooks, electricity challenges, and information overload. These sentiments were pointed out by the University of South Africa.[32]

The librarians that were interviewed indicated that they were trained in accessing and using open textbooks on Open Monograph Press (OMP), but only one librarian's institution is archiving and maintaining the OMP. The other four librarians are just end-users and are not involved in the publication and maintenance of open textbooks. In terms of training, they all indicated that they learned about open access publishing in workshops and webinars. The librarian who is involved in the open access publishing process using Open Monograph Press indicated that they have not faced any challenge yet. The other four librarians stated that they are in the process of creating awareness within their institutions to start the development, archiving, and maintenance of open textbooks using OMP. The librarians also stressed the importance of training both users and lecturers and linking the content to users via the library website as a way of bringing together the scattered resources.

Solutions and Recommendations

The author recommends the adoption and acceptance of open textbooks in institutions of higher learning to improve the accessibility of information by students and researchers. There should be awareness campaigns in institutions of higher learning to educate both students and lecturers on the importance of open textbooks so that they understand how to find and use OER. If people realize the impact of using open textbooks, they would encourage others to use the resources. This is in line with a study that was done by McKenzie,[33] which pointed out that faculty members who are knowledgeable and aware of open educational resources are more likely to adopt them.

Institutions of higher learning should also be involved in the development of open textbooks to encourage their usage since most researchers are satisfied with their own research output. It can also be noted that localized production of open textbooks can help increase the representation of minoritised voices in textbooks by adopting inclusive design principles. This would lead to the launch of open textbooks in many colleges and universities. The researchers would ensure that quality issues are taken care of and the publishing process is thorough enough to make the textbooks acceptable.

There is also a need for capacity-building among librarians and other stakeholders with the institutions to ensure that they are knowledgeable about the Open Monograph system and understand the role they play in the development and use of open textbooks. Building institutional capacity enables support for faculty to adopt open textbooks. The government and other non-governmental organisations (NGOs) should provide funds for the production of open textbooks to offer a more sustainable and affordable solution. This would be a step in the right direction in ensuring that the collection is sustainable and usable.

There should be policies that eliminate taxes on textbooks, such as value-added tax (VAT), replacing textbooks with modules, encouraging the use or purchase of secondhand textbooks, and licensing textbooks that can be copied.

Policies should also be enacted to facilitate national and international collaborations in the development and use of open textbooks. There is also a need to integrate OER into institutional policies, procedures, and practices to encourage lecturers and students to adopt them.

Conclusion

The use of open textbooks is prevalent in institutions of higher learning in Africa, and students and faculty have been benefiting from these services since the beginning of the open science movement. Institutions are supposed to support the initiative and incentivize the researchers who are involved in the development and use of open textbooks as a way of encouraging other members to adopt them. The major advantage of using open textbooks is cost reduction, which alleviates financial pressures, and the prospect of improving teaching and learning. Librarians should also be actively involved in creating awareness and training all stakeholders to enhance the development and use of open textbooks.

Endnotes

1. Kirk Perris and Mpine Makoe, "The case for using open textbooks in HE is growing," University of South Africa, 2, https://www.unisa.ac.za/sites/corporate/default/News-&-Media/Articles/The-case-for-using-open-textbooks-in-HE-is-growing.
2. Glenda Cox, Bianca Masuku, and Michelle Willmers, "Open Textbooks and Social Justice: Open Educational Practices to Address Economic, Cultural and Political Injustice at the University of Cape Town," *Journal of Interactive Media in Education* 1 (2020): 5, https://doi.org/10.5334/jime.556.
3. Perris and Makoe, "The case for using open textbooks," 3.
4. Vivien Rolfe and Beck Pitt, "Open textbooks—an untapped opportunity for universities, colleges and schools," *Insights* 31 (2018): 2, https://insights.uksg.org/articles/10.1629/uksg.427/.
5. Cox et al, "Open Textbooks and Social Justice."
6. Perris and Makoe, "The case for using open textbooks," 4.
7. Farhad Dastur, Rajiv Jhangiani, Richard Le Grand, and Kurt Penner, "Introductory Psychology Textbooks: The Roles of Online vs. Print and Open vs. Traditional Textbooks" (presentation at the 2015 Open Ed Conference, Vancouver, Canada), 2015.
8. Perris and Makoe, "The case for using open textbooks."
9. "What is an open textbook and how do you use it?," OpenEd, 2016, accessed July 2, 2021, https://bcacampus.ca/2016/04/05/what-is-an-open-textbook-and-how-do-you-use-it (site discontinued).
10. "Open textbooks: what if you could change higher education with just one textbook?," BCcampus, 2021, accessed July 2, 2021, https://open.bcampus.ca/files/2016/02/BCOpenTextbookBrochure_Feb2016.pdf (site discontinued).
11. Perris and Makoe, "The case for using open textbooks."
12. Andrew Moore and Neil Butcher, *Guide to Developing Open Textbooks* (British Columbia: Commonwealth of Learning, 2016).
13. Joe Moxley, "Open Textbook Publishing," American Association of University Professors, 2013, 2, https://www.aaup.org/article/open-textbook-publishing#.YE7d0Z0zbIU (page discontinued).

14. Lindsay McKenzie, "Window of Opportunity for OER," *Inside Higher Ed* (August 13, 2020), accessed July 2, 2021, https://www.insidehighered. com/news/2020/08/13/ (page discontinued).
15. "Open Monograph Press," Public Knowledge Press, 2021, 1, accessed July 2, 2021, https://pkp.sfu.ca/omp/.
16. "Open Monograph Press," Public Knowledge Press, 1.
17. Rolfe and Pitt, "Open textbooks," 2.
18. McKenzie, "Window of Opportunity for OER," 2.
19. Ibid., 3.
20. Robin DeRose and Rajiv Jhangiani, "Open Pedagogy," in *A Guide to Making Open Textbooks with Students*," ed. Elizabeth Mays, Rebus Community, 2020, 6, accessed July 2, 2021, https://press.rebus.community/makingopentextbookswithstudents/chapter/open-pedagogy/.
21. Kylienne A. Clark, Travis R. Shaul, and Brian H. Lower, eds., *Environmental ScienceBites* (Columbus: The Ohio State University, 2015), 4.
22. Deepak Prasad and Tsuyoshi Usagawa, "Towards development of OER derived custom-built open textbooks: a baseline survey of university teachers at the University of the South Pacific," Athabasca University, 2014, 2, accessed July 2, 2021, http://www.irrodl.org/index.php/irrodl/article/view/1873/3005.
23. Perris and Makoe, "The case for using open textbooks," 2.
24. "Open learning for post-school education and training," Department of Higher Education and Training, Republic of South Africa, 2021, 1, accessed July 2, 2021, https://www.dhet.gov.za/open_learning.
25. Perris and Makoe, "The case for using open textbooks," 2.
26. McKenzie, "Window of Opportunity for OER," 3.
27. "UCT-SPARC Africa Open Access Symposium 2019," University of Cape Town, 2019, 1, accessed July 2, 2021, https://www.sparcafricasymp.ac.za.
28. Perris and Makoe, "The case for using open textbooks," 2.
29. Prasad and Usagawa, "Towards development of OER," 2.
30. Perris and Makoe, "The case for using open textbooks," 2.
31. Moore and Butcher, *Guide to Developing Open Textbooks*, 13.
32. Perris and Makoe, "The case for using open textbooks," 3.
33. McKenzie, "Window of Opportunity for OER," 5.

Bibliography

BCcampus. "Open textbooks: what if you could change higher education with just one textbook?" 2021. Accessed July 2, 2021. https://open.bcampus.ca/files/2016/02/BCOpenTextbookBrochure_Feb2016.pdf.

Clark, Kylienne A., Travis R. Shaul, and Brian H. Lower, eds. *Environmental ScienceBites*. Columbus: The Ohio State University, 2015.

Cox, Glenda, Bianca Masuku, and Michelle Willmers. "Open Textbooks and Social Justice: Open Educational Practices to Address Economic, Cultural and Political Injustice at the University of Cape Town." *Journal of Interactive Media in Education* 1 (2020): 1–10. https://doi.org/10.5334/jime.556.

Dastur, Farhad, Rajiv Jhangiani, Richard Le Grand, and Kurt Penner. "Introductory Psychology Textbooks: The Roles of Online vs. Print and Open vs. Traditional Textbooks." Presented at the 2015 Open Ed Conference, Vancouver, Canada, 2015.

DeRose, Robin, and Rajiv Jhangiani. "Open Pedagogy." In *A Guide to Making Open Textbooks with Students*," edited by Elizabeth Mays. Rebus Community, 2020, 6. Accessed July 2, 2021. https://press.rebus.community/makingopentextbookswithstudents/chapter/open-pedagogy/.

McKenzie, Lindsay. "Window of opportunity for OER." *Inside Higher Ed* (2020). Accessed July 2, 2021. https://www.insidehighered. com/news/2020/08/13/. Page discontinued.

Moore, Andrew, and Neil Butcher. *Guide to Developing Open Textbooks*. British Columbia: Commonwealth of Learning, 2016.
Moxley, Joe. *Open Textbook Publishing*. American Association of University Professors. 2013. https://www.aaup.org/article/open-textbook-publishing#.YE7d0Z0zbIU.
OpenEd. "What is an open textbook and how do you use it?" BCCampus. 2016. Accessed July 2, 2021. https://bcacampus.ca/2016/04/05/what-is-an-open-textbook-and-how-do-you-use-it. Site discontinued.
Prasad, Deepak, and Tsuyoshi Usagawa. "Towards development of OER derived custom-built open textbooks: a baseline survey of university teachers at the University of the South Pacific." Athabasca University. 2014. Accessed July 2, 2021. http://www.irrodl.org/index.php/irrodl/article/view/1873/3005.
Perris, Kirk, and Mpine Makoe. "The case for using open textbooks in higher education is growing." University of South Africa. 2020. https://www.unisa.ac.za/sites/corporate/default/News-&-Media/Articles/The-case-for-using-open-textbooks-in-HE-is-growing.
Public Knowledge Press. "Open Monograph Press." 2021. Accessed July 2, 2021. https://pkp.sfu.ca/omp/.
Republic of South Africa. Department of Higher Education and Training. "Open learning for post-school education and training." 2021. Accessed July 2, 2021. https://www.dhet.gov.za/open_learning.
Rolfe, Vivien, and Beck Pitt. "Open textbooks—an untapped opportunity for universities, colleges and schools." *Insights* 31 (2018). https://insights.uksg.org/articles/10.1629/uksg.427/.
University of Cape Town. "UCT-SPARC Africa Open Access Symposium 2019." 2019. Accessed July 2, 2021. https://www.sparcafricasymp.ac.za.

CHAPTER 10

Where Are We on the Map?
The State of Open Educational Resources (OER) in Africa

Alkasim Hamisu Abdu

Introduction

Open educational resources (OER) have already shown the potential to alter traditional educational practice to a more diversified and all-inclusive system. Therefore, any attempt for social justice needs to harbour and promote OER. This has already been recognized in the education systems of many countries, especially in Europe and North America. This manifests in the form of public and private funding as well as developing institutional frameworks for the promotion of OER. However, Sub-Saharan Africa (SSA) is lagging behind in almost all the developmental indices. Taking advantage of OER would help to bridge the gap, but the commitment of the region toward the development of OER is either low or not well reported. This chapter attempts to shed more light on the development of OER in SSA. The chapter reports on a mini-survey on teacher education engagements with OER in Kano State, Nigeria. The survey respondents were deliberately chosen because the TESSA (Teacher Education in Sub Saharan Africa) programme is one of the largest and oldest programmes conceptualized to promote the use of OER in teacher education in Sub-Saharan Africa. The results of the survey may be useful to all stakeholders in the educational systems of the region.

Open Educational Resources and the Sub-Saharan Education

Access to quality education is the foundation of global peace and cooperation as enshrined in UNESCO's vision,[1] which emphasizes quality and contextually relevant educational programmes and resources as a right for global citizens.[2] Some claim it has the power to liberate citizens from poverty, diseases, abuse, and all forms of exclusion.[3] Closing access to education in the twenty-first-century connected world may have trans-border effects, such as mass migration and environmental degradation, in addition to aggravating the vulnerability of the vulnerable. Therefore, any attempt to entrench social justice within individual countries and among nations needs a concerted effort to widen and democratize access to education as a tool that possesses great potential to relieve societies from the shackles of poverty and other forms of social exclusion. This calls for more strong political alliances to widen access to education in order to achieve sustainable development goals, especially among the less-developed regions like Sub-Saharan Africa where access to education has been unbearably low due to socio-cultural, political, and economic restrictions. These constraints block Africans' ability to access and benefit from the pool of knowledge generated outside the region, mainly in the Global North, and, conversely, deny the rest of the world the ability to benefit from the more contextual knowledge from Africa.[4]

The emergence of open culture in and around research and pedagogical practices, including open access (OA), open educational practice (OEP), and open educational resources (OER), creates opportunities to reduce or even eliminate the knowledge divide among nations and regions. Already, OER has shown its effectiveness in reducing barriers within educational systems, mostly in connection with reducing the cost of education,[5] which ultimately led to wider enrolment and longer retention. OER also show effectiveness in improving test scores and attainment rates.[6]

This chapter relies on the UNESCO definition of OER: "Learning, teaching and research materials in any format and medium that reside in the public domain or are under copyright that have been released under an open license, that permit no-cost access, re-use, re-purpose, adaptation and redistribution by others."[7] The work of UNESCO in the area of OER is in most cases connected to funding from the William and Flora Hewlett Foundation, which defines OER as

> [Any] teaching, learning, and research resources that resides in the public domain or have been released under an intellectual property license that permits their free use and re-purposing by others.

Open educational resources include full courses, course material, modules, textbooks, streaming videos, tests, software, and any other tools, materials, or techniques used to support access to knowledge.[8]

The focal point of most OER definitions is the license under which a resource has been released.[9] The license needs to be open and allow no-charge and permission-free responsible use and reuse.

In addition to cost reduction, OER allow for quality resources to be shared and contextualized for remote locations that otherwise couldn't have access to similar resources. Despite the presumed benefits of OER in democratizing learning and educational opportunities, the countries of Sub-Saharan Africa (SSA) are not being carried along. Most notable OER initiatives were hosted and led by the European and North American countries. Very few OER initiatives can be found in SSA.[10]

Prospect of OER in the Educational System of Sub-Sahara Africa

The SSA was home to some of the most renowned medieval universities. However, it has been marginalized in the modern educational ecosystem. The education systems of the independent African states continued along the path of their colonial heritage, lacking a close connection with the immediate needs of the indigenous people. Long after independence, school enrolment and higher education attainment in SSA are the lowest compared to other regions of the world. Sub-Saharan Africa has a vast landmass that is cut apart with bad terrain and, in most cases, lacks basic infrastructure such as telecommunication and communication facilities. This creates a need to capitalize on the premise of OER to expand its educational delivery.[11] OER may be reproduced locally or stored in local retrieval systems to bypass the need for an internet connection to be able to sustain the use. Reproducing the resources locally may also reduce the need for importation, mainly from foreign countries that rely on effective communication and transportation facilities.

Whilst the developed nations have already started reaping the fruit of OER in their educational systems, communities of practice have sprung up in those regions. Governments and donor agencies are supplementing the development of OER with funding, subvention, and policy formulation.[12] Consequently, successes in the application of OER have been emerging in different areas.[13] Though open and distance learning is not new in sub-Saharan countries, the OER movement is still conceptual, without much practical application yet. South

Africa is leading the rest of Africa, providing a good example of funding and collaboration between government and publishers in the use of OER.[14] But in the rest of Africa, the application of OER in their education systems and awareness of the movement remain low, even among educational practitioners, while policies are scarcely spotted at institutional and national levels. Some suggest that policymakers' prioritization of on-campus study inhibits the uptake and further development of OER applications across the region.[15] Making the situation worse, the educational policies of most SSA countries leave much to be desired. It is common for children to attend all years of compulsory basic education without attaining a basic literacy level that would underpin future education pursuit and life-long learning, despite the fact that most SSA governments are signatories to international treaties and conventions, such as Education for All (EFA) and the Sustainable Development Goals (SGD).[16]

Some blame the African educational systems for the underdevelopment of the region, contributing to poverty, social exclusion, civil unrest, war, and famine. However, the educational system is challenged with insufficient resources. For a long time, Sub-Saharan African countries relied on developed countries for the supply of educational resources. Unfortunately, most countries in SSA are considered low-income economies and experience unfavourable foreign exchange rates, which diminish their purchasing power.[17] These problems make access to quality materials very difficult, while the few available resources may not have relevance to the local context.[18] Furthermore, the lack of quality resources also makes it difficult for the region to produce the required teachers that would assist in achieving the objectives of the educational policies of the countries. Despite a huge gap in the labor supply to staff the educational systems of SSA, the few available educational institutions are overcrowded and lack equipment and facilities. This may be a result of poor funding, which has characterized the systems.

Furthermore, there are socio-cultural, financial, political, and technological barriers that hinder access to education. For example, violent conflicts that spotted the region in many cases push learners out of school or necessitate the authorities to close schools for a long time.[19] Some schools have been targeted by extremists, making on-the-site study a great risk. For example, in Nigeria, it has become a recurrent pattern for extremists to carry out mass abductions. In these incidents, students are taken to the bush for a long time, experiencing inhumane treatment until a ransom is paid. This trend has instilled fear in students and their families for on-site study and jeopardized the sustainability of educational programmes in Nigeria.[20]

Information and communication technology (ICT) and open educational resources provide opportunities for SSA to achieve inclusive quality education at all levels.[21] With the emerging movement for OER, the role of educators can shift to focus more on student support, assessment, and accreditation. Cost should no longer be a barrier to educational attainment and delivery. Overcrowding of educational facilities may be mitigated by online and distance learning programmes.[22] Open educational resources are crucial to online and distance learning, which are the most viable means to align educational supply with the educational demand of the twenty-first century.[23] The National Universities Commission (NUC) recognised that the need for access to university education couldn't be met through the traditional mode of face-to-face instruction.[24] So, the most viable option to widen access is to shift to open and distance education, with OER at the heart of the system. Thus, the commission has been up and working to guide Nigerian universities to realize the full potential of OER.[25] However, much needs to be done to achieve the potential in the country, as very little manifestation can be seen in the uptake of OER among the Nigerian universities. Manifestations of OER on the websites of the universities are still confusing, and universities have posted all sorts of content they develop as OER without explicit statements on copyright and licence issues. Many times, the digital infrastructure that offers OER are not sound; they lead to broken links or metadata without content.

OER initiatives in SSA need support from relevant stakeholders, including libraries and publishing communities. As the OER movement is consistent with the centuries-old mission of libraries, working toward social justice through free and equitable access to education and learning resources,[26] libraries in some regions wasted no time in joining the crusade with full force. Libraries have already developed expertise in areas such as copyright, metadata development, and information search and retrieval, which are very important to any OER initiative. Libraries have established new posts and roles to accommodate OER and related projects. Several journal publishers and professional conferences have responded by creating opportunities to discuss and publish scholarship related to the open movement. However, similar initiatives and innovations could hardly be identified in the SSA.

It is important to note that OER uptake in SSA has its own unique challenges. OER projects are mainly dependent on digital infrastructure. Unfortunately, internet penetration is still low. Mobile technology is spreading fast in the region, but the average income of the populace is insufficient to afford it. In many parts of the region, especially outside the urban centres, power supply is still a problem.[27] Most engagements with OER in SSA are passive and limited to utilization. The TESSA project has been an exception, but most of the OER giveaways and gateways were delivered from the Global North. On this note, some scholars caution about the possibility that OER could further the knowledge divide between the Global South and the Global North, possibly engendering another phase of knowledge imperialism in which the developed world controls the creation and dissemination of knowledge.[28]

Despite the tremendous challenges that have characterized educational systems and programmes in Sub-Saharan Africa, there may be light at the end of the tunnel. Many sub-Saharan countries have developed administrative provisions and architecture that may underpin OER uptake and mitigate the sustainability challenges that in most cases surrounds the donor-supported OER projects. Nigeria provides a typical example: right from the onset, the constitution and the National Policy on Education put education as a key ingredient for unity and progress. Thus, the policy distributed the responsibility of implementing educational policies across all three tiers of government. The National Council of Education is the apex body for making educational policy; policy is then implemented through various agencies and parastatals under the departments or ministries of education across all the three tiers of government in the country. Under this arrangement, introducing, implementing, and sustaining OER policies and programmes in the country may be easier and more straightforward, provided there is awareness and understanding among policy makers.

OER need to be supported by policy at governmental and institutional levels. The Open Educational Resource Policy for Higher Education in Nigeria was formulated in 2015.[29] However, effective implementation and sustaining educational policy require support from many partners, including the Federal Ministries of Education, the ministries of education at each of the thirty-six states of the federation, and several extra-ministerial agencies. There are significant logistical challenges, but efforts are underway to support OER development in the country.

Empirical Evidence on the Engagement with OER in Sub-Saharan Africa

Nigeria developed a draft policy to strategize OER initiatives in its higher education in 2017, but no empirical studies have yet reported, reviewed, or assessed the initiative.[30] Thus, this chapter provides a result of a micro-survey conducted on the use of OER among teacher educators in Kano State Nigeria. Nigeria is the most populous country in Africa, with an estimated population of 193,392,517 in the year 2016.[31] The country is administratively divided into thirty-six states and 774 local governments. Kano State is the most populous in the country and is demographically cosmopolitan in the sense that the state harbours people from all the other regions of the country. There are eight publicly owned teacher education institutions in the state. Therefore, a survey in Kano may shed light on the Nigerian situation in general.

The survey singled out teacher educators because they play an important role in educational practices and they can facilitate widespread change in teaching methods.[32] In addition, Teacher Education in Sub-Saharan Africa (TESSA) is a prominent Africa-based and donor-supported OER initiative that has been built around and for teacher education in Africa. So, it is presumed that teacher educators may have an edge in interacting with OER.

An online questionnaire drafted with Google Forms was used to collect data. The questionnaire was distributed to the respondents via WhatsApp groups of the respective institutions. A total of fifty-six teacher educators responded to the questionnaire.

Result of the Survey

The fifty-six responses included representation from all of the eight teacher training institutions in Kano State. Looking at the personal information of the respondents, about 68% were male and 32% were female. This is not surprising—the teaching profession in Nigeria is still predominantly male, but females are increasingly striving for parity. Also, the majority of the respondents are middle age; about 38% range from thirty-one to forty years and about 34% range from forty-one to fifty years. Workers within these age ranges are expected to yield a good result for the study as they are more likely to have the digital competencies necessary to partake in OER processes. This is in addition to the fact that the majority of the respondents are not novices in their careers, as only about 38% have ten years or less of working experience, while about 41% range from eleven to twenty years of work experience. Furthermore, a majority of the respondents have either a master's degree or a PhD; 54% have a master's degree, and those with PhDs and bachelor's degrees each represented about 23% of the responses (table 10.1).

Category	Variable	Frequency	Percentage
Gender	Female	18	32.1
	Male	38	67.9
Age	Below 30 years	21	37
	41–50 years	19	33.9
	52–60 years	9	16.1
	Above 60	2	3.6
Work experience	Below 10 years	21	37.5
	11–20 years	23	41.1
	21–30 years	8	14.3
	Above 30 years	4	7.1
Qualification	Bachelor's degree	13	23.2
	Master's degree	30	53.2
	PhD	13	23.2

Table 10.1
Personal information of the respondents.

Four questions were used to measure the awareness of the respondents about OER concepts and services. About 57% of the respondents are aware of the OER as a concept, but only about 21% are aware of the OERAfrica website and services of the South African Institute of Distance Education (SAIDE). Despite the pioneering role and popularity of MIT openCourseWare in delivering OER, only about 30% of the respondents are aware of the service or programme. About 36% of the respondents are aware of the TESSA programme. The result indicates there is a low level of OER penetration among teacher educators in Kano State. TESSA as one of the oldest OER programme designed with and for teacher education in Sub-Saharan Africa; it is expected to become very popular among teacher educators in the region. So, having just 36% of the respondents of this study with knowledge of the service is not encouraging to the development of OER initiatives in SSA. On the other hand, the OERAfrica service is very visible when searching OER in relation to Africa. The programme cuts across many professions as well as areas of practice; however, only 21% of the respondents of this study are aware of the service. This further shows a marginal interaction with OER programmes among professionals in SSA, which calls for governments, teacher training institutions, as well as donors and development partners to intensify efforts toward promoting OER programmes and services in Sub-Saharan Africa as prescribed by UNESCO.[33] More than half of the 57% of respondents who know about OER learned about it by self-exploration through browsing the web, while only about 2% of the respondents of this survey came to know about OER from a government awareness campaign or programme. This demonstrates the need for governmental agencies to do much more to promote OER.

The respondents' conceptualization of OER was tested by requiring the respondents to match OER with the best possible options (table 10.2). Respondents were given the opportunity to select all descriptions that apply, so the total of responses adds up to more than 100 percent. Fifty-three of the respondents responded to the question by selecting at least one of the descriptions. This strategy was adopted to reduce the level of reliance on respondents' self-reporting. The result of matching is presented as follows:

S/N	Concept	Description	Score (%)
1	OER	are websites that are open without password	25%
2	OER	are the free books distributed by the Federal Government of Nigeria	7.7%
3	OER	are educational resources that are free for use and re-purposing	44%
4	OER	are educational resources that are free from financial and copyright restrictions	38%
5	OER	I have no idea	17.8%

Table 10.2
Respondents' conceptualization of OER.

The result is interesting as descriptions in numbers 3 and 4 were chosen the most. These two descriptions portray some of the important premises of OER; therefore, each could be a good description of OER. Nevertheless, the result still indicates a good level of misconception and confusion about OER among the respondents because neither a description in number 1 or number 2 portrays any of the premises of OER, but both were selected by 25% and 7.7% of the respondents respectively. It is worth noting that only about 18% of the respondents on this survey indicated they have no idea of what OER are about, though only about 57% of respondents indicated awareness of OER on a previous question, which suggests some respondents guessed instead of admitting to not knowing.

OER offer great potential, especially in the context of Nigerian higher education. As a result of a lack of relevant, high-quality, and accessible learning resources, teachers have no other options than to create content for their classes in the form of handouts. Thus, this survey reveals that about 79% of the respondents have created educational resources in the course of their teaching activities. Almost all of those who developed the content for their classes affirmed to have no problem in making the content freely available on the internet, though only about 16% of the respondents have ever posted their work on the internet. This may serve as good potential for OER development among the respondents as they create content in the course of their educational service that they are ready to make freely available.

The survey asked whether OER is used as a course or part of a course that is taught at the institutions of the respondents. Despite TESSA's engagement with the National Commission for Colleges of Education, which is the regulatory agency controlling teacher education in Nigeria, only about 9% answered yes to this question. This shows that OER are still not in the mainstream of educational practice in Nigeria, as they are not included in the Teacher Education Curriculum, which is centrally controlled by a national agency. For OER to be streamlined into educational practice, it needs to be integrated into the official curriculum of teacher training institutions. Possibly, the few respondents who affirmed that OER are part of their curricula it might have emanated from the personal endeavours of the respondents.

To understand the willingness of the respondents to utilize OER in the course of their educational services, the survey inquired whether the respondents share internet resources with their students. About 79% responded in the affirmative, which is a potential for integrating the use of OER in teacher education programmes. But the issue of lack of proper understanding of OER provenance resurfaced here as only about 47% of the respondents examine the copyright provision of works before they remix the content and print or save a copy on the local server to share it with their students. Respondents are overwhelmed by the lack of and high cost of educational resources, as many of them indicated that the cost of educational resources and lack of textbooks are among the major problems of teaching and learning at their institutions. Moreover, most of the problems that hinder OER uptake and development in Africa are persisting among the respondents. These include lack of infrastructure, such as electricity and ICTs, lack of supporting policy, and lack of skill and training. Interestingly, the respondents submitted that time constraint is not a problem to them.

Conclusion

This chapter re-emphasises the low level of engagement with OER among professionals of Sub-Saharan Africa. The situation seems to be connected with the low level of awareness and misconceptions about OER among teaching professionals. The educational systems of the region have great potential for the use of OER. The systems have already been denied access to quality and relevant resources, as high-cost materials are made even more expensive by an unfavourable exchange rate. This paved the way for the use of the freely available resources on the internet, which the teachers curated to create handouts for the learners, often without considering copyright implications. To achieve the potential of OER in SSA, which is imperative to achieve social justice in the region, there is a need for a massive campaign on the use of OER in the region. These may include government awareness programmes and policy formulation as well as institutional initiatives such as conferences and curriculum reviews to incorporate OER. Private funders need to increase their efforts in stimulating and supporting OER initiatives in the region. To shy away from these facts means denying millions of people access to quality education in Sub-Saharan Africa, which would keep the world far from achieving social justice for all.

Endnotes

1. "UNESCO in Brief—Mission and Mandate," UNESCO, 2019, https://en.unesco.org/about-us/introducing-unesco.
2. "Education Transforms Lives," UNESCO, 2019, https://en.unesco.org/themes/education.
3. Clayton R. Wright and Sunday A. Reju, "Developing and Deploying OERs in Sub-Saharan Africa: Building on the Present," *International Review of Research in Open and Distributed Learning* 13, no. 2 (2012): 181–220.
4. Jorrit Mulder, "Knowledge Dissemination in Sub-Saharan Africa: What Role for Open Educational Resources (OER)?" (master's thesis, Amsterdam, University of Amsterdam, 2008).
5. Ed Diener, Carol Diener, and Robert Biswas-Diener, "Open-Source for Educational Materials Making Textbooks Cheaper and Better," in *The Philosophy and Practices That Are Revolutionizing Education and Science*, ed. R. S. Jhangiani and R. Biswas-Diener (London: Ubiquity Press, 2017), 209–17.

6. Martin Weller, *The Battle for Open: How Openness Won and Why It Doesn't Feel like Victory* (London: Ubiquity Press, 2014), 75.
7. "Recommendation on Open Educational Resources (OER)," UNESCO, 2019, http://portal.unesco.org/en/ev.php-URL_ID=49556&URL_DO=DO_TOPIC&URL_SECTION=201.html.
8. Weller, *The Battle for Open*, 72.
9. Patricia B. Arinto et al., "Research on Open Educational Resources for Development in the Global South: Project Landscape," in *Adoption and Impact of OER in the Global South*, ed. Hodgkinson-Williams and Patricia B. Arinto (Cape Town: African Minds, 2017), 3–26, doi: 10.5281/zenodo.1005330.
10. Cornelia K. Muganda, Athuman S Samzugi, and Brenda Justine Mallinson, "Analytical Insights on the Position, Challenges, and Potential for Promoting OER in ODeL Institutions in Africa," *International Review of Research in Open and Distributed Learning* 17, no. 4 (2016): 36–49; J. Atenas and Leo Havemann, "Quality Assurance in the Open: An Evaluation of OER Repositories," *International Journal for Innovation and Quality in Learning* 1, no. 2 (2013): 22–34.
11. Joel S. Mtebe and Roope Raisamo, "Investigating Perceived Barriers to the Use of Open Educational Resources in Higher Education in Tanzania," *The International Review of Research in Open and Distance Learning* 15, no. 2 (2014): 43–66, https://doi.org/10.19173/irrodl.v15i2.1803.
12. Geser, Guntram, ed. 'Open Educational Practices and Resources'. Open e-Learning Content Observatory Services (OLCOS), 2012. https://files.eric.ed.gov/fulltext/ED498433.pdf.
13. For examples, Diener, Diener, and Biswas-Diener, "Open-Source for Educational Materials," 209–17.
14. Reported by Sarah Goodier, "Tracking the Money for Open Educational Resources in South African Basic Education: What We Don't Know," in *Adoption and Impact of OER in the Global South*, ed. Cheryl Hodgkinson-Williams and Patricia B. Arinto (Cape Town: African Minds, 2017), 233–49, doi: 10.5281/zenodo.1005330.
15. Tony John Mays, "Mainstreaming Use of Open Educational Resources (OER) in an African Context," *Open Praxis* 9, no. 4 (2017): 387–401.
16. Caleb Imbova Mackatiani, Alfred Nyakangi Ariemba, and Jane Wanjiku Ngware, "African Response to Quality Education: Comparative Perspectives on Quality Primary Education in Kenya," *European Journal of Education Studies* 6, no. 11 (2020), https://doi.org/doi:10.5281/zenodo.3663073.
17. Freda Wolfenden, Alison Buckler, and Fred Keraro, "OER Adaptation and Reuse across Cultural Contexts in Sub Saharan Africa: Lessons from TESSA (Teacher Education in Sub Saharan Africa)," *Journal of Interactive Media in Education* (2012), https://jime.open.ac.uk/articles/10.5334/2012-03/.
18. Sajitha Bashir et al., *Facing Forward: Schooling for Learning in Africa*, Africa Development Forum Series (Washington, DC: World Bank, 2018).
19. Mulder, "Knowledge Dissemination."
20. Nduka Orijinmo, "Nigeria's School Abductions: Why Children Are Being Targeted," *BBC News*, March 2, 2021, sec. News, https://www.bbc.com/news/world-africa-56212645; Vanguard Media Limited, "We Mustn't Allow Boko Haram, Bandits Disrupt Learning," *Vanguard Media Limited*, March 2, 2021, sec. News, https://www.vanguardngr.com/2021/03/we-mustnt-allow-boko-haram-bandits-disrupt-learning-%E2%80%95-tambuwal/.
21. Wright and Reju, "Developing and Deploying OERs," 181–220.
22. Neil Butcher, Asha Kanwar, and Stamenka Uvalic-Trumbic, *A Basic Guide to Open Educational Resources (OER)* (Paris: United Nations Educational, Scientific and Cultural Organization & Commonwealth of Learning, 2015).
23. Patrick Alan Danaher and Abdurrahman Umar, eds., *Creating New Forms of Teacher Education: Open Educational Resources (OERs) and the Teacher Education in Sub-Saharan Africa (TESSA) Programme* (Vancouver: Commonwealth of Learning, 2010).
24. "'NUC Partners University of London on ODL," National Universities Commission (NUC), Institutional, n.d., https://www.nuc.edu.ng/nuc-partners-university-of-london-on-odl/.

25. Suleiman Ramon-Yusuf, "Trend in Open and Distance Learning in the Nigerian University System," in *The National Universities Commission and University Education in Nigeria: Perfectives on the Development of a System* (Abuja-Nigeria: National Universities Commission, 2014), 203–32.
26. Stuart Lawson, "The Political Histories of UK Public Libraries and Access to Knowledge," in *Reassembling Scholarly Communications: Histories, Infrastructures, and Global Politics of Open Access*, ed. Martin Paul Eve and Jonathan Gray (MIT Press, 2020), 161–72.
27. Freda Wolfenden et al., "Teacher Educators and OER Tin East Africa: Interrogating Pedagogical Change," in *Adoption and Impact of OER in the Global South*, ed. Cheryl Hodgkinson-Williams and Patricia B. Arinto (Cape Town: African Minds, 2017), 251–86, doi: 10.5281/zenodo.1005330.
28. Arinto et al., "Research on Open Educational Resources," 3–26.
29. Jane-Frances O. Agbu and Sanjaya Mishra, "Open Educational Resources Policy for Higher Education in Nigeria" (British Columbia: Commonwealth of Learning, 2017), http://oasis.col.org/handle/11599/2798 (page discontinued).
30. "Population 2006–2016," National Bureau of Statistics, Population forecast, Abuja, n.d., https://nigerianstat.gov.ng/elibrary?queries[search]=population.
31. "Annual Abstract of Statistics, 2017," National Bureau of Statistics, Annual Abstract and Statistics, Abuja-Nigeria: National Bureau of Statistics, 2017, https://nigerianstat.gov.ng/elibrary.
32. Wolfenden et al., "Teacher Educators," 251–86, doi: 10.5281/zenodo.1005330.
33. "Recommendation on Open Educational Resources (OER)," UNESCO.

Bibliography

Agbu, Jane-Frances O., and Sanjaya Mishra. "Open Educational Resources Policy for Higher Education in Nigeria." British Columbia: Commonwealth of Learning, 2017. http://oasis.col.org/handle/11599/2798. Page discontinued.

Akinwumi, Femi Sunday, and T. L. Adepoju. "Roles of Educational Agencies in Nigerian Educational System." In *Educational Management: Theories and Tasks*, 165–80. Ibadan: Macmilian Nigerian Publishers, 2009. https://www.researchgate.net/publication/343282455_Roles_of_Educational_Agencies_in_Nigerian_Educational_System.

Arinto, Patricia B., Cheryl Hodgkinson-Williams, Thomas King, Tess Cartmill, and Michelle Willmers. "Research on Open Educational Resources for Development in the Global South: Project Landscape." In *Adoption and Impact of OER in the Global South*, edited by Cheryl Hodgkinson-Williams and Patricia B. Arinto, 3–26. Cape Town: African Minds, 2017. doi: 10.5281/zenodo.1005330.

Atenas, Javiera, and Leo Havemann. "Quality Assurance in the Open: An Evaluation of OER Repositories." *International Journal for Innovation and Quality in Learning* 1, no. 2 (2013): 22–34.

Bashir, Sajitha, Marlaine E. Lockheed, Elizabeth Ninan, and Jee-Peng Tan. *Facing Forward: Schooling for Learning in Africa*. Africa Development Forum Series. Washington, DC: World Bank, 2018.

Butcher, Neil, Asha Kanwar, and Stamenka Uvalic-Trumbic. *A Basic Guide to Open Educational Resources (OER)*. Paris: United Nations Educational, Scientific and Cultural Organization & Commonwealth of Learning, 2015.

Danaher, Patrick Alan, and Abdurrahman Umar, eds. *Creating New Forms of Teacher Education: Open Educational Resources (OERs) and the Teacher Education in Sub-Saharan Africa (TESSA) Programme*. Vancouver: Commonwealth of Learning, 2010.

Diener, Ed, Carol Diener, and Robert Biswas-Diener. "Open-Source for Educational Materials Making Textbooks Cheaper and Better." In *The Philosophy and Practices That Are Revolutionizing Education and Science*, edited by R. S. Jhangiani and R. Biswas-Diener, 209–17. London: Ubiquity Press, 2017.

Down, Lindsey R. "Opening New Path to Success—A Journey with Open Textbooks." WCET Frontiers, 2018. http://wcetfrontiers.org/2018/04/26/opening-a-new-path-to-success-a-journey-with-open-textbooks/.

Global Monitoring Report Team, The. "Education: The Other Global Emergency." *The UNESCO Courier* (2008).

Goodier, Sarah. "Tracking the Money for Open Educational Resources in South African Basic Education: What We Don't Know." In *Adoption and Impact of OER in the Global South*, edited by Cheryl Hodgkinson-Williams and Patricia B. Arinto, 233–49. Cape Town: African Minds, 2017. doi: 10.5281/zenodo.1005330.

Hart, Kerry de, Yuraisha Chetty, and Elizabeth Archer. "Uptake of OER by Staff in Distance Education in South Africa." *International Review of Research in Open and Distributed Learning* 16, no. 2 (2015): 18–45. https://doi.org/10.19173/irrodl.v16i2.2047.

Kleymeer, Pieter, Molly Kleinman, and Ted Hanss. "Reaching the Heart of the University: Libraries and the Future of OER." In *Open ED 2010*, 241–50. Barcelona: Universitat Oberta de Catalunya, 2010.

Lawson, Stuart. "The Political Histories of UK Public Libraries and Access to Knowledge." In *Reassembling Scholarly Communications: Histories, Infrastructures, and Global Politics of Open Access*, edited by Martin Paul Eve and Jonathan Gray, 161–72. MIT Press, 2020.

Mackatiani, Caleb Imbova, Alfred Nyakangi Ariemba, and Jane Wanjiku Ngware. "African Response to Quality Education: Comparative Perspectives on Quality Primary Education in Kenya." *European Journal of Education Studies* 6, no. 11 (2020). https://doi.org/doi: 10.5281/zenodo.3663073.

Marcus-Quinn, A., and Y. Diggins. "Open Educational Resources." In *Procedia—Social and Behavioral Sciences*, 243–46. Turkey: Elsevier, 2013.

Mays, Tony John. "Mainstreaming Use of Open Educational Resources (OER) in an African Context." *Open Praxis* 9, no. 4 (2017): 387–401.

Moon, Bob. "Creating New Forms of Teacher Education: Open Educational Resources (OERs) and the Teacher Education in Sub-Saharan Africa (TESSA) Programme." In *Perspectives on Distance Education: Teacher Education through Open and Distance Learning*, edited by Patrick Alan Danaher and Abdurrahman Umar, 121–42. Vancouver: Commonwealth of Learning, 2010.

Mtebe, Joel S., and Roope Raisamo. "Investigating Perceived Barriers to the Use of Open Educational Resources in Higher Education in Tanzania." *The International Review of Research in Open and Distance Learning* 15, no. 2 (2014): 43–66. https://doi.org/10.19173/irrodl.v15i2.1803.

Muganda, Cornelia K., Athuman S. Samzugi, and Brenda Justine Mallinson. "Analytical Insights on the Position, Challenges, and Potential for Promoting OER in ODeL Institutions in Africa." *International Review of Research in Open and Distributed Learning* 17, no. 4 (2016): 36–49.

Mulder, Jorrit. "Knowledge Dissemination in Sub-Saharan Africa: What Role for Open Educational Resources (OER)?" Master's thesis, University of Amsterdam, 2008.

National Board for Arabic and Islamic Studies (NBAIS). "About Us." Accessed March 30, 2021. https://nbais.com.ng/about-us.

National Board for Technical Education. "About Us." National Board for Technical Education. 2021. https://net.nbte.gov.ng/about%20us.

National Commission for Mass Literacy, Adult & Non-Formal Education. "Mandate." 2020. https://www.nmec.gov.ng/mandate.php.

National Teachers Institute. "About NTI." 2017. http://www.nti.edu.ng/about/about-nti/.

National Universities Commission (NUC). "Nigeria's Draft OER Policy Gets World Acclaim." National Universities Commission. n.d. https://www.nuc.edu.ng/nigerias-draft-oer-policy-gets-world-acclaim/.

Ngimwa, Pauline, and Wilson Tina. "An Empirical Investigation of the Emergent Issues around OER Adoption in Sub-Saharan Africa." *Learning, Media and Technology* 37, no. 4 (2012): 398–413.

Olufunke, Akomolafe Comfort, and Olajire Adeola Adegun. "Utilization of Open Educational Resources (OER) and Quality Assurance in Universities in Nigeria." *European Scientific Journal* 10, no. 7 (2014): 535–43. https://doi.org/10.19044/esj.2014.v10n7p%25p.

Open Education Conference. "Planning Committees." 2021. https://openeducationconference.org/about/planning-teams.

Open Education Global. "Members." Accessed March 20, 2021. https://www.oeglobal.org/members/.

Orijinmo, Nduka. "Nigeria's School Abductions: Why Children Are Being Targeted." *BBC News*. March 2, 2021, sec. News. https://www.bbc.com/news/world-africa-56212645.

Ramon-Yusuf, Suleiman. "Trend in Open and Distance Learning in the Nigerian University System." In *The National Universites Commission and University Education in Nigeria: Perspectives on the Development of a System*, 203–32. Abuja-Nigeria: National Universities Commission, 2014.

Tertiary Education Trust Fund. "Guideline." 2020. https://tetfundserver.com/index.php/guideline-12/.

———. *Guidelines for Higher Education Book Development*. 2nd ed. Abuja-Nigeria: Tertiary Education Trust Fund. 2020. https://tetfundserver.com/index.php/guideline-3/.

Thakrar, Jayshree, Freda Wolfenden, and Denise Zinn. "Harnessing Open Educational Resources to the Challenges of Teacher Education in Sub-Saharan Africa." *International Review of Research in Open and Distributed Learning* 10, no. 4 (2009): 1–15. https://doi.org/10.19173/irrodl.v10i4.705.

Tina, Wilson. "New Ways of Mediating Learning: Investigating the Implications of Adopting Open Educational Resources for Tertiary Education at an Institution in the United Kingdom as Compared to One in South Africa." *International Review of Research in Open and Distributed Learning* 9, no. 1 (2008).

UNESCO. "Education Transforms Lives." UNESCO. 2019. https://en.unesco.org/themes/education.

———. "Forum on the Impact of Open Courseware for Higher Education in Developing Countries." UNESCO. 2002. https://unesdoc.unesco.org/ark:/48223/pf0000128515.

———. "Nigeria Identifies Priority Areas for Open Educational Resources." UNESCO. 2021. https://en.unesco.org/news/nigeria-identifies-priority-areas-open-educational-resources.

———. "Recommendation on Open Educational Resources (OER)." UNESCO. 2019. http://portal.unesco.org/en/ev.php-URL_ID=49556&URL_DO=DO_TOPIC&URL_SECTION=201.html.

———. "UNESCO in Brief—Mission and Mandate." UNESCO. 2019. https://en.unesco.org/about-us/introducing-unesco.

Universal Basic Education Commission. "Annual Report." Abuja: Universal Basic Education Comission. 2018. https://www.ubec.gov.ng/publication/report/.

University of South Africa. "African & SA OER Initiatives." University of South Africa. 2021. https://www.unisa.ac.za/sites/corporate/default/Unisa-Open/African-&-SA-OER-initiatives.

Vanguard Media Limited. "We Mustn't Allow Boko Haram, Bandits Disrupt Learning." *Vanguad Media Limited* (March 2, 2021), sec. News. https://www.vanguardngr.com/2021/03/we-mustnt-allow-boko-haram-bandits-disrupt-learning-%E2%80%95-tambuwal/.

Weller, Martin. "Different Aspects of the Emerging OER Discipline." *Revista Educacao e Cultura Contemporanea* 13, no. 31 (2016): 404–18.

———. *The Battle for Open: How Openness Won and Why It Doesn't Feel like Victory*. London: Ubiquity Press, 2014.

Wolfenden, Freda. "The TESSA OER Experience: Building Sustainable Models of Production and User Implementation." *Journal of Interactive Media in Education* 1 (2008). https://doi.org/10.5334/2008-3.

Wolfenden, Freda, Pritee Auckloo, Alison Buckler, and Jane Cullen. "Teacher Educators and OER Tin East Africa: Introgating Pedagogical Change." In *Adoption and Impact of OER in the Global South*, edited by Cheryl Hodgkinson-Williams and Patricia B. Arinto, 251–86. Cape Town: African Minds, 2017. doi: 10.5281/zenodo.1005330.

Wolfenden, Freda, Alison Buckler, and Fred Keraro. "OER Adaptation and Reuse across Cultural Contexts in Sub Saharan Africa: Lessons from TESSA (Teacher Education in Sub Saharan Africa)." *Journal of Interactive Media in Education* (2012). https://jime.open.ac.uk/articles/10.5334/2012-03/.

World Open Educationl Resources (OER) Congress UNESCO Congress. "2012 Paris OER Declaration." UNESCO. 2012. http://www.unesco.org/new/fileadmin/MULTIMEDIA/HQ/CI/WPFD2009/English_Declaration.html.

Wright, Clayton R., and Sunday A. Reju. "Developing and Deploying OERs in Sub-Saharan Africa: Building on the Present." *International Review of Research in Open and Distributed Learning* 13, no. 2 (2012): 181–220.

SECTION IV
Scaling Up with Institutional Policies (Approaches)

CHAPTER 11

Reflecting on the Institutional Organization of Academic "Knowledge" as a Barrier to OER Construction and Adoption in Higher Education Curricula

Emily M. Doyle, Kristin Petrovic, Tanya Mudry, and Murray Anderson

The concept of open education resources (OER) originated in response to a demand for increased and equitable access to educational materials. The potential value of OER use has since been taken up in post-secondary institutions and linked to increased learner success due to the removal of financial barriers. Within university or college curriculum development, educators can reuse, retain, remix, redistribute, and revise OER to tailor resources to meet the unique teaching and learning activities in their courses.[1-3] The digital nature of OER allows for the continual integration of user feedback, resulting in prompt revisions to increase quality and provide an excellent learner experience.[4]

Integration of OER into course curricula can also facilitate continued access to content for program graduates, as they are digitally accessible, open-licensed, and freely available. As academics in regulated health professions, we endorse the value of open access materials, not only on behalf of the learners that we work with but also for our graduates and other practitioners in our communities of practice (psychology, education, and nursing). For practice-orientated professionals, continued competency requires continuous engagement with developments in research and current trends. Without OER, equitable access to information is of concern post-graduation, when the library resources of the institution are no longer accessible to support this type of engagement with fee-for-service resources in professional life.

Before attempting to specify how OER can contribute to the promotion of social justice through equitable access for health professionals post-graduation, it is critical that we consider how the construction of OER is not currently a supported practice within academia for the majority of those responsible for the generation of the knowledge that is required to be incorporated into educational programs. When the social and institutional barriers to contributing to the construction and implementation of OER are made explicit, we will be better positioned to systematically dismantle them. We propose utilizing this chapter as an opportunity to begin to consider these tensions and immediate barriers, as we currently are experiencing them in our faculty roles in psychology and nursing, with the intention to inform advocacy for new possibilities for how OER can be considered, engaged with, and supported in academia.

Tensions in the Social and Institutional Organization of "Knowledge" in Academia

Definitions of academic "knowledge" are often absent but implicit in the everyday work required of academic faculty. They are taken for granted but tacitly operating in the background, informing what is recognizable as valid and valuable in the everyday work we engage in. If we look closely enough, we can find links to how "knowledge" is implicitly defined within many of the "boss texts"[5]—reproducible written and graphic materials that orient, coordinate, and sometimes constrain our professional activities within both our specific institutions and, more broadly, our professions. These texts provide the context that makes our work recognizable and can include our institution's practices and policies, ethical and values statements, job descriptions, competency assessments, and, at the individual course level, grading rubrics.

Current discourses of "knowledge" within many academic institutions suggest that the institutional value of OER is acknowledged and contextualized as consideration of the future of education in a digital age. As junior academics and curriculum developers, we have been encouraged by faculty leadership to, whenever possible, draw from free OER rather than from costly textbooks or fee-for-services resources with the goal of reducing institutional course material costs. The nature of an OER resource to be personalized[6,7] can facilitate maintained engagement with the learning material in meaningful ways, both as part of educational programs and to inform professional practices after degree completion.

Tensions arise when these acknowledged possibilities for OER integration are contrasted with the definitions of "knowledge" contained in the grading policies and practices upon which grading rubrics are built (boss texts). In these texts, both explicit and implicit requirements are conveyed that operate to constrain how OER can actually be used in our everyday academic work. To illustrate, the following example is drawn from an Athabasca University webpage, created by faculty for use by graduate students in counseling psychology:

> The foundation for scholarly work and practices of intellectual honesty is your grounding in the scholarly literature of the discipline. This involves selecting appropriate sources of information, as well using those sources ethically in your own work. If you fail to use academic sources for your paper, your paper will not be considered graduate level writing, and it will be graded accordingly.... The reference list must include recent scholarly (typically peer-reviewed) sources such as academic journals, books, monographs, and other appropriate sources.... One of the typical features of quality healthcare literature is that it is peer-reviewed. This means that other professionals with relevant expertise have provided feedback on the content and judged its quality as sufficiently rigorous and scholarly to warrant publication. Many books are not peer-reviewed. However, most academic journals are peer-reviewed.[8]

The implicit message conveyed is that the most valid forms of knowledge are contained within peer-reviewed published journal articles. This also extends to the message conveyed by grading rubrics, where graduate students are required to cite a minimum number of "appropriate" sources. Any additional sources—including OER that are not linked to easily recognizable journals—cannot normally be counted toward this minimum quota of scholarly support in how they have come to know the topic they are writing about. The explicit direction, then, for course instructors is that in order for students to demonstrate that they have achieved sufficient competency to pass the assignment (and the course), they must have adhered to the academic definition of knowledge in their work.

In course construction, this grading expectation, in turn, informs the practices of the curriculum developers and instructors, as they were brought up in this academic culture, adhering to these expectations as they select "appropriate" course materials. Current practices of curriculum development are informed by both implicit and explicitly stated guidelines. Although not explicitly stated, the implication is that professionals should disregard other sources that are not institutionally supported. Different institutional messages—both explicit and implicit—are needed for OER to be valued as valid in our everyday work practices. As health disciplines education is intended to inform professional practice after graduation, the implicit meaning becomes that health professionals are required to continue in this regard toward peer-reviewed journals and continuing beyond graduation from an educational program.

Tensions in Developing and Integrating OER for use in Health Disciplines Curricula

In many areas of health education, there has been a move toward evidence-based practice, adopting a "scientist-practitioner" or "Boulder" model of training.[9] This model is becoming increasingly medicalized and aims to teach student-clinicians to adhere to the scientific method in research and practice, which includes drawing from empirically based research in their academic work and utilizing evidence-based assessment, diagnosis (*Diagnostic Manual of Mental Disorders*; DSM-5), and interventions. This medicalization is often in tension with the foundation of counselor education, for example, which tends to be grounded in a plurality of approaches focused on diversity, multiculturalism, and social justice.[10] Even if a counselor-educator is well-grounded in a social justice framework (privileging the voices of marginalized authors, content, modalities, speakers, etc.), the expectation of the discipline to use and teach evidence-based, peer-reviewed literature often wins.

Nursing education is also framed from an evidence-based or evidence-informed perspective, with heavy reliance on the evidence being that of scholarly and peer-reviewed works.[11] These scholarly peer-reviewed works have produced dominant societal norms that do not always represent those who sit within minority groups.[12] When these clinical standards are applied to all clients, a subtle form of racism can come to exist, implicit in how practices have been constructed.[13]

As curriculum developers, we have observed that demand for OER resources exceeds their current availability, rendering the promotion, organization, and findability of OER repositories challenging.[14] Although the use of OER is encouraged by faculty leadership and could address concerns related to equitable access to educational materials, both nursing and psychology professions are still in the beginning stages of developing robust repositories. For example, we conducted a search of the Creative Commons OER e-texts in nursing theory and found only four e-texts and five e-modules on different websites that meet our institutional criteria for use. There are likely more OER, but if they cannot be effectively and reliably located by curriculum developers, students, and practicing professionals, then they will not be integrated with available "knowledge."

Challenges in accessing viable OER for use in the health disciplines educational programs can be linked to the challenges in finding content experts who want to develop an OER, who have institutional support to pursue this development, and who have competence in the process of OER licensing and copyrighting practices.[15,16] Once resources are developed by competent professionals, it can be cost-prohibitive to consider pursuing the OER status that would qualify the publication as a peer-reviewed contribution. The cost of publishing an OER in this manner needs to be absorbed by the academic or the institution; cost ranges have been found of $299 to $5,000 US.[17]

The process of disseminating research through peer-reviewed contributions in reputable journals is particularly relevant, as it is almost exclusively academics who are willing to go through the publication process (largely because their careers depend on it). Peer-reviewed articles comprise the sanctioned body of "knowledge" on a given topic; these contributions become what is available to be cited, included, and learned from in the curriculum. However, it is not exclusively academics (often, it is rarely academics) who are on the front lines of practice. Obscured from view are the experiences of instructors in delivering curricula informed by these sources. Also, the experiences of learners going through these programs are given little attention during new course construction. Finally, it is concerning that the experiences of clients, whom the learners are being trained to serve, are rarely acknowledged; obscuring and/or ignoring the voices of those we serve is not a socially just practice in education.

Many OER are situated as teaching resources. While the role of teaching is critical in research-intensive higher education institutions (in fact, universities would cease to exist if there were not students to engage with in teaching and learning activities), teaching does not hold the same value as research on a curriculum vitae (CV) or application for funding and/or promotion, resulting in less motivation to engage in doing the work of developing OER.[18] When reviewing the structure of academic role appraisals, this does not sit as well as recognized work in the role of the junior academic. New faculty members, in particular, are bound by these tensions. They are assigned courses requiring "new prep," sometimes with little lead time to structure outlines and choose appropriate readings. Typically, new faculty members are required to hit the ground running and without adequate guidance regarding curriculum development as an ongoing professional competency. Teaching and learning departments might offer workshops for faculty members over the course of the year related to curriculum development, but this career development opportunity often does not line up with when course development tasks first take place.

More importantly, the actual time to attend these courses competes for more urgent, immediate, and non-negotiable tasks, with professional development in this area coming second (or third, or not at all), as workdays are allocated to current teaching load, research, and service responsibilities. As a result, previous course offering outlines are typically adapted and modified, which leaves less space for the location and integration of new resources such as OER; out of ease or necessity, the expensive seminal textbooks are often utilized. Additional institutional considerations that may limit the integration of OER into course curricula are beyond the work of course developers. To illustrate, at some institutions, course outlines must be approved by a program director, who might be (implicitly) examining for assigned readings and a rubric that privileges peer-reviewed journals, seminal textbooks, and the scientist-practitioner model. And some universities require course outlines to be approved by the university library's copyright department. When using content that is not in the purchased textbook or not available in the library, librarians need to obtain special copyright permission to include the content. There may even be organizational restrictions to how many special permission pages or chapters can be included in the course.

OER in the Context of "Publish or Perish" Academic Culture

As pre-tenure academics, publication in OER is consistently ranked as a lesser contribution to knowledge in the field, according to this particular piece of academic structure. Or payment is required to the journal or source to achieve OER status that we may not have the funds to support. Additionally, current practices and academic culture can encourage competition versus collegiality, with funding, tenure, promotion, and hiring focused on the contribution to knowledge as represented in a CV. As stated in March 14, 2006, Facebook posts on the page Shit Academics Say:

> Knowledge is power.
> Funding is knowledge.
> Funding is power.
> This is depressing.

Peer-reviewed publications, books, and presentations are often valued by tenure and promotion committees and external reviewers. Similarly, large grants are valued, which are more likely to be awarded through demonstration of expertise in the field, often indicated by publication in high-impact journals.

In traditional textbook development for academia, publishers assume most of the workload and cost of resource development. In OER development, however, responsibilities for publication, licensing, distribution, and revision now become work done at the levels of the institution and individual faculty members. This model can be critiqued for sustainability, questioning whether the cost of educational materials is actually lowered or if it has just shifted with the incorporation of OER. This model can also be critiqued for sustainability as it relates to the "publish or perish" culture that most academic professionals are evaluated within.

Arguably, if the articles are open access, they are more likely to have a higher actual impact. But producing them is costly. Tensions exist in how OER development, distribution, and revision are institutionally viable toward goals of accessibility. Because so much of someone's career depends on the claims they stake, there is limited (and even implicitly discouraged) opportunity for academics to change their minds and/or challenge their own ideas as OER maintenance would require. Creating a research or knowledge product can only be counted once on a CV (the original publication), meaning if the author was to dedicate the time to update a living document or OER, the time in doing so would not be institutionally visible in the ways that a new publication would be.

Tracking research impact has become increasingly viewed as a metric of academic success, which can be done via ORCiD, Google Scholar, as well as H-index. Success is measured by the impact of a published work based on how often it has been cited. Additionally, it can be challenging to be accepted by a high-impact journal, and the process entails lengthy review times once work is submitted. Submission requirements specify that work submitted for review has not been accepted into another journal and once accepted becomes the property of the publisher. This may prevent authors from using their own peer-reviewed work in OER development in substantive ways without complying with or purchasing copyright access rights permitting them to do so.

Professional Licensing Exams as Boss Texts

In both counseling psychology and nursing education programs, tensions in teaching and learning become explicit in the requirement to prepare students-in-training to enter their professional fields. This entails meeting the requirements of the regulatory colleges who will determine the "appropriate" foundational content to enter the discipline. The licensing exams for entrance into the discipline of psychology (Examination for Professional Practice in Psychology (EPPP) and nursing (the National Council Licensure Examination; NCLEX-RN) in Canada are the benchmarks of foundational content requiring competency for entrance.[19,20] These exams are expensive, requiring substantial knowledge that is not available for free or at a reasonable cost, and they cover numerous content areas regardless of their relevance to local practices as they are international examinations. These explicit directions in "appropriate content" are also evident in accreditation standards and guidelines for professional psychology programs and advanced nursing degrees. Curriculum developers, in addition to the other tensions they balance, are required to orient curricula toward licensure exam preparation.[21]

While foundational knowledge and expectations for entrance into the discipline are vital, access to OER covering this foundational knowledge is lacking. Seminal survey textbooks and exam preparation materials that cover the wide gamut of psychological theories and interventions often come with a high price tag. If there is access online through the library, there are often restrictions on the number of pages per day that can be downloaded or a limit to the number of users at a time, making it difficult for students to have their own copy.

OER and Continuing Competencies

Graduates from health disciplines programs, as regulated health professionals, are required to participate in continuing competence and professional development that involves staying abreast of new contributions to their fields. Ongoing professional development (otherwise referred to as continuing education and continuing professional development) is a requirement of psychological registration across all Canadian provinces. To facilitate this process, both the Canadian Psychological Association (CPA) and, regionally, the College of Alberta Psychologists (CAP) promote educational opportunities, including online professional development workshops, convention workshops, sponsored workshops, and seminars. Registered nurses (RN) across Canada are also required to demonstrate ongoing professional development. In Alberta, RNs can choose to demonstrate this through a variety of formal and informal learning opportunities, including formal higher education coursework, employer-delivered professional development, nursing education webinars and workshops, and self-led educational resource reviews.

In Alberta (where three of the four authors reside and practice), this process started with the passing of the Alberta Health Professions Act (HPA—boss text) in 1999, which emphasized the need to engage in continuing competence activities. In 2006, the College of Alberta Psychologists (CAP) developed a Continuing Competence Program (CCP), which describes several competency elements, including assessment of competence in professional practice, development of a learning plan, implementation of the learning plan, documentation of continuing competence activities, assessment of the learning plan, and an ongoing review of the two competence programs.[22] In 2010, the college forwarded the Psychologists Profession Regulation to Alberta Health and Wellness as per procedures outlined in the Health Professions Act entitled the Continuing Competence Program (CCP). As of 2021, the CCP exists as a voluntary practice until formal regulatory approval has occurred. RNs in Alberta participate under the same-titled program of the Continuing Competence Program, where they develop learning plans that highlight self-identified areas of growth from a professional competency set.[23] RNs are then required to report learning activities, assessment of competency, and evaluation as part of yearly license renewal.

There is a clear endorsement of the need for professional development that goes beyond university education that is comprehensive and career-long. A review of the boss texts Health Professions Act (HPA), the Canadian Code of Ethics for Psychologists (2000), and Practice Standards for Regulated Members[24] indicate that the responsibility for continuing professional development does not rest solely with the regulating bodies to provide but rather on the shoulders of the individual health practitioners to seek out. Such activities are relevant to professional practice, education, and science, enable practitioners to keep pace with emerging issues and technologies, and allow practitioners to maintain, develop, and increase competencies in order to improve services to the public and enhance contributions to the profession.

These expectations are reflected in Principle II.9 of Canadian Code of Ethics for Psychologists, which indicates that practitioners should "keep themselves up to date... through the reading of relevant literature, peer consultation, and continuing education activities, in order that their practice, teaching, supervision, and research activities will benefit and not harm others."[25] Psychologists are required to declare that they have participated in these activities during annual licensure renewal while retaining records of participation in case of a future audit. RNs in Alberta must participate in a similar process, including self, peer, and supervisory feedback as well as self-led continuing education activities with review and self-assessment of all competencies. They must keep a record of the full self-assessment, not just the targeted area of growth for the licensing year.

Tensions in Accessing Resources Toward Continuing Competencies

After graduation from a health disciplines program, tensions result from the equity of access to the course material and academic "knowledge" from which students were mentored. For example, at Athabasca University, student alumni access to a set of databases is more limited compared to that of active students. Physical book and journal access are not provided to alumni; instead, alumni are encouraged to reach out to their public libraries for supplemental research resources.[26]

Alumni could use open access resources to meet this need; however, this suggestion creates two tensions. First, while students, they learned to access peer-reviewed scholarly articles as a best practice. The practice of evidence gathering from peer-reviewed sources organized through the search engine is only available to active students, whereas alumni have to learn (without mentorship) a different way to access these resources. In exploring available databases, open access (OA) is not searchable, making it difficult to recognize what is accessible without a membership or additional fees; filtering a search for OA and OER are not yet mainstream library curation practices.[27] Options for alumni would be to access the under-resourced alumni database or, second, to engage in the unfamiliar practice of finding OER (or to pay exorbitant fees to purchase or rent scholarly articles). Along with the unfamiliar practice of access of OER is also the challenge of discerning the quality of the resource when not drawn from a resource they became familiar with during educational training and preparation.[28]

One illustration of tensions of discernment can be observed around the well-known open resource Wikipedia. Rhetoric in academia is that Wikipedia is not considered reputable as it is not under traditional peer-reviewed practices. Yet Wikipedia, on average, has 255 million page views daily[29] and edits are taking place every 1.8 seconds. What if the concern about reputability was mitigated by HCPs and academics having a built-in and recognized role in contributing to the health care articles in Wikipedia? The source then becomes a common source for clients and HCPs to gather information, lessening miscommunication, and the work of writing to explain health concepts in accessible language provides opportunities for academics and HCPs to evolve that skill set.

Using Wikipedia as a common and reputable source of information supports social justice mandates for equity in access to health information by all. Wiki edit-a-thons are recognized as open educational practices for both students and academics in general higher education.[30] As a collaborative project with teachers, students can contribute to Wikipedia pages with revisions and updates. The inclusion of student voices is a powerful opportunity to increase minoritized voices, such as those of students. Though Wiki-edits can provide an opportunity for students to do work that is meaningful in the realm of public knowledge, it is important to consider the traditional power dynamics of teacher and student relationships; student workload and student choice to contribute must be considered.[31]

Possible Paths Forward Supporting OER in the Health Disciplines Education and Academia

Some promising work being carried out in the field of OER is collaborative OER development with students as non-disposable assignments, extra-credit opportunities, mentorship initiatives, and opportunities to amplify minoritized voices in curricula. For example, in an OER nursing textbook development process, there were several positive outcomes, including students experiencing the shift in power in relationships that occurs through these collaborative experiences, socialization to the profession that comes with these experiences, and the experience of interacting with the content in an applied fashion, promoted deeper learning.[32] Students have also described their experiences of collaboration OER development as transformational in their learning about equitable access to education, including the pragmatic understanding of working within OER licensing, copyright, and intellectual property practices.[33,34]

OER has succeeded with some students as they would choose not to purchase traditional textbooks to save on cost. With OER, there is equitable access. However, as many of the OER are provided electronically, if a student wants a physical copy, they must print it themselves. This requires the student to have access to a printer and ink, which is a cost the student has to absorb.

OER are also an excellent opportunity to remove barriers for accessibility to quality evidence-informed information for the public.[35] With health education, this provides the potential to have access to reputable sources written in accessible language while facilitating client empowerment and health ownership. HCPs and health care academics are in an excellent position to contribute to the development and maintenance of these OER.

Conclusion

The tensions that result from the contrast between discourses of OER as valued, valuable, and desired for use in health disciplines education and the implicit academic traditions and pressures contained in the boss texts that organize and constrain how the actualities of the work can be done warrants further consideration. While contributing to the construction of publicly available lay media or professional press has been touted recently as increasingly important in funding applications and can be highlighted in an application for promotion and tenure, OER likely won't receive the same institutional research recognition, despite the possibility of much higher reach; we have yet to see a translation for recognition in academia. As a result, developing these types of "reliable" yet institutionally unrecognizable resources is a time-consuming practice and typically ends up being done off of "the side of one's desk" in the case of junior academics.

With OER sitting in public spaces, both locating resources and discernment of reputability are largely up to the person accessing them. As curriculum developers, we have internalized the discussed pressures to organize our work and our teaching resources, drawing from *validated, best-practice, gold-standard* sources of knowledge, typically found in peer-reviewed contributions. Academia has relied heavily on the peer-review process to discern credible evidence; challenging this traditional institutional practice will likely be a slow-turning ship. And for health care practitioners not attached to academia, participating in this work is even less understood, valued, and recognized.

There is a need for advocacy for change in terms of visibility and value of OER for pre-tenure academics and others in our fields of practice. This includes how to incorporate OER into coursework, with mentorship in how to incorporate them into continuing competency work after graduation. Institutions can purchase open access rights to faculty work so that it can be easily incorporated into curriculum development and in the construction of OER. Challenging the explicit and implicit "gold standards" for recognition as institutionally valuable and recognizable contributions may support academic scholars to both create and maintain OER.

We hope that this contribution does indeed contribute to our ability to unpack the barriers we face to the implementation of OER in health education and for registered health professionals in continued competency development. When we understand how our practices come to be shaped and constrained by the policies, procedures, and other boss texts operating far beyond the frontlines of our everyday work, we can target our advocacy efforts most effectively. As a group of four junior academics, we have embraced the tensions between identifying the importance of these types of contributions and the lack of institutional recognition for holding and disseminating the conversations in an open access space.

Endnotes

1. Thomas Carey, Alan Davis, Salvador Ferreras, and David Porter, "Using Open Educational Practices to Support Institutional Strategic Excellence in Teaching, Learning & Scholarship," *Open Praxis* 7 no. 2 (2015).
2. Tarah Ikahihifo, Kristian J. Spring, Jane Rosecrans, and Josh Watson, "Assessing the Savings from Open Educational Resources on Student Academic Goals," *International Review of Research in Open and Distributed Learning* 18, no. 7 (November 2017).
3. Ray Miller and Lindley Homol, "Building an Online Curriculum Based on OERs: The Library's Role," *Journal of Library & Information Services in Distance Learning* (October 2016).
4. Richard E. West, "Developing an Open Textbook for Learning and Instructional Design Technology," *TechTrends: Linking Research & Practice to Improve Learning* 63, no. 2 (2019).

5. Dorothy Smith and Susan Marie Turner, eds. *Incorporating Texts into Institutional Ethnographies* (Toronto: University of Toronto Press, 2014).
6. Ikahihifo, Spring, Rosecrans, and Watson, "Savings from Open Educational Resources."
7. Miller and Homol, "Curriculum Based OERs."
8. Sandra Collins, "Professional Writing in the Health Disciplines," Athabasca University, accessed March 21, 2021, http://charon.athabascau.ca/gcapgrad/Writing/Professional_Writing.html.
9. "Scientist–practitioner Model," Wikipedia, accessed March 20, 2021, at Wikipedia, https://en.wikipedia.org/wiki/Scientist%E2%80%93practitioner_model.
10. Tom Strong, Konstantinos Chondros, and Vanessa Vegter, "Medicalizing Tensions in Counselor Education," *European Journal of Psychotherapy & Counselling* 20, no. 2 (2018).
11. Samson Wakibi, Linda Ferguson, Lois Berry, Don Leidl, and Sara Belton, "Teaching Evidence-Based Nursing Practice: A Systematic Review and Convergent Qualitative Synthesis," *Journal of Professional Nursing* 37, no.1 (2021).
12. Roberta Waite and Deena Nardi, "Nursing Colonialism in America: Implications for Nursing leadership," *Journal of Professional Nursing* 35 no. 1 (2019).
13. Margareth Santos Zanchetta, Marguerite Cognet, Rezwana Rahman, Aaron Byam, Patricia Carlier, Camille Foubert, Zarina Lagersie, and Ricardo Federico Espindola, "Blindness, Deafness, Silence and Invisibility that Shields Racism in Nursing Education-Practice in Multicultural Hubs of Immigration," *Journal of Professional Nursing* (2020).
14. Lisa Petrides, Letha Goger, and Cynthia Jimes, "The Role of 'Open' in Strategic Library Planning," *Education Policy Analysis Archives* 24 (2016).
15. Drew Paulin and Caroline Haythornthwaite, "Crowdsourcing the Curriculum: Redefining E-Learning Practices Through Peer-Generated Approaches," *Information Society* 32, no. 2 (2016).
16. West, "Developing an Open Textbook."
17. Richard Van Noorden, "Open Access: The True Cost of Science Publishing," *Nature* (March 27, 2013).
18. Gráinne Conole and Mark Brown, "Reflecting on the Impact of the Open Education Movement," *Journal of Learning for Development* 5, no. 3 (2018).
19. *EPPP Candidate Handbook–Examination for Professional Practice in Psychology*, Association of State and Provincial Psychology Boards (ASPPB), 2021.
20. Kristin Petrovic, Emily Doyle, Annette Lane, and Lynn Corcoran, "The Work of Preparing Canadian Nurses for a Licensure Exam Originating from the USA: A Nurse Educator's Journey into the Institutional Organization of the NCLEX-RN," *International Journal of Nursing Education Scholarship* 16, no. 1 (2019).
21. Petrovic, Doyle, Lane, and Corcoran, "Preparing Canadian Nurses."
22. College of Alberta Psychologists, Continuing Competence Program, 2010, 6.
23. College and Association of Registered Nurses of Alberta, Continuing Competence, 2021.
24. College and Association of Registered Nurses of Alberta, *Practice Standards for Regulated Members*, January 2013.
25. Canadian Psychological Association, *Canadian Code of Ethics for Psycho* (2017): 19.
26. "Services for Alumni: Athabasca University Library & Scholarly Resources," Athabasca University, last modified 2018, accessed March 4, 2021.
27. Petrides, Goger, and Jimes, "Role of 'Open.'"
28. Evrim Baran and Dana AlZoubi, "Affordances, Challenges, and Impact of Open Pedagogy: Examining Students' Voices," *Distance Education* 41, no. 2 (2020).
29. Manish Singh, "Wikipedia now has more than 6 Million Articles in English–Tech-Crunch," TechCrunch, accessed March 20, 2021, https://techcrunch.com/2020/01/23/wikipedia-english-six-million-articles/.
30. Maha Bali, Catherine Cronin, and Rajiv Jhangiani, "Framing Open Educational Practices from a Social Justice Perspective," *Journal of Interactive Media in Education* 1, no. 10 (2020).
31. Bali, Cronin, and Jhangiani, "Framing a Social Justice Perspective."

32. Margaret Verkuyl, Jennifer Lapum, Oona St-Amant, Andy Tan, and Wendy Garcia, "Engaging Nursing Students in the Production of Open Educational Resources," *Nurse Education Today* 71 (2018).
33. Benjamin Croft and Monica Brown, "Inclusive Open Education: Presumptions, Principles, and Practices," *Distance Education* 41, no. 2 (2020).
34. Baran and AlZoubi, "Affordances, Challenges, and Impact."
35. Ibid.

Bibliography

Association of State and Provincial Psychology Boards (ASPPB). *EPPP Candidate Handbook–Examination for Professional Practice in Psychology*, 2021. https://cdn.ymaws.com/www.asppb.net/resource/resmgr/eppp_2/10_2020_eppp_candidate_handb.pdf.

Athabasca University, "Services for Alumni: Athabasca University Library & Scholarly Resources." Last modified 2018. Accessed March 4, 2021. http://library.athabascau.ca/ServicesAlumni.html#Access.

Bali, Maha, Catherine Cronin, and Rajiv Jhangiani. "Framing Open Educational Practices from a Social Justice Perspective." *Journal of Interactive Media in Education* 1, no. 10 (2020). https://doi.org/http://doi.org/10.5334/jime.565.

Baran, Evrim, and Dana AlZoubi. "Affordances, Challenges, and Impact of Open Pedagogy: Examining Students' Voices." *Distance Education* 41, no. 2 (2020): 230–44. https://doi.org/10.1080/01587919.2020.1757409.

Canadian Psychological Association. *Canadian Code of Ethics for Psycho* (2017). https://cpa.ca/docs/File/Ethics/CPA_Code_2017_4thEd.pdf.

Carey, Thomas, Alan Davis, Salvador Ferreras, and David Porter. "Using Open Educational Practices to Support Institutional Strategic Excellence in Teaching, Learning & Scholarship." *Open Praxis* 7 no. 2 (2015): 161–71. http://0-search.ebscohost.com.aupac.lib.athabascau.ca/login.aspx?direct=true&AuthType=url,ip,uid&db=eric&AN=EJ1075354&site=ehost-live.

College and Association of Registered Nurses of Alberta. *Practice Standards for Regulated Members*. January 2013. https://nurses.ab.ca/docs/default-source/document-library/standards/practice-standards-for-regulated-members.pdf?sfvrsn=d4893bb4_16.

———. *Continuing Competence*. 2021. https://nurses.ab.ca/become-a-nurse/registration-requirements/continuing-competence.

College of Alberta Psychologists. Continuing Competence Program. 2010. https://www.cap.ab.ca/Portals/0/pdfs/CCP-ProgramDescription.pdf?ver=2019-07-03-130050-563.

Collins, Sandra. "Professional Writing in the Health Disciplines." Athabasca University. Accessed March 21, 2021. http://charon.athabascau.ca/gcapgrad/Writing/Professional_Writing.html.

Conole, Gráinne, and Mark Brown. "Reflecting on the Impact of the Open Education Movement." *Journal of Learning for Development* 5, no. 3 (2018): 187–203. http://0-search.ebscohost.com.aupac.lib.athabascau.ca/login.aspx?direct=true&AuthType=url,ip,uid&db=eric&AN=EJ1197527&site=ehost-live.

Croft, Benjamin, and Monica Brown. "Inclusive Open Education: Presumptions, Principles, and Practices." *Distance Education* 41, no. 2 (2020): 156–70. https://doi.org/10.1080/01587919.2020.1757410.

Ikahihifo, Tarah K., Kristian J. Spring, Jane Rosecrans, and Josh Watson. "Assessing the Savings from Open Educational Resources on Student Academic Goals." *International Review of Research in Open and Distributed Learning* 18, no. 7 (November 2017): 126–40. http://0-search.ebscohost.com.aupac.lib.athabascau.ca/login.aspx?direct=true&AuthType=url,ip,uid&db=eric&AN=EJ1163189&site=ehost-live.

Miller, Ray, and Lindley Homol. "Building an Online Curriculum Based on OERs: The Library's Role." *Journal of Library & Information Services in Distance Learning* (October 2016): 349–59. https://doi.org/10.1080/1533290X.2016.1223957.

Paulin, Drew, and Caroline Haythornthwaite. "Crowdsourcing the Curriculum: Redefining E-Learning Practices Through Peer-Generated Approaches." *Information Society* 32, no. 2 (2016). 130–42. https://doi.org/10.1080/01972243.2016.1130501.

Petrides, Lisa, Letha Goger, and Cynthia Jimes. "The Role of 'Open' in Strategic Library Planning." *Education Policy Analysis Archives* 24 (2016). 36–42. https://doi.org/10.14507/epaa.24.2478.

Petrovic, Kristin, Emily Doyle, Annette Lane, and Lynn Corcoran. "The Work of Preparing Canadian Nurses for a Licensure Exam Originating from the USA: A Nurse Educator's Journey into the Institutional Organization of the NCLEX-RN." *International Journal of Nursing Education Scholarship* 16, no. 1 (2019). https://doi.org/10.1016/S2155-8256(17)30160-6.

Singh, Manish. "Wikipedia now has more than 6 Million Articles in English–TechCrunch." TechCrunch. Accessed March 20, 2021. https://social.techcrunch.com/2020/01/23/wikipedia-english-six-million-articles/.

Smith, Dorothy, and Susan Marie Turner, eds. *Incorporating Texts into Institutional Ethnographies*. Toronto: University of Toronto Press, 2014.

Strong, Tom, Konstantinos Chondros, and Vanessa Vegter. "Medicalizing Tensions in Counselor Education." *European Journal of Psychotherapy & Counselling* 20, no. 2 (2018): 220–43. https://doi.org/10.1080/13642537.2018.1459765.

Van Noorden, Richard. "Open Access: The True Cost of Science Publishing." *Nature* (2013): 426. http://0-search.ebscohost.com.aupac.lib.athabascau.ca/login.aspx?direct=true&db=edsbl&AN=RN329597099&site=eds-live.

Verkuyl, Margaret, Jennifer Lapum, Oona St-Amant, Andy Tan, and Wendy Garcia. "Engaging Nursing Students in the Production of Open Educational Resources." *Nurse Education Today* 71 (2018): 75. http://dx.doi.org/10.1016/j.nedt.2018.09.012.

Waite, Roberta, and Deena Nardi. "Nursing Colonialism in America: Implications for Nursing Leadership." *Journal of Professional Nursing* 35 no. 1 (2019): 18–25. https://doi.org/https://doi.org/10.1016/j.profnurs.2017.12.013.

Wakibi, Samson, Linda Ferguson, Lois Berry, Don Leidl, and Sara Belton. "Teaching Evidence-Based Nursing Practice: A Systematic Review and Convergent Qualitative Synthesis." *Journal of Professional Nursing* 37, no.1 (2021): 135. https://doi.org/10.1016/j.profnurs.2020.06.005.

West, Richard E. "Developing an Open Textbook for Learning and Instructional Design Technology." *TechTrends: Linking Research & Practice to Improve Learning* 63, no. 2 (2019): 226–35. https://doi.org/10.1007/s11528-018-0263-z.

Wikipedia. "Scientist–practitioner Model." Accessed March 20, 2021. https://en.wikipedia.org/wiki/Scientist%E2%80%93practitioner_model.

Zanchetta, Margareth Santos, Marguerite Cognet, Rezwana Rahman, Aaron Byam, Patricia Carlier, Camille Foubert, Zarina Lagersie, and Ricardo Federico Espindola. "Blindness, Deafness, Silence and Invisibility that Shields Racism in Nursing Education-Practice in Multicultural Hubs of Immigration." *Journal of Professional Nursing* (2020). https://doi.org/https://doi.org/10.1016/j.profnurs.2020.06.012.

CHAPTER 12

Beyond Affordability:
Developing Policy to Encourage Faculty to Explore OER as a Means to Create More Diverse, Inclusive, and Socially Conscious Course Materials

Dawn (Nikki) Cannon-Rech

OER as an Affordability Solution

Open educational resources (OER) have been recognized as an important method to ease the growing financial burden on students. As early as 2014, the US Public Interest Research Group (PIRG) published a study detailing the ways the high cost of textbooks can negatively impact students' academic success. A report published in February 2021 found that approximately 60 percent of students are still not buying assigned textbooks, even though they feel that not buying them will negatively impact their grades. The report also showed that approximately 11 percent of students are now deciding to not purchase access codes. These access codes often provide the platform for homework assignments, quizzes, and other important parts of their grades in a class.[1] As a result of this and other studies, many state systems and individual institutions have implemented affordability campaigns and grant monies to incentivize faculty to explore OER options for their courses. Initiatives such as Affordable Learning Georgia (ALG), the UMass Library Open Education Initiative, Temple University

Libraries' Alternate Textbook Project, and SUNY Textbooks all began as part of an active movement to save students money on course materials.[2] Many of these programs have also promoted the use of non-open materials, such as library subscription resources, as these do not incur any additional costs for students.

As the usage of OER materials has increased at these and other institutions, research has shown benefits beyond affordability. These benefits include lower drop/fail/withdraw (DFW) rates, higher engagement with course materials, and an increase in average grades, especially amongst traditionally more at-risk groups such as Pell recipients, non-white students, and part-time students.[3] More of these programs are now beginning to focus on educational equity and accessibility of these materials. ALG has created OpenALG, "a new responsive reading platform developed by Manifold. Manifold features a dark mode, alters font size to fit different screens, and encourages student participation through highlighting and annotation that can be done either individually or as a group."[4] Platforms like Manifold increase accessibility equity with American with Disabilities Act (ADA) best practices built in. These platforms also elevate OER materials from static documents, like PDFs, and create a more engaging learning experience.

During the recent COVID pandemic, OER leaders have documented a notable increase in interest in OER materials. Richard Baraniuk, founder of OpenStax, describes the growth as "off the charts. We're in a special moment in history—a critical time for OER as course modalities are changing rapidly from in-person to hybrid to online."[5] Many feel that this pandemic has permanently changed education, and these hybrid courses will be more the norm than 100 percent face-to-face courses. OER's flexibility and accessibility are the driving forces for this increase in usage since March 2020.

Still, with all the changes the movement has seen, and the knowledge that the benefits of OER go well beyond affordability, the flexibility that OER offer to pedagogy and what is covered in a subject seem to receive the least attention from most stakeholders.

Social Justice in Education

The idea of addressing social justice in education is not new, and it has been an area of contention for some. Twenty-one years ago, Nieto wrote that this controversy revolves around the fact that "it insists that awareness of issues of social justice and power relations in our society, past and present, are crucially relevant to the future of our society and the priorities and values of the next generation."[6] Since this publication, quite a bit has been centered on training K-12 teachers to be culturally responsive and aware of how to present issues of social justice within their curricula. In 2011, Hytten and Bettez published a work attempting to synthesize the works of social justice in education. They divided these works into five different categories, labeled philosophical/conceptual, practical, ethnographic/narrative, theoretically specific, and democratically grounded. Throughout their review of the literature, the authors state more than once that none of the above categories contains an agreed-upon and firm definition of social justice and education.[7] This lack of agreement as to what constitutes social justice in education adds to the complexity of addressing it with any standards that can be fully measured. When we place the concepts of social justice within the frame of what we know about OER, we often return to the fundamental works of "Paulo Freire and bell hooks, [as] we recognize a commitment to diversity, collaboration, and structural critique of both educational systems and the technologies that permeate them."[8]

Diversity, Equity, and Inclusion in Higher Education

Many institutions have developed diversity, equity, and inclusion (DEI) plans and initiatives to advertise a campus welcoming to all individuals. The past few years have seen an increase in uprisings and movements, with an apex of sorts during the summer of 2020 centering around the murders of George Floyd and Breonna Taylor. Since these events, several institutions have specifically added anti-racism plans to extend the standard DEI plans. The Educational Advisory Board (EAB) has since created a specific website dedicated to highlighting resources for institutions, chief diversity officers, and anyone else looking to include social justice within their DEI plans. Their landing page specifically states, "Our goal is to provoke thought and agitate for action across higher education. We believe that diversity, equity, and inclusion, while noble goals and disciplines on their own, must be animated by the ongoing pursuit of justice for those harmed by the racist systems of oppression that operate throughout our society. Colleges and universities have a vital role to play in this work."[9]

The ideas of diversity, equity, and inclusion intersect with the foundational ideas of social justice. Most institutions have developed definitions incorporating statements pertaining to welcoming communities celebrating all diversity while utilizing a purposeful development of resources to enhance student learning. Certainly, OER and the freedoms allotted by their open licenses encompass this portion of these statements, and so again they represent a natural fit to accomplish the goals of enhancing student learning.

Georgia Southern's Diversity, Equity, and Inclusion Journey

Georgia Southern University is a public doctoral and research university located on three campuses in southeast Georgia. Georgia Southern offers 141 degree programs and serves more than 26,000 full-time and part-time students. In 2017, the Board of Regents announced a consolidation between Georgia Southern University, Statesboro, and Armstrong University, Savannah. Complete turnover in administration from the president, provost, and several college-level deans have led to several new initiatives on the campuses. Attempts to blend institutions with different atmospheres and student body dynamics resulted in consulting an outside expert, Dr. Damon Williams, to provide a third-party assessment of diversity and inclusion on the Georgia Southern campuses. This resulting report, completed in 2019, indicated that many Georgia Southern students and faculty did not feel the university was welcoming to all groups or that diversity was being actively promoted and supported.[10] This report included several recommendations, including the development of an Office of Inclusive Excellence and the hiring of an associate vice president for inclusive excellence and chief diversity officer to head this new unit. This plan also recommended the development of a strategic diversity leadership framework that includes accountability measures within.

Social Justice within the Curriculum

As all of these changes were taking place within the administration of Georgia Southern, it should be noted that many faculty were already working to increase diversity and inclusion concepts within the curriculum. Many institutions have been working to ensure that teacher training programs include social justice training for teaching candidates. Georgia Southern's curriculum for their Master of Art in Teaching (MAT) in Elementary Education is centered completely around culturally responsive teaching. One of the first courses listed in the requirements is Culturally Responsive Pedagogy and Classroom Management. In addition, the College of Education (COE) offers a six-course certification program in Curriculum and Pedagogy for Social Justice. The program's website describes the goal of this certification as "designed to provide educators with the theoretical foundations, historical knowledge, practical experience, and supportive infrastructure needed to become reflective practitioners who successfully integrate social justice education into their classrooms. This graduate certificate can be completed as a stand-alone program or along with any of the master's degrees offered in the College of Education. An underlying assumption of this graduate certificate is that educators who engage in social justice education will be able to identify dehumanizing sociopolitical conditions that undermine good teaching and academic achievement and will actively engage in pedagogical practices to alter those conditions to educate all students to reach their highest potential."[11]

Other colleges within the university have addressed social justice issues with grants designed to increase diversity in STEM representation, developing workshops and seminars exposing students to diversity and social justice issues and integrating readings and assignments. The university administration sponsored two full professional development days, one for faculty and one for staff, dedicated to inclusive excellence professional development. Led by campus faculty, the Center for Teaching Excellence (CTE), and some outside experts, these workshops sought to facilitate conversation and teach practical and simple ways for faculty and staff to play a role in social justice education centered around inclusive excellence. As the Affordable Learning Georgia (ALG) Library Champion, I taught two separate workshops on how OER materials support diversity, inclusion, and social justice. This was Georgia Southern's first documented program where OER was introduced as more than just a way to cut student costs.

OER at Georgia Southern

At Georgia Southern, support for open educational resources (OER) traditionally had been offered through passive educational activities, such as maintaining a generic OER website or LibGuide and emailing basic information about OER through institutional listservs. These efforts are coordinated with the statewide Affordable Learning Georgia (ALG) initiative by a "library champion" who works with the campus community and fellow librarians to support OER initiatives campus-wide. In 2017, I was appointed the new ALG "library champion" and began working to increase OER awareness on the consolidated campuses. Since then, the university libraries have taken a more active and integrated approach to support OER education and advocacy through workshops, semester-long learning communities, and one-on-one consultations. Like almost all programs, my initial workshops and educational materials centered around the affordability theme of OER materials, with almost all focus centered around addressing the rising cost of course materials. The ALG initiative itself was originally designed with this goal in mind, and ALG has provided support and recommendations for faculty utilizing library subscription materials as well as OER in place of costly textbooks. Though not true open educational resources, these materials are available for students to use at no additional cost since the subscription fees have been paid by the institution's library. This strong emphasis on affordability from the university system itself adds to the difficulty in helping faculty realize that, while a worthy goal, saving students money is not the only and possibly not even the greatest benefit of OER materials. The university's push to develop its campus-wide inclusive excellence plan opened a door of opportunity to showcase some of the more valuable benefits that OER materials provide for both faculty and students. As feedback came through from various campus units, it became apparent that OER were a perfect fit with the mission and goals of the plan. Feedback comments included, "Pursuing inclusive excellence as a university will teach each of us to recognize some of the conditions that leave some of us feeling less connected and hopefully inspire all of us to do our part to change some of those conditions" and "It's not only seeing diverse faces and including marginalized voices, it is creating a fair and just environment for our whole and varied community to actively and safely engage in."[12] These characteristics named by our university community—recognizing conditions that make others feel less connected, seeing diversity, including marginalized voices, and actively engaging in learning—are the very characteristics that open education resources and open education overall employ, embrace, and empower faculty and students. This is how we knew OER would be a perfect fit within this new plan.

The Inclusive Excellence Action Plan

The newly hired associate vice president for inclusive excellence and chief diversity officer immediately began work on creating a framework that would address the issues brought up in Damon William's report and provide a system of accountability to check if departments, colleges, and other campus units were meeting goals of inclusive excellence. This campus-wide Inclusive Excellence Plan was designed as a blueprint to provide guidance, reflection, and examples of inclusive excellence practices that could be incorporated into the daily routines of the university. The first step in creating this plan was to define the inclusive excellence that Georgia Southern would follow: the recognition that an organization's success is dependent on, and tied directly to, how well it values, engages, and includes the rich diversity of its community members, including its students, faculty, staff, alumni, friends, and affiliates. Included in the plan is Georgia Southern's unique statement of inclusive excellence: Inclusive excellence is a strategic pillar and a core value at Georgia Southern University.

The first drafts of the plan were presented to the entire campus with opportunities for feedback from every entity. The Office of Inclusive Excellence also offered several town hall meetings to discuss the plan and elicit feedback, comments, and address concerns or questions about the plan. These town halls were sent out on a staggered schedule to provide dates/times that would reach as many persons as possible. It was during one of these town hall meetings that I mentioned OER in support of inclusive excellence and that it should not be ignored when developing this plan. This led to a robust set of conversations and working meetings between me and the associate vice president for inclusive excellence and the chief diversity officer.

How OER integrates into the Inclusive Excellence Action Plan

Georgia Southern's Inclusive Excellence Action Plan consists of four comprehensive goals. Each of these goals is followed by a set of strategies to support the goal, and each strategy is followed by a list of actions to be taken in order to meet each strategy. It was important to ensure we incorporated OER into the goals and strategies that made the most sense. The four overarching goals of the plan include the following:

1. Create an equitable and inclusive environment for all.
2. Increase the representation of diverse students, faculty, staff, and community partners at all levels of the university.
3. Facilitate access to achievement, success, and recognition for underrepresented students, faculty, staff, and alumni.
4. Implement strong, genuine, and consistently communicated culturally inclusive practices that reinforce the strategic plan and the inclusive excellence action plan.

A detailed analysis of each goal and the strategies written to support them led us to embed very specific language about OER under goals one and four. Under goal 1, strategy 1-G calls on the community to incorporate practices that support equity, inclusion, and intercultural understanding for all students. Action 5 under this strategy encourages faculty to incorporate and diversify course materials by exploring OER that can be revised and/or restructured to better represent the rich diversity of our students. Under goal 4, strategy 4-C calls on the community to incentivize and require new programming and initiatives for students, faculty, and staff that enhance diversity, equity, and inclusion. Action 10 under this strategy states that the university will provide incentives for faculty to explore using OER as these have specifically been shown to enhance retention and progression of underrepresented student populations. In each of these instances, the wording was carefully constructed to ensure that faculty did not feel any of their academic freedoms were being challenged. Within both actions, faculty are encouraged and offered incentives to explore incorporating OER materials into their courses.

There is zero mandate that OER be used. Instead, our goal is to highlight the ways costly course materials limit their academic freedom and provide background and incentives to encourage faculty to seek alternatives.

We're in the Plan, Now What?

The main campus-wide Inclusive Excellence Action Plan is available to the campus and has been disseminated in a variety of ways. The next steps from the Office of Inclusive Excellence required every academic college, every central until, the faculty senate, and staff council to develop their own Inclusive Excellence Action Plan (IEAP) utilizing a centralized template based on the original plan. Once completed plans are received, the Office of Inclusive Excellence will review each group's IEAP and determine how they have addressed this intersection of OER in their work. Once each group has established a strong IEAP, there will then be quarterly reports from each unit assessing their progress in meeting key performance indicators as determined by each academic college and our central units.

The Office of Inclusive Excellence has also formulated a stronger partnership with the University Libraries and the Center for Teaching Excellence (CTE) to engage faculty in learning opportunities about OER and how the flexibility provided by the 5Rs helps create opportunities to engage in social justice education.

An already strong partnership between the CTE and me has resulted in an asynchronous course offering for faculty who want to learn about OER and how to adopt, adapt, or create for their courses. This course is currently being revised to add a module specifically tied to OER and social justice teachings that embody inclusive excellence. Additionally, I have designed workshops focusing specifically on OER's ability to address social justice, multiculturalism, equity, and inclusion. All these workshops allow faculty to earn credit toward digital badges through CTE, which provides additional incentive to participate.

Per my conversations with the associate vice president for inclusive excellence and the chief diversity officer, the Office of Inclusive Excellence has set aside funding to incentivize faculty interested in pursuing this work. These small internal grants will prioritize proposals that include social justice principles in the planned rework of the course materials and curricula. These grants can be used in conjunction with any additional grants, such as ALG Textbook Transformation Grants, to help pay faculty stipends, award monies for presentations, and to hire student assistants to help revise and/or create materials.

Looking Ahead

As is always the case with course overviews, selections of course materials, OER, and social justice, this is work that is never fully complete. As we wait for the first sets of campus groups IEAPs to come in, plans are already being developed to take this work further. The university is reviewing our core curriculum to identify opportunities for improvement within our current structure and to prepare for possible changes in the program structure as mandated by the University System of Georgia. Currently, the campus-wide General Education Curriculum Committee (GECC) has thirteen sub-committees comprised of faculty working to develop student learning objectives (SLO) that will align a core curriculum with our new strategic plan and mission. Discussion is on the table to explore OER options for this new core curriculum by insisting that faculty submitting courses for possible inclusion in the core show how they are supporting our two action items within the inclusive excellence plan. As stated previously, faculty will not be mandated to use OER, but they will be asked how their materials support the inclusive excellence goals of the university.

Recent recipients of a programmatic textbook transformation grant from ALG will be included in a pilot program between the library, the CTE, and the Office of Inclusive Excellence. Earlier, this chapter mentioned that the MAT in Elementary Education already has a culturally responsive focus to its curriculum. This program is in the process of completely shifting over to OER materials with the help of grant funding from ALG. Additional grant funding from the Office of Inclusive Excellence will provide small faculty stipends to help train the program faculty to utilize these OER materials in their courses in ways that address social justice, culturally responsive teaching habits, and inclusive excellence. I will partner with the CTE and grant team members to present a series of required workshops to the rest of the program faculty, introducing open pedagogy, assessment, alignment, and ways to further increase social justice teachings into the curriculum. We are also working to create a rubric or adopt the one already created by Hays and Mallon that will integrate the inclusive excellence pedagogy with the 5Rs of OER.[13] This rubric will provide a visual for faculty to measure their curriculum design while also providing measurable outcomes to show progress toward meeting the defined actions, strategies, and goals of the inclusive excellence action plan. It is hoped that this programmatic overhaul will become a model for other programs to follow suit and overhaul their own curriculum to incorporate OER as a means to create more inclusive, culturally responsive materials to address social justice issues with their students.

Finally, we'd like to begin adding the student voices to this project. Our Student Government Association (SGA) is only recently active again since consolidation, and plans are developing to reach out to SGA officers as well as the Office of Student Activities. The Office of Inclusive Excellence is setting aside small funding opportunities to acknowledge student contributions to materials that will be utilized by other student organizations and future SGA officers. The university has set a goal to ensure that students also begin to review their contributions to the campus through cultural diversity, equity, and inclusive best practices.

Conclusion and Hopes

Georgia Southern University is at the very threshold of a very ambitious campus-wide Inclusive Excellence Plan. This plan has called for the campus community to collectively evaluate all our current practices through the lenses of social justice, equity, and inclusion. The campus has previously encouraged faculty to explore OER options strictly within the perimeters of reducing course materials costs for students. With the embedding of specific OER language in our new Inclusive Excellence Action Plan, we have an opportunity to highlight not only the equity and inclusiveness of materials being affordable but also to help our faculty develop pedagogically superior course materials that reflect social justice issues, multiculturalism, and the strength of our collective life experiences. We have an opportunity to ensure that our students can truly see themselves being represented in every aspect of their education, and with that representation, they can see themselves successful in this learning environment. By working the fundamentals of OER into the fabric of our inclusive excellence journey, we hope to offer a level of accountability that promises our students that we care about what we teach, how we teach, and we also care about their unique contributions to the knowledge field. OER's flexibility allows this and more. We're excited about this journey and look forward to what learning opportunities this will provide for all of us utilizing OER.

Endnotes

1. Cailyn Nagle and Kaitlyn Vitez, *Fixing the Broken Textbook Market*, U.S. PIRG Education Fund, 2021.
2. "List of North American OER Policies & Projects," SPARC, https://sparcopen.org/our-work/list-of-oer-policies-projects/.
3. Nicholas Colvard, C. Edward Watson, and Hyojin Park, "The Impact of Open Educational Resources on Various Student Success Metrics," *International Journal of Teaching and Learning in Higher Education* 30, no. 2 (2018): 262, https://search.informit.org/documentSummary;res=APO;dn=183991.
4. Ben Dedman, "Affordable Learning Georgia: Increasing Equity and Improving Pedagogy through Open Educational Resources," Association of American Colleges & Universities, 2020.

5. Lindsay McKenzie, "Window of Opportunity for OER," *Inside Higher Ed* (2020), accessed March 15, 2021, https://www.insidehighered.com/news/2020/08/13/pandemic-drives-increased-interest-open-educational-resources.
6. Sonia Nieto, *Affirming Diversity: The Sociopolitical Context of Multicultural Education*, 3rd ed. (New York: Longman, 2000).
7. Kathy Hytten and Sylvia C. Bettez, "Understanding Education for Social Justice," *Educational Foundations* 25, no. 1-2 (2011): 7–24.
8. Robin DeRosa and Rajiv Jhangiani, "Open Pedagogy," Open Pedagogy Notebook, accessed March 15, 2021. http://openpedagogy.org/open-pedagogy/.
9. "The Diversity, Equity, Inclusion and Justice Resource Center," EAB, https://eab.com/research/strategy/resource-center/diversity-equity-inclusion-and-justice-initiatives-in-higher-education/.
10. Damon Williams, *3 Campuses One Heartbeat: Towards Inclusive Excellence at Georgia Southern*, Georgia Southern University, 2019.
11. "Curriculum and Pedagogy for Social Justice Certificate," Georgia Southern University, https://catalog.georgiasouthern.edu/graduate/education/curriculum-foundations-reading/curriculum-pedagogy-social-justice-certificate/.
12. "2020–2024 Inclusive Excellence Action Plan," Georgia Southern University, https://drive.google.com/file/d/1fmIOT7VzKVFNymkSQqk6Y3U69Le1JgK0/view.
13. Lauren Hays and Melissa N. Mallon, "Using OER to Promote Inclusion in Higher Education Institutions," *Currents in Teaching & Learning* 12, no. 2 (2021): 20–33, https://search.ebscohost.com/login.aspx?direct=true&AuthType=ip,shib&db=edo&AN=148965069&custid=gso1.

Bibliography

Colvard, Nicholas, C. Edward Watson, and Hyojin Park. "The Impact of Open Educational Resources on Various Student Success Metrics." *International Journal of Teaching and Learning in Higher Education* 30, no. 2 (2018): 262. https://search.informit.org/documentSummary;res=APO;dn=183991.

Dedman, Ben. "Affordable Learning Georgia: Increasing Equity and Improving Pedagogy through Open Educational Resources." Association of American Colleges & Universities. https://www.aacu.org/aacu-news/campus-model/affordable-learning-georgia-increasing-equity-and-improving-pedagogy-through-open.

DeRosa, Robin, and Rajiv Jhangiana. "Open Pedagogy." Open Pedagogy Notebook. Accessed March 15, 2021. http://openpedagogy.org/open-pedagogy/.

EAB. "Diversity, Equity, Inclusion and Justice Initiatives in Higher Education." Accessed March 15, 2021. https://eab.com/research/strategy/resource-center/diversity-equity-inclusion-and-justice-initiatives-in-higher-education/.

Georgia Southern University. *2020-2024 Inclusive Excellence Action Plan*. Office of Inclusive Excellence. 2020.

———. "Curriculum and Pedagogy for Social Justice Certificate." https://catalog.georgiasouthern.edu/graduate/education/curriculum-foundations-reading/curriculum-pedagogy-social-justice-certificate/.

———. "Inclusive Excellence." Accessed March 15, 2021. https://www.georgiasouthern.edu/inclusive-excellence/.

Hays, Lauren, and Melissa N. Mallon. "Using OER to Promote Inclusion in Higher Education Institutions." *Currents in Teaching & Learning* 12, no. 2 (2021): 20–33. https://search.ebscohost.com/login.aspx?direct=true&AuthType=ip,shib&db=edo&AN=148965069&custid=gso1.

Hytten, Kathy, and Sylvia C. Bettez. "Understanding Education for Social Justice." *Educational Foundations* 25, no. 1-2 (2011): 7–24.

McKenzie, Lindsay. "Window of Opportunity for OER." Accessed March 15, 2021. https://www.insidehighered.com/news/2020/08/13/pandemic-drives-increased-interest-open-educational-resources.

Meindel, Claudia. *Executive Summary*. München: Verlag C. H. Beck, 2018. http://bvbr.bib-bvb.de:8991/F?func=service&doc_library=BVB01&local_base=BVB01&doc_number=030287166&sequence=000001&line_number=0001&func_code=DB_RECORDS&service_type=MEDIA.

Nagle, Cailyn, and Kaitlyn Vitez. *Fixing The Broken Textbook Market*. U.S. PIRG Education Fund. 2021.

Nieto, Sonia. *Affirming Diversity*. 3rd ed. New York: Longman, 2000.

SPARC. "List of North American OER Policies & Projects." Accessed March 10, 2021. https://sparcopen.org/our-work/list-of-oer-policies-projects/.

Walz, Anita, Kristi Jensen, and Joseph A. Salem. *SPEC Kit 351: Affordable Course Content and Open Education Resources*. Washington DC: Association of Research Libraries, 2016.

Williams, Damon. *3 Campuses One Heartbeat: Towards Inclusive Excellence at Georgia Southern*, Georgia Southern University. 2019.

CHAPTER 13

OER, Social Justice, and Online Professional Development to Enhance Equity, Diversity, and Inclusion at a University

Samantha Harlow and Melody Rood

Until recently, it has commonly been assumed that open educational resources are inherently equitable due to their constitution toward accessibility. Recent literature, however, challenges the idea that access is synonymous with equity and social justice. While definitions of open education and openness vary from source to source, in general, traditionally, there is a focus on providing entry to educational materials to underprivileged populations in an effort to save money. Sarah Lambert, author of *Changing our (Dis)Course: A Distinctive Social Justice Aligned Definition of Open Education*, likens the phenomenon of assumed justice in OER to technological determinism, which she defines as "a problematic and ultimately ineffective approach to technology implementations, which assumes that the particular capabilities of new technologies will always improve the situations into which they are brought."[1] Similarly, *openness determinism* assumes that being open is intrinsically "good"—thus, open educational resources will naturally foster justice. Lambert argues that the open community should avoid openness determinism to reflect contributions to social justice and equity and instead consider how OER applies to redistributive justice, recognitive justice, and representational justice.

Redistributive justice relates to the allocation of resources and can be applied to OER through free textbooks and other educational resources that can lift a financial burden from those who cannot afford them. Recognitive justice refers to the inclusion of diverse perspectives in open content. Due to the ability to revise and remix OER, recognitive justice provides the opportunity to intentionally include marginalized populations through images, histories, studies, and more. Finally, representational justice is similar to recognitive, but it takes it a step further by allowing marginalized and oppressed populations to use their own voices to create firsthand knowledge. Representational justice invites the creation of equitable educational resources that move beyond the white, Western, and cishet male (cisgender and heterosexual)-centered voice that is traditionally found in academic canon. The addition of more learning opportunities and professional development around recognitive and representational justice is an ongoing goal for University of North Carolina Greensboro librarians tasked with the OER initiatives and thinking through the challenges of virtually engaging audiences with these concepts.

Kristina Clement echoes the importance of justice in the article, *Interrogating and Supplementing OER through a Decolonized Lens*, by questioning if open materials are actually perpetuating inequity in education: "While the affordability of OER can increase accessibility for marginalized learners, implementing OER in the classroom that are heavily colonized and center a white patriarchal epistemology does nothing to increase or foster equity for marginalized learners. It merely gives marginalized students increased access to an educational environment that continues to systematically devalue them."[2] The online learning and student success librarians intend to build opportunities for conversations and improvements into general education about OER as well as presenting more social justice-centered educational sessions.

Background

The University of North Carolina Greensboro (UNCG) is a mid-sized public university located in central North Carolina. UNCG is a minority-serving institution, with a large population of Pell Grant-eligible students and a large rural student population. As of fall 2020, around 13 percent of UNCG students are classified as fully online distance students, and in fall 2019, around 30 percent of students were first-generation.[3] Based on demographics, UNCG has an active student success center and offers many programs centered around student experience, including high-impact practices (HIPS), a Course-Based Undergraduate Research Experience (CURE) grant from the University of North Carolina (UNC) system, and a Ronald E. McNair Post-baccalaureate Achievement Program focused on an immersive and advanced research experience for underrepresented and first-generation students.[4] As well as recruiting and giving strong support to a diverse student body, UNCG has committed to building a more diverse faculty. Based on UNCG's student population and dedication to equity, diversity, and inclusion (EDI) through student success initiatives, the UNCG University Teaching and Learning Commons (UTLC) has long offered EDI programming, professional development, and pedagogy training. Some EDI workshops that have been offered in fall 2019 and spring 2020 include trauma-informed curriculums, Indigenous pedagogy, and an EDI online course through the UNCG learning management system (LMS), Canvas. With most courses moving to an online format due to COVID-19, these sessions became more important and popular than ever before.

The switch to online course delivery has brought an opportunity for instructors to learn about and implement low- and no-cost online course materials for their students. Open educational resources (OER) are "educational materials made freely and legally available on the Internet for anyone to reuse, revise, remix and redistribute."[5] OER educational programs within libraries have been around for well over a decade. The United Nations Educational, Scientific and Cultural Organization (UNESCO) Forum on the Impact of Open Course-ware for Higher Education in Developing Countries first mentioned OER in 2002.[6] Many university libraries have established OER programs, faculty stipends for implementing OER, training workshops, or have librarians who are committed to helping instructors find OER to replace textbooks and costly course materials. Instructors are usually quick to agree that eliminating a textbook will help students save money, and when surveyed, they think that OER is important to student success.[7] As OER has grown and become established within higher education, the national importance of equity, diversity, and inclusion (EDI) pedagogies have also become vital to teaching and learning, including critical race theory, anti-racism pedagogy, and universal design for learning (UDL). This EDI expansion has taken root through university programming and teaching and learning centers in the form of courses, curricula workshops, presentations, and webinars.

At UNCG University Libraries, OER programming has been well-established in services and support since 2010. The former libraries associate dean of technical services was heavily ingrained in the national OER community but left for another position in mid-2019. This paved the way for the online learning librarian and the student success librarian (both housed in the Research, Outreach, and Instruction department) to form a partnership to lead OER for UNCG Libraries. This workflow also includes managing and implementing the OER faculty stipends of $1,000 per instructor to eliminate a textbook in a course through a program called "OER Mini Grants." UNCG Libraries has awarded approximately seventy instructors in eighty different courses these stipends, saving UNCG students over $2 million in textbook costs between 2013 and 2020.

Though many courses and students have been positively impacted by these grants, the online learning and student success librarians wanted to alter certain aspects of the implementation of the grant. One plan for improvement was increased and more visible marketing of the grant to new instructors, adjuncts, and teaching assistants. As of fall 2019, no online courses had ever been awarded an OER Mini Grant, but OER can have a significant impact on online students. Online students at UNCG and nationally are largely non-traditional; non-traditional students include those over twenty-four, whose entry to college was delayed by at least one year following high school, single parents, those employed full-time, those attending a postsecondary institution part-time, those with dependents, those who are financially independent, and those who do not have a high school diploma.[8] Another desired shift in OER and UNCG Libraries services was to improve alignment with UNCG professional development opportunities, including student success initiatives and EDI programming.

To refresh OER at UNCG and to better meet the needs of diverse student populations, we wanted to make the vital connection of uplifting teaching with OER to contribute to EDI and social justice conversations throughout campus by developing and hosting online professional development opportunities. Migrating all OER educational programming to virtual starting in 2020 was developed out of the public health needs of COVID-19 but led to librarians being able to reach a broader audience and to better advocate to lessen the cost of course materials to students during a pandemic and beyond. This chapter covers how these UNCG librarians incorporated virtual OER programming and asynchronous, interactive tutorials through a collaborative workflow to allow a more holistic EDI approach to student success; these changes to UNCG Libraries' OER services and programming continue to save students money but also encourage better representation in course materials and curricula. COVID-19 has forever shifted online learning within academia, and this chapter delves into the successes and challenges of implementing this kind of online training and future directions of how instructors and librarians can take OER beyond textbook replacement.

We intend to build upon the previous foundation to further promote open education and social justice. While it is useful to show stakeholders the culmination of costs saved due to OER adoption, especially when funds for grants are being determined by the return on investment, that conversation should be a starting point. Sarah Crissinger, author of *A Critical Take on OER Practices: Interrogating Commercialization, Colonialism, and Content*, urges librarians to be honest about the limitations of OER, urging advocates to be transparent about open content as enhancements to the classroom and not the solution to inequitable education systems.[9] We who are tasked at UNCG with leading the OER program are attempting to understand the nuance of adjusting conversations depending on the audience. While it might be appropriate to emphasize the return on investment when speaking to the Provost's Office, a different approach should be used for faculty and students. Regardless of the stakeholder, we want to be inspired by this OER, social justice, and EDI research and literature and build these theories into virtual professional development and dialogue at UNCG and beyond.

OER, Online Learning, and COVID-19

COVID-19 caused a large shift in global academia. According to the College Crisis Initiative, 44 percent of universities and colleges in the United States of America (out of around 3,000 institutions surveyed) were delivering courses fully or primarily online in fall 2020, with only 4 percent staying completely in-person.[10] In spring 2020, most courses at UNCG (around 90 percent) moved online due to the COVID-19 pandemic. Going into the fall 2020 semester, about 50 percent of courses were online, with many of the face-to-face classes being hybrid or hyflex, where courses give students the flexibility to attend in person or online; this transition meant that UNCG Libraries moved many services to virtual, including all information literacy instruction and research programming being offered at a distance, through synchronous or asynchronous methods.

Moving academic courses online quickly causes stress for many university stakeholders, including instructors, librarians, and students. According to a survey sent out to adults (over 18) in the United States in June 2020, it was found that "40.9% of respondents reported at least one adverse mental or behavioral health condition, including symptoms of anxiety disorder or depressive disorder (30.9%), symptoms of a trauma- and stressor-related disorder (TSRD) related to the pandemic."[11] When library patrons are stressed, getting them to attend and take part in virtual training on research and OER is a challenge; university libraries are forced to shift mindsets in terms of how they best help patrons with research and all academic services.

Though pandemics cause strain on communities, online learning provides a way to better reach out to students and instructors across campus and beyond during these challenging times. While students were at home and most likely experiencing high levels of stress, units across UNCG's campus came up with a variety of programs and resources to address student and instructor needs, as well as address social justice and equity issues in higher education. The University Teaching and Learning Commons (UTLC) came up with a series of online classes for instructors to help with ways to better understand how to incorporate equity, diversity, and inclusion (EDI) within their curricula, pedagogy, and syllabi. The UNCG High Impact Practices (HIPs) committee brought in virtual guest speakers to showcase specific strategies of HIPs in action to help students. Even very physical and high-touch university services, such as advising, counseling, and tutoring, moved services online to better help students. With the quick shift to online learning, UNCG Online, Information Technology Services (ITS), and instructional technology consultants created a Keep Teaching website and offered many virtual workshops about creating courses online as well as on the learning management system (LMS) Canvas, Google Suite, video options, and more.[12]

UNCG Libraries shifted all information literacy instruction online during COVID-19, including professional development and research workshops for patrons. The online learning librarian has been offering two webinar series for almost four years: one is entitled Online Learning and Innovation and the other one is a series on Research and Applications. These series have also included a variety of virtual panels of instructors, showcasing examples of collaborations between various online learning departments around campus. During COVID-19, all campus undergraduate programming moved fully online, including all orientations, campus workshops, and welcoming events. This positioned UNCG Libraries to promote more virtual programming to ease research and assignment anxiety for students and instructors.

To connect OER to a social justice framework, as well as promote more instructors at UNCG to use OER during the pandemic, we sought to educate and train all UNCG Libraries employees. In spring 2020, we collaborated with a university library technician in the UNCG Libraries Technical Services department to do an OER educational session for the whole library. This was part of the newly formed virtual training program for internal library workers called University Libraries Virtual Learning Community (ULVLC) and a collaboration with a university library technician to showcase the Course Adopted Text program. This is a program where e-books are purchased by the library and adopted and used by UNCG instructors for use in the classroom as a "free for students" alternative to traditional textbooks.

In summer 2020, we did a two-part synchronous Zoom workshop for UNCG library liaisons and other librarians and archivists working with courses and research in academic departments. Part one was an introduction to searching for OER so librarians could help instructors locate OER for courses, with interactive activities in open repositories. The second part of the series was on the basics of OER creation as well as reviewing OER research guides and webpages at other universities to compare with what the UNCG Libraries offer. After this liaison and librarian workshop series, the need became clear for more collaboration with OER across departments and to provide more educational opportunities to all library personnel. Based on feedback from the Access Services library

OER, Social Justice, and Online Professional Development   235

department about patrons requesting textbooks, a virtual meeting was planned for everyone working at the checkout desk to discuss the most common issues brought up by patrons. From this meeting, an infographic of major OER repositories was developed in collaboration with this department and the Student Success Librarian. See figure 13.1 for a view of categories for arts and humanities, business, social sciences, and science and math that were included on the infographic.

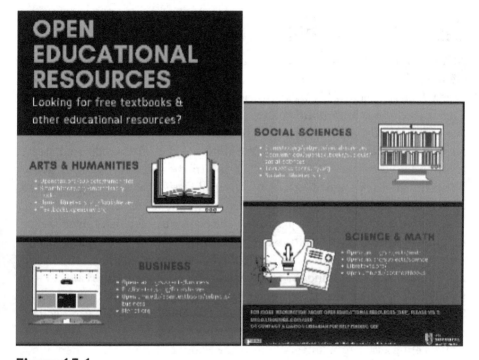

Figure 13.1
View of the options included on the OER infographic developed in collaboration with UNCG Access Services.
For the full infographic, go to http://go.uncg.edu/oerinfo.

The push to get more instructors to use OER to help students during the stress of the pandemic and promote better social justice in the classrooms also exists at the state level. The online learning and student success librarians got involved in various University of North Carolina (UNC) system OER collaborative projects to create more virtual training for instructors teaching online during the pandemic and beyond. The first undertaking, in summer 2020, was the creation of a series of online course packs to help instructors throughout North Carolina use and create OER in large lecture courses. In fall 2020, a series of OER training modules was created to guide instructors through finding, creating, and evaluating OER. There is also an ongoing project creating a UNC system OER Commons hub for instructors to ingest and share their open educational materials. In spring 2021, these projects and training are being pushed out across the system through educational webinars and academic unit deans; these projects can be found on the UNC System and OER Collections webpage.[13]

Designing and Implementing OER Tutorials

UNCG Libraries also resourced and created a variety of materials to help contribute to student success and teaching or researching online during COVID-19. When virtually helping library patrons with research and assignments, liaison librarians rely heavily on asynchronous research tutorials—specifically, the newly designed UNCG Libraries Research Tutorials.[14] These tutorials and modules are on research concepts to help students find, evaluate, use, credit, and create research based on the UNCG Libraries' information literacy learning goals. The platform was designed based on Universal Design for Learning (UDL) to be accessible and interactive as well as have multiple means of representation, engagement, and action and expression.[15] The platform uses a rich content editor to implement a variety of multimedia content; this works well for adapting and using openly licensed resources. Content from YouTube, Google, and beyond can be easily embedded, and the open-source tool H5P is used to create interactive, HTML5 "quick checks" on every page so that users can test their learning. The creation workflow of the modules (housed within tutorials) is also a collaboration between all UNCG liaison librarians.

Educating a variety of university and state-wide academic stakeholders about OER contributes to student success, but in order to promote the social justice components of OER during a pandemic, it's important to create a variety of online components, including showcasing open pedagogy and social justice frameworks. With the combination of UNCG recognizing the importance of OER, EDI, and online learning to student success and accessibility, the online learning librarian created a suite of online modules on OER, housed within the UNCG Libraries Research Tutorials platform. The Finding, Creating, and Evaluating modules help users get started with OER. The Finding module provides OER definitions and addresses searching for open materials for courses within repositories. The Creating module trains instructors and students on best practices of producing open materials, applying Creative Commons licenses, and technologies and accessibility strategies for designing OER. The Evaluating module helps educators discern which OER materials are appropriate for college-level courses within a variety of educational settings. See figure 13.2 for how the OER modules are organized within the overall tutorial in the UNCG Libraries Research Tutorial platform.

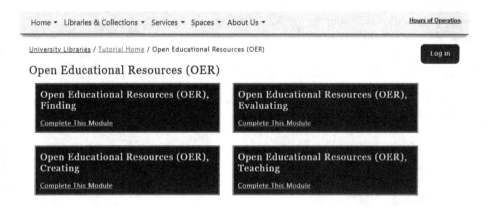

Figure 13.2
UNCG open educational resources (OER) tutorial homepage.

To show how incorporating open education is vital to teaching with an EDI lens, whether virtual or face-to-face, the Teaching module was created. This module centers on open pedagogy and helps connect OER to social justice in course design. Open pedagogy is the "use of open educational resources (OER) to support learning, or the open sharing of teaching practices with a goal of improving education and training at the institutional, professional, and individual level."[16] Many times, open pedagogy goes beyond teaching with open materials; it also includes students in the process of creating OER for assignments while contributing to the materials available for their disciplines. Therefore, this module aligns with the UNCG UTLC equity, diversity, and inclusion training and professional development opportunities; contributes to online learning and instructional design training; and helps to advocate for student success and empathy during a global pandemic. The module pages include an introduction to open pedagogy; open pedagogy tools such as H5P, Timeline JS, and Pressbooks; considerations for open pedagogy such as understanding digital tools, scaffolded learning, and copyright education; a section on equity, diversity, inclusion, social justice and OER, which includes information about inclusive teaching, readings on OER and social justice, a webinar on OER and student equity, and a comprehensive breakdown of the social justice principles applied to OER, assessing OER and learning outcomes; and finally, teaching with OER help at UNCG. See figure 13.3 for a screenshot of how the OER Teach module looks on the open pedagogy page.

Figure 13.3
Screenshot of the "Introduction to Open Pedagogy" page from the UNCG Libraries OER Teach module.

Due to the flexible nature of the tutorials, the OER modules were created and published throughout fall 2020. Librarians were able to use the modules with specific classes in order to get feedback and see how they worked with students and instructors. In fall 2020, the online learning librarian worked with the UNCG music librarian on an open pedagogy music Ear-Training course, which was moved online due to COVID-19. This course focuses on music reading, and the instructor had students create materials to contribute to an open textbook on music dictation. The online learning librarian presented a virtual, interactive synchronous session on searching for open musical materials for students to adapt for this course, and the Finding OER module was pulled down from Canvas Commons and adapted to train undergraduate music students about OER. This example shows how open pedagogy can be used virtually and how the OER tutorials' flexibility contributes to students being contributors to OER in their fields.

Virtual Programming and OER

After the original design of the asynchronous online tutorials on OER, an increase in EDI programming at UNCG, and the shift in courses due to COVID-19, the need became apparent for more virtual professional development for instructors. Based on this demand, the student success librarian designed a lesson plan for an online workshop that highlights how open pedagogy can be used to challenge traditional academic canon, which tends to center the overrepresented white Western narrative. Drawing on the instructional theory of constructivism, which encourages people to construct their own knowledge, the session encouraged faculty to empower students to be collaborators and contributors to knowledge, further promoting opportunities to center marginalized voices. Using examples of student-created open content, this webinar wanted to show faculty the multitude of ways in which their assignments can contribute to EDI learning objectives and curricula. This webinar was then presented in a campus-wide professional development series in winter 2020.

This synchronous professional development webinar introduced Lambert's principles of social justice, with a focus on representational justice. Attendees were encouraged to consider why representation matters and how insidious an impact a lack of representation can have on marginalized and oppressed populations. This was followed by a brief discussion about how a lack of representation upholds problematic assumptions, such as whiteness as neutral or standard. The presentation also reviewed the 5Rs of openness to make sure that attendees understood the components that make open pedagogical assignments possible. The definitions of open pedagogy used in this presentation were intentionally chosen for their acknowledgment of social justice: "'Open Pedagogy,' as we engage with it, is a site of praxis, a place where theories about learning, teaching, technology, and social justice enter into a conversation with each other and inform the development of educational practices and structures."[17] Audience members were asked to consider overlaps with other learning theories such as constructivism.

The presentation used a variety of examples with varying levels of openness to showcase assignments that contribute to recognitive and representational justice. The anthology, *My Slipper Floated Away*, uses a non-commercial and no-derivatives Creative Commons license (CC-BY-NC-ND), which means that the work can be distributed with credit but cannot be changed. Despite the anthology being the least "open" example presented, it has a high representational justice impact, allowing students to tell their own stories. For further discussion on why materials with high representational impact may select less-open terms, see Shanna Hollich's chapter, "The Unrealized Promise of OER: an Exploration of Copyright, the Open Movement, and Social Justice." *My Slipper Floated Away* is a collection of student-written essays, where the writers are immigrants, children of immigrants or people of color, showcasing their "intense longing to belong in America and their passion to succeed in this country, while dealing with myriad challenges."[18]

This example addresses how the discourse around open educational resources needs to move beyond openness as a measure of equity. While the ability to remix and revise allows opportunity toward recognitive and representational justice, the level of openness is not what makes the resource equitable. As Lambert states, "A social justice-oriented definition would be useful then to shift the debate from what openness might look like, to whom we want our openness to ultimately serve and how our openness might achieve greater educational and societal equality."[19] Other examples, like the "Timeline of African American Rights Movement 1950–1980," as well as open case studies on social justice movements from the University of British Columbia allowed attendees to see a multitude of renewable assignments that engage students and add value to their disciplines as specific examples that contribute to social justice beyond redistribution.[20]

Assessment and Future Directions of OER

When thinking about OER, EDI, social justice, and assessment at a university, thinking through the return on investment for OER programming is crucial to ensure continued institutional support. When we took over the OER grant and initiatives, the return on investment from the stipends already had a significant financial impact, with the program saving students over $2 million in course materials and textbook costs from 2013 to 2020. Financial savings and academic student success are a major focus at UNCG, which is why it is crucial to incorporate the redistributive justice principle within OER programming. Workshops promoting the grant cover introductory information about OER, the increased rates of educational materials in the last forty years, statistics from the Florida Distance Learning Consortium that look at the student success impact due to required textbook costs, and information about grant applications and where to seek guidance.[21] In the current application for the OER Mini Grants to be awarded in 2021–2022, a question was added for applicants to specifically address how the grant will help support equity, diversity, and inclusion for UNCG students, allowing the reviewers to prioritize applications that consider opportunities for recognitive and representational justice, such as open pedagogy assignments.

Beyond the return on investment of OER Mini Grants, looking at the assessment of the OER virtual tutorials and programming that has been performed over the last year is crucial to move the program forward. A survey is sent out after all the library's virtual professional development offerings, which include the synchronous sessions done on OER and open pedagogy during the 2020–2021 academic year. The survey showed success for the open pedagogy and social justice webinar; everyone who attended was very satisfied with the content, pace, and timing of this webcast being around forty-five minutes. Since their implementation in fall 2020, the OER tutorials on the website application are being used more heavily than Canvas Commons. The OER website tutorials, published throughout fall 2020, have received 312 unique views as of February 2021. More people are signing up for virtual OER training than in past years. For example, the February 2021 OER virtual training workshops for instructors interested in applying to the OER Mini Grant had the highest registration and attendance since the grant's inception.

Continuing these types of synchronous workshops and programs are integral to securing the funds needed for the continuation of the OER Mini Grants, but moving forward, we plan to place a stronger emphasis on professional development and workshops that highlight how open education can utilize the principles of recognitive and representational justice. This includes adding information about inclusive teaching and learning with links to perspectives on open education and equity into every presentation, using UNCG specific examples of renewable assignments, teaching with OER virtual modules, and incorporating open pedagogy. Integrating with other EDI virtual events on campus will be crucial to keep the momentum going; for example, we plan on presenting to instructors at an annual UNCG virtual meeting on teaching and research called ADAPT, within the EDI track, to showcase how OER goes beyond freeing the classrooms from textbooks.

Online programming provides access based on restrictions due to COVID-19, creating more opportunities for instructors to attend and engage in these concepts, but for OER to better contribute to social justice, there need to be more chances for students to learn and create OER in their disciplines. In February 2019, the student success librarian created an event called the OER Valentine's Day Pop-Up where they gave out treats and coffee to students passing through the library that included cards with basic information on OER. There was also a whiteboard where students could interact with the question, "What would you buy if you didn't have to buy expensive textbooks?" By the end of the day, the whiteboard was packed with answers. Students who interacted with the pop-up were generally interested in free educational resources; this activity focused on financial savings, and we were able to gather specific quotes and needs of the UNCG student population. A picture of the whiteboard with student feedback has been used in OER programming for instructors and administrators, helping different audiences better connect to the needs of UNCG students. The success of the interactions and pop-up nature of this OER event for students has not been replicated virtually but provides a model for organically connecting to students to help them better advocate for themselves to eliminate costly course materials. In the future, this librarian will experiment with student pop-up virtual events and develop alternative attendance incentives geared toward students.

To allow students to have a clearer voice within OER, continuing events like the Valentine's Day pop-up will be crucial, as will increasing the incentive for professors to use OER and open pedagogy in their courses. Since taking over OER initiatives on campus, we have noticed specific examples of teachers using open pedagogy in a variety of disciplines. A Kinesiology course on "Foundations of Sports Coaching" won an OER Mini Grant, eliminated a textbook, and allowed students to create digital timelines on women sports coaches to fill a gap in coaching literature; this assignment gave the students voice while showcasing the need for more diversity in sports textbooks on underrepresented populations. Another example is the art history course "Modern and Contemporary African Art History" from fall 2019. In this class, each student substantially edited and improved an article for a modern or contemporary African artist in Wikipedia over the course of the semester; one exception was a student who created a new article for an artist who did not have one. To achieve this, the course instructor, the director of the UNCG Digital ACT Studio, and the art and visual resource librarian collaborated on the assignment design and assessment and scheduled six workshops during the semester on Wikipedia and art history research. This group of collaborators is currently working on an article that covers the assessment of the course and open pedagogy assignment; ultimately, the students were able to connect their Wikipedia work to many competencies with art history education and information literacy, as found through an assessment using rubrics and by surveying students in this course.

Open pedagogy gives students a voice, teaches them about OER, and allows them to participate within their course and discipline, but it's challenging to track and assess open pedagogy assignments at any given university. For example, the Music Dictation and Reading course was able to use the tutorials for their open pedagogy assignments and even implemented an open pedagogy project. The instructor of this course did this, with help from the library, without winning the UNCG Libraries OER Mini Grant. Since liaison librarians do not always know of open pedagogy and OER being implemented into curricula and courses, it's difficult for them to assess and improve on what has been done. Moving forward, better tracking of who is using OER and open pedagogy in courses will be key, possibly by surveying instructors outside of the OER Mini Grants. Ideally, this will also lead to showcasing the known UNCG open pedagogy assignments for the campus community and beyond through resources such as the UNCG OER Mini Grant website and the Open Pedagogy Notebook. Finding ways to build incentives for resource sharing could be another improvement to the grant and OER programming at UNCG and beyond.[22]

Some assessment data has been collected on OER and online programming at UNCG. An assessment form is sent out after the course is complete to instructors who won grants. Overall, instructors generally agree that the OER Mini Grants contribute to student success, and most continue to not use textbooks in their courses. This year, a COVID-19 question was added into the survey sent to the grant winners to assess if the pandemic shifted their original plan. The survey is mostly composed of open-ended questions, so reviewing the responses for social justice and EDI connections will be helpful to better promote OER as a crucial aspect of helping students moving forward, whether instructors continue to teach online, hybrid, or face-to-face. In the future, a qualitative study on instructors using OER and open pedagogy at UNCG or throughout all of North Carolina or the Southeast, would lead to interesting findings on accessibility and student success connections.

Conclusion

In 2019, the online learning and student success librarians took the already established OER program at UNCG Libraries and built upon it to include new advocacy and education for a variety of audiences, including other library personnel, students, teaching faculty, and student success stakeholders campus-wide as well as at a state-level. The librarians moved beyond the traditional introductory-level workshop that placed an emphasis on affordability to provide more content on the connection between open educational resources, EDI, and social justice. The additional programming placed a focus on Lambert's three principles of social justice: redistributive, recognitive, and representational. As this move coincided with the global COVID-19 pandemic, it was important to consider both synchronous and asynchronous virtual professional development opportunities. The online learning librarian created online modules on OER that can be accessed asynchronously through the UNCG Libraries Research Tutorials Platform. The Teaching with OER module provides information for instructors that introduces open pedagogy, the connection to social justice and EDI, tools for open pedagogical considerations, assessment, and learning outcomes. As for a synchronous learning opportunity, the student success librarian created a lesson plan for a webinar as part of the UNCG Libraries winter 2020 professional development series, which looked at student-created open content and the representation of marginalized and oppressed groups. Even though the OER program at UNCG has predominantly focused on redistributive justice until recently, the librarians plan to evolve education and professional development opportunities to include more conversations about recognitive and representational social justice. They recognize that equity, diversity, and inclusion also impact student success, even though the research around OER tends to connect financial savings to student success alone. The suite of asynchronous OER modules, as well as the lesson plan on open pedagogy and EDI, are the beginning steps toward a more social justice and EDI-aligned OER program at UNCG.

Endnotes

1. Sarah Roslyn Lambert, "Changing Our (Dis)Course: A Distinctive Social Justice Aligned Definition of Open Education," *Journal of Learning for Development* 5, no. 3 (November 19, 2018): 229.
2. Kristina Clement, "Interrogating and Supplementing OER Through a Decolonized Lens," *OER & Beyond* (blog), December 30, 2020, accessed January 31, 2021, https://ijoerandbeyond.org/interrogating-and-supplementing-oer-through-a-decolonized-lens/.
3. "UNCG Enrollment Data Factbook Dashboard," UNCG Office of Institutional Research & Analytics, 2020, https://ire.uncg.edu/factbook/dashboards/.
4. "About," National McNair Scholars website and University of Central Florida, 2021, https://mcnairscholars.com/about/.
5. Heath Wickline, "Open Educational Resources: Breaking the Lockbox on Education," *Hewlett Foundation* (blog), 2013, para. 1, https://hewlett.org/open-educational-resources-breaking-the-lockbox-on-education/.
6. Mei-Hung Chiu, ed., *Science Education Research and Practice in Asia: Challenges and Opportunities* (Singapore: Springer, 2016), https://doi.org/10.1007/978-981-10-0847-4.
7. Samuel Abramovich and Mark McBride, "Open Education Resources and Perceptions of Financial Value," *The Internet and Higher Education* 39 (October 1, 2018): 33–38, https://doi.org/10.1016/j.iheduc.2018.06.002.
8. Susan Choy, "Nontraditional Undergraduates, National Center for Education Statistics," Findings from the Condition of Education, 2002, https://nces.ed.gov/pubs2002/2002012.pdf.
9. Sarah Crissinger, "A Critical Take on OER Practices: Interrogating Commercialization, Colonialism, and Content—In the Library with the Lead Pipe," *In The Library With The Lead Pipe* (October 21, 2015), accessed January 31, 2021, http://www.inthelibrarywiththeleadpipe.org/2015/a-critical-take-on-oer-practices-interrogating-commercialization-colonialism-and-content/.
10. "College Crisis Initiative (C2i), Data Dashboard," Davidson College, 2020, https://collegecrisis.shinyapps.io/dashboard/.
11. Mark É. Czeisler et al., "Mental Health, Substance Use, and Suicidal Ideation During the COVID-19 Pandemic—United States, June 24–30, 2020," *Morbidity and Mortality Weekly Report* 69, no. 32 (August 14, 2020): 1049, https://doi.org/10.15585/mmwr.mm6932a1.
12. "Keep Teaching: During Campus Service Interruptions," University of North Carolina Greensboro (UNCG), 2021, https://keepteaching.uncg.edu/.

13. "UNC System Course Enhancement and OER Collections," University of North Carolina, System Office, UNC System, 2020, https://www.northcarolina.edu/unc-system-course-collection-libraries/.
14. "University of North Carolina at Greensboro (UNCG), University Libraries, Research Tutorials," UNCG Libraries, The University of North Carolina at Greensboro (UNCG), University Libraries, Research Tutorials, 2021, http://libapps4.uncg.edu/tutorials/.
15. "CAST: About Universal Design for Learning," CAST, 2020, http://www.cast.org/our-work/about-udl.html#.XA_Sx9tKjIU.
16. "What Is Open Pedagogy? BCcampus OpenEd Resources," British Columbia (BC) Campus, 2020, para. 1, https://open.bccampus.ca/what-is-open-education/what-is-open-pedagogy/.
17. Robin DeRosa and Rajiv Jhangiani, "Open Pedagogy Notebook," Open Pedagogy Notebook, 2020, para. 2, http://openpedagogy.org/.
18. Justine Hope Blau, ed., *My Slipper Floated Away: New American Memoirs* (CUNY Manifold Project), sec. Introduction, accessed January 31, 2021, https://cuny.manifoldapp.org/projects/my-slipper-floated-away.
19. Lambert, "Changing Our (Dis)Course," 239.
20. "Timeline of African American Rights Movement 1950–1980," Knightlab, accessed February 19, 2021, https://cdn.knightlab.com/libs/timeline3/latest/embed/index.html?source=1h-he4rDYiUwaTSwCMzKcnaVhWrrNBxP7dvg1_u-tuzFU&font=Default&lang=en&initial_zoom=2&height=650; "Open Case Studies at UBC," University of British Columbia, Vancouver, accessed March 1, 2021, https://cases.open.ubc.ca/.
21. Robin Donaldson, John Opper, and E Shen, "2018 Florida Student Textbook & Course Materials Survey" (Florida Virtual Campus, 2018).
22. DeRosa and Jhangiani, "Open Pedagogy Notebook."

Bibliography

Abramovich, Samuel, and Mark McBride. "Open Education Resources and Perceptions of Financial Value." *The Internet and Higher Education* 39 (October 1, 2018): 33–38. https://doi.org/10.1016/j.iheduc.2018.06.002.

British Columbia (BC) Campus. "What Is Open Pedagogy? BCcampus OpenEd Resources." 2020. https://open.bccampus.ca/what-is-open-education/what-is-open-pedagogy/.

CAST. "CAST: About Universal Design for Learning." 2020. http://www.cast.org/our-work/about-udl.html#.XA_Sx9tKjIU.

Chiu, Mei-Hung, ed. *Science Education Research and Practice in Asia: Challenges and Opportunities*. Singapore: Springer, 2016. https://doi.org/10.1007/978-981-10-0847-4.

Choy, Susan. "Nontraditional Undergraduates, National Center for Education Statistics." Findings from the Condition of Education. 2002. https://nces.ed.gov/pubs2002/2002012.pdf.

Clement, Kristina. "Interrogating and Supplementing OER Through a Decolonized Lens." *OER & Beyond* (blog), December 30, 2020. Accessed January 31, 2021. https://ijoerandbeyond.org/interrogating-and-supplementing-oer-through-a-decolonized-lens/.

Crissinger, Sarah. "A Critical Take on OER Practices: Interrogating Commercialization, Colonialism, and Content." *In The Library With The Lead Pipe* (October 21, 2015). Accessed January 31, 2021. http://www.inthelibrarywiththeleadpipe.org/2015/a-critical-take-on-oer-practices-interrogating-commercialization-colonialism-and-content/.

Czeisler, Mark É., Rashon I. Lane, Emiko Petrosky, Joshua F. Wiley, Aleta Christensen, Rashid Njai, Matthew D. Weaver, et al. "Mental Health, Substance Use, and Suicidal Ideation During the COVID-19 Pandemic—United States, June 24–30, 2020." *Morbidity and Mortality Weekly Report* 69, no. 32 (August 14, 2020): 1049–57. https://doi.org/10.15585/mmwr.mm6932a1.

Davidson College. "College Crisis Initiative (C2i), Data Dashboard." 2020. https://collegecrisis.shinyapps.io/dashboard/.

DeRosa, Robin, and Rajiv Jhangiani. "Open Pedagogy Notebook." Open Pedagogy Notebook. 2020. http://openpedagogy.org/.

Donaldson, Robin, John Opper, and E Shen. "2018 Florida Student Textbook & Course Materials Survey." Florida Virtual Campus. 2018.

Hope Blau, Justine, ed. *My Slipper Floated Away: New American Memoirs*. CUNY Manifold Project. Accessed January 31, 2021. https://cuny.manifoldapp.org/projects/my-slipper-floated-away.

Knightlab from Northwestern University. "Timeline of African American Rights Movement 1950–1980." Accessed February 19, 2021. https://cdn.knightlab.com/libs/timeline3/latest/embed/index.html?source=1hhe4rDYiUwaTSwCMzKcnaVhWrrNBxP7dvg1_u-tuzFU&font=Default&lang=en&initial_zoom=2&height=650.

Lambert, Sarah Roslyn. "Changing Our (Dis)Course: A Distinctive Social Justice Aligned Definition of Open Education." *Journal of Learning for Development* 5, no. 3 (November 19, 2018): 239.

National McNair Scholars. "About." University of Central Florida. 2021. https://mcnairscholars.com/about/.

UNCG Libraries. "University of North Carolina at Greensboro (UNCG), University Libraries, Research Tutorials." The University of North Carolina at Greensboro (UNCG), University Libraries, Research Tutorials. 2021. http://libapps4.uncg.edu/tutorials/.

UNCG Office of Institutional Research & Analytics. "UNCG Enrollment Data Factbook Dashboard." 2020. https://ire.uncg.edu/factbook/dashboards/.

University of British Columbia. "Open Case Studies at UBC." University of British Columbia, Vancouver, Canada." Accessed March 1, 2021. https://cases.open.ubc.ca/.

University of North Carolina Greensboro (UNCG). "Keep Teaching: During Campus Service Interruptions." 2021. https://keepteaching.uncg.edu/.

University of North Carolina, System Office. "UNC System Course Enhancement and OER Collections." UNC System. 2020. https://www.northcarolina.edu/unc-system-course-collection-libraries/.

Wickline, Heath. "Open Educational Resources: Breaking the Lockbox on Education." *Hewlett Foundation* (blog), 2013. https://hewlett.org/open-educational-resources-breaking-the-lockbox-on-education/.

SECTION V
Building and Decolonizing OER Platforms

CHAPTER 14

Decolonizing Wikipedia

Ian Ramjohn

Wikipedia is the largest, most widely available reference work of its kind. Its ubiquity ensures its use by almost everyone and shapes the way information is presented in everything from public websites to scholarly literature.[1] Wikipedia is the most widely available of open educational resources (OER) and is used by learners in both formal and informal settings. But unlike most OER, which are selected and assigned by the instructor, the content students find on Wikipedia is outside the control of instructors.

When I taught introductory biology, students would send me emails asking to explain things I had neither covered in class nor discussed in the textbook. Sure enough, I would find the terminology or concept they asked about when I checked Wikipedia. As a Wikipedian, I found this validating—after all, you contribute to Wikipedia in the hope that someone will find your additions useful. But as an instructor, I found it alarming that students were learning from a source created outside the norms of knowledge creation and curation.[2,3] Wikipedia's incredible value as an OER is tempered by the fact that a large part of the knowledge curation is done by interested amateurs.

Wikipedia's coverage of the world's knowledge is uneven in systemic ways that reflect the world's broader systemic inequalities. This is particularly true on the English Wikipedia, the largest language version with more than six million articles. Perhaps the best-known issue is the gender gap[4]—Wikipedia has fewer articles about women, the women who have biographies on Wikipedia are more notable than the men who do, articles about women are more likely to discuss their husbands (and their husbands' jobs), their role in mentoring, and the fact that they were role models to other women.[5]

Less well-known are the biases in geographic content. Most geotagged articles on Wikipedia are in the global north. The densely populated parts of Asia are less well-represented, while coverage of much of Africa is especially poor.[6] Looking across language versions, European countries are best covered in their

249

native languages, while countries in the Global South are usually covered best in a foreign language, frequently the language of their former colonizers.[7] This disparity is made more acute since topics that are well-covered attract more traffic and receive more edits. This results in a positive feedback cycle in which poorly covered topics fall further behind.[8]

Origin Stories

Wikipedia's origin has been called a "happy accident." Jimmy Wales had set out to build "the finest encyclopedia in the history of humankind" that could be available throughout the world for only the cost of printing, but the project struggled to find expert contributors and reviewers able to volunteer their time.[9] So on January 15, 2001, a new, simpler project was launched. Based on simple wiki software that anyone could edit, the project grew rapidly into a useful encyclopedia. As Joseph Reagle's analysis of the first ten thousand edits to Wikipedia has shown, there was a lot of "dreck" amidst the early contributions, but the good content grew quickly and blossomed into something usable.[10]

While the Wikipedia community included academics, even in its earliest days, a lot of the people who joined were simply enthusiastic people interested in building a better internet. People wrote about topics they were familiar with, often drawing on what they knew or could find online. While the community was international from its inception, it also reflected the fact that only a small part of the world's population was online in 2001, and many were still using dial-up modems and paying by the minute for their internet access. When I made my first edits to Wikipedia in 2004, I was doing both these things while based in Trinidad and Tobago.

Beyond this, the adoption of the model of Wikipedians as volunteers may have posed an additional barrier to involvement, since volunteerism tends to be seen as a mode of contribution in which privileged individuals, especially from the Global North, "give back" to those who are less well off. A more cooperative frame for collectively building a shared project may be a more effective way to attract people from less individualistic cultures.[11] All of these factors resulted in a community of contributors who were not representative of the world whose knowledge they were trying to document. While the online community has changed a lot in the last twenty years, Wikipedia's volunteer community remains unrepresentative of the world at large.

In its early period, Wikipedia needed content. More content drew more traffic, which in turn attracted more contributors.[12] While much of this was produced by volunteer editors, public domain sources provided a valuable way to supplement their contributions. The 1911 edition of *Encyclopaedia Britannica* and the 1913

Catholic Encyclopedia were both out of copyright and became available online after they were scanned and digitized. As a work produced by the US federal government, the *CIA World Factbook* was another source whose content could be incorporated into the nascent Wikipedia. Much of this content has been reworked or rewritten since then, but the influence of these sources remains, often with a somewhat nineteenth century feel to their prose. With 11,843 articles tagged as incorporating text from the 1911 *Encyclopaedia Britannica*, and 4,870 incorporating text from the 1913 *Catholic Encyclopedia*,[13] that influence isn't trivial.

When Wikipedians rely on older sources, they run the risk of importing outdated attitudes into the encyclopedia. The "Geography of Trinidad and Tobago" article until recently still included a line, "Area—comparative: slightly smaller than Delaware."[14] The article on Sir Norman Lamont says, "He went out to Trinidad where he owned a sugar plantation"[15]—language reminiscent of a time when Britain was the center of an empire.[16] Coming from Trinidad and Tobago, this sort of writing reinforces the sense that I come from somewhere lesser and implicitly questions my right to contribute to the project *as an equal*.

A Colonizing Encyclopedia?

Wikipedia asks you to imagine, in the words of Jimmy Wales, "a world in which every single person on the planet is given free access to the sum of all human knowledge,"[17] but it is important to consider who collects that knowledge, and how it is collated and curated. The realities of the digital divide mean that billions of people without internet access are excluded from the process of writing Wikipedia.[18]

Carwil Bjork-James describes his encounter with the 2005 debate on the English Wikipedia over which topic should exist at the page named "Java" on Wikipedia. Until September 12, the article about the Indonesian island had occupied that space, but on that day someone replaced it with an article about the programming language. In the ensuing debate, one Wikipedian commented, "I don't know of a single person who is familiar with the island."[19]

The fact that reasonable voices won out and the community decided to retain the island as the primary topic for Java is a testament to the reasonableness of the Wikipedian community, but the fact that this was something worthy of debate illustrates a fundamental weakness. The community that writes Wikipedia is disproportionately white, male, well-educated, and lives in the Global North. The community is disproportionately technology-oriented. The idea that we should weigh the merits of an island with 150 million people against those of a programming language is absurd on its face, but not if you apply rules to decide that are based on coverage in sources—worse yet, when you're contrasting the sources that were available online in late 2005.

This wasn't an intentional effort to marginalize the people of Indonesia. The person who said they didn't know anyone familiar with the island wasn't trying to elicit a spit-take; it seems likely that they expected most people to be in a similar position to them. And they saw shared ignorance as a valid argument: no one like me knows anything about this, so it can't be important.

In an environment like this, a person of color or an editor from the developing world feels like an outsider. Your labor is welcome, of course, because the uncredited labor of people like you has always been welcome in building the edifices of the Global North. But if you choose to join the conversation about shaping the direction of the encyclopedia (or even the main topic for "Java"), you need to carefully consider how to present yourself. If I declare my identity, I risk being labeled as someone seeking to advance my agenda at the expense of Wikipedia's best interests. But if I don't declare it, I implicitly validate the idea that white men from the Global North are the best people to decide what the world of knowledge should look like.

Debates on Wikipedia can be heated, and editors often mention the need for a thick skin. Despite the existence of a policy banning personal attacks,[20] comments may become personal and can cross the line into misogynistic, homophobic, transphobic, or racially charged language. This creates added barriers for precisely the types of editors that Wikipedia needs to diversify the editing community.[21]

Wikipedia is, in the words of Alexandria Lockett "a subtle form of information warfare against colonized populations" who are conditioned to "[feel] as if you cannot and should not 'disrupt' the information architecture."[22]

The Wikipedia community has always been aware of the problems posed by this systemic bias.[23] A WikiProject[24] aimed at countering systemic bias has existed on the English Wikipedia since October 4, 2004, when a Wikipedian who went by the username ChrisG gathered several existing conversations into a centralized location.[25] Similarly, the Wikimedia Foundation addresses this issue as part of its mission for "knowledge equity."[26] But the problem is intertwined with the policies that make Wikipedia what it is and, potentially, those who have allowed it to function as a high-quality reference work.

The Problems with Policy

An encyclopedia that *anyone* can contribute to only works if you have rules that determine what can and cannot be included. A traditional encyclopedia relies on the authority of the subject matter experts who are its contributors. They act as gatekeepers, determining what is worthy of inclusion and deciding how to weigh the competing arguments in the literature. These contributors are recruited for their subject matter expertise, and their time is a major bottleneck in the process of completing the final product. In Wikipedia's model of commons-based peer production,[27] contributors can fill neither of these roles on their own authority because the identity of individual contributors is subsumed into the mass of faceless contributors hidden behind pseudonyms.[28]

When you can't rely on the authority of your editors, the only way to avoid anarchy is through a rules-based system of contributions. While these rules have made Wikipedia possible, they also pose a barrier to the work of decolonization.

To be covered in the encyclopedia, a topic must be "notable." In the context of policy on the English Wikipedia,[29] notability is a term of art that usually refers to the general notability guideline (usually abbreviated GNG) which says, "A topic is presumed to be suitable for a stand-alone article or list when it has received significant coverage in reliable sources that are independent of the subject."[30] To further complicate the matter, "significant coverage," "reliable sources," and "independent of the subject" are all terms whose precise meanings are worked out, in context, through a consensus-building process (or failing that, a vote).

The goal of this policy is to provide a barrier against the inclusion of trivia. The idea is that if a topic has been covered by reliable sources, it is probably important enough for Wikipedia to cover. And if it hasn't been covered, it probably isn't. This policy builds on an older policy—verifiability.[31] The verifiability policy exists to keep hoaxes out of Wikipedia, but it is also effective in excluding topics that haven't been covered by mainstream publications.[32]

While the notability and verifiability policies define two of the three borders of what Wikipedia can cover, the sourcing policy creates the third and perhaps the most challenging border. Source quality is culturally determined—the community decides whether to accept a source as reliable or not. But it's not just the "community" in a broad sense, it's the portion of the community that is interested enough to show up to discuss the quality of a source. Participation, and the degree to which the participants are knowledgeable about a source, can have a huge impact on the acceptability of less well-known sources.[33] This is particularly true for sources in languages other than English; not all articles that should meet the notability threshold (e.g., articles about towns in Libya or national politicians in Laos) will do so if we only rely on English-language sources.

A combination of the notability, verifiability, and reliable sources policies ensure that inclusion on Wikipedia is based on (mostly) external criteria. This allows the community to outsource some of the decision-making about what to cover. The problem, though, is that this means that the biases present in outside sources are reproduced in Wikipedia's coverage. It is difficult for Wikipedia to do a better job than the available sources. Fixing the gap in Wikipedia's coverage for women would require, according to Katherine Maher, "journalists, book publishers, scientific researchers, curators, academics, grant-makers and prize-awarding committees [to] recognize the work of women."[34] And while this can be addressed for contemporary people, the contributions of underrepresented people in history may be lost forever to Wikipedia.

Throughout all this, the problem remains that Wikipedia's inclusion policies are "bias[ed] toward Western, rational, and print-centric knowledge-making practices."[35] While these policies play a crucial role in keeping hoaxes out of Wikipedia, they also ensure that its content coverage will be based on a system that gives priority to the interests of media and academics in the Global North.[36]

A Cost and Benefit of Openness

Wikipedia's image selection in articles is decidedly dated. People have often asked why Wikipedia tends to use historic photographs, even to illustrate modern landscapes. Why the preference for out-of-date images? The answer, which is surprising to many people (but not to people in the OER community) is that Wikipedia uses these images because their copyrights have expired. Openness has been an immense benefit to Wikipedia and has been important in its growth into a near-ubiquitous resource.

An old image of a familiar landscape can draw the viewer to consider what has changed. But an old image of an unfamiliar landscape can reinforce existing perceptions. Images of urban rail in Casablanca or Addis Ababa can challenge these stereotypes,[37] but they are only available to challenge these perceptions because someone chose to upload their images to Wikimedia Commons (or released them under a compatible license on Flickr), which meant that they were available for a participant in Wiki Education's Student Program to add to the article they were expanding on urban rail in Africa.[38]

Many parts of the world have modernized at a remarkable pace in the last few decades, but you might not know that from Wikipedia. The use of historic imagery reinforces the perception that the developing world is backward. Photographic contests like the annual Wiki Loves Africa contest[39] have done a lot to expand coverage, but because they are contests, they favor the inclusion of spectacular, interesting, or exoticizing imagery over the mundane. When the contests are judged through the eyes of the Global North, the effect is heightened—no one wants to give awards for the kind of thing they can see regularly in their own backyards. But as long as the developing world is portrayed on Wikipedia through this lens, it remains *exotic*.

If we want to push back against the perception of the developing world as backward, we need to improve the way we present it visually.

Governance

The Wikimedia Foundation (WMF) is a central player in the governance of Wikipedia and its sister projects. Their control of the movement strategy process and funds dissemination to chapters, thematic groups, and user groups within the movement makes them a powerful player both in efforts to decolonize Wikipedia and as a force that preserves the status quo. While its staff and board of trustees are diverse by American standards, they are not representative of the world at large. For example, there is zero representation from African, Caribbean, or Pacific countries (OACPS countries) on either the board[40] or the leadership team.[41]

While they had good intentions, the nature of the power structure reinforces the colonized nature of Wikipedia. They cannot tell *our* stories if *we* are not represented. At the same time, if they stray too far outside the Wikimedia community, they risk drawing criticism for putting power in the hands of individuals and groups who don't understand the community. In the short term, this causes tensions between elements of the community who are concerned about being marginalized in a project they built and elements in the community who see the need to devolve power to the global majority as part of the mission to work toward knowledge equity.

The future of governance within the movement lies not with the resolution of tensions between these groups but rather in the true decolonization of the governance process. At this point, we stand where the global empires stood on the eve of the modern era of decolonization—aware of the moral imperative to devolve power and extend some measure of home rule to the global majority but imagining a special role for themselves during a decades-long transition to responsible governance.

If the lessons of history are meaningful, the Wikimedia community should be prepared for a shift in power that could happen much quicker than people imagine. We seem to assume that people in the Global South don't know "how to Wikipedia," and that while they may eventually be able to learn, it will happen through the dissemination of knowledge from colonizer to colonized. But power meant to be carefully devolved can also be claimed by the grassroots.[42]

Diversifying the Voices

When Emmanuelle Charpentier and Jennifer Doudna's win of the 2020 Nobel Prize for Chemistry was announced, I felt an immediate sense of gratitude for work done by Laura Hoopes two years earlier when she had participated as a Wiki Scholar in a program run by Wiki Education. As part of the course, Hoopes rewrote Doudna's biography, expanding its coverage of her work on CRISPR—very useful information for any reader coming to Wikipedia to learn about this new Nobel laureate. But equally important, Hoopes reframed Doudna's biography so that she was no longer interpreted through the lens of the men in her life.[43]

Through its Student Program, Wiki Education brings about 16,000 student editors to Wikipedia each year: 59 percent of these students identify as women and 42 percent as non-white. These students make up about 19 percent of active editors on the English Wikipedia. Although limited to college and university students in the United States and Canada, this influx of student editors makes a significant impact on the demographics of Wikipedia's editors.[44] These students have access to the latest scholarly literature and are supervised by faculty members who can help steer them toward modern, inclusive scholarship.

Other groups working in a similar space to diversify the population of Wikipedia contributors include AfroCROWD, Women in Red, Black Lunch Table, Art + Feminism, and Whose Knowledge. AfroCROWD works to diversify Wikipedia's contributor base by expanding participation and awareness among people of African descent.[45] Women in Red is a WikiProject that works to reduce systemic bias by improving coverage of women on Wikipedia.[46] Black Lunch Table[47] and Art + Feminism[48] work to improve the coverage of the arts and artists, while Whose Knowledge works to make the internet "less white, male, straight, and Global North in origin."[49]

Adding more diversity to Wikipedia's pool of contributors while recruiting these contributors to fill gaps in Wikipedia's coverage is a valuable part of the toolkit to decolonize Wikipedia. But as Bjork-James points out, this strategy "shouldn't form the only horizon of our work."[50] Academia needs to focus on ways to write marginalized people back into history, and Wikipedia needs to collaborate more closely with the academics who are doing this work. An interesting example of this is the work by Cipta Media Ekspresi and Wikimedia Indonesia to implement research projects that documented oral indigenous knowledge.[51] Not only were they able to document traditional songs (which were never recorded in a format compatible with Wikipedia) they also documented traditional birthing practices from the last practitioner familiar with the entire process.

Speaking for Ourselves

What brought me to Wikipedia was a chance to invert the traditional model of knowledge creation as it applies to the developing world—or at least one little corner of the developing world. Here was a chance to shape the way the Caribbean was presented to the world, instead of being observed and written about by outsiders. I set out to change the way the Caribbean, its society, its history, and its peoples were represented.[52] I believe I have made a valuable contribution to Wikipedia, but the contributions of any one person aren't enough. Samuel Baltz created 264 new pages for women political scientists in 2020, but only boosted the proportion of women in the category by about 5 percent.[53]

Working with the Wikimedians of the Caribbean user group (WikiCari) over the last two years has opened my eyes to new opportunities and new limitations. Most people know that they *can* make edits to Wikipedia, but they don't know that Wikipedia *needs them*, especially if they have specialized knowledge to offer. Caribbean academics and their students are uniquely positioned to contribute decolonized perspectives to Wikipedia. But there is also a wealth of knowledge that has never been documented in reliable sources. Worse yet, there is information that was documented inaccurately, either by well-meaning academics who didn't get things right or by biased sources that happen to be the only ones that meet Wikipedia's standards. At the same time, there are practitioners and artists, historians, archaeologists, environmentalists, naturalists, and folklorists, many of them with experience in higher education, who nonetheless have never recorded this knowledge in what the Wikipedia community could consider a reliable source.

A group like WikiCari can either adopt the role of client, relying on good relations within the movement to open doors for more people like us, or it can work as part of a movement to re-center knowledge production on the voices and sources of the Global South. There's work to be done, but there's also the opportunity for us, as colonized people, to tell our stories as Wikipedia editors. Because when you see yourself in the world, when you take the plunge and participate in the process as an equal, it changes things for you, and it changes things for those who come after you.[54]

Acknowledgments

I would like to thank LiAnna Davis, Brandon Sullivan, Carol Ramjohn, and Linsday Hill-Ramjohn whose feedback substantially improved my earlier draft.

Endnotes

1. Neil Thompson and Douglas Hanley, "Science is Shaped by Wikipedia: Evidence from a Randomized Control Trial," MIT Sloan Research Paper No. 5238-17 (February 2018).
2. Jake Orlowitz, "How Wikipedia Drove Professors Crazy, Made Me Sane, and Almost Saved the Internet," in *Wikipedia @ 20: Stories of an Incomplete Revolution*, eds. Joseph Reagle and Jackie Koerner (Cambridge, MA: The MIT Press, 2020), 128.

3. Robert E. Cummings, "The First Twenty Years of Teaching with Wikipedia: From Faculty Enemy to Faculty Enabler," in *Wikipedia @ 20: Stories of an Incomplete Revolution*, eds. Joseph Reagle and Jackie Koerner (Cambridge, MA: The MIT Press, 2020), 142.
4. As of September 21, 2020, the only 18.6% of biographies on the English Wikipedia were of women. Denelezh, "Gender Gap on Wikidata," accessed March 1, 2021, https://denelezh.wmcloud.org/gender-gap/?sort=percent_females.
5. Claudia Wagner, Eduardo Graella-Garrido, David Garcia, and Filippo Menczer, "Women through the glass ceiling: gender asymmetries in Wikipedia," *EPJ Data Science* 5, no. 5 (2016).
6. Mark Graham, Bernie Hogan, Ralph K. Straumann, and Ahmed Medhat, "Uneven Geographies of User-Generated Information: Patterns of Increasing Informational Poverty," *Annals of the Association of American Geographers* 104, no. 4 (2014), 746–64.
7. Martin Dittus and Mark Graham, "Mapping Wikipedia's Geolinguistic Contours," *Digital Culture and Society* 5, no. 1 (November 2019), 147–64.
8. Kai Zhu, Dylan Walker, and Lev Muchnik, "Content Growth and Attention Contagion in Information Networks: Addressing Information Poverty on Wikipedia," *Information Systems Research* 31, no. 2 (2020): 491–509.
9. Joseph Reagle, "Wikipedia: The Happy Accident," *Interactions* 16, no. 3 (May 2009), 42–45.
10. Joseph Reagle, "The Many (Reported) Deaths of Wikipedia," in *Wikipedia @ 20: Stories of an Incomplete Revolution*, eds. Joseph Reagle and Jackie Koerner (Cambridge, MA: The MIT Press, 2020), 10–11.
11. For example, *gayap* is a mode of shared work in Trinidad and Tobago in which each member of the community contributes labor, with the understanding that this pool of shared labor is available to anyone in the community. This builds a sense of collective ownership of the success of a project that isn't available in the same way with the individualistic concept of "donation." See Lise Winer, "Gayap," *Dictionary of the English/Creole of Trinidad & Tobago* (Montreal & Kingston: McGill-Queen's University Press, 2009), 377.
12. Larry Sanger, "The Early History of Nupedia and Wikipedia: A Memoir," in *Open Sources 2.0: The Continuing Evolution*, eds. Chris DiBona, Mark Stone, and Danese Cooper (Cambridge, MA: O'Reilly Media, 2005), 307–38.
13. For the most part, these tags were added years after the content was added to Wikipedia, and tags may also have been removed by editors at some point in time. For these reasons, the numbers of articles tagged should be taken as a minimum estimate.
14. Wikipedia contributors, "Geography of Trinidad and Tobago," Wikipedia, The Free Encyclopedia, accessed February 26, 2021, https://en.wikipedia.org/w/index.php?title=Geography_of_Trinidad_and_Tobago&oldid=1006288922.
15. Wikipedia contributors, "Sir Norman Lamont, 2nd Baronet," Wikipedia, The Free Encyclopedia, accessed February 26, 2021, https://en.wikipedia.org/w/index.php?title=Sir_Norman_Lamont,_2nd_Baronet&oldid=992720771.
16. It often feels like there's a large dose of nostalgia for glories of the British Empire both in the article space in Wikipedia and in the structure of the category tree.
17. Roblimo, "Wikipedia Founder Jimmy Wales Responds," interview, Slashdot, July 28, 2004, https://slashdot.org/story/04/07/28/1351230/wikipedia-founder-jimmy-wales-responds.
18. Dittus and Graham, "Mapping Wikipedia's Geolinguistic Contours," 148.
19. Carwil Bjork-James, "New maps for an inclusive Wikipedia: decolonial scholarship and strategies to counter systemic bias," *New Review of Hypermedia and Multimedia*, 2–4, doi: 10.1080/13614568.2020.1865463.
20. Wikipedia contributors, "Wikipedia:No personal attacks," *Wikipedia: The Free Encyclopedia*, accessed September 1, 2021, https://en.wikipedia.org/wiki/Wikipedia:No_personal_attacks.
21. Zachary J. McDowell and Matthew A. Vetter, *Wikipedia and the Representation of Reality* (New York: Routledge, 2022), 76–79.
22. Alexandria Lockett, "Why Do I Have Authority to Edit the Page? The Politics of User Agency and Participation on Wikipedia," in *Wikipedia @ 20: Stories of an Incomplete Revolution*, eds. Joseph Reagle and Jackie Koerner (Cambridge, MA: The MIT Press, 2020), 216.

23. Phoebe Ayers, Charles Matthews, and Ben Yates, *How Wikipedia Works: And How You Can Be a Part of It* (San Francisco: No Starch Press, 2008), 355–61.
24. WikiProjects are groups of Wikipedians who come together to focus on improving some area of knowledge on Wikipedia.
25. Wikipedia contributors, "Wikipedia:WikiProject Countering systemic bias," *Wikipedia: The Free Encyclopedia*, October 4, 2005, accessed February 26, 2021, https://en.wikipedia.org/w/index.php?title=Wikipedia:WikiProject_Countering_systemic_bias&oldid=6332105.
26. Jackie Koerner, "Wikipedia Has a Bias Problem," in *Wikipedia @ 20: Stories of an Incomplete Revolution*, eds. Joseph Reagle and Jackie Koerner (Cambridge, MA: The MIT Press, 2020), 312–14.
27. Yochai Benkler, "From Utopia to Practise and Back," in *Wikipedia @ 20: Stories of an Incomplete Revolution*, eds. Joseph Reagle and Jackie Koerner (Cambridge, MA: The MIT Press, 2020), 43.
28. Not really though. Page histories, diffs, and various plug-ins allow you to identify who wrote what. And many contributors have connected their usernames with their real identities.
29. This section refers specifically to policy on the English Wikipedia. Other language communities have their own policies.
30. Wikipedia contributors, "Wikipedia:Notability," *Wikipedia: The Free Encyclopedia*, accessed February 25, 2021, https://en.wikipedia.org/wiki/Wikipedia:Notability.
31. Wikipedia contributors, "Wikipedia:Verifiability," *Wikipedia: The Free Encyclopedia*, accessed February 25, 2021, https://en.wikipedia.org/wiki/Wikipedia:Verifiability.
32. Koerner, "Wikipedia Has a Bias Problem," 316–17.
33. Ian A. Ramjohn and LiAnna L. Davis, "Equity, Policy, and Newcomers: Five Journeys from Wiki Education," in *Wikipedia @ 20: Stories of an Incomplete Revolution*, eds. Joseph Reagle and Jackie Koerner (Cambridge, MA: The MIT Press, 2020), 304–05.
34. Katherine Maher, "Wikipedia is a mirror to the world's gender biases," *Wikimedia Foundation* (October 18, 2018), accessed February 25, 2021, https://wikimediafoundation.org/news/2018/10/18/wikipedia-mirror-world-gender-biases/.
35. Matthew Vetter, "Possible Enlightenments: Wikipedia's Encyclopedic Promise and Epistemological Failure," in *Wikipedia @ 20: Stories of an Incomplete Revolution*, eds. Joseph Reagle and Jackie Koerner (Cambridge, MA: The MIT Press, 2020), 286.
36. For an in-depth discussion of how these policies impacts inclusion and exclusion of content and contributors to Wikipedia, see Zachary J. McDowell and Matthew A. Vetter, *Wikipedia and the Representation of Reality* (New York: Routledge, 2022).
37. Wikipedia contributors, "Urban rail transit in Africa," Wikipedia, The Free Encyclopedia, accessed February 26, 2021, https://en.wikipedia.org/w/index.php?title=Urban_rail_transit_in_Africa&oldid=1004047527.
38. Ian Ramjohn, "Expanding Wikipedia's coverage of African topics," *Wiki Education* (December 10, 2020), accessed February 26, 2021, https://wikiedu.org/blog/2020/12/10/expanding-wikipedias-coverage-of-african-topics/.
39. Commons contributors, "Wiki Loves Africa," *Wikimedia Commons*, accessed February 26, 2021, https://commons.wikimedia.org/wiki/Commons:Wiki_Loves_Africa.
40. Board of Trustees, Wikimedia Foundation, accessed February 26, 2021, https://wikimediafoundation.org/role/board/.
41. Leadership Team, Wikimedia Foundation, accessed March 1, 2021, https://wikimediafoundation.org/role/leadership/.
42. Credit to Brandon Sullivan for helping me sort some of these ideas out.
43. Ian Ramjohn, "How a Wiki Scholar improved a Nobel laureate's biography," *Wiki Education* (October 7, 2020), accessed February 26, 2021, https://wikiedu.org/blog/2020/10/07/how-a-wiki-scholar-improved-a-nobel-laureates-biography/.
44. LiAnna Davis, "Wiki Education brings 19% of English Wikipedia's new active editors," *Wiki Education* (October 5, 2020), accessed February 26, 2021, https://wikiedu.org/blog/2020/10/05/wiki-education-brings-19-of-english-wikipedias-new-active-editors/.

45. AfroCROWD, Afro Free Culture Crowdsourcing Wikimedia, accessed February 26, 2021, https://afrocrowd.org/.
46. Wikipedia contributors, "Wikipedia:WikiProject Women in Red," *Wikipedia: The Free Encyclopedia*, accessed February 26, 2021, https://en.wikipedia.org/wiki/Wikipedia:WikiProject_Women_in_Red.
47. Jina Valentine, Eliza Myrie, and Heather Hart, "The Myth of the Comprehensive Historical Archive," in *Wikipedia @ 20: Stories of an Incomplete Revolution*, eds. Joseph Reagle and Jackie Koerner (Cambridge, MA: The MIT Press, 2020), 260–61.
48. Siân Evans, Jacqueline Mabey, Michael Mandiberg, and Melissa Tamani, "What We Talk About When We Talk About Community," in *Wikipedia @ 20: Stories of an Incomplete Revolution*, eds. Joseph Reagle and Jackie Koerner (Cambridge, MA: The MIT Press, 2020), 221–23.
49. Camille E. Acey, Siko Bouterse, Sucheta Ghoshal, Amanda Menking, Anasuya Sengupta, and Adele G Vrana, "Decolonizing the Internet by Decolonizing Ourselves: Challenging Epistemic Injustice through Feminist Practice," *Global Perspectives* 2, no. 1 (2021): 1–8.
50. Bjork-James, "New maps for an inclusive Wikipedia," 17–18.
51. Ivonne Kristiani, "Encouraging indigenous knowledge production for Wikipedia," *New Review of Hypermedia and Multimedia* 27:3 (2021), https://www.tandfonline.com/doi/full/10.1080/13614568.2021.1888320.
52. Ramjohn and Davis, "Equity, Policy, and Newcomers," 298–99, 302.
53. Samuel Baltz, "Wikipedia's political science coverage is biased. I tried to fix it," *The Washington Post* (February 24, 2021), accessed February 26, 2021, https://www.washingtonpost.com/politics/2021/02/24/wikipedias-political-science-coverage-is-biased-i-tried-fix-it/.
54. Ian Ramjohn, "Seeing yourself in the world," *Wiki Education* (October 25, 2018), accessed February 26, 2021, https://wikiedu.org/blog/2018/10/25/seeing-yourself-in-the-world/.

Bibliography

Acey, Camille E., Siko Bouterse, Sucheta Ghoshal, Amanda Menking, Anasuya Sengupta, and Adele G Vrana. "Decolonizing the Internet by Decolonizing Ourselves: Challenging Epistemic Injustice through Feminist Practice." *Global Perspectives* 2, no. 1 (2021): 1–8.

AfroCROWD. Afro Free Culture Crowdsourcing Wikimedia. Accessed February 26, 2021. https://afrocrowd.org/.

Ayers, Phoebe, Charles Matthews, and Ben Yates. *How Wikipedia Works: And How You Can Be a Part of It*. San Francisco: No Starch Press, 2008.

Baltz, Samuel. "Wikipedia's political science coverage is biased. I tried to fix it." *The Washington Post* (February 24, 2021). Accessed February 26, 2021. https://www.washingtonpost.com/politics/2021/02/24/wikipedias-political-science-coverage-is-biased-i-tried-fix-it/.

Benkler, Yochai. "From Utopia to Practise and Back." In *Wikipedia @ 20: Stories of an Incomplete Revolution*, edited by Joseph Reagle and Jackie Koerner. Cambridge, MA: The MIT Press, 2020, 43–54.

Bjork-James, Carwil. "New maps for an inclusive Wikipedia: decolonial scholarship and strategies to counter systemic bias." *New Review of Hypermedia and Multimedia*, 2–4. doi: 10.1080/13614568.2020.1865463.

Commons contributors. "Wiki Loves Africa." *Wikimedia Commons*. Accessed February 26, 2021. https://commons.wikimedia.org/wiki/Commons:Wiki_Loves_Africa.

Cummings, Robert E. "The First Twenty Years of Teaching with Wikipedia: From Faculty Enemy to Faculty Enabler." In *Wikipedia @ 20: Stories of an Incomplete Revolution*, edited by Joseph Reagle and Jackie Koerner. Cambridge, MA: The MIT Press, 2020, 141–49.

Davis, LiAnna. "Wiki Education brings 19% of English Wikipedia's new active editors." *Wiki Education* (October 5, 2020). Accessed February 26, 2021. https://wikiedu.org/blog/2020/10/05/wiki-education-brings-19-of-english-wikipedias-new-active-editors/.

Denelezh. "Gender Gap on Wikidata." Accessed March 1, 2021. https://denelezh.wmcloud.org/gender-gap/?sort=percent_females.

Dittus, Martin, and Mark Graham. "Mapping Wikipedia's Geolinguistic Contours." *Digital Culture and Society* 5, no. 1 (November 2019), 147–64.

Evans, Siân, Jacqueline Mabey, Michael Mandiberg, and Melissa Tamani. "What We Talk About When We Talk About Community." In *Wikipedia @ 20: Stories of an Incomplete Revolution*, edited by Joseph Reagle and Jackie Koerner. Cambridge, MA: The MIT Press, 2020, 221–38.

Graham, Mark, Bernie Hogan, Ralph K. Straumann, and Ahmed Medhat. "Uneven Geographies of User-Generated Information: Patterns of Increasing Informational Poverty." *Annals of the Association of American Geographers* 104, no. 4 (2014), 746–64.

Koerner, Jackie. "Wikipedia Has a Bias Problem." In *Wikipedia @ 20: Stories of an Incomplete Revolution*, edited by Joseph Reagle and Jackie Koerner. Cambridge, MA: The MIT Press, 2020, 311–21.

Kristiani, Ivonne. "Encouraging indigenous knowledge production for Wikipedia." *New Review of Hypermedia and Multimedia* 27:3 (2021). https://www.tandfonline.com/doi/full/10.1080/13614568.2021.1888320.

Lockett, Alexandria. "Why Do I Have Authority to Edit the Page? The Politics of User Agency and Participation on Wikipedia." In *Wikipedia @ 20: Stories of an Incomplete Revolution*, edited by Joseph Reagle and Jackie Koerner. Cambridge, MA: The MIT Press, 2020, 205–20.

Maher, Katherine. "Wikipedia is a mirror to the world's gender biases." *Wikimedia Foundation* (October 18, 2018). Accessed February 25, 2021. https://wikimediafoundation.org/news/2018/10/18/wikipedia-mirror-world-gender-biases/.

McDowell, Zachary J., and Matthew A. Vetter. *Wikipedia and the Representation of Reality*. New York: Routledge, 2022.

Orlowitz, Jake. "How Wikipedia Drove Professors Crazy, Made Me Sane, and Almost Saved the Internet." In *Wikipedia @ 20: Stories of an Incomplete Revolution*, edited by Joseph Reagle and Jackie Koerner. Cambridge, MA: The MIT Press, 2020, 125–39.

Ramjohn, Ian. "Expanding Wikipedia's coverage of African topics." *Wiki Education* (December 10, 2020). Accessed February 26, 2021. https://wikiedu.org/blog/2020/12/10/expanding-wikipedias-coverage-of-african-topics/.

———. "How a Wiki Scholar improved a Nobel laureate's biography." *Wiki Education* (October 7, 2020). Accessed February 26, 2021. https://wikiedu.org/blog/2020/10/07/how-a-wiki-scholar-improved-a-nobel-laureates-biography/.

———. "Seeing yourself in the world." *Wiki Education* (October 25, 2018). Accessed February 26, 2021. https://wikiedu.org/blog/2018/10/25/seeing-yourself-in-the-world/.

Ramjohn, Ian A., and LiAnna L. Davis. "Equity, Policy, and Newcomers: Five Journeys from Wiki Education." In *Wikipedia @ 20: Stories of an Incomplete Revolution*, eds. Joseph Reagle and Jackie Koerner. Cambridge, MA: The MIT Press, 2020, 297–310.

Reagle, Joseph. "The Many (Reported) Deaths of Wikipedia." In *Wikipedia @ 20: Stories of an Incomplete Revolution*, edited by Joseph Reagle and Jackie Koerner. Cambridge, MA: The MIT Press, 2020, 9–20.

———. "Wikipedia: the happy accident." *Interactions* 16, no. 3 (May 2009), 42–45.

Roblimo. "Wikipedia Founder Jimmy Wales Responds." Interview, Slashdot, July 28, 2004. Accessed February 25, 2021. https://slashdot.org/story/04/07/28/1351230/wikipedia-founder-jimmy-wales-responds.

Sanger, Larry. "The Early History of Nupedia and Wikipedia: A Memoir." In *Open Sources 2.0: The Continuing Evolution*, edited by Chris DiBona, Mark Stone, and Danese Cooper. Cambridge, MA: O'Reilly Media, 2005, 307–38.

Thompson, Neil, and Douglas Hanley. "Science Is Shaped by Wikipedia: Evidence from a Randomized Control Trial." MIT Sloan Research Paper No. 5238-17 (February 2018).

Wagner, Claudia, Eduardo Graella-Garrido, David Garcia, and Filippo Menczer. "Women through the glass ceiling: gender asymmetries in Wikipedia." *EPJ Data Science* 5, no. 5 (2016).

Valentine, Jina, Eliza Myrie, and Heather Hart. "The Myth of the Comprehensive Historical Archive." In *Wikipedia @ 20: Stories of an Incomplete Revolution*, edited by Joseph Reagle and Jackie Koerner. Cambridge, MA: The MIT Press, 2020, 259–72.

Vetter, Matthew. "Possible Enlightenments: Wikipedia's Encyclopedic Promise and Epistemological Failure." In *Wikipedia @ 20: Stories of an Incomplete Revolution*, edited by Joseph Reagle and Jackie Koerner. Cambridge, MA: The MIT Press, 2020, 285–95.

Wikimedia Foundation. Board of Trustees. Accessed February 26, 2021. https://wikimediafoundation.org/role/board/.

Wikipedia contributors. "Geography of Trinidad and Tobago." Wikipedia, The Free Encyclopedia. Accessed February 26, 2021. https://en.wikipedia.org/w/index.php?title=Geography_of_Trinidad_and_Tobago&oldid=1006288922.

———. "Sir Norman Lamont, 2nd Baronet," Wikipedia, The Free Encyclopedia. Accessed February 26, 2021. https://en.wikipedia.org/w/index.php?title=Sir_Norman_Lamont,_2nd_Baronet&oldid=992720771.

———. "Urban rail transit in Africa." *Wikipedia, The Free Encyclopedia*. Accessed February 26, 2021. https://en.wikipedia.org/w/index.php?title=Urban_rail_transit_in_Africa&oldid=1004047527.

———. "Wikipedia:Notability." *Wikipedia: The Free Encyclopedia*. Accessed February 25, 2021. https://en.wikipedia.org/wiki/Wikipedia:Notability.

———. "Wikipedia:Verifiability." *Wikipedia: The Free Encyclopedia*. Accessed February 25, 2021. https://en.wikipedia.org/wiki/Wikipedia:Verifiability.

———. "Wikipedia:WikiProject Countering systemic bias." *Wikipedia: The Free Encyclopedia*. October 4, 2005. Accessed February 26, 2021. https://en.wikipedia.org/w/index.php?title=Wikipedia:WikiProject_Countering_systemic_bias&oldid=6332105.

———. "Wikipedia:WikiProject Women in Red." *Wikipedia: The Free Encyclopedia*. Accessed February 26, 2021. https://en.wikipedia.org/wiki/Wikipedia:WikiProject_Women_in_Red ().

Winer, Lise. "Gayap." *Dictionary of the English/Creole of Trinidad & Tobago*. Montreal & Kingston: McGill-Queen's University Press, 2009.

Zhu, Kai, Dylan Walker, and Lev Muchnik. "Content Growth and Attention Contagion in Information Networks: Addressing Information Poverty on Wikipedia." *Information Systems Research* 31, no. 2 (2020): 491–509.

CHAPTER 15

Using Open Educational Resources (OER) to Bring Marginalized Voices into the Music Theory Curriculum

Barbara Murphy and Claire Terrell

In fall 2019, Philip Ewell began an address to the Society of Music Theory (SMT) saying, "Music Theory is white."[1] He explained that the field currently requires those calling themselves music theorists to practice this whiteness "in the composers we choose to represent our field inside and outside of the classroom, and in the music theorists that we elevate to the top of our discipline."[2] The composers that musicians choose to play or teach constitute the musical canon, the "sanctioned or accepted group or body of related works" used in music classes.[3] The musical canon has historically been European, white, and male-biased. Roxanne Prevost and Kimberly Francis, talking about the effect of the narrowness of the musical canon, state, "By continuing to promote certain pieces and repertoire as representative of the best works, canons not only promote certain repertoire but also give the impression that this repertoire is of the highest quality, diminishing the value of those works not considered."[4] Choosing mainly European, white, male composers implies that music written by other populations, such as women and people of color, is of lesser quality and should not be played or studied. Therefore, the lack of diversity in the musical canon must be addressed.

Prevost and Francis infer that music theory teachers can be catalysts for change since they "decide what [musical compositions] their students will analyze" in their classes."[5] Instead of using pieces in the current European, white, male canon, theory instructors could use a broader range of compositions as examples for topics being taught and include examples written by a wider variety of composers. However, the process of locating new examples suitable for use in theory classes is a difficult and time-consuming task. What instructors need is a source of musical examples and recordings representing a wide range of composers that have already been vetted for use in theory classes. Ideally, these materials would be open educational resources (OER), licensed by authors and creators to be shared and freely used by others. One such OER of musical examples is the website Music Theory Materials.[6] This website contains, among other class materials, scores and recordings of a wide variety of compositions, including pieces by under-represented composers (e.g., women, and Black, Indigenous, People of Color—BIPOC) for use in music theory classes.

The purpose of this chapter is to discuss the importance of expanding the musical canon and the efforts to do this through the continuing development of the Music Theory Materials website. The chapter begins with a description of the musical canon—its current state and the need for increased diversity in the represented composers in the canon. The Music Theory Materials website is then described and the efforts to expand its contents are explained. This chapter concludes with a discussion of the advantages of creating these materials as OER, illustrating how the Music Theory Materials website and similar initiatives can contribute to a richer and more diverse musical canon by bringing marginalized voices into the music curriculum.

The Musical Canon

As stated above, a canon can be defined as a "sanctioned or accepted group or body of related works."[7] Marcia Citron adds that musical canons are "exemplary, act as models, instruct, represent high quality, endure, and embody at least some degree of moral and ethical force."[8] In addition, Citron says canons exert "tremendous power" over "what is considered worthy of inclusion."[9] Canons are therefore exclusive. "Works that do not measure up are excluded, either in the sense of deliberately omitted or ignored and hence forgotten." By including or excluding certain works, canons "represent certain sets of values or ideologies, which in turn represent certain segments of society."[10] She states that "as models to be emulated, [canons] replicate their encoded values in subsequent exemplars. As canonic values become entrenched over time, the prescriptive and normative powers of canons become even greater."[11] Thus, canons are self-perpetuating, tenacious, authoritative, and create an impression that they are timeless and immutable.

There is not just one type of canon. Although Edward Komars lists up to ten types of canons (i.e., potential, accessible, official, personal, critical, selective, closed, pedagogical, diachronic, and nonce),[12] Citron suggests only two types of canons for music: disciplinary and repertorial.[13]

The disciplinary canon refers to the "goals, methodologies, research convention, institutions, social structures, belief systems, underlying theories, audience, language, subjects for study, and various other parameters that shape and define a discipline's self-view of what is standard, acceptable, or even desirable."[14] For music, the disciplinary canon includes the collection of music scores, recordings, manuscripts, treatises, etc. used in the study and performance of music.

Repertorial canons are "canons or works performed by professional groups and individuals, and each performing area has its own canon."[15] Examples of repertorial canons could include the orchestral canon, the choral canon, and the wind band canon. Furthermore, Citron says, "There are canons for groups that inhabit a particular historical niche"[16] and canons that "occur in academic teaching of music in the classroom," with textbooks and anthologies as the "repository" of these canons.[17] These last examples blur the lines between disciplinary canon and repertorial canon. For example, the field of music contains subdisciplines, e.g., music history/musicology, music theory, music education, and performance, with even more subcategories in this last subdiscipline (e.g., woodwind, brass, string, keyboard, chamber music). Each of these areas can have its own canon of music, which, according to the examples given by Citron above, might be considered repertorial canons and not disciplinary canons. In this research, we will consider the disciplinary canon the body of works for music in general or a sub-discipline of music (e.g., music history, music theory) and the repertorial canon the works that are performed by particular instruments or ensembles (e.g., woodwinds, brass, wind band, chamber music), acknowledging that there will sometimes be an overlap in the music contained in the two types of canons.

Bias in the Repertorial Canon

In both the disciplinary and repertorial canons in music, there has been a historical bias toward compositions written by European, white, male composers. This bias is apparent in the pieces that are performed by ensembles, both professional and academic, and is documented over a period of 150 years. In a study of both the number and distribution of composers who had their pieces performed by ensembles, Pierre-Antoine Kremp wrote on the lack of innovation of twenty-seven prominent American orchestras from 1879 to 1959. Of the composers performed in the latter years of his study, the 1950s, "twelve of the twenty most popular composers chosen were among the 20 most played in the 1880s."[18] Kremp found that 1,612 composers' pieces were played in the eighty-year time span, but thirteen composers constituted more than half of the performances.[19] He concluded that orchestras were not being innovative in their programming, choosing instead to continue to play pieces by the "greats" of the canonical (European, white, male) past. These orchestras' continued success despite this lack of innovation reinforces the canon since a sentiment of "don't fix what isn't broken" likely pervades the field. This bias is also often explained by public preference for the aesthetic of the "classical" past, generally the Baroque, Classical, and Romantic periods. However, orchestras in the late twentieth century sought novelty in the form of "resurrected composers," composers of the past who were not previously included in the canon,[20] shattering the idea of a preference for a certain musical aesthetic. The availability of music by non-European, non-male, and non-white composers in periods of the "greats" proves that the root of canonical bias cannot be restricted to an aesthetic preference of certain time periods. Kremp's definition of the orchestral performance canon as "a narrow set of mostly Austro-German composers (the classics)" exemplifies the exclusionary makeup of the orchestral performance canon.[21]

To determine if the choice of composers whose pieces are played by ensembles has changed in more recent years, we set out to gather statistics of our own. Innovation was not an explicit concern in this study; our purpose was to discover the diversity of the choice of composers. Given that those enforcing the professional performance canon are trained musicians who likely have music degrees, we propose that academia must have some effect on creating the musical canon performed by professional musicians and ensembles. Therefore, we looked to academia, not professional orchestras, to determine the diversity of composers performed by ensembles.

To investigate the diversity of composers performed by academic institutions, we studied the compositions played by large ensembles at large and/or prominent American universities. For each university, we looked at the composers programmed from August 2018 to March 2020 by the institution's major ensembles. This timeframe was selected because it reflects recent programming, and it ends in March 2020 due to the international pandemic that disrupted the typical performance season. To select the universities for this study, we created a list of approximately forty large universities with the capacity for multiple large ensembles and/or universities with a prominent music program. Since this study began at the University of Tennessee (UT), we looked for university music programs comparable or larger in size to UT or that had nationally prominent music programs. Since we needed access to concert programs for the desired timeframe, either publicly available online or through the music library of each school, the list of schools narrowed to the universities shown in table 15.1.

School	Location
Boston University	Boston, MA
Eastman School of Music (University of Rochester)	Rochester, NY
Indiana University	Bloomington, IN
The Ohio State University	Columbus, OH
University of California, Los Angeles	Los Angeles, CA
University of Hawai'i at Mānoa	Honolulu, HI
University of Massachusetts at Amherst	Amherst, MA
University of North Texas	Denton, TX
University of South Carolina	Columbia, SC
University of Tennessee	Knoxville, TN
University of Texas at Austin	Austin, TX
University of Wisconsin-Madison	Madison, WI
Washington University in St. Louis	St. Louis, MO

Table 15.1
List of selected universities.

To determine which ensembles to include in this study, we considered the original question: How does academia create and/or indoctrinate its students into a pre-established canon? Since the shared ensemble performance experience was the most likely influence on students, we included in the scope of this study the large ensembles music majors are most likely required to join—choirs, bands, orchestras, and opera programs. We felt that the programming of these ensembles represents the music emphasized by the institution since the pieces chosen for performance are usually chosen by the conductor or faculty member rather than by the students. In contrast, chamber ensembles and student recitals reflect the interests of the individuals and, therefore, were not included in this study. It should be noted, before delving into the programmatic data, that several of the studied universities, most notably the University of California, Los Angeles, and the University of Hawai'i have a plethora of chamber groups focused on music cultures outside of the Western art canon, though most of the universities include at least one such ensemble. However, to ensure equity of ensembles, these admirable groups were excluded.

Once the institutions with accessible concert programs were identified, the pieces on the programs were listed and the composers identified by gender and race. The data in table 15.2 shows the gender of programmed composers in raw numbers as well as percentages of the whole. Table 15.3 shows the race of programmed composers in raw numbers, delineated by each race, and percentages of the whole (designated as white and non-white).

University	Total No. of Composers	No. Male Composers	Percentage of Male Composers	No. Female Composers	Percentage of Female Composers
University of Hawai'i at Mānoa	48	40	83.33%	8	16.67%
Eastman School of Music	153	131	85.62%	22	14.38%
University of California, Los Angeles	41	36	87.8%	5	12.2%
University of Tennessee	127	112	88.19%	15	11.81%
University of Wisconsin-Madison	128	113	88.28%	15	11.72%
University of Massachusetts at Amherst	85	76	89.41%	9	10.59%
University of North Texas	252	226	89.68%	26	10.32%
Washington University at St. Louis	72	65	90.28%	7	9.72%
University of South Carolina	69	63	91.3%	6	8.7%
University of Texas at Austin	149	137	91.95%	12	8.05%
The Ohio State University	137	128	93.43%	9	6.57%
Indiana University	176	165	93.75%	11	6.25%
Boston University	66	64	96.97%	2	3.03%
Averages			90.00%		10.00%

Table 15.2
The number and percentage of composers programmed by each university by gender.

As can be seen in table 15.2, the percentage of women composers ranges from a low of 3.03% (Boston University) to a high of 16.67% (University of Hawai'i) with an average of 10% female composers programmed at each university. Even though these numbers are relatively low, they may be a bit inflated. For example, the high percentage of women composers at the University of Hawai'i represents only eight female composers of a total of 48 composers programmed. Likewise, the percentage of female composers at UCLA (12.2%) represents only five female composers of 41 composers. Four universities did have "higher" numbers, i.e., over 10% female composers of over 100 total composers programmed: University of North Texas, 10.32% of 252; Eastman School of Music, 14.38% of 153; University of Wisconsin-Madison, 11.72% of 128; University of Tennessee, 11.81% of 127. Even so, the lowest percentage of male composers is a shockingly high number (83.33%).

University	Total No. Composers	No. White Composers	Percentage White Composers	No. Asian Composers	No. Black Composers	No. Latin(a/o) Composers	Percentage Non-White Composers
University of Wisconsin-Madison	128	111	86.72%	4	6	7	13.28%
Eastman School of Music	153	137	89.54%	4	4	8	10.46%
The Ohio State University	137	123	89.78%	6	3	5	10.22%
University of California, Los Angeles	41	37	90.24%	2	1	1	9.76%
Washington University at St. Louis	72	66	91.67%	0	2	4	8.33%
University of Hawai'i at Mānoa	48	44	91.67%	3	1	0	8.33%
University of South Carolina	69	64	92.75%	0	4	1	7.25%
University of Tennessee	127	118	92.91%	2	5	2	7.09%
Indiana University	176	164	93.18%	6	5	1	6.82%
University of North Texas	252	236	93.65%	4	9	3	6.35%
University of Massachusetts at Amherst	85	80	94.12%	3	1	1	5.88%
University of Texas at Austin	149	141	94.63%	4	3	1	5.37%
Boston University	66	63	95.45%	0	2	1	4.55%
Averages			92.02%				7.98%

Table 15.3
The number and percentages of white vs non-white (Asian, Black, and Latin(a/o)) composers programmed at each university.

The data on white versus non-white composers shown in table 15.3 also reveals the bias of the musical canon. The percentage of non-white composers programmed ranges from 4.55% (Boston University) to 13.28% (University of Wisconsin-Madison) with an average of 7.98% non-white composers. Eight of the schools programmed pieces by fewer than ten non-white composers. Again, even the lowest percentage of white composers, 86.72%, is still very high.

In a moderately large study such as this one, it is common to find outliers. However, the spread of the percentages is relatively small (for gender: max = 96.97%, min = 83.33%, range = 13.64%; for ethnicity: max = 13.28%, min = 4.55%, range = 8.73%) indicating that there are no universities that are programming a great deal more female and non-white composers than the others. The small percentage ranges of female and non-white composers also illustrate that the bias toward European, white, male composers pervades academia, with no marked difference in region or between institutions. Therefore, this issue of diversity must be addressed by *all* institutions, rather than just a problematic few.

Though the average number of compositions for both gender (male = 90%, female = 10%) and ethnicity (white = 92.02%, non-white= 7.98%) is shocking, it seems that there is slightly more inclusion of women than non-white composers into the canon. This bias is likely not a conscious preference for female composers over non-white composers but, instead, may result from the fact that the wealth of academic canonical music comes from Romantic-era Europe, specifically Germany—a predominantly white population—and that there has been consistent pressure to recognize popular female composers in the past few years. Therefore, more white women may be included than people of color (male or female). The effort to include composers of color is much more recent, possibly explaining why programs have not included more composers of color.

The above data also does not take into consideration composers who are programmed multiple times. However, in our raw data, we kept track of the names of the programmed works of music themselves, thus allowing us to see multiple works by the same composer. Tables 15.4 and 15.5 contain the total number of composers included in this study, summed between all thirteen universities, and shows repeated composers as well as the number of non-repeated (different) individual composers. Table 15.4 categorizes the total number of composers and the total number of different composers by gender; table 15.5 categorizes the two sums by race. The difference between these two numbers indicates the number of times a composer was repeated between universities.

There were hundreds of composer repetitions among universities, as illustrated by the data. Generally, comparing the total number of composers to the total number of different composers rarely changed the number of female or BIPOC composers but greatly reduced the number of programmed white, male composers. This finding echoes that of Kremp who indicated that certain (canonical) composers, largely white and male, were programmed repeatedly.[22]

Bringing Marginalized Voices into the Music Theory Curriculum 271

	Total No. of Composers	No. of Non-repeated Composers	No. of Repeated Composers	Percentage Repeated Composers
Male	1,356	779	577	42.55%
Female	147	98	49	33.33%

Table 15.4
Sum of total composers included in the study categorized by gender.

	Total No. of Composers	No. of Non-Repeated Composers	No. of Repeated Composers	Percentage Repeated Composers
Asian	38	30	8	21.05%
Black	46	31	15	32.61%
Latin(a/o)	35	26	9	25.71%
White	1,383	790	593	42.59%

Table 15.5
Sum of total composers included in the study categorized by race.

Though these percentages are not quite as staggering as the previous tables, they do show that throughout the entire scope of this study, even among universities, there is a marked bias toward programming white, male composers repeatedly. For example, male composers (42.55%) were repeated 9.22% more than women (33.33%). The raw numbers of repeated composers indicate this bias perhaps even more clearly. Male composers were repeated 577 times—577 separate times an administrator or conductor from one of the thirteen included universities chose to program a male composer more than once within two years. Similarly, white composers were repeated 593 separate times as opposed to 32 repetitions for Asian, Black, and Latin(a/o) composers combined. *Repetitions* of male and white composers outnumber the *sum* of the number of every programmed female and non-white composer. Included in the above data are 12 female composers of color. This number is alarmingly low, though understandable when taking a cross-section of two already small percentages of a whole. These 12 women of color were programmed a total of 22 times. The relatively large recurrence of women of color can likely be attributed to the recent efforts to include women in concert programs and a limited knowledge or recognition of female composers of color.

Both the research of Kremp with professional orchestras and our research with academic ensembles indicate a clear bias toward programming the works by white, male composers. In addition, the research on composers programmed repeatedly at universities serves as further evidence of Kremp's assertion that ensemble administrators choose to program certain composers repeatedly rather

Chapter 15

than expand their performative canon. As students sit in ensembles, they are indoctrinated into this canonical value system, one dominated by European, white, male composers.

Bias in the Theory Classroom

The lack of diversity in composers chosen for ensemble performances is echoed in the musical examples seen in music theory textbooks. Citron notes these biases: "Anthologies [and textbooks] have stressed Western art music and generally ignored other idioms, such as folk music, popular music and world music. Music by women and other 'minorities' in Western culture has also been overlooked, and this shows the biases in gender, class and race."[23] Philip Ewell provides statistics that demonstrate the bias toward white composers (table 15.6). He found that, of the 2,979 musical examples in the seven music theory textbooks that have 96% of the market share, only 49 examples (1.67% of the total) are by non-white composers.[24]

Textbook	Percentage of Market Share	Total No. of Examples	No. of Examples by Non-Whites	Percent of Examples by Non-Whites
Aldwell and Schachter, 4th ed. (2011)	5	465	0	0%
Benward and Saker, 9th ed. (2015)	13	333	8	2.40%
Burstein and Straus, 1st ed. (2016)	11	304	1	0.33%
Clendinning and Marvin, 3rd ed. (2016)	25	504	15	2.98%
Kotska, Payne, and Almen, 8th ed. (2018)	29	370	10	2.70%
Laitz, 4th ed. (2015)	8	550	2	0.36%
Roig-Francoli, 2nd ed. (2010)	5	404	13	3.22%
TOTALS	96	2,930	49	1.67%

Table 15.6
Ewell: Racial demographic data for musical examples from seven American music theory Textbooks. Philip A. Ewell, "Music Theory and the White Racial Frame," *Music Theory Online* 6, no. 2 (September 2020): table 1.

Ewell's statistics do not include the number of examples by female composers. Statistics on the gender of the composers in the same textbooks as those reviewed by Ewell indicate that women composers fare slightly better than non-white composers (see table 15.7). The total number of examples by women composers (99) across all textbooks is 3.02% of the total number of examples (3,275)—almost double that of non-whites found by Ewell (1.67%)[25]—but still a very low number. Some compositions by women composers were referenced more than once. Therefore, the number of different compositions by women was also counted, showing that only 93 different music compositions by women were used.

In his statistics, Ewell also did not list the number of white or non-white *composers* (i.e., he counted the number of *examples*). In our statistics, the number of women *composers* was counted in each textbook; this number ranged from 0 to 36, 0% to 24.53%, of the total number of composers in these textbooks. Across all textbooks, 51 different women composers had pieces used as examples.

Textbook Author	Text Title	Total No. of Composers	Total No. Examples	No. of Women Composers	No. of Examples by Women	Percentage of Women Composers	Percentage of Examples by Women
Roig-Francoli	Harmony in Context, 3rd ed.	53	404	13	21	24.53%	5.20%
Burstein, Straus	Concise Introduction to Tonal Harmony, 2nd ed.	129	414	30	36	23.26%	8.70%
Benward, Saker	Music in Theory and Practice, 10th ed., Vol. 2	62	205	6	6	9.68%	2.93%
Clendinning, Marvin	Musician's Guide to Theory and Analysis, 3rd ed.	111	507	9	16	8.11%	3.16%
Benward, Saker	Music in Theory and Practice, 10th ed., Vol. 1	95	360	7	7	7.37%	1.94%
Kotska, Payne, Almen	Tonal Harmony with an Intro to Post-tonal Music, 8th ed.	96	358	4	11	4.17%	3.07%
Laitz	The Complete Musician, 4th ed.	89	545	1	2	1.12%	0.37%
Aldwell, Schachter, Cadwallader	Harmony and Voice Leading, 5th ed.	40	482	0	0	0%	0%
Total		675	3,275	70	99	10.37%	3.02%

Table 15.7
Gender demographic data for musical examples from seven music theory textbooks.

The lack of diversity in the current choice of composers performed by large ensembles and used in theory textbooks for musical examples is very disconcerting. It is through the ensembles in which university students play and the courses they take that music students are exposed to new music. Limiting the diversity of composers and compositions creates a hidden curriculum. Cora S. Palfy and Eric Gilson define a hidden curriculum as "a concept or idea that, though not explicitly taught to students, is communicated by the classroom or curricular design."[26] Such a hidden curriculum can "impart and reinforce a message about who is and can be important."[27] The composers who are included in their classes are understood by students to be "artistic greats who have composed standard masterworks" that should be studied.[28] Since, as Citron states, the university will shape "the aesthetic values of future professionals as well as audience members and consumers of music,… the teaching canon, as a major influence on the future musical culture, is extremely important."[29] The current teaching canon, as represented by the statistics shown in the tables above, needs to be much more diverse and include a wider variety of composers and pieces, especially compositions by women, people of color, and other under-represented populations. Music theory teachers can be catalysts for such change since their classes—the undergraduate music theory sequence—are some of the few classes that all music majors are usually required to take.[30]

Diversifying Music Theory

Diversifying the field of music theory has been a topic of discussion since the 1990s.[31] However, in the last year, the diversification of music theory has become a major theme in many conversations. Philip Ewell's keynote speech at the 2019 National Convention for the Society for Music Theory[32] caused a great deal of dialogue on the biases in the field of music theory. In his talk, he argued that "music theory will only diversify through 'deframing and reframing' that 'structural and institutionalized' framework that Schenker helped build. He also pushed for a more diverse music theory curriculum."[33] Several articles in Volume 12 of the *Journal of Schenkerian Studies*, responding critically to Ewell's speech,[34] caused even more conversations on the lack of diversity in music theory. The death of George Floyd and the Black Lives Matter movement prompted more discussions on diversity, equity, and inclusion and, in the spring and summer of 2020, sparked talks of how to diversify music in general and theory specifically. Groups of theorists and theory organizations (e.g., Composers of Color Resource Project, Society for Music Theory) began open conversations and workshops on how to diversify the collection of pieces to be used in theory classes. Several websites[35] were created or expanded to include more women, Black, Indigenous, and People of Color (BIPOC) composers. One such effort that is still ongoing is the expansion of the Music Theory Materials website to include compositions by under-represented composers.

The Music Theory Materials Website

Music Theory Materials is a website containing open educational resources (OER) for use in music theory classes. OER can be defined as "materials for teaching or learning that are either in the public domain or have been released under a license that allows them to be freely used, changed, or shared with others."[36] The site was originally designed to contain a collection of musical scores and recordings (i.e., an online anthology) for the teaching of musical form and analysis in music theory classes.[37] The musical examples provided on the site are complete compositions or movements, not excerpts of pieces as on other websites or in some anthologies. Included for each music composition is a copy of the score and a link to a recording of the piece. The original musical examples on this site were standard examples used in music theory classes and, therefore, were, for the most part, compositions written by European, white, male composers. Seeing the need for more diversity in the composers listed, the examples on Music Theory Materials are being expanded to include under-represented composers, specifically women and BIPOC composers.

Marcia Citron discusses two methods for adding examples to the musical canon: the "decentered author" model and the "add-and-stir" approach.[38] The decentered author model "removes the author-function," the "organization of history and culture according to authors, or composers," as the main means of structuring the curricula.[39] Since most music theory classes are not organized around composers or even specific compositions but instead arranged according to topic, the decentered author method of adding to the canon of music theory classes does not apply to the addition of examples on Music Theory Materials.

The "add-and-stir" approach is exactly what it sounds like: "adding" something to a mixture that already exists and "stirring" the new mixture to incorporate the added material into the old. Using this method to introduce new compositions into the canon has been criticized for "mechanically adding new works,… especially those of outside groups such as women, without questioning" what was already included and creating ways to use the new pieces.[40] It is important, therefore, when "adding and stirring" new compositions into music classes that the questions of "how and why [these pieces are added are] addressed, not just the what and how many."[41] Although it is the "add-and-stir" method that is being used to expand the content of Music Theory Materials, care is being taken to avoid the "mechanical" addition of new music. Each added composition is vetted to ensure that it covers relevant material for music theory classes and the topics the composition covers are noted on the website.

The Process of Adding to Music Theory Materials

The process of adding new musical examples to the Music Theory Materials website consists of several steps: identifying composers, locating scores and recording of compositions by those composers, determining the copyright of the scores and recordings, analyzing the compositions, and making a decision about the relevance of the piece for use in music theory classes.

First, under-represented composers are identified. To find as many "new" composers as possible, we begin by searching the web for lists of composers who are women or BIPOC and then gather the names of the composers into one master list. Also included in this list are the composers' birth and death dates, gender, and ethnicity.

Once composers are located, we search for compositions by each composer, specifically looking for pieces for which we can locate scores. We concentrate the search on compositions that are in the public domain (i.e., compositions that were written in or before 1925[42] or are not under any other copyright) as these pieces are the easiest to use on an OER website. Several websites exist that are compilations of such compositions (e.g., The Public Domain Information Project: https://www.pdinfo.com/), the most well-known of which is *IMSLP: The International Music Score Library Project* (http://imslp.org/). IMSLP, a free repository of mostly public domain or Creative Commons-licensed classical music, currently contains "175,229 works, 556,792 scores, 65,996 recordings, 21,621 composers, and 563 performers."[43] Although websites such as IMSLP are wonderful sources of scores, they are not indexed by topic and so cannot easily be used to find class examples.

To use a composition once a score is found, a recording of the piece must also be available. As music is an aural art, compositions must be heard while being analyzed and studied. Therefore, having a quality recording of the piece is essential. Finding recordings of music by under-represented composers, however, is not always easy. Sometimes a recording of the piece is available on the website where the score is found. For example, there are recordings of barbershop quartets on the Barbershop Harmony Society's page of free music scores.[44] Most often, however, recordings are located on sites such as YouTube. Although any recording is useful, links to YouTube recordings are not ideal since these recordings can be removed and the links to them then break. However, for many compositions, another recording of the work is either inaccessible or non-existent and so the YouTube recording must be used.

To mitigate this problem of using YouTube recordings or finding no recording available, the UT Recording Project was initiated. For this project, faculty and students at the University of Tennessee School of Music are asked to consider recording pieces for use on the Music Theory Materials website. For these recordings to be used, copyright permission must be obtained from the performer(s), the mixer/sound producer, and the composer/copyright holder of the score used in the performance. If the composition is in the public domain, then the last copyright, the copyright of the score, is not a problem. The copyright release of the mixer/sound recorder is also not a problem since, at UT, this person is an employee of the university and, therefore, recordings of recitals made by them at the university are considered property of the university and can be used on the website. Therefore, only the copyright release of the performer(s) needs to be obtained. Partnering with the University of Tennessee's Office of the General Counsel,[45] we created a Talent Release Form and a process for acquiring the permissions needed to use recital recordings on the Music Theory Materials website.[46] This process consists of obtaining the signature(s) of the performer(s) on the Talent Release Form and having the performer(s) submit copies of the first few pages of each score from which they are playing (i.e., the pages that contained the copyright information) to check that the piece is either in the public domain or usable under copyright laws. Once the signatures are obtained and the availability of the composition is confirmed, then, and only then, can the recording be posted on the website.

After a score and a recording are procured, the composition is analyzed to determine its applicability for use in a music theory class. Form, harmonic content, and other stylistic characteristics are noted along with specific analytical methods that can be used to study the piece (e.g., set theory, linear analysis). If the composition contains elements that are covered in music theory classes, then the piece is added to the website. All compositions on the site are indexed according to composer, time period, composer category (e.g., gender, ethnicity), and the form and theoretical elements contained in the piece.

In summary, a piece is included on the Music Theory Materials website only if both a score and a recording for the piece can be located and used according to copyright rules and the piece contains musical elements that are studied in music theory classes. All compositions are assessed before they are "added and stirred" into the mix of compositions available for music theory examples.

The Advantages of Music Theory Materials as OER

The Music Theory Materials website was created to be an OER for use in music theory classes; it was intended to be a compilation of class materials—specifically, compositions and recordings—that could be used freely by students and faculty alike. Using public domain compositions and recordings (or obtaining copyright permission to use both the score and recording of the piece), therefore, makes sharing these compositions possible. Other advantages of creating this site as an OER include the reduction of financial burden for the student, the reduction of time spent in lesson planning for the teacher, the adaptability and responsiveness of a website, and the possibility of promoting social equality and social justice within the classroom.

The main advantage of using OER in the music theory classroom is to reduce the financial burden of the student. Students in music theory courses are often required to purchase several books, including a textbook, a workbook, and an anthology. Although some textbooks include anthologies as part of the book, these anthologies may not provide enough musical examples for study. When a student reaches upper-division courses in music theory, more and complete musical examples are needed and so a separate anthology may be required. Print anthologies can be very expensive. Prices for music anthologies range from approximately $40 to $200, with the average price approximately $97.[47] The anthology used at the University of Tennessee (before converting to the use of Music Theory Materials) was Burkhart and Rothstein's *Anthology for Music Analysis*, the highest-priced anthology ($199.95). Thus, using the compositions found on Music Theory Materials has saved each of our students approximately $200, potentially allowing some students who could not afford to purchase the text a way to fully participate in a course. In the current culture, $200 over several semesters may not seem unreasonable for a college course, but when coupled with the price of the other texts the students are required to purchase—at UT, the Roig-Francoli e-textbook ($70) and workbook ($91.33)[48]—the total initial cost of the student's music theory texts sums to $361.28, a high cost for one class's textbooks. Thus, the shift to an OER relieves some of the financial burden for the student.

For the instructor, the use of a web-based OER (or OER in general) can reduce the amount of time spent in class preparation. As noted above, the process of finding and vetting new compositions for use in music theory classes is time-consuming. However, an OER such as Music Theory Materials has already gathered and assessed the material needed for class, reducing preparation time for the instructor. An instructor can search the composition index and find several pieces that apply to a specific topic (e.g., ternary or binary form, augmented sixth chords, Neapolitan chords), eliminating time the instructor would have spent searching for pieces containing the specific teaching topic.

A web-based OER also has the advantage of adaptability and responsiveness. Web-based resources, such as Music Theory Materials, can be updated and added to at any time, adapting and responding quickly to the needs of faculty and students. The only true time limitation is how quickly the manager of the site can find, assess, and upload new pieces. The updating of a textbook or anthology, on the other hand, can be a much longer process. Time is needed by the author to assemble and categorize works and by the publisher to print and distribute the new edition. The speed of publishing new editions of anthologies, according to our research on fifteen popular anthologies, is a minimum of two years. A web-based OER avoids the publishing process and therefore is able to adapt much more quickly to changes in music and teaching.

The use of OER in general, and Music Theory Materials in particular, can also help to reduce some of the academic bias the instructor may unconsciously carry into their classroom by increasing the diversity of the pieces and composers used as musical examples. Any music theory teacher who has taught the same topic more than once may fall into the habit of using the same musical examples each semester (or the ones provided by their textbooks), which may create a hidden curriculum of European, white, male music that they are unwittingly perpetuating. The ready availability of musical examples, vetted, categorized, and added to on a regular basis, by non-white, non-male, or non-European composers allows instructors to choose a wider variety of compositions by a more diverse group of composers in their classes. New pieces by under-represented composers can be introduced into the curriculum regularly and with ease, expanding the teaching canon and reducing bias in the theory curriculum.

Next Steps Toward Equity in the Music Theory Classroom

The project described above, the addition of compositions by under-represented composers to the Music Theory Materials website, has resulted in the inclusion, to date, of approximately seventy compositions or movements of pieces by women and BIPOC composers to the website. Much more work on this project is planned for in the near future. More than 250 pieces by under-represented composers have been located and will soon be assessed for inclusion on the website. However, the addition of examples using the "add-and-stir" method should only be thought of as a first step in truly changing the way music theory is taught. The addition of these examples, though effective in reducing some of the bias against minority composers within the theory classroom, does not change the bias of the music theory curriculum teaching pieces that fit only the European tradition of music and music theory. The "add-and-stir" method adds composers that are designated worthy of inclusion into *our* canon; it does not introduce the teaching of music and theories outside the Western Art Music tradition.

As Citron said, "Anthologies [and textbooks] have… generally ignored other idioms, such as folk music, popular music and world music."[49] The teaching of non-Western music in most music schools happens mainly in ethnomusicology classes. Discussions of non-Western music and music theories rarely occur within music theory classes. In the ever-changing and rapidly globalizing world, students' careers would only be helped by the incorporation of non-Western theories and music into more classes in the curriculum. Robin Attas[50] and Tomoko Deguchi[51] discuss the merits of incorporating non-Western art music into the theory curriculum, including an increase in student engagement as well as "enhancing global education for our students."[52] Attas discusses the use of popular music by a Black artist, Kendrick Lamar, as an avenue through which the music theory class can engage in questions about race, power, and bias in addition to the theoretical aspects of this music. She encourages instructors to not shy away from this discussion or other non-Western music out of lack of expertise in the theories behind them. Music theory teachers, she says, are not meant to be experts in every music aesthetic; they just need to be able to teach a student how to engage with a piece theoretically.[53] Adding new types of music theories will change the entire curriculum, and such a change can, and most likely should, be introduced incrementally. Deguchi presents a method for gradually integrating East Asian composers and East Asian theory into a class on music form and analysis. She suggests beginning with the discussion of a piece by an East Asian composer that is rooted more in the Western music tradition, then progressively choosing pieces that are less and less Western, explaining the theory behind the East Asian music as the class continues. Using this method, Deguchi actually changes the theory curriculum by adding discussions on Eastern music theories to those of the Western tradition.[54] Through their teaching examples, Attas and Deguchi demonstrate that the theory curriculum can be expanded to include a more diverse set of compositions and theories.

Although ideas for large-scale change to the entire theory curriculum are laudable and should be the goal, expansive curricular changes take time to achieve. In the meantime, smaller steps can be made to begin changing the musical canon and, thus, the theory curriculum, contributing to social change in the field of music theory. The process described in this chapter of adding under-represented composers to an OER website is an example of the small, achievable steps that can help achieve the ultimate goal of bringing marginalized voices into the theory classroom.

Endnotes

1. Philip A. Ewell, "Music Theory and the White Racial Frame," *Music Theory Online* 6, no. 2 (September 2020): 1.1.
2. Ewell, "Music Theory," 1.1.
3. "Canon," Merriam-Webster Dictionary, accessed February 18, 2021, https://www.merriam-webster.com/dictionary/canon.
4. Roxanne Prevost and Kimberly Francis, "Teaching Silence in the Twenty-First Century: Where are the Missing Women Composers?," in *The Oxford Handbook of Music Censorship* ed. Patricia Hall (New York: Oxford University Press, 2017), 645.
5. Prevost and Francis, "Teaching Silence," 646.
6. Barbara Murphy, Music Theory Materials, University of Tennessee, accessed February 23, 2021, https://musictheorymaterials.utk.edu/.
7. "Canon," Merriam-Webster.
8. Marcia Citron, *Gender and the Musical Canon* (Champaign, IL: University of Illinois Press, 2000), 15.
9. Citron, *Gender*, 15.
10. Ibid.
11. Ibid.
12. Edward Komara, "Culture Wars, Canonicity, and 'A Basic Music Library,'" *Notes* 64, no. 2 (December 2007): 236–37.
13. Marcia Citron, "Women and the Western Art Canon: Where Are We Now?" *Notes* 64, no. 2 (December 2007): 210.
14. Citron, *Gender*, 19.
15. Ibid., 23.
16. Ibid.
17. Ibid., 24.
18. Pierre-Antoine Kremp, "Innovation and Selection: Symphony Orchestras and the Construction of the Musical Canon in the United States," *Social Forces* 88 no. 3, (2010): 1051, https://doi.org/10.1353/sof.0.0314.
19. "These composers include Wagner, Beethoven, Brahms, Mozart, Tchaikovsky, Strauss, Bach, Berlioz, Debussy, Ravel, Schumann, Schubert, and Mendelssohn," Kremp, "Innovation and Selection," 1077, footnote 1.
20. Kremp, "Innovation and Selection," 1052.
21. Ibid.
22. Ibid., 1068.
23. Citron, *Gender*, 26. Although we do agree with Citron that anthologies and textbooks have historically ignored idioms other than Western Art Music, we do feel that this is changing. We do not address the inclusion of other types of musics here since this is not the focus of this article.
24. Ewell, "Music Theory," table 1.
25. The differences in number of examples between tables 15.6 and 15.7 may be due to the editions of the books or the way in which the examples were counted.
26. Cora S. Palfy and Eric Gilson, "The Hidden Curriculum in the Music Theory Classroom," *Journal of Music Theory Pedagogy* 32 (2018): 81.
27. Palfy and Gilson, "Hidden Curriculum," 81.
28. Ibid., 84.

29. Citron, *Gender*, 27–28.
30. Other sequences of courses that music majors are required to take include music history/musicology, piano class, and major ensembles (e.g., band, orchestra, choir, and opera).
31. Ewell, "Music Theory," 1.2.
32. Philip Ewell, "Music Theory's White Racial Frame," Plenary speaker at the annual meeting of the Society for Music Theory, November 7–10, 2019, http://philipewell.com/wp-content/uploads/2019/11/SMT-Plenary-Slides.pdf.
33. Colleen Flaherty, "Whose Music Theory?," *Inside Higher Ed* (August 7, 2020), https://www.insidehighered.com/news/2020/08/07/music-theory-journal-criticized-symposium-supposed-white-supremacist-theorist.
34. Flaherty, "Whose Music Theory?"
35. Some of these websites are Composers of Color Resource project: https://composersofcolor.hcommons.org/; Music Theory Examples by Women: https://musictheoryexamplesbywomen.com/.
36. Sarah D. Sparks, "Open Educational Resources (OER): Overview and Definition," *Education Week* (April 12, 2017), https://www.edweek.org/teaching-learning/open-educational-resources-oer-overview-and-definition/2017/04.
37. The website has been expanded to include handouts, explanatory videos, powerpoint presentations on theoretical topics and analytic methods, and exercises for aural skills training.
38. Citron, "Women and the Western Art Canon," 210.
39. Ibid., 211.
40. Ibid., 210.
41. Ibid.
42. Composition written in or before the year 1925 entered the public domain in the United States on January 1, 2021, https://www.pdinfo.com/.
43. "IMSLP: About," IMSLP, https://imslp.org/wiki/IMSLP:About.
44. "Free Sheet Music," Barbershop Harmony Society, https://www.barbershop.org/music/free-music-and-tags/free-sheet-music.
45. We would like to thank Frank Lancaster (https://counsel.tennessee.edu/contact/frank-lancaster/), Associate General Counsel for Copyrights and Patents, for his work on the Talent Release forms used in this project.
46. The final version of the form is available at https://musictheorymaterials.utk.edu/musictheory-materials-utk-edu-recording-project/. The form gives the authors of the MusicTheoryMaterials.utk.edu website and the University of Tennessee School of Music the right to use the video/sound recordings as well as photographs on their website. The student or faculty, however, retain the rights to the recordings under a CC-BY-NC-SA license.
47. These figures are based on the pricing of 14 widely used anthologies sourced from publishers: Owen, *Music Theory Resource Book*, 2000 ($107.95); Briscoe, *New Historical Anthology of Music by Women*, 2004 ($39.95); Burkhart and Rothstein, *Anthology for Music Analysis*, 2012 ($199.95); Bribtzer-Stull, *Anthology for Analysis and Performance*, 2013 ($152.95); Santa, *Hearing Form*, 2016 ($56.95); Laitz and Sewell, *Score Anthology to Accompany the Complete Musician*, 2016 ($59.95); Cutler, *Anthology of Music for Analysis*, 2018 ($106.25); Benjamin, Horvit, Koozon, and Nelson, *Music for Analysis*, 2018 ($147.95); Dorf, MacLachlan, and Randel, *Anthology to Accompany Gateways to Understanding Music*, 2020 ($74.95); Clendinning and Marvin, *Musician's Guide to Theory Analysis Anthology*, 2021 ($58.75); Roig-Francoli, *Anthology of Post-Tonal Music* Ed. 2, 2021 ($59.95).
48. Miguel Roig-Francoli, *Harmony in Context*, 3rd ed. (New York: McGraw-Hill Education, 2020), accessed February 28, 2021, https://www.mheducation.com/highered/product/harmony-context-roig-francoli/M9781260055764.html#textbookCollapse.
49. Citron, *Gender*, 26.
50. Tomoko Deguchi, "Promoting Diversity in the Undergraduate Classroom: Incorporating Asian Contemporary Composers' Music in a Form and Analysis Course," *Journal of Music Theory Pedagogy* 32 (2018): 1.2.

51. Robin Attas, "Strategies for Settler Decolonization: Decolonial Pedagogies in a Popular Music Analysis Course," *Canadian Journal of Higher Education* 49, no. 1 (2019): 22.
52. Deguchi, "Promoting Diversity," 22.
53. Attas, "Strategies for Settler Decolonization," 5.3.
54. Deguchi, "Promoting Diversity," 36.

Bibliography

Aldwell, Edward, Carl Schachter, and Allen Cadwallader. *Harmony & Voice Leading*, 5th ed. Boston, MA: Cengage, 2019.

Attas, Robin. "Strategies for Settler Decolonization: Decolonial Pedagogies in a Popular Music Analysis Course." *Canadian Journal of Higher Education* 49, no. 1 (2019): 125–39.

Barbershop Harmony Society. "Free Sheet Music." Accessed February 23, 2021. https://www.barbershop.org/music/free-music-and-tags/free-sheet-music.

Benjamin, Thomas, Michael Horvit, Timothy Koozin, and Robert Nelson. *Music for Analysis*. New York: Oxford University Press, 2018.

Benward, Bruce, and Marilyn Saker. *Music in Theory and Practice, Volume 1*, 10th ed. New York: McGraw Hill Education, 2021.

———. *Music in Theory and Practice, Volume 2*, 10th ed. New York: McGraw Hill Education, 2021.

Bribtzer-Stull, Matthew. *Anthology for Analysis and Performance*. New York: Oxford University Press, 2013.

Briscoe, James R., ed. *New Historical Anthology of Music by Women*. Bloomington: Indiana University Press, 2004.

Bristow, Richard, Chris Fish, and Richard Knight. *AQA AS and A-Level Anthology of Music (Theory)*. London: Faber Music, 2016.

Burkhart, Charles, and William Rothstein. *Anthology for Music Analysis*. Boston, MA: Cengage, 2012.

Burstein, L. Poundie, and Joseph Straus. *Concise Introduction to Tonal Harmony*, 2nd ed. New York: W.W. Norton & Company, 2020.

Campbell, Patricia Shehan, David Meyers, and Ed Sarath. *Transforming Music Study from Its Foundations: A Manifesto for Progressive Change in the Undergraduate Preparation of Music Majors: Report of the Task Force on the Undergraduate Music Major*. College Music Society (2014). https://www.music.org/pdf/pubs/tfumm/TFUMM.pdf.

Clendinning, Jane Piper, and Elizabeth West Marvin. *The Musician's Guide to Theory and Analysis*, 3rd ed. New York: W.W. Norton & Company, 2016.

———. *The Musician's Guide to Theory Analysis Anthology*, 3rd ed. New York: W.W. Norton & Company, 2020.

Citron, Marcia J. *Gender and the Musical Canon*. Champaign, IL: Illinois University Press, 2000.

———. "Women and the Western Art Canon: Where Are We Now?" *Notes* 64, no. 2 (December 2007): 209–15. https://www.jstor.org/stable/30163078.

Composers of Color Resource Project. "Composers of Colors Analysis-a-thons Google Doc." Accessed February 23, 2021. https://docs.google.com/spreadsheets/d/1pgqCqnVkXDz5tWhe0RxY0UGSkVjki5adltlGWPdQKU8/edit#gid=0.

Cutler, Timothy. *Anthology of Music for Analysis*. New York: W.W. Norton & Company, 2018.

Deguchi, Tomoko. "Promoting Diversity in the Undergraduate Classroom: Incorporating Asian Contemporary Composers' Music in a Form and Analysis Course." *Journal of Music Theory Pedagogy* 32 (2018).

Dorf, Samuel N., Heather Maclaclan, and Julia Randel, *Anthology to Accompany Gateways to Understanding Music*. Milton Park, Abington, UK: Routledge, 2021.

Ewell, Philip A. "Music Theory and the White Racial Frame." *Music Theory Online* 6 no. 2 (2020). doi: 10.30535/mto.26.2.4.

———. "Music Theory's White Racial Frame." Plenary speaker at the annual meeting of the Society for Music Theory, November 7–10, 2019. https://vimeo.com/372726003.

Flaherty, Colleen. "Whose Music Theory?" *Inside Higher Ed* (August 7, 2020). Accessed February 23, 2021. https://www.insidehighered.com/news/2020/08/07/music-theory-journal-criticized-symposium-supposed-white-supremacist-theorist.

Komara, Edward. "Culture Wars, Canonicity, and 'A Basic Music Library'." *Notes* 64, no. 2 (December 2007): 232–47. https://www.jstor.org/stable/30163081.

Kostka, Stefan, Dorothy Payne, and Byron Almen. *Tonal Harmony with an Introduction to Post-Tonal Music*, 8th ed. New York: McGraw-Hill Education, 2018.

Kremp, Pierre-Antoine. "Innovation and Selection: Symphony Orchestras and the Construction of the Musical Canon in the United States (1879–1959). *Social Forces* 88 no. 3, (2010): 1051-1082. https://doi.org/10.1353/sof.0.0314.

Laitz, Steven G. *The Complete Musician: An Integrated Approach to Theory, Analysis, and Listening*, 4th ed. New York: Oxford University Press, 2016.

McClary, Susan. "Terminal Prestige: The Case of Avant-Garde Compositions." *Cultural Critique* 12 (Spring 1989): 57–81. https://www.jstor.org/stable/1354322.

———. *Score Anthology to Accompany the Complete Musician*. New York: Oxford University Press, 2016.

Merriam-Webster Dictionary. "Canon." Accessed February 18, 2021. https://www.merriam-webster.com/dictionary/canon.

mtew.org. "Music Theory Examples by Women." Accessed February 23, 2021. https://musictheoryexamplesbywomen.com/.

Murphy, Barbara. "Music Theory Materials." Accessed February 23, 2021. https://musictheorymaterials.utk.edu/.

Owen, Harold. *Music Theory Resource Book*. New York: Oxford University Press, 2000.

Palfy, Cora S., and Eric Gilson. "The Hidden Curriculum in the Music Theory Classroom." *Journal of Music Theory Pedagogy* 32 (2018): 79–110. https://jmtp.appstate.edu/hidden-curriculum-music-theory-classroom.

PD Info: Public Domain Information Project. "Public Domain Music." Accessed February 23, 2021. https://www.pdinfo.com/.

Prevost, Roxanne, and Kimberly Francis. "Teaching Silence in the Twenty-First Century: Where are the Missing Women Composers?" In *The Oxford Handbook of Music Censorship*, edited by Patricia Hall, 637–56. Oxford: Oxford University Press, 2017.

Project Petrucci LLC. "IMSLP:About." Accessed February 23, 2021. https://imslp.org/wiki/IMSLP:About.

Roig-Francoli, Miguel. *Anthology of Post-Tonal Music*, 2nd ed. Milton Park, Abington UK: Routledge, 2021.

———. *Harmony in Context*, 3rd ed. New York: McGraw-Hill Education, 2020.

Santa, Matthew. *Hearing Form*. Milton Park, Abington UK: Routledge, 2017.

Society for Music Theory. "SMT Demographics." Accessed February 23, 2021. https://societymusictheory.org/administration/demographics.

Sparks, Sarah D. "Open Educational Resources (OER): Overview and Definition." *Education Week* (April 12, 2017). https://www.edweek.org/teaching-learning/open-educational-resources-oer-overview-and-definition/2017/04.

CHAPTER 16

An Institute-Based Approach to OER in Digital Caribbean Studies

Perry Collins, Hélène Huet, Laurie Taylor, Brittany Mistretta, Hannah Toombs, Anita Baksh, Nathan H. Dize, Juliet Glenn-Callender, Ronald Angelo Johnson, Aaron Kamugisha, K. Adele Okoli, Laëtitia Saint-Loubert, and Keja Valens

In May 2019, more than forty educators, scholars, and librarians came together for a week-long workshop to collaboratively explore the potential—and the limitations—of digital pedagogies within Caribbean Studies. Hosted by the University of Florida (UF) and the Digital Library of the Caribbean (dLOC), "Migration, Mobility, Sustainability: Caribbean Studies & Digital Humanities" delved into digital projects amplifying community narratives across the Caribbean diaspora, low-barrier tools to enable student-instructor co-creation, and efforts to subvert colonialist legacies as we build and describe digital collections. This face-to-face experience offered a rich starting point for a two-year institute that fostered virtual dialogue, course development, and publication of a contextualized selection of open educational resources (OER).

With a multi-institutional, international group of participants working across the Caribbean and the United States, institute leaders took a flexible approach to topical coverage, schedule, and anticipated outcomes that invited individual perspectives and experience to shape the conversation. This approach drove the capacious framing of OER, continued in this chapter, simply as content available freely online and useful to teachers and students. Rather than attempting to normalize vocabulary or prescriptively define what might "count" as an OER, the institute broadly encouraged knowledge-sharing around access to digital collections, technology, and models for leveraging both in the classroom. Presentations on courses and projects served as boundary objects, offering common ground where participants could explore potential next steps and opportunities for collaboration from multiple vantage points.[1]

This chapter focuses on the institute as a case study for OER development that centers relationship-building, lived experience, empathy, and flexibility as foundational principles, grounded in feminist approaches to digital pedagogy.[2] Attention to social justice permeates this work, both in amplifying Caribbean voices across the diaspora and in leveraging approaches in the digital humanities (DH) that call on students to challenge reductive or colonialist perspectives. These values mirror those embodied by participants' own research and teaching, and the following sections draw heavily on the publicly available reflections, syllabi, assignments, and other materials they contributed.[3]

Institute Overview

The goals and underlying values of the institute followed very closely those of dLOC. Indeed, dLOC's original mission and vision were twofold: making materials accessible while ensuring their preservation, which would help grow capacity and community for Caribbean Studies. As dLOC grew into a major resource for Caribbean resources, enabling new work, dLOC team members started collaborating with scholars in various areas to discuss and plan how to best support teaching and research by using materials in dLOC.

These threads came together in a roundtable discussion at the West Indian Literature Conference in 2016.[4] In response to the question "What are the next steps?", several people agreed that the community needed to have a forum for learning tools and meeting collaborators. They shared that the preferred format was a training institute for scholars, librarians, archivists, graduate students, and others from the shared community of practice. This institute would be focused on learning digital tools and collaborative practices, and the goal would be to create new teaching resources. Moreover, they emphasized that the institute could not be exclusive to the US. It must include people from the Caribbean and be designed in such a way that a lack of travel funding would not prevent people from applying and participating. Their scoping served as the basis for the Migration, Mobility, and Sustainability: Caribbean Studies Digital Humanities Institute grant, which was funded by the National Endowment for the Humanities in 2018 through the Institutes for Advanced Topics in the Digital Humanities program.[5]

Many people collaborated on writing the grant proposal, working closely with the official grant investigators to plan the program. The collaborators identified the optimal structure for the institute, including a project or deliverable in the form of an OER that ideally would utilize open access primary materials, in dLOC or elsewhere, to then provide the framework and context for teaching with those materials. As explained in the grant proposal, the overall goal was for participants to learn and adapt DH tools and practices, as made possible by the work of the institute, which would

> 1) introduce participants to the processes of finding and using open access materials from digital repositories to provide a foundation for teaching through, and building with, DH; 2) provide intensive training on tools and practices for analyzing, mapping, and presenting materials in relation to the themes of migration, mobility, and sustainability; and, 3) provide intensive training in DH teaching methods for incorporating these practices and themes into classrooms as part of the ongoing process for sustaining a community of practice in Caribbean Studies.[6]

Collaborators specifically designed the institute to consider how resources supported individuals and the community of practice. As such:

> The Institute's featured technologies were selected based on the following criteria for enabling a community of practice across many fields, disciplines, and geographical regions: 1) no-cost; accessible across classes and institutions (e.g., not institutional subscriptions/single-institution limited services); sufficiently accessible for students such that the technology can be taught as coupled with the subject matter for teaching and integration; 2) usable after the students and teaching team complete the class, to continue building for future courses; and, 3) ideally, usable on lower-bandwidth and without software beyond a web browser, to remove barriers to collaboration.[7]

As described further below, these criteria shaped development of the institute curriculum, including a five-day, face-to-face workshop, a series of virtual guest webinars, as well as expectations for participants to contribute back to the community by sharing their own teaching materials.

How Did Participants Engage with Existing OERs, Especially Digital Collections, as a Shared Knowledge Base?

Building Awareness of Collections

Collaborators explicitly planned the institute to utilize and promote a selection of existing digital collections. The institute's digital collections included dLOC, The Diaspora Project, the Dutch Caribbean Digital Platform, and Chronicling America. While Chronicling America is focused on US newspapers (including Puerto Rico and the Virgin Islands), the papers include stories from and about the wider Caribbean. In addition to these, participants also shared information about other collections they were familiar with. The institute presented both these platforms and the materials they contain as OER, ready for reuse in the classroom.

Indeed, in working with our broader community of practice before the institute, we realized that many teachers identify open access primary resources as OER in and of themselves because they are foundational to creating equitable courses and assignments that may be shared back with the community. For example, one early list of OER in dLOC is the *List of Anglophone Caribbean Novels Published Before 1950* by Leah Rosenberg.[8] Rosenberg first shared this list online in dLOC in 2012 to assist the library and technical teams in locating and prioritizing the digitization of important Caribbean novels. Rosenberg then updated the list in 2014 and 2016 to reflect newly identified items and to add links to newly digitized items. This list has been a frequent starting point in discussions because access to primary resources is a critical concern for teaching Caribbean studies.[9] In fact, this list helped to spark conversations on collaborative teaching that, while enabled by technologies in the digital age, were insufficient unless shared texts could be available for all students. With access to core primary texts made possible, and promoted through Rosenberg's list of novels, new conversations emerged on collaborative teaching and on teaching with digital collections like dLOC. These conversations led to a 2013 Distributed Online Collaborative Course, Panama Silver, Asian Gold: Migration Money and the Making of the Modern Caribbean, which underwent updated iterations in 2016 and 2017.[10] These deeply collaborative courses informed development and goals for the institute.

Instructors frequently note that a core obstacle to teaching is the lack of access to such primary sources. These materials, including photographs, maps, diaries, newspapers, etc., serve a range of purposes, from offering insight into the lives of everyday people in the Caribbean and Caribbean diaspora over time to facilitating students' awareness and critique of long histories of colonialism and structural racism. While many educators readily share syllabi and teaching materials throughout their teaching communities, facilitating access to primary sources is often beyond the abilities of any single person or institution. This is why the institute was designed in a way that would enable participants to familiarize themselves and connect with digital collections, built as OER through the work of many individuals, communities, and institutions.

Our experiences leading up to the institute affirmed that we most often will not hear from people teaching with OER, whether from dLOC or other sources. As a matter of fact, we regularly need to reach out to teachers to request syllabi for review in order to evaluate the use of OER. This is due, in part, to demanding workloads for teaching, and some of this is due to communication needs, as teachers do not necessarily use the term OER. Explaining the request can therefore require a bit of translation and time. With the sudden move to remote work and teaching with the pandemic in 2020, we have heard anecdotally about the increased use of dLOC and other online resources in teaching. However, work to collect and review inclusion in syllabi remains pending.

Leveraging Free/Open Source Software for Open Pedagogy

Most participants looking to incorporate digital humanities tools in their teaching were doing so in the context of courses designed around specific topics in the history, literature, language, religion, and culture of the Caribbean and Caribbean diaspora. This is distinct from courses focused on digital methods, where many weeks might be granted to scaffolding that supports students' understanding and application of specific software. Especially for undergraduate or K-12 students unfamiliar with using web-based tools in the humanities classroom, it was crucial that the institute highlight tools students could learn quickly, allowing them to focus on interpretation and storytelling. One institute participant, K. Adele Okoli, described how, following the institute, she "went on to apply these inclusive digital pedagogies in my French seminar, 'Literature and Culture of the Creole Atlantic,' for which one nontraditional student from Senegal [Aïssatou Lo] created, illustrated, and recorded her reading of a French-language digital storybook dedicated to her children featuring a transatlantic Black woman, the shapeshifting Princess Mbaïta. A high number of my students in Caribbean Studies-focused French courses are from West and Central African countries, and they often report that learning about Caribbean history, literature, and culture, especially through digital materials and projects accessible through minimal technologies, gives them an empowering global perspective of their own sense of Black identity and Diasporic connection."[11]

Though numerous tools and platforms were mentioned at the institute, the agenda allotted significant time to showcasing and experimenting with two tools developed by the Knight Journalism Lab at Northwestern University: TimelineJS and StoryMapJS. Constraints of local IT support, web connectivity, and lack of funding for commercial products are frequently cited challenges for the dLOC community; these tools are accessible to a broad swath of educators when considering resource inequities across institutions and geographies. While open source, neither of these tools requires downloading or installation, and they make use of familiar web browser and Google spreadsheet interfaces. Beyond specific technical considerations, mapping and timeline applications are especially appealing for instructors looking to engage students in low-barrier tools that juxtapose primary and secondary sources with students' original research.

In the assessment interviews and the syllabi and assignments contributed after the institute, many participants reported incorporating these tools into their courses. For instance, Takkara Brunson assigned students in her course, African Cultural Perspectives, to develop StoryMaps that synthesized primary sources and data tied to specific locations in order to build an argument around "an issue of religious, gender, or ethnic identity; precolonial, colonial, or post-colonial society; politics, music, or the visual arts."[12] Juliet Glenn-Callender's reflection describes how she was able to develop an alternative assignment asking students to use StoryMapJS to trace the Bahamian route to independence. She notes that the "institute really brought home the concept of minimal computing… [and] highlighted resources that were either free or at minimal cost and with minimal training that could be used to capture digital data and make it accessible to users."[13]

Participants also made use of other open source platforms, such as Omeka, to engage their students in developing original, public scholarship. Graduate students in Keja Valens' course, Roots of the Commonwealth: Caribbean Provisions from the British Empire to the 21st Century, worked in small teams to curate exhibits on regional foodways. Valens noted that by showcasing dLOC as a research publication platform as well as a trove of primary sources, she "was able to present to my students a real community that they could understand as their interlocutors and where they could see their work being published. This meant that when they searched for material and reviewed other projects through dLOC, they did so with a profound interest and engagement, and as they completed their exhibits, they did so with a specific venue and audience in mind, and it was one in which they already felt invested and engaged and also one that they felt was urgent to participate in with care and integrity."[14]

How Did the Institute Structure Facilitate Collaboration among Members of the Cohort, and How Have Participants Built Upon this Foundation to Co-create Course Materials?

To put our principles of empathy and flexibility into action, institute hosts built in many opportunities for participants to iteratively discuss and reflect in small groups, to present or report out to the larger group, and to informally chat between sessions. Especially during the week-long, in-person phase of the institute, this structure cultivated a supportive network for participants to share educational resources and to envision their humanities projects in new ways. Many participants responded positively to their hands-on experience working with digital tools during the institute and learning from a diverse set of member projects that demonstrated how others had translated courses, assignments, and research could for digital platforms. Further, participants reported an interest in DH not only to engage students and research participants in their classrooms or the field but also as a set of methods and tools that created more collaborative opportunities and greater access to learning technology among under-resourced communities and institutions. Overall, institute participants' reflections and contributions to the website demonstrate a shared interest in applying digital tools for the public humanities, with potential to co-create with one another as well as community members and students.

Multilingual Translation as Digital Pedagogy

Participant reflections also expressed that experiencing the institute as a cohort fostered a sense of community among members that encouraged further partnerships. One example of such a partnership, still in the planning phase, is co-developed by literary scholars Anita Baksh and Laëtitia Saint-Loubert.[15] This "connected classrooms" course, Transoceanic Experience of Indenture in Indo-Caribbean, Indo-Mauritian and Indo-Reunionese Writing, was designed using the Collaborative Online International Learning model (COIL) developed at the State University of New York (SUNY) to foster digital engagement between students with various linguistic backgrounds as part of global learning initiatives.

Developed about fifteen years ago, COIL has produced resources to support international, virtual collaboration between instructors and students across borders.[16] A major goal of this course will be for students to learn about indentured labor from a transoceanic perspective and to further decolonize curricula. In this case, Baksh's students will complete the course as part of a capstone at a two-year institution in the US. For Saint-Loubert, it is likely that students will come from a predominantly French-speaking linguistic background. Students will spend several weeks working with their international student partners to translate English and French twentieth- and twenty-first-century literary texts that focus on narratives of indenture.

Engaging with this literature will expose students to indentured experiences through laborer perspectives and introduce them to words and expressions from various languages, including Creoles, Hindi, and Bhojpuri. Literature analysis and interpretation will give students insights into key themes of indenture, such as culinary and cultural traditions, gendered experiences, inter-ethnic relationships, and working conditions. Translation projects will be shared with digital tools (e.g., StoryMapJS, TimelineJS, and WordPress) to contextualize historical texts through time and space and to make translations more accessible for continued annotation and feedback between students. In addition to producing projects, students will be asked to write a reflection of their experiences with digital tools, collaboration, and how international partnerships and new knowledge of indentured experiences informed their assessment of peer translations.

Developing a Community OER
COLLECTION OF INTERVIEWS AND REFLECTIONS

A primary goal of the institute was to foster an enhanced community of practice for digital humanities and digital pedagogy specific to the needs and concerns of Caribbean studies. Critical pieces contributing to this outcome and to institute assessment have been maintaining communication with participants since the in-person meeting through interviews, the contribution of relevant teaching and research materials, and public collection of reflections on participants' experience. By documenting lessons learned and by asking participants to directly reflect on the institute in their own words, we hope to promote an institute model as a framework that others in the field may replicate and build upon.

To support program assessment, twenty-seven follow-up interviews were conducted with participants via Zoom from May to August of 2020, focused on understanding the impact of the institute on teaching and learning and on potential improvements for future iterations. Conversations highlighted the wide range of DH skills participants adopted in their research and courses and surfaced potential OER deliverables from these projects, including syllabi, assignment samples, and reflections. Importantly, participants noted that they were able to draw on skills acquired during the institute to continue working and teaching remotely during the COVID-19 pandemic.

Again, frequently mentioned benefits included opportunities for institute participants to interact with one another. The institute allowed established scholars, graduate students, and instructors from institutions within and beyond the Caribbean diaspora to collaborate during and after the in-person institute, beginning new research relationships that may not have otherwise been possible. As then-doctoral candidate Nathan Dize put it, "The institute could have gone on for another two weeks and I'm not sure that I would have tired of the group of people that were brought together. Not only was it a pleasure to learn with and from the other scholars, but the selection of folks in terms of career level and path… made the experience for me as a graduate student quite formative. In this way, I felt the learning environment was reciprocal."[17]

INSTITUTE WEBSITE DEVELOPMENT

As part of planned deliverables, UF OER librarian Perry Collins, graduate students Brittany Mistretta and Hannah Toombs, and designer Tracy MacKay-Ratliff developed a website to serve as a user-friendly access point for institute documentation and a thematic OER collection. This site includes presentations delivered in person and virtually as well as teaching materials and reflections contributed by participants. To address concerns about the discoverability of institute materials in a larger digital repository such as dLOC, it was determined that a separate website could contextualize materials and related resources within the institute's initiatives. This site was published in March 2021 by LibraryPress@UF, an open access imprint of the UF Libraries and UF Press, as the first in a new OER-focused series. With this goal in mind, the website was designed to work as a nexus that links institute information and products in a meaningful way to increase their accessibility and to amplify participant contributions.

Leveraging WordPress's strengths, the website's content was organized into pages and posts, with pages acting as entryways to groups of posts. Participant contributions were incorporated as posts and organized into content categories such as Projects & Courses, Tools & Topics, and Institute Reflections. The selected categories focus on various examples, resources, and experiences relevant to digital pedagogy, teaching, and the institute. Each post was also tagged with identifiers that include author names, educational resources (e.g., lesson plans, videos, presentations), resource audiences (e.g., graduate, undergraduate, K-12), and specific topics (e.g., mapping, oral history, decolonization). Tags connect posts to individual participant pages, creating a layered network that highlights shared and related content from various participants. In this way, the website structure puts people, projects, and topics in conversation with one another and encourages a sustained dialogue beyond the institute. A virtual launch event reinforced this goal as an opportunity to share a concrete outcome constructed by many hands and to reflect on the institute's impact on participants and their students.

While we are proud of the website as a community-driven resource, we are also mindful of its limitations. Even as educators aim to promote social justice for their students by crafting and adapting freely available, more inclusive course materials, they are also impacted by inequities that hamper OER creation. Throughout the website development and OER publication process, we strived to offer flexibility that acknowledged not only time constraints but also different comfort levels with OER and potential dynamics of participants' respective labor situations (with positions varying from contingent instructors to professional staff to high school educators to tenured professors). We encouraged all participants to contribute *something* to the website that could inform others' teaching (even a short reflection or course syllabus), but we did not demand that anyone circulate full courses or other content they might not have been willing to share publicly. We also did not require or even request that all materials be made available under a Creative Commons license; while some participants chose to do so to enable downstream adaptation, we strongly felt that, as with all dLOC projects, contributors should have autonomy in licensing their work. This is a challenge that cuts across disciplines in OER, as we aim to balance respect for instructors' labor and rights to their course materials with a desire to maximize impact by sharing widely.

As Institute Participants Navigate Long-Term Crises, How Have They Engaged and Supported Students through Digital or Open Pedagogies?

Two recent disasters, the COVID-19 global pandemic and Hurricane Dorian, took a major toll on the personal and professional lives of institute participants and their students over the course of our two-year project. The impacts of each have persisted long-term, demanding adaptation to new modes of teaching and exacerbating historical inequities in students' access to technology. Participant reflections report course delays and challenges for students in completing coursework. Of course, we cannot know the full extent of personal trauma and grief among the community of institute participants as they have carried on in teaching and leadership roles over the past several years.

Dorian especially affected participants living in the Caribbean, particularly those based at the University of the Bahamas-North. Here, much of the campus, including a substantial portion of the library's collection, was destroyed by the hurricane. Participants Juliet Glenn-Callender and Sally Everson were unable to undertake the course project they had originally planned; however, both were able to implement alternative assignments that engaged students in co-creating digital, public humanities resources. Both contributed to Everson's online course, Climate and Inequality, where students created a Zotero digital library and undertook community-based research to document stories incorporated into an exhibit developed in partnership with the Rutgers Humanities Action Lab.[18]

Of course, hurricanes and attendant issues such as climate change have long affected the Greater Caribbean, reinforcing a damaging legacy of colonialism and requiring institutions to account for disaster as a recurring reality.[19] One institute guest expert, Schuyler Esprit, described the impact of both Tropical Storm Erika and Hurricane Maria in just three years following the founding of Create Caribbean.[20] This program, which takes a "for students, by students" approach, invites interns at Dominica State College to teach technology workshops for K-12 students and to develop digital scholarship research. One major project, Carisealand, engages students in developing "regional resources that actively support or raise awareness about sustainable development in the era of climate change disaster."[21] The damage Maria caused to Dominica and to the Create Caribbean space forced a period of rebuilding and compounded existing access barriers; however, Esprit and her students have moved forward with support from local and global networks. In a later keynote at the 2020 Digital Humanities annual conference, Esprit described the work of Create Caribbean in "moving students closer to a sense of shared responsibility for the political, economic, and cultural future of their Caribbean home."[22]

These examples reflect how recent disasters have made the development of OER and digital pedagogical models both more challenging and more immediately urgent. Crucially, they also describe local responses by instructors best positioned to understand what students and communities have lost, their specific needs, and the possibilities for digital and open pedagogies in engaging students with immediate issues of climate and social justice. Complementing and supporting these local endeavors, dLOC offers shared community infrastructure not only to digitally preserve materials potentially vulnerable to disaster but also to advocate for partner needs and additional capacity, including for OER development. In a 2020 podcast on disaster research and cultural memory, Haitian studies scholar and institute co-organizer Crystal Felima noted that "dLOC is a really great example of looking at how social justice and the library works, where you have different partners collaborate [and] share resources.... You have this working relationship where institutions are in conversation with each other, whether they're in Haiti or Puerto Rico."[23]

Increasingly, these relationships include knowledge exchange around teaching resources and the need to document and preserve course modules, lesson plans, lecture videos, etc., alongside digitized collections. Even within a supportive community, the burden often falls on individuals to create course materials, sometimes with limited resources or institutional support. As described throughout this chapter, an emphasis on collaboration and co-creation—with other educators, with students, and across institutions—surfaces again and again as a response to community educational need throughout ongoing crises. This need has also motivated a more ambitious vision for the public institute website, which complements teaching resources available through dLOC. While many institute participants were able to contribute materials to the community website, we know the gaps in this collection reflect the obstacles of COVID in particular, with materials collected during a pandemic peak from mid-2020 to early 2021. With a commitment to sustaining the website long-term, we hope to continue building on this project to assess the OER needs of a wider Caribbean studies network and to implement effective and ethical ways of sharing.

Acknowledgments

The authors thank all those who contributed time and expertise to the institute, including the listed co-authors as well as Miguel Asencio, Sharon Wright Austin, Ricia Anne Chansky, Bastien Craipain, Bess de Farber, Rachel Denney, Schuyler Esprit, Yanie Fécu, Crystal Felima, Alex Gil, Tao Leigh Goffe, Katerina Gonzalez Seligmann, Mirerza González-Vélez, Margo Groenewoud, Molly Hamm-Rodríguez, Melissa Jerome, Natasha Joseph, Sophonie Milande Joseph, Rosamond S. King, Debbie McCollin, Audra Merfeld-Langston, Lisa Ortiz, Paul Ortiz, Nadjah Ríos Villarini, Mary Risner, Shearon Roberts, Leah Rosenberg, Hadassah St. Hubert, Margarita Vargas-Betancourt, Jose R. Vazquez, and Erin Zavitz.

Funding was provided by the National Endowment for the Humanities (HT-261817-18).

Conflicts of Interest

Collins worked concurrently as an employee of the NEH and UF during part of the award period but was not involved in the funding or administration of the grant or compensated by grant funds.

Endnotes

1. Susan Star and James Griesemer, "Institutional Ecology, 'Translations' and Boundary Objects: Amateurs and Professionals in Berkeley's Museum of Vertebrate Zoology, 1907–39," *Social Studies of Science* 19, no. 3 (1989): 387–420, doi:10.1177/030631289019003001.
2. Liz Polcha, "On Respecting 'Deep Knowledge' in Collaborative Feminist Work: A Discussion with Jacque Wernimont," *NULab for Texts, Maps, and Networks* (blog), March 23, 2017, https://web.northeastern.edu/nulab/on-respecting-deep-knowledge-in-collaborative-feminist-work-a-discussion-with-jacque-wernimont/.
3. Because the chapter draws heavily on the discussion, presentations, course materials, and reflections contributed, participants were invited via the institute email list to communicate if they wished to be listed as co-authors. This approach supports the overarching principles of the institute and adapts more inclusive authorship models increasingly implemented in other scholarly publishing contexts (e.g., the CRediT taxonomy, which has defined a series of contributor roles for scientific research).
4. "Roundtable Discussion on Teaching with Caribbean Digital Libraries & Archives" (refereed presentation within Roundtable for the West Indian Literature Conference (WILC), University of the West Indies, Western Jamaica Campus, Montego Bay, Jamaica, October 7, 2016), http://dloc.com/AA00040791/00001/allvolumes.
5. "Institutes for Advanced Topics in the Digital Humanities," Office of Digital Humanities, National Endowment for the Humanities, https://www.neh.gov/grants/odh/institutes-advanced-topics-in-the-digital-humanities.
6. "Migration, Mobility, and Sustainability: Caribbean Studies Digital Humanities Institute" (grant proposal), Digital Library of the Caribbean, 2018, 15, https://dloc.com/IR00010262/00001.
7. "Migration, Mobility, and Sustainability," Digital Library of the Caribbean, 3.
8. Leah Rosenberg, "List of Anglophone Caribbean Novels Published Before 1950," Digital Library of the Caribbean, 2012–2016, https://www.dloc.com/AA00011396/00001.
9. Leah Rosenberg, "Refashioning Caribbean Literary Pedagogy in the Digital Age," *Caribbean Quarterly* 62, no. 3-4 (2016): 422–44, https://doi.org/10.1080/00086495.2016.1260282.
10. Laurie Taylor, "Topical Collection Page for 'Panama Silver, Asian Gold, Migration, Money, and the Making of the Modern Caribbean'" (course material), Digital Library of the Caribbean, 2020, https://dloc.com//AA00037039/00001.
11. K. Adele Okoli, email message to author, September 17, 2021.
12. Takkara Brunson, "Digital Mapping Project and Presentation," Migration, Mobility, Sustainability: Caribbean Studies and Digital Humanities, Digital Library of the Caribbean and LibraryPress@UF, 2021, https://nehcaribbean.domains.uflib.ufl.edu/projects/digital-mapping-project-presentation/.
13. Juliet Glenn-Callender, "Reflection," Migration, Mobility, Sustainability: Caribbean Studies and Digital Humanities, Digital Library of the Caribbean and LibraryPress@UF, 2021, https://nehcaribbean.domains.uflib.ufl.edu/blog/reflection-juliet-glenn-callender/.
14. Keja Valens, "Reflection," Migration, Mobility, Sustainability: Caribbean Studies and Digital Humanities, Digital Library of the Caribbean and LibraryPress@UF, 2021, https://nehcaribbean.domains.uflib.ufl.edu/blog/reflection-keja-valens/.
15. Anita Baksh and Laëtitia Saint-Loubert, "A Connected Classrooms Project on 'Transoceanic experiences of indenture in Indo-Caribbean, Indo-Mauritian and Indo-Reunionese writing'" (lesson plan), Migration, Mobility, Sustainability: Caribbean Studies and Digital Humanities, Digital Library of the Caribbean and LibraryPress@UF, 2021, https://nehcaribbean.domains.uflib.ufl.edu/projects/a-connected-classrooms-project-transoceanic-experiences-of-indenture/.
16. SUNY COIL, State University of New York, accessed September 13, 2021, https://coil.suny.edu.
17. Nathan Dize, "Reflection," Migration, Mobility, Sustainability: Caribbean Studies and Digital Humanities, Digital Library of the Caribbean and LibraryPress@UF, 2021, https://nehcaribbean.domains.uflib.ufl.edu/blog/reflection-nathan-dize/.

18. Sally Everson et al, "Climates of Inequality in The Bahamas" (resource library), Zotero, 2019-2020, https://www.zotero.org/groups/2403887/climates_of_inequality_in_the_bahamas; Ian Strachan, Ian Anthony Bethell-Bennett, Sally Everson, Juliet Glenn-Callender, and Andrew Moxey et al, "Climates of Inequality" (exhibit website), Sustainable Grand Bahama Conference, 2020, https://www.sustainablegb.org/clmates-of-inequality.
19. Levi Gahman and Gabrielle Thongs, "In the Caribbean, colonialism and inequality mean hurricanes hit harder," *The Conversation*, September 20, 2017, https://theconversation.com/in-the-caribbean-colonialism-and-inequality-mean-hurricanes-hit-harder-84106.
20. Schuyler Esprit, "Using Digital Repositories to Teach DH and Caribbean Studies" (presentation, Migration, Mobility, Sustainability: Caribbean Studies and Digital Humanities), Digital Library of the Caribbean and LibraryPress@UF, 2021, https://nehcaribbean.domains.uflib.ufl.edu/projects/using-digital-repositories-to-teach-dh-and-caribbean-studies/.
21. Schuyler Esprit, "Climate Change, Recovery and Creative Intervention: A Note from the Director," *Create Caribbean* (blog), September 10, 2018, http://createcaribbean.org/create/blog/2018/09/10/climate-change-recovery-and-creative-intervention-a-note-from-the-director/.
22. Schuyler Esprit, "Keynote: Digital experimentation, courageous citizenship, and Caribbean futurism," *Digital Scholarship in the Humanities* 36, Supplement 1 (June 2021): i9-i14, https://doi.org/10.1093/llc/fqaa034.
23. Crystal Felima and Nicole Kang Ferraiolo, "How We Tell the Story of Disaster," *Material Memory* (podcast transcription), 2020, Council on Library and Information Resources, https://material-memory.clir.org/wp-content/uploads/sites/28/2020/12/S2-E3-Transcript.pdf.

Bibliography

Baksh, Anita, and Laëtitia Saint-Loubert. "A Connected Classrooms Project on 'Transoceanic experiences of indenture in Indo-Caribbean, Indo-Mauritian and Indo-Reunionese writing'." Lesson plan. Migration, Mobility, Sustainability: Caribbean Studies and Digital Humanities. Digital Library of the Caribbean and LibraryPress@UF. 2021. https://nehcaribbean.domains.uflib.ufl.edu/projects/a-connected-classrooms-project-transoceanic-experiences-of-indenture/.

Brunson, Takkara. "Digital Mapping Project and Presentation." Migration, Mobility, Sustainability: Caribbean Studies and Digital Humanities. Digital Library of the Caribbean and LibraryPress@UF. 2021. https://nehcaribbean.domains.uflib.ufl.edu/projects/digital-mapping-project-presentation/.

Digital Library of the Caribbean. "Migration, Mobility, and Sustainability: Caribbean Studies Digital Humanities Institute." Grant proposal. 2018. https://dloc.com/IR00010262/00001.

Dize, Nathan. "Reflection." Migration, Mobility, Sustainability: Caribbean Studies and Digital Humanities. Digital Library of the Caribbean and LibraryPress@UF. 2021. https://nehcaribbean.domains.uflib.ufl.edu/blog/reflection-nathan-dize/.

Esprit, Schuyler. "Climate Change, Recovery and Creative Intervention: A Note from the Director." *Create Caribbean* (blog), September 10, 2018. http://createcaribbean.org/create/blog/2018/09/10/climate-change-recovery-and-creative-intervention-a-note-from-the-director/.

———. "Keynote: Digital experimentation, courageous citizenship, and Caribbean futurism." *Digital Scholarship in the Humanities* 36, Supplement 1 (June 2021): i9-i14. https://doi.org/10.1093/llc/fqaa034.

———. "Using Digital Repositories to Teach DH and Caribbean Studies." Presentation. Migration, Mobility, Sustainability: Caribbean Studies and Digital Humanities. Digital Library of the Caribbean and LibraryPress@UF. 2021. https://nehcaribbean.domains.uflib.ufl.edu/projects/using-digital-repositories-to-teach-dh-and-caribbean-studies/.

Everson, Sally, et al. "Climates of Inequality in The Bahamas" (resource library). Zotero. 2019-2020. https://www.zotero.org/groups/2403887/climates_of_inequality_in_the_bahamas.

Felima, Crystal, and Nicole Kang Ferraiolo. "How We Tell the Story of Disaster." *Material Memory*. Podcast transcription, 2020. Council on Library and Information Resources. https://material-memory.clir.org/wp-content/uploads/sites/28/2020/12/S2-E3-Transcript.pdf.

Gahman, Levi, and Gabrielle Thongs. "In the Caribbean, colonialism and inequality mean hurricanes hit harder." *The Conversation*. September 20, 2017. https://theconversation.com/in-the-caribbean-colonialism-and-inequality-mean-hurricanes-hit-harder-84106.

Glenn-Callender, Juliet. "Reflection." Migration, Mobility, Sustainability: Caribbean Studies and Digital Humanities. Digital Library of the Caribbean and LibraryPress@UF. 2021. https://nehcaribbean.domains.uflib.ufl.edu/blog/reflection-juliet-glenn-callender/.

National Endowment for the Humanities. "Institutes for Advanced Topics in the Digital Humanities." Office of Digital Humanities. https://www.neh.gov/grants/odh/institutes-advanced-topics-in-the-digital-humanities.

Polcha, Liz. "On Respecting 'Deep Knowledge' in Collaborative Feminist Work: A Discussion with Jacque Wernimont." *NULab for Texts, Maps, and Networks* (blog), March 23, 2017. https://web.northeastern.edu/nulab/on-respecting-deep-knowledge-in-collaborative-feminist-work-a-discussion-with-jacque-wernimont/.

Rosenberg, Leah. "List of Anglophone Caribbean Novels Published Before 1950." Digital Library of the Caribbean. 2012-2016. https://www.dloc.com/AA00011396/00001.

———. "Refashioning Caribbean Literary Pedagogy in the Digital Age." *Caribbean Quarterly* 62, no. 3-4 (2016): 422–44. https://doi.org/10.1080/00086495.2016.1260282.

Rosenberg, Leah R., Laurie N. Taylor, Nicole N. Alioe, Elizabeth Maddock Dillon, Dania Dwyer, Nadjah Ríos Villarini, Mirerza González, and Rhonda Cobham-Sander. "Roundtable Discussion on Teaching with Caribbean Digital Libraries & Archives." Refereed presentation within Roundtable for the West Indian Literature Conference (WILC). University of the West Indies, Western Jamaica Campus, Montego Bay, Jamaica. October 7, 2016. http://dloc.com/AA00040791/00001/allvolumes.

Star, Susan, and James Griesemer. "Institutional Ecology, 'Translations' and Boundary Objects: Amateurs and Professionals in Berkeley's Museum of Vertebrate Zoology, 1907-39." *Social Studies of Science* 19, no. 3 (1989): 387–420. doi:10.1177/030631289019003001.

Strachan, Ian, Ian Anthony Bethell-Bennett, Sally Everson, Juliet Glenn-Callender, and Andrew Moxey, et al. "Climates of Inequality." Exhibit website. Sustainable Grand Bahama Conference. 2020. https://www.sustainablegb.org/clmates-of-inequality.

SUNY COIL. State University of New York. Accessed September 13, 2021. https://coil.suny.edu.

Taylor, Laurie. "Topical Collection Page for 'Panama Silver, Asian Gold, Migration, Money, and the Making of the Modern Caribbean.'" Course material. Digital Library of the Caribbean. 2020. https://dloc.com//AA00037039/00001.

Valens, Keja. "Reflection." Migration, Mobility, Sustainability: Caribbean Studies and Digital Humanities. Digital Library of the Caribbean and LibraryPress@UF. 2021. https://nehcaribbean.domains.uflib.ufl.edu/blog/reflection-keja-valens/.

About the Authors

Kevin Adams is an information literacy librarian at Alfred University. His research focuses on critical librarianship and critical information literacy.

Murray Anderson is an assistant professor in the Faculty of Health Disciplines at Athabasca University. He has 20-plus years of experience as both a private and public health care practitioner, including roles as a coordinator, outreach worker, and crisis response clinician. His research focuses on the stigma and trauma attached to those dealing with issues related to clutter and hoarding. He also maintains a small, private practice where he works with couples, addiction issues, and those dealing with life transitions.

Elissah Becknell is a faculty librarian at Minneapolis Community & Technical College Library and teaches in the Library Information Technology and Information Studies departments. She is an advocate for teaching information as a discipline and liberal art in its own right. Critical information literacy and culturally responsive pedagogy greatly influence the content of Elissah's teaching. She uses open education resources and zines in her classroom and advocates their use on her campus.

Dawn (Nikki) Cannon-Rech is a research services librarian at Georgia Southern University. She has been an instructional STEM librarian for nearly sixteen years. Ms. Rech is a strong advocate for active and engaging learning as well as open education. She holds a Creative Commons Certification from creativecommons.org and is also a 2020 graduate of the SPARC Open Education Leadership Fellows Program. Ms. Rech welcomes collaborations concerning open education, especially as it intersects with social justice.

Josiline Chigwada is the deputy librarian at Chinhoyi University of Technology in Zimbabwe. She is an open science advocate with fifteen years of experience in higher and tertiary education. She holds a doctorate in information science from

...ity of South Africa (UNISA). She has published two books, nineteen ...chapters, ten journal articles, and six conference proceedings.

Perry Collins et al. The authors of this chapter represent a subset of contributors to Migration, Mobility, Sustainability: Caribbean Studies + Digital Humanities, an institute exploring the potential to enrich students' understanding of history, literature, and other disciplines and to weave their own narratives through digital collections and tools. Perry Collins, Hélène Huet, Laurie Taylor, Brittany Mistretta, Hannah Toombs, all affiliated with the University of Florida at the time of writing, facilitated the institute over the course of two years. Anita Baksh, Nathan H. Dize, Juliet Glenn-Callender, Ronald Angelo Johnson, Aaron Kamugisha, K. Adele Okoli, Laëtitia Saint-Loubert, and Keja Valens were selected as institute participants through a competitive process and participated alongside other cohort members and expert instructors. Within eight colleges and universities in four countries, they planned or implemented lessons and full courses shaped in part by the institute, and they have shared back their experiences, teaching materials, and lessons learned. This chapter draws heavily on written and oral components of the institute from co-authors and those listed in the acknowledgments, as well as the original grant proposal to the National Endowment for the Humanities; the group of authors who have agreed to be listed here represents this varied set of contributions. More information about all who made the institute possible may be found at https://nehcaribbean.domains.uflib.ufl.edu/contributors/.

Glenda Cox is a senior lecturer in the Centre for Innovation in Learning and Teaching (CILT: http://www.cilt.uct.ac.za/) at the University of Cape Town (UCT) and her portfolio includes curriculum projects, teaching innovation grants, open education resources (OER), and staff development. She holds the UNESCO chair in Open Education (2021-2024). She has an NRF C rating and is recognised as being an established researcher in the field of open education. She is passionate about the role of open education in the changing world of higher education. Dr Glenda Cox is currently the principal investigator in the Digital Open Textbooks for Development (DOT4D) initiative. Her current research includes analysing the role of open textbooks for social justice. With more than ten years of experience in working on open education initiatives at UCT, she is an active member of the international open textbook and OER community.

Samantha Dannick is the engineering and scholarly communication librarian at Alfred University. Her areas of interest include open access, open educational resources, and science communication.

Emily M. Doyle is a registered psychologist and member of the Faculty of Health Disciplines at Athabasca University. Her program of research focuses on the social and institutional organization of experience.

Katya Gorecki is a senior user experience researcher working in education technology where she focuses on integrating design justice and humanities methodologies into UX research. She received her PhD from Duke University in American literary and cultural studies with a focus on digital media, technology, and culture in 2020. She also holds an MA in cultural studies from Carnegie Mellon University.

Kimberly S. Grotewold has worked as an academic librarian for nearly fourteen years and is currently employed as the subject specialist research librarian for education and human development programs at Texas A&M University-San Antonio. Prior to her academic librarian experience, she has been a small public library director, a school librarian, and an English and social studies teacher at the middle and high school levels. She holds an MLS degree from the University of Maryland and an MS in higher education administration degree from Drexel University. A true life-long learner, she has recently begun a PhD program in learning technologies through the University of North Texas with hopes of graduating in 2025.

Alkasim Hamisu Abdu was born in Kano State Nigeria. Alkasim earned a BA in library science in 2003; a master of library and information science in 2018; a post-graduate diploma in banking and finance; and is now pursuing a PhD in library and information science all at Bayero University Kano, Nigeria. In 2015, Alkasim earned a post-graduate diploma in education from Federal College of Education Kano, Nigeria. Alkasim worked with Kano State Senior Secondary School Management Board as a classroom teacher from 2005 to 2013 before joining the Yusuf Maitama Sule University Library, where he is currently the coordinator of branch libraries. In 2014 he participated in a short course for the next generation librarians organized by the University of Pretoria with sponsorship from Carnegie Corporation of New York. Alkasim is currently the Secretary of the Nigerian Library Association Kano State Chapter. His major area of research interest is scholarly communication and open education with keen interest in advocating for the use of OER in the Nigerian Educational System. Alkasim is married to Fatima with three children, Maimunah, Omar, and Muhammad-Mufid.

Harlow is an assistant professor and online learning librarian at the University of North Carolina Greensboro (UNCG) University Libraries. She is also a liaison librarian to community and therapeutic recreation, Kinesiology, and public health education. She works with the Research, Outreach, and Instruction (ROI) UNCG University Libraries department to train and assist liaison librarians with online learning, including creating accessible digital objects, teaching online through Zoom and the university learning management system (LMS) Canvas, and hosting a variety of virtual events for online and face-to-face students and instructors. She recently won the national Routledge Distance Learning Librarianship Conference Sponsorship Award and works with the student success and OER librarian Melody Rood on open education and pedagogy resources and services.

Ryan Henyard, MA (he/him/his), is an educational innovator, technologist, artist, and social justice advocate at the University of Michigan's Center for Academic Innovation. He received a bachelor's degree in Asian languages and cultures (Japanese) as well as a master's degree in higher education (student access and success) from the University of Michigan Ann Arbor. He is interested in creating innovation opportunities and learning experiences that align with the needs of marginalized communities, combining a wide range of interdisciplinary skills to create impact while centering compassion, authenticity, and equity.

Shanna Hollich is currently serving as the director of the Guthrie Memorial Library in Hanover, PA. They have been doing research, reform, and advocacy work in the field of copyright and open licensing for several years. They hold an MLIS from Rutgers University and a master's in data analytics from Penn State. You can find them on Twitter @srhlib.

CJ Ivory is an associate professor and librarian at the University of West Georgia where she teaches information literacy and research with a focus on social justice. She is also an advocate for open education on her campus and works with faculty across disciplines to support the implementation of open textbook alternatives. She holds a bachelor's degree in economics from the University of Central Florida and MLIS from Florida State University. Her research interests include information literacy instruction, social justice education, and open pedagogy.

Karen L. Kohler is an assistant professor of curriculum and instruction at Texas A&M University-San Antonio. Her research interests include family engagement, teacher preparation, open education resources (OER), and educational collaboration between teachers.

Elisabeth M. Krimbill is an assistant professor in the Education Leadership Program at Texas A&M University-San Antonio. Throughout her career, she has been a teacher, assistant principal, and principal. Dr. Krimbill now works with aspiring school leaders and is the interim director of the Superintendency Certification Program. Her research focuses on law, ethics, and school leadership. She embraces the OER movement and hopes to inspire others to do the same.

Rebecca March is a librarian at Minneapolis Community & Technical College and teaches in the Information Studies and Library Information Technology departments. She is fascinated by the meaning, power, and impact of how information is packaged, delivered, and received. Rebecca wants information to be open and freely available to all.

Bianca Masuku is a PhD candidate in anthropology at UCT and a junior research fellow in the DOT4D project. Her research background and varied research experiences fuel her more recent interests in open education, open textbooks, and open scholarship with a keen interest in the inclusion and recognition of student voices.

Julia Maxwell is the first year experience librarian at California State University, San Francisco, and is a recent graduate of the University of Michigan, where she received an MA in education and an MS in information science. During graduate school, she created digital learning objects at U-M's Center for Academic Innovation and assessed library teaching and learning through the IMLS-funded Library as Research Lab project. Her research interests include undergraduate self-efficacy and belonging in library spaces and in information literacy learning, learner experience design (LXD) and user experience design (UX) in academic library spaces, and the assessment of library-mediated learning in higher education.

Benjamin Morse is the design management lead in the Center for Academic Innovation (CAI) at the University of Michigan. He holds a master's of science from the School for Environment and Sustainability in Behavior, Education & Communication and a master's of public policy from the Gerald R. Ford School of Public Policy at the University of Michigan.

y is a registered psychologist and assistant professor of counseling ...gy at the Werklund School of Education at the University of Calgary. ...ne supervises and trains counseling psychology students and practices family therapy at the Calgary Family Therapy Centre. Tanya's research and writing have focused on family therapy, excessive behaviours, addiction and recovery from addiction, and the relational recovery of critical care survivors and their families.

Barbara Murphy is an associate professor of music theory at the University of Tennessee, Knoxville, teaching undergraduate classes in music theory and graduate classes in theory pedagogy, analytical techniques, and technology in music research. Recent research projects include creating open educational resources (OER) for use in music theory classes, the inclusion of jazz theory into the music theory core curriculum, and the incorporation of theatrical improvisation in theory pedagogy. She is currently the co-editor of the *Journal of the Association for Technology in Music Instruction*. Along with Brendan McConville, she has authored an e-book, *Foundations of Music Theory: An interactive e-book* (through Kendall-Hunt Publishing). She has articles published in *Journal of Music Theory Pedagogy*, *College Music Symposium*, *Sacred Music*, the *Journal of Research in Music Pedagogy*, and the *Journal of Research in Music Education*.

Mary Jo Orzech is the scholarly communications librarian at Drake Memorial Library, SUNY Brockport. Her academic interests include planning and assessment as well as open access, open educational resources, and digital scholarship.

Angela Pashia has over a decade of experience as an academic librarian focusing on teaching critical information literacy, mentoring colleagues, working against structural oppression within libraries, and growing as a collaborative leader. Angela's first co-edited book (with Jessica Critten), *Critical Approaches to Credit-Bearing Information Literacy Courses*, was selected as an ACRL Instruction Section, Teaching Methods Committee Selected Resource in 2020. Angela currently works as professor and head of the learning and research support department at Ingram Library, University of West Georgia, and is beginning to explore opportunities to support other scholars as a book and career coach.

Kristin Petrovic is a master's prepared nurse educator at an online university in Canada. Students in her program are furthering their nursing education from practical nurses to bachelor's prepared registered nurses. Kristin has a passion for online learning where students can work around barriers for access and participation in post-secondary education. Kristin is a doctorate in distance education student. Her research focuses on how digital nursing education can mitigate sociocultural barriers in the educational system. She also wants to better understand the impact of nursing ethical principles of practice on nursing educator praxis.

Ian A. Ramjohn is the senior Wikipedia expert at Wiki Education. He has been a contributor to Wikipedia since 2004, an administrator since 2005, and is a founding member of Wikimedians of the Caribbean. He has a PhD in ecology from Michigan State University and a bachelor's from the University of the West Indies and spent a decade teaching in higher education before joining Wiki Education in 2014.

Melody Lee Rood is the student success and open education librarian at the University of North Carolina at Greensboro where she serves as a liaison to the International and Global Studies Program, the Library and Information Science Program, as well as the library's Open Educational Resources Initiatives. Her research interests include outreach for nontraditional students, open pedagogy, equity, diversity, inclusion, and social justice.

Claire Terrell is a master's candidate in music theory at the University of Tennessee, Knoxville, where she completed her bachelor of music degree in composition in 2020. Her research interests range from music theory pedagogy—specifically, the diversification of the music theory curriculum, to studies in popular music and twentieth- and twenty-first-century atonal composers. She premiered several compositions in the University of Tennessee New Sounds Concert Series (2016–2018) as well as her solo recital in 2020. Claire was also commissioned to processional for UTK's Chancellor's Investiture Ceremony in 2019.

Thomas C. Weeks is an assistant professor and reference and instruction librarian at Augusta University, where he serves the Department of Social Sciences and graduate students in the College of Education. In addition, he is a doctoral student in curriculum studies at Georgia Southern University, where he researches the sexuality curriculum of teen media. He is interested in the ways cultural politics influence educational institutions, including libraries.

Michelle Willmers has a background in academic and scholarly publishing and has worked in scholarly communication initiatives since 2008. She is currently the publishing and implementation manager of the Digital Open Textbooks for Development project in the Centre for Innovation in Learning and Teaching at the University of Cape Town.

od earned her bachelor's degree in psychology from St. Joseph's ...01, her MSW from Stony Brook University in 2009, and her PhD ...ocial welfare from Stony Brook University in 2014. While pursuing her doctorate, Jennifer was in clinical practice on Long Island. In 2014, Jennifer began teaching in the BSW and MSSW programs at West Texas A&M University, serving as the graduate program director from 2016 to 2018. In 2018, Jennifer returned to New York to teach at SUNY Brockport. She lives in Brockport with her husband and rescued bulldog.